THE VIEW
FROM WITHIN

MENACHEM FISCH

and

YITZHAK BENBAJI

THE VIEW

FROM WITHIN

Normativity and the Limits of Self-Criticism

University of Notre Dame Press

Notre Dame, Indiana

Library of Congress Cataloging-in-Publication Data

Fisch, Menachem.
   The view from within : normativity and the limits of self-criticism /
Menachem Fisch and Yitzhak Benbaji.
      p.   cm.
   Includes bibliographical references (p.   ) and index.
   ISBN-13: 978-0-268-02904-3 (pbk. : alk. paper)
   ISBN-10: 0-268-02904-0 (pbk. : alk. paper)
   1. Normativity (Ethics)   2. Criticism (Philosophy)
I. Benbaji, Yitzhak.   II. Title.
   BJ1458.3.F57   2011
   170'.44—dc23

                                        2011034654

for

HANNA

and

HAGIT

Contents

PART III. NORMATIVE SELF-CRITICISM

Preface and Acknowledgments

This book has been long in the making. A commitment to grounding agency in a capacity for normative self-criticism had permeated our work long before we decided to explore the prospects of joining forces in summer 2001. The initial idea to collaborate was Fisch's, who, as reader of Ben baji's dissertation on moral relativism, suggested that something along the lines of the generalized Popperian perspective he had been working with in the philosophy of science might prove the key to resolving Ben-baji's deliberation between external and internal reasons in ethics. Ben-baji, by then a postdoctoral research assistant at the Institute for Advanced Study, Princeton, agreed to try. Needless to say, what looked to us then like the outline of an elegant solution served merely to aggravate the problem. Taking the internalist perspective seriously—along Frankfurtian lines, for instance—seemed to render normative commitment immune in principle to self-critique, certainly in the light of Popper's analytical construal. We swiftly found ourselves forced back to the drawing board to rethink from scratch the very notions of normative commitment and critical discourse we were working with. This proved a daunting yet greatly rewarding task that required us to seriously engage the work of some of the most interesting and demanding thinkers working in these areas today. The project transformed our teaching, thinking, and writing, forcing us to divide the labor while bridging as best we could our own very different styles and philosophical temperaments. But it worked—at least to our own, admittedly blinkered satisfaction.

In the course of its long gestation, many colleagues and friends have invested time, effort, and good cheer in commenting on various aspects and extracts of the project. These include Hagit Benbaji, Yemima Ben Menahem, Akeel Bilgrami, Bill Child, Lorraine Daston, Michael Friedman, Ariel Furstenberg, Noah Efron, Paul Franks, Snait Gissis, Niccolò Guicciardini, Zoe Gutzeit, Oren Harman, David Heyd, Don Howard, Andrew Janiak, Bernard Katz, Ehud Lamm, Menachem Lorberbaum, Avishai Margalit, Adi Ophir, Gideon Rosen, Carol Rovane, Eric Schliesser, Alfred Tauber, Nehama Verbin, and Michael Walzer. Good, hard-hitting, and informed criticism, as we argue toward the end of chapter 7, is one of the greatest gifts a person can give to another, because self-criticism is something none of us are very good at and have great difficulty applying effectively. So thanks, dear colleagues and friends, for your invaluable critiques. We have also had the great privilege of receiving two extraordinarily insightful and engaging, yet alas anonymous, referee reports commissioned by the University of Notre Dame Press that have contributed decisively to improving this work. We thank you, kind readers, and only wish we could have done so in person.

Finally, it is a great pleasure to acknowledge our debt to the people at Notre Dame responsible for seeing the book through the Press: Charles Van Hof, acquisitions editor; Rebecca DeBoer, managing editor; and Sheila Berg, copyeditor.

Overviews of the argument, as well as more focused segments of it, were presented at conferences, seminars, and colloquia at the Universities of Tel Aviv, Bar Ilan, Ben Gurion, Notre Dame, Virginia, Cape Town, and Bergamo, the Hebrew University, Jerusalem, Muhlenberg College, and the Bar Hillel Colloquium, where we enjoyed much lively discussion. We thank the organizers, hosts, and participants.

This book is the result of a truly collaborative undertaking. We each wrote separately but read and commented on each other's drafts several times. Fisch was responsible for the initial drafting and final versions of chapters 1, 5, 6, 7, 8, and 9; Benbaji, for those of chapters 2, 3, and 4.

Credits

An early version of chapter 2 appeared as "Through Thick and the Thin: A New Defense of Cultural Relativism," *Southern Journal of Philosophy* 42, no. 1 (2004): 1–24.

Chapter 3 first appeared as "Factuality without Realism: Normativity and the Davidsonian Approach to Meaning," *Southern Journal of Philosophy* 43, no. 4 (2005): 505–30.

The main argument of chapter 9 is anticipated in the latter part of "Taking the Linguistic Turn Seriously," *European Legacy* 13, no. 5 (2008): 605–22 (Special Issue, "The Languages of the Sciences and the Humanities," ed. Oren Harman); and is summarized, along with some of the relevant strands of chapter 8, in "Toward a History and Philosophy of Scientific Agency," *The Monist* 93, no. 4 (October 2010): 518–44.

▬   ▬   ▬

As this book goes to print, the collaboration that sired it disbands, with each of us, well embarked on new projects, heading our separate ways to well-earned sabbatical leaves—Benbaji at the Yale Law School and Fisch at the Institute for Advanced Study, Princeton, and Collegium Budapest. Benbaji's new project is a book on the ethics of war, the point at which normative diversity ceases to pose a constructive challenge and deteriorates into violence. Fisch's new book will further develop the account of scientific paradigm shifts outlined in chapter 9, in application to a series of interrelated nineteenth-century case studies. We thus each return to our original fields—Benbaji to ethics and Fisch to the history and philosophy of science. But we do so enriched and positively "ambivalated" by a study partnership, not unlike the one described by Abot de Rabbi Nathan at the end of chapter 7, that yielded a project neither of us was capable of undertaking alone. The collaborative partnership we succeeded in forging would not have been possible, however, without the loving support of our families, especially the sustaining and inspiring force of our partners in marriage—Hanna and Hagit—to whom this book is dedicated with our deepest gratitude and love.

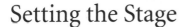

CHAPTER ONE

Setting the Stage

The Problem with Rationality

Two Concepts of Rational Action

Theories of rational action fall under two main headings. The first pronounces an action rational if, given the circumstances, it is perceived to be the right or proper thing to do. To act rationally is to act in ways that, given the actor's needs, desires, and, situation, meet expert approval. On this view, what is scrutinized in assessments of rationality are the merits of the actor's actual performance rather than the quality of the data at her disposal, her level of expertise, or the quality of her reasoning. It is the end result that counts. To be considered rational in this sense, it is enough for an act to be deemed effective or worthwhile. What is appraised is per formance, not agency. Action taken or withheld thoughtlessly, instinctively, or unwittingly may also be considered rational as long as it is deemed appropriate. Rationality thus construed is, therefore, not limited, in principle, to human action. Instinctive animal behavior can be deemed rational in this respect. Likewise, properly functioning computer programs, automatic pilots and thermostats, programmed to "sense," "assess," and respond to a situation effectively, are often said to perform rationally without doing too much violence to the term. It is a notion of rationality used widely in talk of skillful feats one trains to perform instinctively without having to ponder on them each time anew. It matters little how the skill was originally acquired. Often, as Michael Polanyi famously argued, the learning process may itself remain tacit.[1] Most of us learn to perform highly complex feats of logical reasoning, for example, without ever having studied logic as such. The move from tacit human knowledge acquisition to preprogrammed, hardwired animal and artificial skilled response is then quite natural.

To paraphrase Bernard Williams's well-known distinction, it is not X's reasons for ϕ-ing that are being judged but the extent to which ϕ-ing is considered the reasonable thing for X to do.[2] Rationality on such a showing is hence a matter of situation analysis. It has to do with the weighing of possibilities and calculation of possible outcomes. Due to the supposedly calculable, algorithmic nature of its underlying logic, this notion of rationality has attracted enormous attention in recent years, especially among decision and game theorists.

Thus construed, rationality still requires reflection and sound assessment, but it is not the actor who is required, or, in most cases, even qualified to do so. To be considered rational she is expected to act *in conformity* with what is considered appropriate by the best means available but without necessarily having to have worked it out for herself. Indeed, unless the actor happens to be the referring expert herself, her own account of her actions will be of little if any relevance to their rationality.[3]

Nor need the required approval be unanimous, or granted immediately. Approval, and with it assessments of rationality, may be conceded by some and not by others and, even then, only long after the event. Rationality, in this sense of the term, is time- and context-dependent, in principle, and is hence interestingly relativized despite its supposedly objective, calculable nature. Actions deemed inappropriate and hence irrational by some may come in time to be considered fitting and perfectly rational by others—and vice versa.

Although the rationality of the *type* of action in question may have been ascertained long before the specific act under consideration was performed (as in the case of standard countermoves in chess, or an appropriately applied well-honed mathematical technique), evaluations of this first category of rationality are always backward-looking. What is deemed rational is forever what the actor ended up doing or refraining from doing.

One does not embark on a process of deliberation that can be deemed rational before it is completed and its outcome independently assessed. Rationality, in this sense of the term, is always decided after the event. It is not a prospective evaluative category of acting but a retrospective evaluative category of types of actions. What makes for the rational is not what goes into practical reasoning, if you wish, but what comes out. It is the move the actor actually makes that is assessed regardless of the manner in which she reasoned or conducted herself prior to making it.

The second approach to rationality is less liberal. It insists, as Robert Brandom puts it, on distinguishing human rationality from "the mere reliable differential responsiveness that we share with non-conceptual creatures such as pigeons—or as far as that goes, with photocells and thermostats."[4] It demands of moves deemed rational to be more than merely right or efficient. It is trickier than the first, and is less prone to calculation. To be considered rational, it is not enough for a move to gain retroactive approval; an action is required to be the outcome of considered deliberation. Rationality is made to turn not on what the actor ends up doing but on the manner in which she arrives at her decision to do so—gauging the quality of reasoning culminating in the act rather than the merit or effectiveness of the act once made.[5] Here, by contrast, agency reigns supreme. Thoughtless action, appropriate, effective, and meritorious as it may turn out to be, will never be deemed rational.[6] There are other evaluative categories by which to commend action that merely fits the bill. Rationality is here construed as an evaluative category reserved exclusively for *considered* action, action taken self-consciously and reflectively.

Rationality's Authority

But by what standards are we to judge an actor's considered deliberation? The answer, obviously, is by appealing again to expert opinion. An action will be deemed rational only when taken by virtue of such feats of practical reasoning that meet authoritative approval. The canons of rationality appealed to here differ substantially from those of the first-order situational analyses that gauge the first model. Here the actor is not expected to act merely in conformity with the outcome of expert diagnosis, but to emulate expert diagnosing. To paraphrase Bernard Williams again, to be deemed rational, it is not enough for a move to be considered reasonable by approved standards; it is required to be reasoned for approvingly. The first sense of rational conduct required actors merely to *act* as would an expert, the second requires of them to *reason* as experts do.

The two notions of rationality differ significantly. At best, the class of activity deemed rational by the second forms but a tiny subset of that deemed rational by the first. (But even that is not entirely true, for according to the second, an action may be considered rational even when unsuccessful, or deemed mistaken, which for the first would be unthinkable.) The demands on the actor are in a sense far more stringent in the second than in the first. But the two do have one important feature in common: they are both ultimately gauged by appeal to authoritative approval. The foci of approval are very different in each case, and, consequently, so are the criteria by which it is leveled. Still, gauging the rationality of a move by appeal to accepted standards renders rationality inherently context-dependent. It matters little if the standards invoked are the accepted canons of appropriate action or those of appropriate reasoning. In either case, rationality becomes a matter of conforming to the currently accepted standards and hence, by definition, wholly dependent on time, place, and opinion.

Indeed, why not? Do not all our evaluative categories invoke standards and norms, and are not all our standards and norms culturally determined? Is it not obvious that action considered appropriate in one context may well be deemed unfounded in another; that conduct deemed reasonable in one cultural setting may be considered outrageous in another?[7] Needless to say, the arguments for the relativity of the normative in this regard are powerful. With respect to rationality, however, there is a price to pay.

Second-Order Pondering

To see this we need to take a closer look. As noted, the context-dependency of the first notion of rationality makes perfect sense. If the rationality of a move is thought to be calculable by the most recent decision-theoretic or game-theoretic approach, it should be expected to change as the theory is further developed or replaced. If rationality amounts to acting in accord with expert opinion, then, by definition, it *is* a matter of opinion. What allegedly saves rationality from becoming *merely* a matter of opinion is, of course, the fact that it is made to turn, not just on anyone's opinion, but on that of reliable assessors who are expected to form their opinions rationally. But if rational action is action taken in conformity with approved standards of performance, how is the work done *on* those very standards to be rated? Since standards of adequate performance of both acting and reasoning undergo changes from time to time, by what means, and with respect to which measures, can their second-order scrutinization and replacement be deemed rational, arbitrary, or capricious? This is where the first notion of rationality converges on the second, and where both become problematic.

Our reason for focusing on expert, rather than personal, common, communal, or majority, opinion is to lay special emphasis, if only metaphorically, on the special role played by informed specialists in devising, reviewing, and occasionally revising the standards, norms, and methods of their fields of expertise. Even the most avid supporters of the first notion of rationality will allow thoughtless, mindless action to be considered rational only if it can be said to merit the authoritative approval of someone who has competently thought it through. Unconsidered action, or activity performed thoughtlessly by an entire community that is merely following custom, instinct, or habit, will not be considered rational by either model. The two approaches differ with respect to the level of reasoning, consciousness, and agency they demand of whoever (or whatever) performs the action in question. But both agree that to be deemed rational, an act must be actively and consciously approved. Rationality, on either showing, would seem to require more than knowingly or unwittingly following a rule or a ruling; it requires that the rule or ruling followed be fittingly *approved and endorsed.*

An approved norm, rule, or ruling is a considered one, one that at some point was weighed and deliberated, compared and tested for situations and tasks resembling those at hand. What makes for rational action, according to both understandings of the term, is the fact that it is *reasoned.* Although we side with the second approach—insisting that for action to be deemed rational the actor herself be required to perform the reasoning—we shall press the matter here no further. Rather than attempt to adjudicate between theories of rationality, let alone propose one of our own, this book, as stated at the outset, focuses on what we hold both approaches to rationality have in common: namely, a requirement that the rational turn centrally on some form of second-order, deliberative assessment and what Christine Korsgaard terms "reflective endorsement" of the sort exemplified most fully in prudent expert evaluation.[8] The phrase "have in common" could be misleading, though. For we believe that this type of reflective deliberation is more than something theories of rationality just happen to share. On the contrary, it is our contention that the various approaches to rationality exhibit wide if at times implicit agreement that this type of reasoning is, in the last analysis, rationality's widely shared defining feature. It is where humankind's capacity to reason (minimally) enters the picture to make the rational what it is and to mark it off from what it is not.

The sort of evaluative approval to which we refer requires a stepping back from the well-honed ways of old with a view to considering them to some degree anew. If rational action is action taken with a view to effectively meeting a need or accomplishing a goal, then to approve such action amounts, minimally, to critically reviewing the means selected to do so. A more robust evaluation might question the needs and goals themselves.[9] But let us concentrate for the time being on the minimal case.

This type of reasoning, located at the heart of rational endeavor, aims at carefully reviewing the actor's circumstances, values, assets, and goals, with a view to assessing the aptness of her response to the specific task at hand.[10] If the exercise is not an empty one, it will always involve, if but fleetingly, a critical weighing of alternatives. In routine situations it will amount to no more than a nodding acknowledgment of the selection by the actor of the standard tool for the job. But not all situations are routine. Some of the time much more will be at stake and much more will be involved. Each time the actor's specific circumstances, needs, or purposes defies standard procedure, standard procedure will itself become the object of reflection. Most often even then little more will be required than adjusting and tuning standard tools and methods to meet specific conditions in routine and well-rehearsed ways. But often it is not. And when it is not, that is when the standards and the norms constitutive of the field are liable to be called into question. These are moments when experts are required to reflect critically on the tools of their trade rather than expertly apply them.

In facing such outstanding problems they will often have to rely on the findings of sister disciplines. Peter Galison has drawn attention to the way well-managed "trading zones" are established wherein practitioners of different disciplines communicate and "trade" by means of suitably watered-down, pidgin versions of their different professional vocabularies.[11] But dependent as a field may be on other fields for *solving* problems, it is seldom the case that the problems themselves are comprehended outside it. No one is better placed than the foremost practitioners of a field to encounter, experience, and acknowledge difficulties that arise within it, just as it is they who will subsequently be charged with the task of considering, debating, and eventually approving their solutions.[12]

Needless to say, fields operate by means of norms, standards, and procedures some of which are more easily modified than others. Some fields of activity   those that constitute language games in the more literal sense of the word, such as in sports and some arts—maintain rigid rules and regulations in order to increase the challenge and the competition artificially.[13] But the norms, standards, and procedures that regulate the activity in most fields are not maintained merely for the sake of making the play more difficult or challenging, and yet they are not regarded by practitioners as sacred absolutes imposed from without. Rather, they are endorsed and maintained normatively as well-considered means to well-considered ends.[14] And just as they are seriously endorsed and maintained as such, they, too, are liable to come under serious review from time to time in response to problems encountered.

It should not come as a surprise that the mode of reasoning that makes for rationality thus turns out to be the very same mode of reasoning that accounts for the studied operation and the reasoned fashioning and refashioning that occurs in all fields of considered human endeavor. If to act purposefully is to apply a means to an end, and if what makes for the rationality of such a move is that it be competently reviewed and approved, then the two modes of reasoning are not merely similar, but in this sense fully coincide.[15] Competent assessors of rational action are experts, by definition. And the role they are expected to play in assessing such action is precisely the same role they are expected to play *within* their respective fields. The point we wish to emphasize, however, is less the actual agreement between the two roles, which is pretty obvious, than the wide spectrum of activity of which they consist. This, we have seen, extends from the nodding approval of standard uses of standard tools and methods, at its lowest point, all the way up to the studied, at times anxious, rethinking of the field's very foundations in the face of outstanding difficulties.

Note, however, that we do not demand that to be deemed rational action must be approved or reasoned for *correctly* in any absolutist or foundationalist sense of the term—only that it be approved, reasoned, questioned, and reflected on *authoritatively,* that it be normatively endorsed. Rationality thus construed would hence seem quite susceptible to the cultural relativity of the normative central to much latter-day philosophy of language, mind, self, and culture. Or so it would seem. We shall return shortly to the three master ideas that animate this study: (a) the central identification of an action or a belief's rationality, with it being *considered,* that is, embarked on or endorsed for a reason; (b) the essential *normativity* of such reasoning; and (c) the inevitable role of *normative self-criticism* in the rational modification or replacement of normative commitment. But first a word on relativism, or what we prefer to refer to as *Normative Diversity.*

Normative Diversity: An Introduction

In what follows, we take *relativism* in the sense endorsed and held in esteem by Richard Rorty, as opposed to the sense he rejects (despite his objection to the very use of the term).[16] The notion of relativism in which we are interested, and with which we sympathize, differs from the thesis sometimes termed "cultural" or "moral relativism," alleged to claim that any viewpoint is as good as any other.[17] Such a position begs the question, if only by presupposing a transcultural notion of 'good'. According to the more stringent position we shall be interested in, such a "view from nowhere"—to use Thomas Nagel's oxymoronic metaphor from which the title of the present study takes its cue—is humanly unavailable. A culture, a language game, a form of life, a normative outlook, it argues, can only be viewed from within, or, alternatively, from the necessarily biased perspective of another. From these two humanly available perspectives (which roughly map onto Korsgaard's distinction between first- and third-person perspectives with regard to the normative),[18] mutual understanding and normative evaluations and preferences are quite coherently forthcoming but, by definition, are never "objective" in the transcultural, framework-independent sense of the term. Relativism, as we refer to it here, is the position claimed to follow from the very idea by which cultural relativism is rejected, namely, the denial of the availability of a normative vocabulary that "has nothing to do with agency, values or interests,"[19] and that can, therefore, not be shared by radically different normative outlooks. It is the position we dub in what follows "Comparative Normative Irrealism," one that denies thin normative concepts like 'true', 'good', 'despicable', 'rational', and 'sound' the capacity to compare and rank diverse normative systems, in a manner acceptable to both. "Dewey," writes Rorty,

> thought that the Kantian notion of "unconditional obligation" . . . could not survive Darwin. . . . For him, all obligations were situational and conditional. This refusal to be unconditional led Dewey to be charged with 'relativism.' If 'relativism' just means failure to find a use for the notion of 'context-independent validity,' then this charge was entirely justified.[20]

Such a position, it is argued further, entails that meaningful discussion of and reflection on one's own normative vocabulary (or language game, "system of belief," "form of life," or "final vocabulary" as such frameworks are variously termed) is necessarily determined by and contained within it to the extent that, as Rorty rather forcefully puts it, "all we can allow ourselves" is to "limit the opposition between rational and irrational forms of persuasion to the interior of a language game, rather than try to apply it to interesting and important shifts in linguistic behavior."[21] It is only "within a language game, within a set of agreements about what is possible and important, [that] we can usefully distinguish reasons for beliefs from causes for belief which are not reasons."[22] Relativism, as we take it here, is the view according to which, to paraphrase Hilary Putnam, "elements of what we call 'language' or 'mind' penetrate so deeply into what we call 'reality' that the very project of representing ourselves as" capable of rationally reviewing and revising those elements "is fatally compromised from the start."[23]

A Two-Step Argument

In other words, such relativist construals of the normative, it is argued, severely constrain the extent of rational review and revision to which a normative framework can admit from within. It is a two-step argument. The first consists of the sobering neo-Kantian realization that all meaningful normative discourse is determined by, and hence relative to, the particular normative vocabulary it draws on. Following such thinkers as Rorty,[24] Davidson, Williams, Putnam, Michael Friedman, Charles Taylor, Michael Walzer, and Brandom, whose work we shall discuss in some detail, we fully concede this first step. In doing so, we shall be arguing against the opposition, leveled most interestingly from more orthodox latter-day Kantian quarters, such as in the work of Korsgaard and John Rawls and his school and, to a more limited extent, John McDowell's recent work.

The second, more radical step of the argument urges us to realize that by virtue of their constitutive role in the discourses they support, our normative vocabularies are themselves rendered largely immune to normative critical appraisal from within those discourses. In being constitutive of all rational reasoning and reckoning within their scope, it is argued, they defy becoming the *objects* of rational reasoning and reckoning from within. Therefore, though obviously the products of *human* endeavor, they cannot be considered the products of *rational* human endeavor. Scrutinized by their users, a normative vocabulary may be found to harbor inconsistencies, incoherence or, from a Taylorian or Brandomian perspective, felt to be in need of further explication. Problems may also arise regarding the relative priority ascribed to norms. But by virtue of its constitutive role in determining the good, the right, and the appropriate, a normative vocabulary, it is argued, cannot be deemed from within to be bad, wrong, or unfitting. A final vocabulary—to use Rorty's coinage—namely, the set of words with which people justify their actions, and about which "if doubt is cast . . . their user has no noncircular argumentative resource,"[25] is not and, in principle, cannot be the out-come of considered, reflective deliberation of the kind we locate at the heart of rationality.

Many oppose the type of relativism of which we speak—some dis-missively, some thoughtfully. But many concede it—more, perhaps, than one would have thought, as we shall argue in some detail in upcoming chapters. Among those who concede it, none, to the best of our knowl-edge, have taken issue with the second step of the argument, although only very few acknowledge it explicitly; Rorty and Davidson stand out in this respect.[26] Work on rationality among those we class as normative irrealists shows little interest in and exhibits virtually no discomfort with the idea that our normative vocabularies elude rational scrutiny. The ex-ceptions, as we shall see, are Friedman's work on the rationality of scien-tific framework transitions and Brandom's common law, Hegelian model of "historical" rationality.[27] However, even their notions of rationality, as we shall argue in some detail, are wholly lacking of the normative self-critical aspect of rational evaluation on which we insist.

Put briefly, the aim of the present study is to explore the possibility of resisting the second step of the argument while fully endorsing the first; to salvage, in other words, a viable notion of normative self-criticism, ap-plicable to both intersubjective and intrasubjective normative discourse, yet without resorting to an external or comparative normative foothold. Normative vocabularies, we shall show, are susceptible to normative criti-cism from within, despite their essential incomparability to sufficiently diverse alternatives. But before explaining in more detail why, and out-lining how we intend to do so, a little more needs to be said about step 2 in order to get a better sense of the difficulties involved in contesting it. We do so by way of an introduction by appealing to the work of its most outspoken and eloquent advocate, Richard Rorty.

Rorty's Relativism

Richard Rorty, a primary proponent for the two-step argument, does not regard its conclusion in any way problematic. On the contrary, the "iro-nist" strong poet, whose image he portrays and promotes in *Contingency,*

Irony, and Solidarity, and with whom he fully identifies,[28] is someone who knowingly conducts herself in accord with and in full awareness of this constraint on her rationality. She is someone who fulfills three conditions:

> (1) She has radical and continuing doubts about the final vocabulary she currently uses . . . ; (2) She realizes that arguments phrased in her present vocabulary can neither underwrite nor dissolve these doubts; (3) Insofar as she philosophizes about her situation, she does not think that her vocabulary is closer to reality than others, that it is in touch with a power not herself. (73)

She is portrayed as self-critical but only in the sense of tracing the outer borders of self-criticism. Aware of her final vocabulary's inherent contingency, she doubts it persistently and spends "her time worrying about the possibility that she has been initiated into the wrong tribe, taught to play the wrong language game." However, and this is the crucial point, "she cannot give a criterion of wrongness" and thinks, therefore, that there "is no reason to think that Socratic inquiry into the essence of justice or science or rationality will take one much beyond the language games of one's time" (74–75). She therefore experiments in fashioning new vocabularies by blindly casting around for new metaphors to redescribe herself and her world. Unable to question, she dabbles; unable to troubleshoot, she tinkers. She gropes blindly because she assumes, with Rorty, that from the vantage point of her current vocabulary—which is the only committed vantage point available to her—it is impossible to articulate what might be wrong with it, or in what ways it might be improved, and that, subsequently, "the creation of . . . a new vocabulary, will have its utility explained only retrospectively" (55), and, again, only from within. Rorty's ironist aims ultimately to *improve* on her vocabulary, rather than merely change it for another, but can only do so aimlessly. She can envisage change, but, unable to set herself a prospective goal, other than change itself, she cannot envisage progress. All she can do is to do her best to be original, to keep telling her story differently.[29] She works on her vocabulary but cannot appraise it critically.[30] She can, therefore, not proceed rationally in improving it, in the sense we have described and shall explain further below. She can only blindly redescribe with the hope of hitting unwittingly on an option that in retrospect she will find worthwhile.

Rorty refers frequently and glowingly to the work of Thomas Kuhn, whom he describes as "one of [his] idols," "a great philosopher," "the most influential . . . to write in English since the Second World War."[31] Most of the time Kuhn is praised for redescribing science to show that "the subject of truth claims cannot be a relation between beliefs and a putatively mind-independent or 'external' world,"[32] thus contributing to the idea central to Rorty's entire project that "correspondence to reality is a term without content."[33] When he does refer to Kuhn's description of paradigm shifts he is less clear than one would expect, however, tending to slide too easily into Kuhn's collectivist idiom and shift attention from the "strong poets" responsible for fashioning the paradigm shift to the community that ends up endorsing it. This is to blur the difference between rational inquiry and rational acceptance; between perceiving and responding to problems, on the one hand, and being willing to entertain their solution once proposed.[34] Rorty thus creates the false impression that the issue is essentially sociological. "As Kuhn argues in *The Copernican Revolution*," Rorty writes, "we did not decide on the basis of some telescopic observations, or on the basis of anything else, that the earth was not the center of the universe, that macroscopic behavior could be explained on the basis of microstructural motion, and that prediction and control should be the principal aim of scientific theorizing." One wonders who the "we" are to whom Rorty refers. He quickly clarifies: "Rather, after a hundred years of inconclusive muddle, *the Europeans* found themselves speaking in a way which took these interlocked theses for granted. Cultural change of this magnitude does not result from applying criteria. . . . We should not look within ourselves for criteria of decision in such matters any more than we should look to the world."[35]

The question addressed here is how to explain how a community, or a society at large ("the Europeans"), acquires and internalizes a newly fashioned final vocabulary *after* it was formed rather than the very different and far more radical question, so central to his book, regarding the manner in which such radically new vocabularies are fashioned by their authors in the first place.[36] Rorty's reference here to "the Europeans," rather than to the individuals who set the scientific revolutions he mentions in motion, creates the false impression that his reference to Kuhn pertains to the first rather than to the second question.[37] The passage immediately preceding the one quoted, goes beyond Kuhn to include paradigm shifts outside the sciences but remains similarly misleading: "Europe did not *decide* to accept the idiom of Romantic poetry, or of socialist politics, or of Galilean mechanics. That sort of shift was no more an act of will than it was a result of argument. Rather, Europe gradually lost the habit of using certain words and gradually acquired the habit of using others."[38] Discerning how professional communities and the educated public at large lose and acquire such habits of thought and speech is a complex and fascinating story in itself, of course, to which we return if briefly in chapter 9. But the real challenge to rationality is that of Galileo, the poets, and the social reformers themselves, who spent a lifetime deliberating, contriving, and perfecting these new vocabularies. Can Galileo's creative enterprise be deemed "no more an act of will than it was a result of argument"? Can his lifework also be described as a matter of merely losing "the habit of using certain words" and acquiring "the habit of using others"? When these early passages of *Contingency, Irony, and Solidarity* are reread in the light of the self-portrayal of Rorty's ironist developed later in the book, the answer turns out to be a clear and disturbing "Yes!" And indeed, a little later in the first chapter, he says so explicitly. Wittgenstein's analogy between a vocabulary and a tool, he says, "has one obvious drawback."

> The craftsman typically knows what job he needs to do before picking or inventing tools with which to do it. By contrast, someone like Galileo, Yeats or Hegel . . . is typically unable to make clear exactly what it is that he wants to do before developing the language in which he succeeds in doing it. *His new vocabulary makes possible for the first time a formulation of its own purpose.*[39]

Only after a new vocabulary is up and running, as it were, can its creators appreciate retrospectively what it is good for and how it fares better than the vocabulary it replaced. Although few would disagree that there is always more to a tool than what goes into it and that it is never possible to anticipate all its uses before it is actually employed, Rorty's position is far more radical. Only after an alternative vocabulary is endorsed and employed can the problems solved by its endorsement even be formulated. A functioning final vocabulary can only be deemed normatively wanting from the perspective of another.

In other words, a final vocabulary cannot be normatively trouble-shot and modified from within but only by someone working from the outside, someone whose final vocabulary it no longer is. A person can be "ironically" suspicious of her final vocabulary and desire to experiment with other ways of life, as Rorty's ironist is. But she can never do so *for a reason*. One is unable ever to state what is, or might be, wrong with one's normative commitments (other than to find them incongruous with other of one's norms or in need of further clarification). In short, a language game cannot be reflected upon, it cannot admit of normative shortcomings, cannot be criticized, and cannot be improved upon from within, except in the trivial sense of troubleshooting for consistency, coherence, or clarity. Language games may be fashioned by humans but never for a purpose other than for their sheer novelty. And thus, as Rorty is the first to admit, precious as it may be, our admirable capacity for self-criticism and self-improvement is required by his philosophy to stop short of its seemingly profoundest, to be replaced by the aimless experimentation of clueless irony.

At one point Rorty briefly explains why. Quoting Davidson's "Paradoxes of Irrationality,"[40] and alluding to the distinctions between thick and thin normative concepts as well as to that, late of Frankfurt, between first- and second-order desires, Rorty presents a strictly coherentist account of in-house critical reflection. He notes that if we reserve the term *rational*

> to mean something like "internal coherence," ... then we shall be forced to call "irrational" many things we wish to praise. In particular we shall have to describe as "irrational" what Davidson calls "a form of self-criticism and reform which we hold in high esteem, and that has even been thought to be the very essence of rationality and the source of freedom."[41]

The process by which "a person forms a positive or negative judgment of some of his own desires," and acts to change them, he explains, is limited to acts of self-criticism and self-improvement pertaining to a "higher-level" desire capable of mediating and rationalizing the contesting lower first- and second-level desires. However, working up the hierarchy one necessarily reaches a point where the only candidates for such highest-level desires are abstract and empty as to have no mediating powers: They are typified by 'I wish to be good', 'I wish to be rational', and 'I wish to know the truth.' Because what will *count* as 'good' or 'rational' or 'true' will be determined by the contest between the first- and second-level desires, wistful top-level protestations of goodwill are impotent to intervene in that contest. (49)

The possibility of rational appraisal doing real normative work swiftly evaporates as normative concepts become "thinner." And thus, just at the point that our highest and most relished norms and standards "thicken" out to acquire the precise meanings they have for us, they freeze and fossilize, and, for lack of independently meaningful higher standards by which to judge them, are rendered immune to the normative scrutiny of those whose form of life they govern.

Given these constraints on rational self-criticism and self-improvement, Rorty is left no choice but to portray the self-consciously critical pathbreaking work of a Galileo or a Hegel as the outcome of the aimless tinkering of a Rortian ironist. He is aware of how outrageous he must sound but sees no reason to reconsider. He voices the natural objections, only to dismiss them, not by taking anything back, but by rejecting the vocabulary by which they are voiced. Going as it does to the heart of the problem, his comments here are worth quoting at length.

To accept the claim that there is no standpoint outside the particular historical conditioned and temporary vocabulary we are presently using from which to judge this vocabulary is to give up on the idea that there can be reasons for using languages as well as reasons within languages for believing statements. *This amounts to giving up the idea that intellectual or political progress is rational, in any sense of "rational" which is neutral between vocabularies.* But because it seems pointless to say that all the great moral and intellectual advances of European history—Christianity, Galilean science, the Enlightenment, Romanticism, and so on—were fortunate falls into temporary irrationality, the moral to be drawn is that the rational-irrational distinction is less useful than it once appeared. Once we realize that progress, *for the community as for the individual,* is a matter of using new words as well as arguing from premises phrased in old words, we realize that a critical vocabulary which revolves around notions like "rational", "criteria", "argument", and "foundation" and "absolute" is badly suited to describe the relation between the old and the new.[42]

The problem regarding our critical vocabulary is, of course, not at all that of describing "the relation between the old and the new" but that of describing the effort invested in forming and fashioning the new as an activity thoughtfully and meaningfully performed on, and from within the old. It is not that of overcoming the incommensurability between two normatively incongruous existing frameworks but that of deeming the search or creation of one as rationally motivated while committed to the other.

Nor has the question, as we pose it and shall elaborate further in upcoming chapters, anything to do with "foundations" or "absolutes." *Rational,* as we insist on employing the term, is a category of action and agency, not of the relations obtaining between statements, languages, or paradigms.[43] The question is not whether the new can be understood or inferred from the old but whether its fashioning can be described as the outcome of the reasoned deliberation of anxious practitioners committed to and working from within the old.

Rorty flatly denies that it can. He is clearly aware that in saying so he is doing violence not only to the term *rationality,* but to everything we know about the way in which creative individuals critically reflect on, not merely toy with, their norms, their standards, their tools, and their methods. It strikes us not merely as irrelevant or superfluous—or as pointless, as Rorty has it—to describe such "great moral and intellectual advances of European history" as the fortunate falls of aimless, blind tinkering but as downright absurd! Rorty, one feels, should not be allowed to get away with it by merely switching terminologies or refusing to use certain words (a move *he* makes quite purposefully, one should add, not as a result of blindly toying).[44]

The question, however, is not a matter of sticking with or abandoning certain words, and certainly not that of approving or disapproving such evasion tactics. The problem is a major one. Rorty's problem is that, absurd as it may seem to some, the philosophy of language and mind to which he subscribes will not allow him to view normative vocabularies as subject to reasoned modification or replacement (except, again, in the uninteresting sense of testing for consistency, coherence, or clarity). For him, dropping the troublesome terminology is not an evasion tactic. His philosophy leaves him no choice.

Does our commitment to the rational appraisal of the standards and norms we employ leave *us* no choice but to drop Rorty's troublesome philosophy? The answer is neither a simple yes nor a simple no. So far all we have established is that Rorty's normative relativism is incompatible with the notion of rational appraisal when applied reflexively to the normative vocabulary by which it speaks. If that was all we were claiming, it would have been a matter of deciding to which horn of the dilemma we were more deeply committed. But the matter is not so simple for the simple reason that Rorty's normative relativism is not an option easily set aside. So far we have stated our own preferences and described Rorty's contrasting account of the dynamics of normative vocabularies and contrasted it with our own. We have not yet argued for either. It is now time to say a little more about our point of departure, and to examine a little more closely the theories of thought, meaning, and commitment that ground the type of position Rorty represents. Only then will we be in a position to take fuller stock of the dilemma and the prospects of confronting it anew by means of more than a change of words.

The Road Taken

Those who accept (some version of) the first, neo-Kantian step in Rorty's argument but, like us, are unwilling to accept his radical conclusions have one of two nondismissive options. One option is to argue for there being some kind of foothold external to one's normative vocabulary capable of facilitating its critique from within.[45] The modest absolutism premised, for instance, by Dworkin's Rawlsian critique of Walzer's interpretivist ethics is one such approach.[46] The external foothold, as we shall see, need not be absolutist, however. Michael Friedman's *Dynamics of Reason,* though limited exclusively to science, belongs in this subtler category (see chapter 5 below).

The second option is to meet the challenge head-on by opposing Rorty's conclusions without contesting the premises that support them (or, as described above, by conceding the first step and contesting the second of the two-step argument). This, as we have stated, is the option adopted here.

Our interests naturally lie beyond the specifics of Rorty's own position. It is the *type* of challenge his work poses to rationality that animates this study, one we wish first to reformulate in a way that we find most general and effective. Properly constructed, it is a challenge we find deep and far-reaching, to a large extent valid, and not at all easily dismissed. In our reading, it comprises two oft-conflated theses that, we believe, can and need to be properly formulated, analyzed, and distinguished. The first, mentioned briefly above, is the denial of a normative scale on which two maximally coherent yet sufficiently diverse normative outlooks can be ordered in a manner acceptable to both. It claims, in other words, that there is no purely normative relevant comparative property that is shared by significantly conflicting normative outlooks, and, therefore, is capable of ranking them. We call this meta-normative position *Comparative Irrealism*. Comparative Irrealism, however, entails that because (unbiased) normative comparisons of sufficiently diverse (and sufficiently coherent) outlooks are not forthcoming, an outlook cannot be deemed normatively wanting from within *in comparison to a superior alternative*.[47]

The second claim, to which the present work devotes itself to contesting, is that since an outlook cannot be found normatively wanting by comparison, it cannot be found normatively wanting at all! The logic is simple: if for lack of a suitable comparative normative vocabulary, an outlook cannot be deemed by its adherents normatively inferior to another, then, for the very same reason, neither can they find it normatively wanting *in itself*. For the question would always be: wanting in comparison to what? A normative outlook may be judged from within to be inconsistent, incoherent, or unacceptably inexplicit, and, to some extent, even lacking in comparison to another. But, lacking a comparative dimension, the argument goes, it cannot be deemed *wrong, false*, or *unjust*. And if an outlook cannot be deemed *normatively* problematic by its own lights, its present normative state can never be deemed to be the outcome or the subject matter of rational scrutiny as defined at the outset.

The ultimate aim of the following pages is to drive a wedge between Comparative Irrealism and the claim claimed to follow from it, according to which all normative criticism is by nature comparative. We thus seek to salvage a robust notion of normative self-criticism while fully conceding the broadly conceived neo-Kantian and neo-pragmatist premises of the first step of Rorty's argument.

Before outlining the argument unfolded in the following chapters, let us reiterate our point of departure and motivation for taking the road that we take. We set forth from what we characterized above as rational action's defining feature (even for those who do not require agency in the actual performance of the acts they consider rational), namely, that it is (at least in the last analysis) *considered* action,[48] action taken on reflection, for which a person is liable to be prompted and to be willing to give his *reasons* for taking.[49] In other words, we take rational action to be action deemed appropriate. Which, in yet other words, is to take it to be inherently *norm governed*. From which follows that for an act to be deemed rational, standards of propriety must be in place at least prior to the deeming. It is in this sense that we take normative commitment to be *constitutive* of rationality. Hence the problem of revising normative commitment rationally.

Moreover, although the point is little stressed in the literature, we insist in addition, as noted above and as the language of the previous paragraph implies, on taking rationality to be, in essence, a *prospective* category of acting. There is a crucial difference between action opted for for a reason and action taken thoughtlessly and justified only after the event, between the exercise of reason in *evaluating* a move and in *making* it.[50] Retrospective justification, or rationalization, can justify an act only in the sense of deeming it in retrospect to have been the *right* thing to do, but it cannot count as the actor's *reason* for so acting. If to act rationally is to act *for* a reason, *because* prompted or motivated by that reason, then action reasoned for only by hindsight, for which reasons are assigned only after the event, falls short of full-blooded rationality.[51]

The problem that animates this study arises when commitment to the prospective nature and inherent norm-governed-ness of rationality comes to bear in considering the possibility of rational norm revision. No such problem arises for those who deny Normative Diversity and/or the very possibility of rationally contrived normative realignment. But for those of us who do not, the problem of rational norm revision, as we shall explain immediately, is a major one, deemed by most insurmountable.

But first two points of clarification. First, in what follows normative diversity, that is, the plurality of incompatible normative outlooks, will be assumed, not proven or even justified. We take *normativity,* the self-committed, and commitment-driven nature of human agency, to be a human universal, in the sense of being definitive of sapience. And we join Taylor, Brandom, and others in viewing normativity further as grounded in our discursive capacities. But, bracketing contingently shared areas of "minimal code," we take no normative *content* to be fixed or universal.

The second point concerns the possibility of rational norm revision. It is important to understand that the aim of this study is *not* to *prove* that framework transitions can be genuinely motivated by rational argument and deliberation. We know that they can. The problem we set ourselves is primarily not that of convincing our readers that norm revision can be rational but that a compelling philosophical *account of* their rationality is forthcoming—passé Rorty—from the broadly neo-Kantian and neo-pragmatist perspective from which we write. Of all the thinkers whose work is engaged in what follows, Friedman's *Dynamics of Reason* steers closest to us in this respect. Friedman does not ask whether framework transitions in physics are rational but rather how to make philosophical sense of their rationality from the essentially Kuhnian perspective to which he is committed. Like Friedman's, our work too is primarily a work of philosophy.

The Problem

Revisable normative frameworks are adjusted and changed in a variety of ways, some surreptitious and unwitting, some contrived and deliberate. Concentrating on the *rationality* of framework revision, we focus naturally on a subset of the latter category: namely, cases in which a functioning framework is modified or replaced *for* a reason. Now, the only *prospective* reason practitioners might have for wanting to alter or replace their framework is to find it in some sense sufficiently wanting to be reconsidered (as opposed to cases, of which Rorty makes much, in which replacing the old framework is justified in retrospect from the now-perceived superior perspective of the new).

There are three senses in which a functioning normative framework can, in principle, be faulted from within: it could be found *incoherent,* in some sense *lacking,* or in some sense *wrong.* The first two are relatively unproblematic because they do not involve deeming any part of it to be normatively flawed. They are also, as we shall see, largely uninteresting.

Formal failings—inconsistency, incoherence, or insufficient clarity— may well require modifying or even relinquishing lower-level commitments in the light of higher-level standards.[52] But doing so proves the framework to be considered right, not wrong! All the more so in cases where, in engaging other cultures, one's framework is supplemented by unforeseen normative possibilities encountered. Here, too, amendment is achieved without any part of the original framework being normatively condemned.[53] In the first case, lower-level commitments may well be relinquished, but they will be dropped because they are found expendable, not because they are deemed normatively wanting. In the second, a commitment is added but none renounced.

Both cases obviously represent rational forms of normative adjustment. But they are powerless to account for the rationality of transitions between incommensurable or normatively incompatible alternatives, cases in which practitioners contrive to locate or to fashion frameworks significantly different from their own—as in the case of scientific revolutions. Troubleshooting for inconsistency or incoherence can result in normative reprioritizing within a given system, and in extreme cases, in pruning certain of its expendable elements. Awakening to new possibilities can at most result in *supplementing* the existing system (but never, as we shall argue at length, in rationally motivating *replacing* one of the system's existing elements, which would be in blatant violation of Comparative Irrealism). It is, therefore, to the third option that we direct our attention—where frameworks are revised or replaced, because deemed normatively wanting, an option that would seem to characterize processes of rational norm revision far better than the other two, yet is considered notoriously problematic to the point of incoherence.

Framework transitions to normatively incompatible alternatives, involve, by definition, substituting major elements of the system by others—which to be deemed *rational* must be undertaken for a reason. Here, in particular, the difference between prospective and retrospective justification is crucial, because the norms governing the reasoning are replaced in the course of the transition. Finding reason retrospectively for having relinquished norms or standards to which one is *no longer* committed is a matter quite different from finding normative reason to do so while they still bind one.

Hence the problem. To insist that rationality be both prospective and norm-governed and that norm revision can be rational is hence to insist that rational agents not only exercise their norms and standards *in* self-criticism but also make them the *object* of such criticism, that one can coherently deem wrong one's very standards of right and wrong! No viable philosophical account of personal identity makes room for such feats of self-negation. On the other hand, no amount of mere prioritizing or supplementation, we insist, can get one rationally from Aristotelian to Newtonian physics, for example. It follows that if troubleshooting (prospectively) for coherence or (retrospectively) for lacunae is held to exhaust the range of *rational* normative revision, then Rorty must be granted his point that the classical examples of framework replacement in science and philosophy, or the type of deep social reform explored by Walzer, can simply not be considered rational—a conclusion we firmly contest.

No work to date has addressed this dilemma openly and systematically. This is our aim in what follows. But we do so with a bias. If one is committed, as we are, to the possibility of rational norm revision (pace Rorty), one has one of two options:

(a) to argue for a viable philosophical account of normative self-criticism capable of meeting the obvious objections, or
(b) to argue that the rationality of radical framework transition can be fully and viably accounted for without resort to normative self-criticism, on the basis solely of troubleshooting for normative coherence, and openness to noncritical normative supplementation.

Many, including Brandom, Friedman, and McDowell, whose work we discuss and build on, opt for (b). The bias of the present study is firmly in favor of (a).

The Argument

The remainder of this book consists of three parts. Part I, "Through Thick and Thin," purports rigorously to make the case for Comparative Normative Irrealism: the principle, to which this study remains committed throughout, according to which two sufficiently diverse normative outlooks are normatively unrankable. Chapters 2 and 3 argue for Comparative Irrealism on semantic grounds, from the different perspectives of two major theories of meaning that dominate approaches that take seriously the neo-Kantian idea of the constitutive role of language. By utilizing the distinction introduced by Bernard Williams and Michael Walzer between thick and thin normative concepts, we are able to chart a robust framework-dependent notion of normative realism, as well as to make a compelling case for Normative Diversity with reference to the former (e.g., concepts such as modesty, valor, or holiness). The idea is to show that with respect to both theories—those that ground meaning in communal norms and idiolect-based theories late of Davidson—the very assumption of Normative Diversity entails Comparative Irrealism, that is, the unrankability in principle of sufficiently alien normative outlooks. The upshot of Part I is, therefore, that if normative self-criticism is at all possible, it cannot be comparative.

The three chapters in Part II, "Rationality from Within," assess and engage three important latter-day philosophical positions, all of which share premises significantly akin to our own and bear directly on issues central to the question we raise.

Normative Diversity, the incomparability in principle of sufficiently different normative outlooks, and the transformative role of "connected" normative criticism from within are the very principles on which the so-called interpretive approach to ethics is built. Chapter 4 purports, first, to substantiate the interpretive account (in its Walzerian rather than Taylorian form)[54] in terms of the thick/thin distinction developed in Part I, and in a manner applicable to normativity in general. The second and more critical objective of chapter 4 is to expose and analyze the constraints interpretivism seems inevitably to impose on the kind of normative self-criticism it seeks to promote, which we ultimately find too restrictive. Under an interpretivist construal, normative criticism can venture no further than to challenge other articulations of a given way of life and is powerless to challenge the way of life itself.

Friedman's work on the rationality of framework transitions in science is the topic of chapter 5. Though limited to science, Friedman's Kuhnian point of departure steers closest to the presuppositions that animate the present study: forcefully conceding the framework-dependency of science late of Kant, as well as the Normative Diversity and Comparative Irrealism of a science's successive frameworks—at least to a certain extent. Also appealing is his willingness to deem rational framework transitions exceedingly more radical than those allowed by interpretivists. And yet, as we argue in some detail, unlike interpretivists, Friedman's account succeeds in steering wide of any mention of the problem of normative self-criticism by focusing exclusively on the so-called problem of incommensurability, namely, that of explaining how, *once formed*, a new scientific framework can be considered retrospectively a "live option" by practitioners of the old. Lacking from Friedman's picture is any attempt to account *prospectively* for the rational incentive *to seek or form* an alternative to a functioning scientific framework in the first place—without which, we argue, no account of the rationality of scientific paradigm shifts can be considered complete. To do so, we insist, the problem of normative self-criticism is unavoidable.[55]

Chapter 6 is devoted to Robert Brandom's inferentialist normative pragmatism (appropriately extended from conceptual norms to normativity in general, as suggested by the work of Jeffrey Stout, as well as by some of Brandom's own more recent writing), in which, we argue, the interpretivist position receives powerful (if unacknowledged) articulation. Brandom's system offers a rich account of rational action as *reasoned* action that, not unlike Friedman's, appears to make no room for criticism. But unlike Friedman's account, we find in Brandom's "deontic scorekeeping" (especially when its Kantian and Hegelian underpinnings are sufficiently exposed) an articulation of reasoned discourse that tacitly attributes to its participants an essentially self-critical motivational stance.[56] Making Brandom explicit in this regard, so to speak, paves the way for the constructive account of normative self-criticism we propose and develop in Part III.

In chapter 7, the first of the three concluding chapters of the book, we propose, in outline, an essentially pragmatist phenomenology of (prudent) criticizing as a discursive move, or speech-act, clearly distinguished from doubting, questioning, testing, and being merely pressed for one's reasons. Criticism is analyzed as an *addressed* act of speech, directed to alerting its addressees to the existence of a problem or shortcoming within the compass of their responsibility and, in doing so, prompting them to take action. When properly distinguished from, say, mere testing, all criticism is shown to contain an element of rebuke. To be criticized is to be held, to some extent, *responsible* for the shortcomings exposed; to be prompted not only to attend to those shortcomings, but in some sense also to mend one's ways. Hence, all criticism, it is argued, comprises some measure of *normative* criticism. And because the aim of all prudent criticism is to convince its addressee to take action, to achieve its desired transformative effect, it must be endorsed by its addressee as *self-criticism*. Normative self-criticism is, therefore, at least to some degree, of the very nature of *all* criticism.

Placing the onus of rationality on criticism, as we do, ultimately locates the transformative locus of rational reckoning in the realm of intrapersonal deliberation rather than interpersonal discourse. Participation in the public game of giving and asking for reasons is certainly *the* sure sign of rational engagement. But the outward critical scrutiny of one another's reasoning will have its rational transformative effect only when accompanied by a parallel, resonating self-scrutinizing of one's commitments and entitlements. Indispensable as participation in the public game of giving and asking for reasons is to demonstrating one's rationality, it is only in the intrasubjective processes of normative self-scrutinizing that rationality can properly be said to reside and assert itself.

In chapter 8 we therefore turn our attention inward. Focusing on the so-called hierarchical account of personhood, identity, and normativity developed by Charles Taylor, Christine Korsgaard, and especially Harry Frankfurt, the chapter explores the prospects and especially the limitations it imposes on a person's capacity for normative self-criticism. We find Frankfurt's intrapersonal, volitional account of human agency to resonate well and to an extent to reflect, if implicitly, central aspects of the neo-Kantian, pragmatist, and interpretivist pictures of interpersonal normative discourse explored in Part II.

The problem is that no account of human selfhood will suffice of itself to adequately account for the possibility of genuine normative self-criticism—not even Frankfurt's—for the simple reason that left to her own devices, a person is indeed incapable of taking genuinely critical normative stock of her own normative commitments. The central claim of chapter 8, which is the central claim of the entire study, is that a viably philosophical account of normative self-criticism does indeed present itself but only when the two pictures are amalgamated: when a detailed Frankfurtian picture of the reflective self is grafted onto an equally detailed picture of the kind of critical discursive environment pictured by Brandom and Walzer. This has so far never been seriously attempted. Those, like Taylor, Korsgaard, and Frankfurt, whose interest lies in the kind of reflective, intrasubjective self-reckoning central to questions of self, agency, and practical reasoning, have given little if any thought to the possible bearings on it of the external intersubjective discursive contexts in which the selves they study constantly partake. Conversely, thinkers like Brandom, McDowell, and Walzer, whose interests lie in the social, dialogical arenas of communal critical discourse, show no interest in following through their possible transformative impact on the personal commitments and self-reasoning of individual discussants.[57] Intrasubjective reflection and intersubjective discourse are studied by philosophers quite independently, as if the extent and quality of a person's dialogical dealings had no bearing on his reflective capacities, and vice versa.

Combining the two realms of discourse does not, however, yield as straightforward a solution to the problem of normative self-criticism as one might expect. For the very same reason that it is impossible to argue normatively against the norms to which one is committed, it is impossible to be convinced to do so by others. If normative *self*-criticism is unthinkable, it remains unthinkable when leveled by others. But if normative criticism is incapable of *convincing* in what sense can it be said to be *rationally* internalized and endorsed?

The answer proposed in chapter 8 follows on the heels of the conclusions of chapter 7. For their criticism to be endorsable by those they criticize, we argue there, prudent critics must base their case on premises *their addressees* hold true. But in the case of normative criticism, this is never an option. No premises exist to which a person is liable to agree, that entail a denunciation of his very norms. Sensing this, normative critics tend to argue from premises close to what their addressees hold true, yet sufficiently different to allow their arguments to stick. (Arguing from the left, critics will surreptitiously premise certain liberal norms to make their case, whereas arguing from the right, they will tend to smuggle in just enough conservative value to prove their point.) Normative criticism thus typically conveys a portrayal of its addressees' relevant commitments that differs minimally yet crucially from their own self-image. Because normative criticism challenges heartfelt norms, it is powerless to *convince,* but if *trusted,* we argue at length, the discrepancy between the two portrayals, as in the case of a disturbing playback (an analogy explored in some detail), is capable of undermining its addressees' initial commitment and of rendering them ambivalent toward those norms. Herein, we argue, lies the destabilizing, or "ambivalating," potential of trusted normative criticism. And, as Frankfurt famously argues, norms to which one becomes ambivalent lose their wholehearted volitional grounding and normative hold and demand to be reassessed.

Chapter 9 takes stock of the book's project by revisiting the dynamics of scientific framework transitions in light of the conclusions of chapter 8. If, as McDowell puts it, an ability to "reflect about and criticize the standards by which, at any time, [we take ourselves] to be governed . . . from the midst of the way of thinking [we are] reflecting about,"[58] becomes a philosophically articulable option only when a critically motivated version of Brandom's interpersonal deontic interrogation is allowed to bear on a Frankfurtian normative dialogue of self (or some similarly hierarchical equivalent), then, to be considered rational, Friedman's Kuhnian picture paradigm shifts require substantial supplementation on both counts. Friedman, as we argue in chapter 5, reduces the problem of rational framework replacement in science to that of communicating rationally across an already existing divide. We take it primarily to be that of the rational *incentive* to create a new framework in the first place. To answer this question, one cannot avoid asking what fault such a person could have found in the framework to which he was still committed—which in light of the conclusions of chapter 8, we argue, can now be addressed from within Friedman's approach, in ways that have so far been unavailable from that perspective.

It is not an easy fit, however. As we have seen, the sort of self-critical disposition needed for setting a paradigm shift in motion requires the challenging environment of trusted, potentially ambivalating criticism. With all due respect to the importance Walzer assigns to the "connected-ness" of effective critics, from the neo-Kantian perspective we share with Friedman, such criticism will clearly not be forthcoming from within the "normal," paradigm-governed discursive settings of one's own field. The initial source of destabilization has to be external. On the other hand, a scientific field can only be transformed from within. Only physicists can change physics! Accordingly, chapter 9 proposes in rough outline a two-stage format for studying scientific paradigm shifts, in which practitioners of voice and standing are first ambivalated by external critics and later (inadvertently) succeed in promulgating their newfound indecision within their communities by means of a particular form of published work. Both stages represent irreducible moments of intense *intrasubjective* deliberation, which do not admit easily to the collectivist modes of explanation that have come to dominate science studies since Kuhn.

To account for the first stage, we propose an extension and reworking of Peter Galison's novel notion of the scientific "trading zone"—the "locales" of professional engagement outside one's home community, as when bidding for financial support, "trading" with neighbor disciplines for techniques or instruments, offering scientific opinion, engaging students, and so forth. The point we stress is how when "trading" abroad one is frequently exposed to the friendly and trustedly bemused questioning of genuinely curious professionals, on whose thinking the framework constitutive of one's own may have far less of a grip. Here, we show, lies the destabilizing and ambivalating potential of science's external critics.

The second stage is achieved when the doubts and indecision of duly ambivalated individuals come tacitly to inform their creative efforts to overcome them. Such efforts are shown to typically take the form of un-easily split, hybrid attempts to re-represent their field's basic assumptions by retaining some of the old while groping imaginatively toward other possibilities. When analyzed *prospectively,* such works can be seen to represent anxious yet highly creative departures from heartfelt commitments capable of motivating others to seeker cleaner, more radical breaks with the old. Classical examples we mention briefly are Tycho's planetary theory, Galileo's analysis of projectile motion, and Poincaré's geometrical conventionalism, all of which we show unwittingly preserved, and therefore propagated, the keen ambivalence that begot them, prompting others to take a firmer stand.

The philosophical problem this study raises and purports to address— that of articulating the possibility of normative self-criticism from a broadly neo-Kantian perspective—is deemed by those who deny Normative Diversity to be misconceived, others (Popper's school, for instance) deem it trivial, but most (explicitly or implicitly) hold it to be insurmountable. Because we concede Normative Diversity and refuse to limit self-criticism to *instrumental* reason, in what follows the work of the first two groups is largely ignored.[59] We contest the third group's conclusions but not by accusing them of misconceiving the problem or of reasoning it through mistakenly. For we fully concede their claim (or assumption, or tacit presupposition) that, of her own accord, a person is indeed incapable of mounting a normative argument against her own norms and, consequently, of being *convinced* to do so by others. If we accuse them of anything, it is of oversight, of failing to notice how the destabilizing impact of rational discourse can extend *rationally* beyond the realm of reasoned exchange. This is the modest undertaking of the chapters that follow.

PART I

Through Thick and Thin

Introduction

The special character of moral diversity and moral disagreement has long been considered the basis for a normative irrealism that has led several writers to deny in general that normative discourse is factual. In their opinion, our diverse normative commitments are to be explained by appealing to noncognitive mental states such as desires rather than to belief in independent moral facts. And since desires, unlike beliefs, do not (of themselves) track truth or propriety,[1] disagreement, deliberation, and change of commitment in the normative realm are not expected to yield to rational consideration. From such a perspective, our commitment to the diversity of normative outlooks would seem quite at odds with the very idea of rational normative revision that animates this study. The two chapters comprising Part I propose a less crude notion of normative irrealism with regard to which the possibility of rational normative revision remains at least an open question. But first a word about the opposition. Such a combination of antirealism (regarding the factuality of moral properties) and noncognitivism (regarding the source of moral commitments) as described above is typical, for example, of Gilbert Harman's approach.[2] Harman's version of ethical relativism comprises three main claims:[3]

1.   If a person fails to comply by a moral demand D that applies to him, it will be due either to ignorance of the relevant facts, to a failure to reason something through, or to some mental defect or disorder like irrationality, stupidity, confusion, or illness.
2.   Nonetheless, not all are necessarily subject to D. For it is possible that for two people A and B (both subject to some moral demands) D applies only to A but does not to B, because B does not accept D.
3.   There exists no more basic moral principle D^* such that D^* applies to A and B and explains why D applies to A but not to B.

The difficulty seems straightforward: if A is subject to D and B is not, there must be something true of A but not of B that accounts for the difference. There should be a way of arguing that due to certain features lacking in B, A is subject to D while B is not. A description of these features along with their moral implications would constitute the moral principle D^* that applies to A and B and explains their different relationships to D. To this Harman replies as follows:

4. A but not B may be subject to D because it is rational for A to accept D, but not rational for B to do so, and this is sometimes . . . due simply to the fact that A and B start out accepting sufficiently different moral demands in the first place.[4]

Harman's use of "rational" notwithstanding, his answer calls for further elaboration. How do A and B view each other in this respect? Is it not the case that if A regards D as morally compelling, he must also believe that B should accept D as well, otherwise he is liable not to conceive his own subjection to D as moral. But if Harman's relativism is valid, A must be wrong. The source of his mistake, suggests Harman,[5] is that he conceives his acceptance of D as being due to moral facts; he believes that certain modes of conduct are good and others bad *as a matter of fact*. But this is not so. According to Harman, there is no such thing as a moral property or a moral fact. In insisting that D applies to B, A fails to realize that the source of his own commitments is noncognitive. Accepting D is the right thing to do for A, not by virtue of objective facts, but due to his particular set of desires. For B, who lacks this set of desires, it is not. It is easy to see how such a combination of noncognitivism and antirealism applies to all manner of normativity. For the sake of brevity, we shall call this position "standard normative irrealism."

Many find this combination of premises too high a price to pay. We agree. But is there a way of being more selective without surrendering Normative Diversity altogether? To take normative diversity seriously obviously requires premising some form of normative antirealism. On the other hand, the source of discomfort with the standard view is the lack of seriousness with which it treats the fact that people regularly justify their ethical commitments with reference to what they take to be cognitions of normative facts. The standard view hails this as an illusion. In what follows we shall argue for a more nuanced and selective form of normative relativism, which remains equally committed to normative diversity while conceding normative factuality and in doing so declaring neither of them mistaken. The idea is to grant factuality to all normative properties *except those* employed in comparing and ranking different normative outlooks. Our argument aspires to refine, pinpoint, and, most important, reduce to a bare minimum the worrisome, wholesale antirealism too easily granted by the standard view, by specifying where exactly the phenomenon of normative diversity should compel one to be skeptical about the reality of the normative.

But we aim at more than merely presenting Comparative Irrealism as an option. In upcoming chapters we present two different versions of the argument, leveled from two different major approaches to meaning and normativity. The two chapters in Part II argue for Comparative Irrealism from the semantic points of view of community-based and Davidsonian approaches to meaning. Taken together, the two accounts leave little room for those who are unwilling to dismiss the phenomenon of radical normative diversity as an illusion and to draw the realist-antirealist divide with regard to the normative any tighter. The upshot is clear enough. Within the very broadly conceived boundaries of current neopragmatist philosophies of language, mind, and action, the very acknowledgment of normative diversity should compel one to deem normative vocabularies immune to critical evaluation from within, just as Rorty suggests. If thin normative concepts are incapable of comparing and ranking normative vocabularies, then, viewed from within, a normative vocabulary cannot, in principle, be deemed wrong, or mistaken in relation to another. Making this claim in detail is the objective of the two chapters that follow, which together furnish the point of departure for the remainder of the book, namely, that if Rorty's challenge is to be met, it must be met *noncomparatively.*

CHAPTER TWO

Comparative Irrealism and Community-Based Semantics

Kripkenstein and Beyond

Normativity through Thick and Thin

Imagine a "conservative" and a "liberal" community who happen to share the same territory.[1] Their relationship and proximity are "accidental"; they just happen to be neighbors, although they share different cultural heritages and are privy to different historical memories. Suppose further that the ethical outlook of the conservative community is shaped by such concepts as family honor, tradition, and modesty, which are not used at all by the liberals, whose ethical outlook is shaped, conversely, by such concepts as spontaneity, freedom, and creativity, for which the conservatives, in turn, have no use. These are thick normative concepts. Thick, in that they characterize the particularity of the normative thought and discourse of the two communities; they play major roles in the ways they narrate their histories and conceive their collective identities. They are normative, or action guiding, in the sense that they constitute facts "that supply concrete justifications for acting one way or another.... They function as reasons, in the basic, normative sense of considerations that speak in favor of a given course of action."[2]

Following Williams, Scanlon, and others, normative irrealists argue for the primacy of the thick. (The reverse, however, is not always the case. Scanlon, to take the obvious example, seems to grant primacy to the thick without becoming an irrealist.) There is no one substantive property—the property of being good or valuable—that in and of itself provides reasons for action. That is to say, there is no master property that constitutes or explains the concrete value of particular actions. Rather, reasons are provided by what are regarded as the natural properties of actions and things.[3] After all, there is a vast diversity of things that we take to be good, appropriate, or valuable. "Why do moral agents require special procedures for deliberating about what to do? Won't it suffice to apply our general procedures of normative reflection to such concrete values (and dis-values) as loyalty, suffering, betrayal, need, dependence, autonomy and choice . . . ?"[4]

The main argument for the primacy of the thick draws on the nature of practical deliberation: what motivate us are not truths about the good or the bad but rather concrete judgments about what would hurt one's feelings or be demeaning or cruel or helpful, and so on.[5]

Abstract concepts expressed by words like 'good', 'right', 'desirable', and 'rational' are thin. Generating thin concepts requires no anthropological involvement; they are designed to describe human agency and its normative aspects rather than any particular exemplification of them.[6] That is, despite fierce adherence to their respective positions, members of both communities agree that, wrong as they may think their neighbors are, people behave in the light of what *they* think is good. Thus, everyone who understands the phrase 'better than' would agree that if a person rates *a*-like conduct better than *b*-like conduct in *C*-like circumstances, then other things being equal, he would choose *a* rather than *b* in *C*. Hence, people in both communities find thin concepts helpful for describing themselves and others as agents as normatively committed people who have goals and final ends.

Note that 'good', 'right', and 'rational' function not only as thin predicates in the above sense roughly depicted but also as placeholders, as tools for shortening long stories composed of thick judgments. To say that something is good is merely shorthand for saying that certain of its substantive properties constitute concrete considerations that speak in its favor. As placeholders, such predicates also serve to express decisions between conflicting thick considerations. If immodest behavior becomes necessary for defending one's honor, a member of the conservative community might rate it appropriate, obligatory, or good. "Appropriate" and "good" function here as shorthand for the ranking and prioritizing of first-order obligations by which such conflicts are adjudicated. When they function as placeholders, thin predicates stand for different properties in communities that employ different thick concepts. They play the same semantic role in all communities qua their role as placeholders rather than by virtue of their extensions.

Here, however, we shall be interested in their role as thin concepts rather than as placeholders. To emphasize again: in addition to the different roles they play *within* different normative outlooks, they also have a crucial role to play in describing the goals people set themselves in ways that are unrelated to any particular communal framework.[7]

Normative Diversity

With these distinctions between the thick and the thin in mind, different sets of thick normative concepts can be said to constitute different "normative outlooks"—or different "conceptions of the good." We assume that people share a "form of life" insofar as they utilize, at least to a significant degree, the same set of thick concepts. Sharing a form of life in this respect does not imply, of course, that the members of the community will never find themselves in disagreement as to what should be done at a given moment. What it implies is that in any such case they will be able to state their disagreements by appealing to their shared vocabulary of thick concepts.[8]

We further stipulate that different forms of life are *in conflict* if enough of the thick beliefs that constitute the shared normative sensitivities of the one generate thin judgments that contradict the thin judgments generated by the thick beliefs of the other. More precisely, consider a certain mode of behavior, call it *b*, which is at once a paradigm case of immodesty and a paradigm case of creativity and spontaneity. Assume, for the sake of simplicity, that part of being considered a paradigm case of immodesty is that if a person holds *b* to be immodest, then he also holds that, all things considered, *b* as such is undesirable.[9] And similarly for creativity: if one considers *b* to be a paradigm case of creativity, then he deems it to be, all things considered, desirable. Under these assumptions, adhering to both judgments necessarily involves holding two contradictory beliefs.

Our stipulation is this: forms of life in which there are enough *b*-like cases are in conflict. Note that no contradiction follows from our characterization of conflicting forms of life. We are not arguing inconsistently that *b* is, all things considered, bad (due to being immodest) and that *b* is, all things considered, good (due to being spontaneous) but only that conservatives (liberals) who believe that *b* is paradigmatically immodest (spontaneous) would believe it to be bad (good).

Assuming that such normative diversity in fact exists (we address arguments to the contrary, such as David Wiggins's, in the fourth section below), what are its theoretical consequences? To stay with our schematic example, a general theory of normative diversity should be able to account for the disagreement between liberals and conservatives with respect to *b*. On the face of it, the two communities differ as to whether or not *b* is morally desirable. But such a theory must go beyond their first-order moral choices and give a reasonable account for their conceptualization of their very normative diversity. In other words, it must deal with the question of whether the liberals deny the conservative thick judgment that *b* is immodest, and, conversely, whether the conservatives reject the liberal assessment of *b* as spontaneous.

A negative answer to both questions could be reasoned for as follows: one might quite plausibly assume that possessing a concept consists in the capacity to apply it correctly to paradigm cases. Call this "the paradigm case maxim": *If one understands the predicate* 'F' *one believes that* Fa, *if* a *is paradigmatically F and one is acquainted with* a. (Confronted by children torturing their pets—a paradigm case of cruelty—one would expect a person who understands the word *cruel* and is acquainted with pets to form the belief that the children are acting cruelly.) Now recall that to form the thick judgment that *b* is immodest consists, among other things, in deeming *b* to be undesirable (which is simply to assume that the concept of modesty is normative or "action guiding"). It follows that a liberal who believes that *b* is spontaneous, but possesses the concept of modesty, will be expected to also deem *b* to be immodest. But this would commit her to believing absurdly that, all things considered, *b* is both good and bad.

An immediate and natural response would be to claim that while a liberal may be fully capable of *recognizing* immodesty and therefore of being in full possession of the concept of immodesty, recognition per se does not constitute a normative, reason-giving judgment for everyone. Being the liberal she is, for *her*, such a judgment, though fully comprehensible, carries no normative content. Such a move is in line with the so-called prescriptivist analysis of thick normativity. Prescriptivists maintain that thick normative judgments are conjunctions of descriptive and normative elements. The claim that *b* is immodest or cruel is conceived by them as comprising a value-free description of *b*, in conjunction with a *thin* moral proposition about every action that satisfies the description. No absurdity is involved in the liberal's judgment, the response would go, since when a liberal assents to '*b* is immodest' she should be understood as believing a *descriptive* proposition expressed by the statement, without assenting to the normative import it has for her conservative neighbors.

Perspectivism, however, fails to fully capture the feature of thick normative belief in which we are most interested. Remember that what requires explanation, as we stated our problem at the outset, is the nature of the liberal's belief that *b* is immodest. Immodesty, as understood by conservatives, like spontaneity in liberal discourse, is a genuinely descriptive predicate, which, as Williams has it, "may be rightly or wrongly applied, and people who have acquired [them] can agree that [they] apply or fail to apply to some new situation. . . . [T]he use of the concepts is . . . controlled by the facts or by the user's perception of the world."[10] At least on the face of it, in applying these concepts people do not make value-free judgments. Rather, they perform single, unified acts of value-laden perception. Even when the liberals of our example perceive behavior as immodest it strikes us as inadequate, at least phenomenologically, to describe them as merely entertaining a purely descriptive proposition.

Even if there are some underlying descriptive facts upon which thick normative properties supervene, people who perceive and think in terms of thick concepts are typically unable to identify them. There may be some measure of theoretical merit to carving up the use of thick normative concepts into purely descriptive and purely normative components, but such distinctions are quite irrelevant to accounting for what it is for someone to *possess* a thick concept, to have it at his or her linguistic disposal, as it were. Indeed, for a liberal to possess the notion of modesty is (also) for her to be capable of identifying and forming the belief that b is immodest. And to analyze such belief as belief in a value-free proposition seems to us to distort its very meaning.

Note, however, that adopting this line of argument does not commit one to the *reality* of thick ethical properties. Philosophers like Blackburn and Gibbard grant that judgments that feature thick ethical concepts are world guided, so far as their descriptive content goes, while objecting insistently to granting any form of factuality to their normative import. Blackburn and Gibbard hence remain full normative antirealists and still concede everything we have been saying about the nature of thick normative beliefs. We do not need to take issue with their normative antirealism here.[11] Our aim in the present study is to propose a minimalist version of irrealism that remains invariant to the question of the reality of the thick normative properties while denying the reality of comparative thin normative properties. We need not argue for the reality of thick.

On the other hand, our argument does depend on accounting clearly for normative diversity. We thus need a clear picture of what it is for our liberals to be able to *understand* the notion of modesty and be able to apply it. Hence, we need a picture of what it is for them to believe that a (*paradigmatically* immodest) mode of behavior *is* immodest. The perspectivist account fails, we have argued, because for a liberal to believe that b is paradigmatically immodest is for him to entertain more than a merely descriptive proposition.

The main reason for rejecting the prescriptivist's phenomenology is that there seems to be a much better way of accounting for our conservative-liberal debate. When on trial for publishing illegal material, Oscar Wilde was asked whether he didn't think that a certain scene in his *Importance of Being Earnest* should be rated obscene.[12] From the prosecutor's point of view, it was a paradigm case of obscenity. Wilde replied that obscenity was a notion he did not use. Now, it is clear that Wilde knew very well what the word meant and implied; he merely refused to apply it in an evaluative capacity. This strongly suggests that one can grasp a thick evaluative concept not merely as a value-free description but as *someone else's* evaluative category, even though it does not shape one's own normative thinking. In Wilde's case, understanding the meaning of *obscenity* consisted in a capacity for understanding and predicting how those who do use the notion apply it. Such a capacity might be as perceptual, and as directly world guided, as Bernard Williams would have it be.[13]

Indeed, it is our contention that people are generally capable of grasping the meaning and of learning to correctly apply the thick normative concepts of different communities without those concepts having to shape their own normative outlooks. Wilde understands very well what *obscenity* means but refrains, in principle, from using it himself. True, understanding another person's normative concepts involves some measure of sharing her normative outlook and the perceptual sensitivities it demands. Yet an outsider might acquire these sensitivities by willfully undertaking to observe another community, and, for a time, to experience their way of doing things without ever having to adopt their normative outlook. This is how Wilde identifies obscenities, by "listening in" on those who use the concept while refusing to do so himself.[14]

In light of the Wilde example, we suggest that the conservative/liberal debate is about which set of thick concepts to use and how to shape one's ethical thought rather than a debate about the viability of this or that "first-order" normative proposition. *A conflict between forms of life is a normative disagreement with regard to which set of thick ethical concepts one should use.* This is to say that the liberals think that *b* is morally good (the conservatives, that *b* is morally bad). Yet the liberals do not deny that *b* is immodest (after all it is paradigmatically immodest). Nor do they deny that immodesty is bad (after all immodesty is action guiding). In their view, *b* is good despite being "immodest," not because they fail to fully grasp the concept of modesty, but because they hold that one should not use it.

Comparative Irrealism: The Philosophical Thesis

The philosophical thesis premised by the restricted version of Normative Irrealism we wish to propose is based on this account of Normative Diversity in the following way. Faced by the liberal counterexample, conservatives claim that a form of life within which the notion of (say) modesty shapes normative thought is better than forms of life that lack it. In so doing, conservatives attribute to their own form of life the additional property of being *better than* that of the liberals. Comparative Irrealism, as we dub our position, denies the existence of any such property. It does not claim that thin predicates like 'good' or 'right' *never* express concepts. It is only when they are employed as if they were regular predicates capable of attributing normative comparative properties to entire normative outlooks that they are denied reference. In other words, it is a thesis that aims at establishing a contrast between the relevant uses of thin normative predicates like 'good' and 'unworthy' on the one hand and those of such predicates as 'red,' 'heavy', or 'square' on the other, both of which are used by very different communities and can be found in many different languages. The application of the latter, however, is governed by the same standards for all. By contrast, predicates of the former kind, such as 'better than' and 'good', while enjoying similar universal use, are not governed by similar universal standards. For reasons we shall explore below this difference yields a specific form of Normative Irrealism.

Harman's position no longer seems to require across-the-board normative irrealism. There is a demand D, 'avoid b-like behavior', that applies to our conservatives but not to the liberals—and there is no normative principle D^* (which applies to both) that explains why. The reason is that the demand, 'avoid b-like behavior', applies to the conservatives because b-like behavior is clearly immodest. D does not apply to the liberals because they do not use the concept of modesty. Should the liberals use it? Well, if they should, it is, presumably, because doing so is deemed by them to be morally preferable than not doing so. But to express such a preference is to attribute a normative comparative property to a form of life. If our modified version of normative irrealism is viable—as shall be argued shortly—such properties do not exist, and no more would be needed to ground Harman's relativism. Before doing so, however, a different kind of objection needs to be met.

Could Normative Diversity Be a Myth?

Are there really rival forms of life in the sense defined here, or is our story just another philosophical caricature? Many philosophers choose the second option.[15] Wiggins, for example, claims that there is only one possible moral assessment of children torturing cats—that it is cruel. Williams agrees that those who possess the notion of cruelty will necessarily adhere to such a judgment but denies there being anything in the situation to cause someone who does not yet possess the concept of cruelty to use it.[16]

Wiggins remains unconvinced. There is only one moral perspective, he maintains: it is impossible for a person to have a conception of the good yet lack the notion of cruelty, for instance. Williams "would have to show the workability of [an alternative] scheme of moral ideas. . . . [H]e will discover that workability of moral ideas cannot be judged idea by idea." Wiggins considers the question of the possibility of alternative moral attitudes to paradigm cases to be merely rhetorical, one to be answered univocally in the negative.[17]

If there is only one normative perspective, a person capable of forming a conception of the good cannot really refuse to use *any* normative concept. Thus, if Wilde's case is indeed a paradigm case of obscenity, then, in Wiggins's view, there are only two options: either Wilde should agree that the passage in his play is obscene and is thus prima facie objectionable or insist that there is nothing bad in obscenity (i.e., that obscenity is not a normative concept at all). Since the latter option is implausible, Wilde should be viewed, Wiggins would say, not as rejecting the moral claim implicit in his prosecutor's judgment, but as arguing that it is weak, or that, all things considered, it is irrelevant in the light of a higher good achieved by the play—such as the exposition and denouncement of greater evils. Wilde, on such a showing, would not be understood as contesting the principle that obscenity, on and for its own sake, is clearly bad.

In essence, the Williams/Wiggins debate is about historical narratives; they have different views as to how ethical diversity should be described. Wiggins's monism rests less on an argument than on a confident assertion that in their moral judgments all moral people do in fact aspire to a single ethical system to which no alternatives in fact exist.[18]

We do not deny, of course, that many disagreements are far less dramatic than the one we have been describing. Very different communities will often share a battery of thick ethical concepts. Yet they will understand them to have somewhat different extensions, or to differently represent the moral considerations that they entail. Consider a less extreme scenario than the one we have been discussing in which liberals actively use a concept of modesty. It differs from the conservatives' notion with regard only to certain specific modes of behavior and to the overall moral weight liberals attach to undisputed cases of immodesty. In such scenarios, conflicts are due not to differences in the two communities' thick moral vocabulary so much as to disagreements about how to interpret a *shared* vocabulary and the precise weight that it should assign to various considerations it picks out as morally relevant. Wiggins claims that, in principle, these are the *only* ways in which communities ethically diverge.

We believe that Wiggins is mistaken. There are, we insist, many extreme cases of normative disagreement between communities that arise from real differences between their thick normative vocabularies; communities whose disagreement is most naturally interpreted as a disagreement about the normative value of using certain concepts. Such communities will disagree, often bitterly, as to whether a form of life that is structured around certain concepts is better than one that lacks them. And it is with respect to these cases that we argue that normative irrealism can be articulated as skepticism regarding the reality of comparative thin properties of normative vocabularies taken whole. The very viability of our irrealistic argument depends, however, on whether Wiggins is right or wrong in asserting that such cases do not in fact exist.

Refuting Wiggins's position, as he himself indicates, is a matter of counterexample rather than of counterargument. Here is one. Consider the opposition central to (Isaiah Berlin's interpretation of) Machiavelli's *The Prince,* between the Christian praise of righteousness and the ideal of fame typical of high Roman culture. Indeed, in certain societies the religious values of holiness, quietism, and humbleness constitute a complete, closed normative perspective that leaves members of other normative communities wholly unaffected. Pace Wiggins, such examples, it seems to us, are both convincing and in abundance. If this is correct, and we assume it is, the thick/thin distinction as drawn here seems to be the best tool for describing the gulf between incompatible conceptual schemes.

Needless to say, the conservative/liberal debate outlined above is highly schematized and utterly unrealistic. The role played by thick and thin concepts in the real world is far more complex and considerably more nuanced than we make out here. But the schematization is help-ful; it captures one of the deepest aspects of normative thought. What is strictly true about our conservative/liberal debate is approximately true about the largely incompatible forms of life that populate the real world.

In Defense of Comparative Irrealism

We have pointed out that normative diversity and disagreement have led philosophers to doubt the factuality of normative discourse. What we seek to argue in this section is that such irrealistic intuitions can be explained and justified by appeal to the conceptual relationship between *meaning* and *agreement*. The untraditional picture of meaning Kripke advances on behalf of the later Wittgenstein is, perhaps, the clearest statement for this conceptual connection: meanings and (hence) concepts can only be at-tached to words apropos given "forms of life" or "sets of agreement within a community." Put differently, the relations between what we call cultural relativism and the nontraditional conception of meaning suggested by Kripke are crucial in that they explain why the phenomenon of normative diversity leads philosophers to ponder the very reality of moral properties. Hence, in addition to the rough outline of normative diversity defended above, our argument for cultural relativism also presupposes a particular version of Kripke's skeptical solution to the rule-following paradox he finds in Wittgenstein.[19] In what follows we neither defend this concep-tion of meaning, which we grant for the sake of the argument, nor pres-ent it in full.

Kripke's Rule-Following Paradox

The paradox Kripke attributes to Wittgenstein has more than one version, and there is a fair amount of disagreement as to whether it represents Wittgenstein's views at all.[20] Without entering that rather heated debate, we present here a version of the paradox best suited to our needs. We begin with a simple thought experiment. Consider two functions, one ex-pressed by the conventional 'plus', the other, 'quus', defined in terms of the 'plus' function as follows:

For y or x>1,000,000, quus<x,y> = 4
in all other cases, quus<x,y> = x + y.

After studying hard, the twins Castor and Pollex acquire the ability to add numbers. They do well in their studies and regularly come up with the expected answers to the arithmetic tests and quizzes they are given. Being only six years old, however, the sums they are dealt in these tests are always relatively small. As they grow older and their mathematical skills improve, it becomes apparent that Castor uses quus whenever he says he is adding. He insists, for example, that '1,000,000 + 7 = 4', and it proves useless to tell him otherwise. When asked to extend to all sums what he does when adding figures smaller than a million, he assures us that that is exactly what he does. He has no objection to conforming to the accepted way of adding numbers, once it is explained to him. Yet he insists that in doing so he will be applying a new concept. The twins were trained together, by the same teachers and the same methods; they were exposed to the same "data" and examples and acquired and developed their concepts by observing the linguistic behavior of the same people. And still, they seem to have acquired different concepts.[21]

Unless this little story is inherently incoherent, the immediate question it raises is epistemological: how can one ever know in advance what a person means exactly when he or she says "plus"? But according to Kripke's Wittgenstein, doubts run much deeper. The most perplexing question, argues Kripke, is not whether a person's concepts can ever be known by observing his behavior but whether there is anything at all to know! On the face of it, it looks as if one of the twins possesses the appropriate meaning of '+', while his brother fails to do so. Kripke's main efforts are directed to showing that there is no such fact about Pollex that distinguishes him from Castor.

Kripke puts it thus: "agreement is essential for our game of ascribing rules and concepts to each other. . . . [T]he set of responses in which we agree, and the way they interweave with our activities is our *form of life*."[22] The question raised by the rule-following paradox is how is this agreement to be explained.

On Wittgenstein's conception, a certain type of traditional and overwhelmingly natural explanation of our shared form of life is excluded.

We cannot say that we all respond as we do to '68+57' *because* we all grasp the concept of addition in the same way. . . . There is no objective fact . . . that explains our agreement in particular cases. Rather our license to say of each other that we mean addition by '+' is part of a 'language game' that sustains itself only because of the brute fact that we generally agree.[23]

Kripke's way of addressing the paradox is a striking example of reversing the order of explanation so common in philosophy since Hume. To recall, Hume rejects the conviction that we are justified in judging that an *a*-like event will follow a particular event *b* because of the causal relations between *a*-like and *b*-like events. It is the other way around: *a* is causally related to *b* by virtue of our tendency to expect the occurrence of *a*-like event after experiencing a *b*-like event—an expectation that is based on regularity, which is, according to Hume, merely a *brute fact*.

What is known as "the skeptical solution" to the rule-following paradox follows a similar format: the fact that it is considered the right answer does *not* explain the fact that people tend to respond with '125' to '67 + 58 = ?'. The fact that people attach the same meaning to '+' cannot explain why their answers to arithmetical exercises tend to coincide. It is the other way around: it is the wide agreement among them that makes it the case that individuals attach the same meaning to '+'.[24] All we can say is that "[t]he community attributes a given concept to an individual so long as he exhibits sufficient conformity, under test circumstances, to the behavior of the community."[25] This is what having a concept or grasping a sense comes down to, nothing more than behaving linguistically in conformity with the community's received standards.[26]

One lesson can be safely deduced from what we believe are the more solid aspects of the argument. Considered in isolation, there is no sense in which a person can be said to be following a rule or ascribing meaning. To use Kripke's words again:

It turns out that the skeptical solution does not allow us to speak of a single individual, considered by himself and in isolation, as ever meaning anything. . . . [There is no] condition in the world which constitutes my meaning addition by 'plus'—there is no such fact no such condition in either the 'internal' or the 'external' world.[27]

But if this is true, then questions such as "What are the rules that a community, as a whole, follows?" or, "When would we say that the 'community' is mistaken in applying a concept?" are also rendered meaningless. The "community's behavior" is a blunt given in this respect.[28] There can be no point in questioning or attempting to justify the community's linguistic behavior by appealing to underlying rules or standards.[29]

What, then, is the difference between Castor and Pollex? If Castor and Pollex disagree regarding the correct answer to '67 + 58 = ?' only one of them can be right — the one who conforms to the shared practice.

> All that is needed to legitimize assertions that someone means something is that there be roughly specifiable circumstances under which they are legitimately assertable, and that the game of asserting them under such conditions has a role in our lives.[30]

> Any individual who claims to have mastered the concept of addition will be judged by the community to have done so if his particular responses agree with those of the community in enough cases, especially the simple ones. . . . [A]n individual who passes such tests in enough other cases is admitted as a normal speaker of the language and member of the community.[31]

It is important to note that, according to this notion of meaning, there is no clear-cut answer as to whose standards should be used to determine a speaker's concepts. This is made clear by considering a totally isolated speaker. The fact that someone stranded like Robinson Crusoe is physically isolated does not imply that he cannot follow rules or have concepts. Physically isolated individuals can be said to follow rules; only an individual *considered in isolation* cannot be said to do so. Hence, attributing concepts to Robinson Crusoe involves selecting the community with reference to whose practices they are to be attributed. But which is the relevant community for determining the rules Robinson Crusoe should be understood as following? In his case the answer is pretty obvious. But there is no standard and straightforward general answer to such a question — and this in itself bespeaks the fundamental indeterminacy that the community-based conception of meaning normally allows. If one's behavior or biography do not direct us to a linguistic community, nothing can. And if there is no such community that is clearly relevant to his case, there simply can be no clear answer as to which concepts he applies.

An Argument for Comparative Irrealism

This conception of meaning supports the type of Comparative Irrealism we are proposing.[32] Recall that we have argued that the liberal/conservative dispute regarding the undesirability of immodest behavior stems from a more basic dispute as to which of the two sets of thick ethical concepts is morally preferable. At the heart of their numerous first-order moral disagreements, liberals and conservatives are fundamentally divided as to whether the form of life within which, say, the concept of modesty shapes normative thought is better or worse than the form of life within which the concept of creativity was generated. The thin predicates ('. . . better or worse than . . .') utilized in this debate are capable of being formed by any individual sophisticated enough to reflect on human agency, and to distill what is essential to being an agent (among other things, having ends and normative commitments) from his or her own experience.

Our thesis is that the juxtaposition of this account of normative diversity and the kind of community-based conception of meaning we have roughly outlined yields the conclusion that thin concepts—when used to express comparative properties of normative outlooks—cannot be said to express properties at all. The liberals and conservatives of our thought experiment are in error if they suppose that normatively comparative judgments regarding normative outlooks are factual.

The argument runs as follows: according to the community-based conception of meaning, a predicate expresses a concept (i.e., using this predicate is rule governed) only if its correct use can be vouched for by the standards of a given a community of users. To say of thin predicates that they express real properties of normative outlooks is to say that their extension is governed by what the competent speakers of the relevant community take to be their correct application. But since the community relevant to the type of usage of thin predicates comprises, by definition, different communities whose normative outlooks are in conflict, it follows that there can be no shared standards from which the correct application of such concepts can be studied.

Here is the argument in a more structured form:

(i)   According to the community-based conception of meaning, a predicate expresses a concept (i.e., using this predicate is rule governed) only if its correct use can be vouched for by the standards of a given a community of users.

(ii)   With regard to the thin predicates used, say, by liberals and conservatives in comparing their ethical outlooks, the relevant community minimally comprises the combined community of both liberals and conservatives.

(iii) This latter metacommunity uses thin predicates to compare moral outlooks but, again by definition, exhibits no agreement as to how such comparisons should go.

(iv)   Which, in light of (i) is to say that when used to compare normative outlooks, thin predicates simply have no extension.[33]

The advantage of arguing thus is immediately visible: on our construal thick ethical properties are real — and their application is both action guiding and world guided. Relativism results from antirealism only with respect to the thin ethical properties employed in comparative moral assessments of closed fully fledged ethical outlooks, and can now stand unhampered by much unnecessary antirealist baggage other than a bare and (relatively) reasonable minimum. This minimum is enough for motivating the following form of relativism: there might be a normative demand D (avoid b-like behavior) that applies to A while not applying to B, just because A was initiated into a normative outlook in which D is in use. Suppose that D is 'avoid immodest behavior'. This moral demand does not apply to B if B does not use the concept of modesty, since he has no *moral* reason to use it.

One natural objection to the argument might focus on premise (iii). It could be stated thus: suppose we take a community of utilitarians who use 'good' and 'better than' in accordance with the utilitarian moral theory. The same, it could be argued, goes mutatis mutandis for a community of deontologists. Clearly, both groups are using thin moral concepts in a way that pins down their extension. Yet goodness for the first group is tied to facts about the effects of actions upon overall welfare. Their use of thin ethical concepts is guided by utilitarian concerns. And the same can be said (again, mutatis mutandis) for the deontologists. There seems, then, to be a definite and shared judgment each group makes comparing its own normative outlook to the other. And, in performing it, the two groups appear to express a definite normative comparative property that each of them attributes to its own form of life. If this were true, premise (ii) would be refuted.

Note first that in the scenario described it is conceded that the respective uses of the two groups' thin concepts are thoroughly relativized. Whereas the extension of one's use of 'better than' is determined by utilitarian criteria, that of the other is determined by deontological criteria. Rather than view the two groups as trying to use one concept, as we propose, such an objection implies that they are using different concepts entirely. Indeed, the objector avoids a Mackie-style error theory regarding comparative thin normative properties. A closer look reveals, however, that the price to pay for such a strategy is far too high.

In the last analysis there is no sense at all in which the two groups can be said to be *trying* to designate the same comparative property. Hence the objector renders them gravely wrong with regard to each other's thoughts. When an imagined utilitarian argues that her own normative outlook is better than that of a deontologist, she believes that the deontologist denies this very proposition. She believes that they genuinely disagree. Yet, if the objector is right, this is an error; the deontologist has never entertained the proposition the utilitarian attributes to her! We conclude (and our objector must *agree*) that radically different ethical outlooks have no comparative properties with regard to which their adherents can be said to *disagree*.

It might still be argued, however, that the community-based conception of meaning leaves normative absolutism untouched. Recall that this conception of meaning allows freedom in stipulating a community with reference to whose practices concepts are attributed. Given, on the one hand, the universal use of 'better than' (applied to forms of life) and the lack of any set of actually practiced universal standards by which to interpret it, on the other, perhaps the meaning of 'better than' should be fashioned by appeal, not to actual communities, but to *the* perfect one—to the "Kingdom of Ends." Perhaps diversity should not lead us to deny extension to thin predicates (as expressing comparative normative properties of normative outlooks) but rather urges us to raise our sights and speculate on how the normatively perfect community would conduct itself, and on the ways its members would use these terms.[34] If so, the community-based conception of meaning should lead us not to Comparative Irrealism at all but to a form of realism with respect to the ideal.

There are serious reasons for rejecting the Kantian option. Recall that we have assumed that every intelligent person can form thin concepts. Suppose that a set of fitting standards for applying thin normative concepts existed. Then people who failed to apply them correctly would be considered mistaken. Hence, if two conceptions of the good are incompatible in the sense defined above, we would be forced to conclude that (at least) one of them is radically mistaken.

But what is it to even talk of a mistake under such circumstances? In cases of erring in applying color concepts, erring in a simple calculation, or erring as regards the location of one's wallet, we assume cognitive explanations: lack of normal conditions for recognizing colors in the first, negligence or incompetence in the second, a lapse of memory in the third. Ultimately, the cognitive causes for these errors are elucidated by the neurology and physiology of memory, visual capacities, and mathematical skills. Such explanations are required even when different communities use conflicting sets of color concepts. Scientists have a neutral vocabulary—the language of wavelengths—in order to formulate the differences. With the help of these formulations, anthropologists, physiologists, and psychologists might describe and explain how different networks of color concepts fit into one world.

Could we expect such an explanation for errors in applying the notion of 'good' (used as a comparative property of forms of life)? Could there be a cognitive explanation for a group's failure to use a network of thick normative concepts? Williams's answer is negative: there is no "practicable theory" of error or account of how each party fails to perceive things that other parties perceive. "We could not, as in the case of secondary qualities, fit together into one world the qualities that they are supposedly perceiving and those that we are supposedly perceiving," Williams submits.[35] Subsequently, it would simply be wrong to attribute to people who use the predicate 'good' a concept that they systematically err in applying—since no explanation of such an error is available.[36]

A similar argument can be elaborated as follows. Compare 'good' to '+'. At a certain point, Kripke wonders whether quus-like behavior is at all intelligible to us. On the one hand, we can imagine a community within which it feels natural to continue a series in quus-like fashion. After all there are no facts about meaning, the grasping of which necessitates continuing a series in one way rather than another. Still,

> it is supposed to be part of our very form of life that we find it natural and indeed inevitable that we follow the rule of addition in the particular way that we do. . . . [T]hen it seems that we should be unable to understand 'from the inside' . . . how any creature could follow a quus like rule. We could describe such behavior extensionally and behavioristically, but we would be unable to find it intelligible how the creature finds it natural to behave in this way. . . . What it seems may be unintelligible to us is how an intelligent creature could get the very training we have for the addition function, and yet grasp the appropriate function in a quus like way.[37]

Now, as we have described Normative Diversity, if in the liberal community a paradigmatic case of immodesty is said to be good, the conservatives would take this judgment to be a quus-like employment of 'good'. The same goes for the liberals; from their standpoint, the conservatives apply 'good' in quus-like fashion. Hence, the concepts they express by these predicates cannot be the same. This contradicts our assumptions with regard to thinness. It turns out that the comparative concept expressed by the liberals' 'good' was not formed by conservatives, despite them being sophisticated enough to reflect on human agency as such. The lesson we urge diversitists to draw is that thin normative comparative predicates, as we have defined them, do not express concepts at all.

It follows that the shared usage of thin predicates cannot be explained by designating a shared *extension*. Once this is realized, the community-based conception of meaning would prompt us to account for the semantics of such expressions by searching for uses of them that are universally rule governed. And these are not hard to find. Clearly members of every community, whatever normative profile it has, agree that if *x* rates *a*-like conduct better than *b*-like conduct in *C*-like circumstances, then, other things being equal, *x* would choose *a* rather than *b* in *C*. According to the community-based conception of meaning, this suggests that from a semantic standpoint, in some contexts, the phrase '*x* thinks that *a*-like actions are good' is more basic than 'good'.

As we have noted,[38] Williams has been accused of oscillating between the horns of a false dilemma. Putnam, for instance, complains that, according to Williams, our values are either merely contingent or else products of a search for the best normative outlook from "an absolute point of view." That is, we have to painfully digest the fact "that this outlook is ours just because of the history that has made it ours."[39] But, Putnam says, our outlook might be "more or less *warranted* without being *absolute*. . . . What goes missing in Williams's entire discussion is the very possibility of pragmatism."[40] We have shown, however, that given the plausible analysis of radical normative diversity, and given our notion of error in applying the concepts we possess, community-based conceptions of meaning render Comparative Irrealism a real threat even to pragmatists like Putnam. The argument that we have put forward is not prejudiced by any absolutist conception of the world, nor does it overuse (what philosophers conceive as) the model of scientific justification.

Conclusion: Irrealism and Relativism

It seems plausible that human beings become initiated into the realm of thick normative considerations by their particular upbringing. The lesson from our argument is that one's adherence to a certain set of thick normative concepts—one's overall conception of the good—cannot be explained, justified, or criticized by normatively thin comparative judgments. Hence, properly modified, Harman's general formulation, that there might be a normative demand *D* that applies to *A* but not to *B*, just because *A* was initiated into one normative outlook rather than another, is well motivated.

But this raises the more general worry, to which this study is ultimately addressed. In the absence of substantive comparative thin concepts, and in view of the existence of rival normative outlooks, our upbringing within a culture might be conceived as blind training. And this might lead to a Rortian relativism according to which reasoning becomes irrelevant when we "raise the question of how we get from one vocabulary to another, from one dominant metaphoric to another."[41]

Had thin ethical concepts been substantive, we could have boasted the existence of a theory of normative diversity, capable of accommodating the entire spectrum of humanly possible schemes of thick normative concepts. But they are not. The diversity of our normative intuitions and practices flies in the face of any such accommodation. But what about our local, specific stories? To what extent are the thick beliefs that constitute a form of life subject to ongoing modification, elaboration, and revision? Should the notion of a form of life be understood as marking the limits of reflection (as Rorty would have us believe)? Does the fact that a normative outlook cannot be ranked *worse* than another suggest that reflection itself is limited by the particular configuration of a community's thick normative concepts? Are the (fairy-tale) liberals of our (fairy-tale) example incapable, in principle, of ever considering, say, religious attitudes toward sexual permissiveness as more than "unnatural" quus-like applications of the notion of 'good'?

Of themselves, community-based approaches to meaning have little to offer in this respect. If meaning is defined by and confined to communal boundaries in the manner they describe, it is hard to see how reason can transcend them. But do other approaches to meaning fare better in this regard? In the next chapter we consider one such approach.

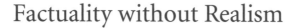

CHAPTER THREE

Factuality without Realism

Normativity and the Davidsonian Approach to Meaning

The Argument

The restricted version of normative relativism presented in the previous chapter was argued for on the basis of two main premises: acknowledgment of the phenomenon of Normative Diversity and commitment to a community-based approach to meaning. The aim of the present chapter is to argue that despite his decidedly non-community-based approach to concepts and properties, and opposition to the very idea of a diversity of reason-giving conceptual schemes (normative or other), Davidson's theory of meaning fares no better than the opposition. Not only does it not provide a safeguard *against* Normative Diversity, but, we shall argue, it turns out that from a Davidsonian standpoint, not only is normative factuality compatible with Comparative Normative Irrealism, but on the assumption that radically different conceptions of the good life indeed exist, normative factuality in fact *leads* to Comparative Normative Irrealism.

To recall, the version of Normative Irrealism of which we speak maintains that in comparing conflicting and fully fledged coherent normative outlooks, people commit themselves to nonexistent normative comparative properties. It thus denies the existence of the possibility of a normative ranking of maximally coherent systems of values acceptable to both. The argument we shall present—this time from a Davidsonian perspective—is, again, that rather than lead us to deny the factuality of normative discourse, Normative Diversity should lead us to deny its realistic character.

Obviously, for many of Davidson's readers such a claim will come as a surprise. On the standard reading, supported by some of his own texts, Davidson himself would seem to reject the very idea of Normative Diversity. If a normative outlook is understandable (by us), it cannot be radically different (from our own). Susan Hurley expresses this conviction thus:

> Alternative reason giving concepts . . . must be local alternatives; we cannot make sense of the possibility of an entirely alien scheme of reasons for action, without losing our grip on the very idea of intentional action. To be a reason for action is just to be one of our reasons, related to one another in roughly the ways they are.[1]

Let us say at the outset, what we shall be presenting is a Davidsonian approach to normativity rather than an attempt to account for Davidson's own views on the matter. Having said that, however, we do insist that although Davidsonians will not allow radically different conceptual schemes, they should allow radically different *theoretical* conceptions of the world and (analogously) radically different conceptions of the good life. But we shall be arguing from within the Davidsonian framework for more: not merely for the *possibility*, but the *inevitability* of normative (and theoretical) diversity. This combination of diversity and factuality will form the first component of our argument for Comparative Normative Irrealism with regard to the thin.

The other crucial element of our argument draws on Davidson's theory of meaning. In some of his writings Davidson famously develops an idiolect-based conception of meaning. One essential element of this conception comes down to the following. For the individual speaker to possess a concept is for him to have the capacity to apply it correctly in "normal" cases. Failure can be attributed only to ignorance of relevant facts, a failure to reason something through, or some other sort of defect or disorder such as stupidity, confusion, or illness. The individual speaker's coherence in applying a concept and his having all the information he takes to be relevant guarantee *the truth* of the application. It follows, we shall argue, that to concede Normative Diversity implies that two conflicting, yet fully coherent, conceptions of the good life held by different people must both be true. In skeleton form, the argument runs as follows:

(i)   *Normative Diversity:* Conflicting conceptions of the good life can be radically different from each other.
(ii) *Factuality:* (And yet) normative discourse is factual (truth apt).
(iii) *Idiolect-Based Conception of Meaning:* Coherence (in a very broad sense) and full information of the individual speaker in applying a concept guarantee the truth of its application.

From which follows, we shall argue:

(iv) *Normative Irrealism:* Since conflicting conceptions of the good life can all be true, there can be no one normative order that ranks them.

Our further objective is to show that from within a Davidsonian framework, what clinches the argument for Normative Irrealism is Davidson's strict normative *internalism*. Unhampered by community-based constraints on meaning, Davidsonians can accept Normative Diversity without confining meaning and reasoning to communal boundaries. It would seem possible for them, therefore, to remain normative realists by arguing that although fully rational people can live in accordance with radically conflicting conceptions of the good life, since normative discourse is factual at least one of two conflicting conceptions of the good life is simply false by virtue of external reasons shared by both. We argue that although such a line of reasoning is open to them in principle, Davidsonians have good reasons for resisting it in favor of the version of Normative Irrealism of which we speak.

Let us briefly sketch how we believe their argument should go. A person is said to have an internal reason for acting in a certain way only if his conclusion to act thus can be reached by a sound deliberative route from his *actual* conative states (or motivational set, to use Williams's coinage). Had he deliberated rationally he would have been *motivated* to act thus. An external reason for acting in a certain way has no such dependence on one's actual conative states: even if the agent had no element in his motivational set that supports this line of action, he would still have reason to take it.[2] Internalists believe that there are only internal reasons for action. By contrast, externalists claim that we have a reason, say, to improve the condition of our health, whatever our conative state happens to be. Internalists do not necessarily disagree but insist that this type of reason follows merely from our shared psychology, and hence, though universal, it remains forever internal.

Both sides would agree, however, that if Normative Diversity is admitted, one cannot be said to shift allegiance from one self-sufficient and coherent normative outlook (or conception of the good life) to a conflicting one solely on the basis of internal reasons. This is because a self-sufficient value system supports a corresponding fully coherent motivational set.

Let us demonstrate this connection between Normative Diversity and normative externalism by means of an imagined, concrete, if schematic example. Consider an unruly motorcyclist whose wild driving habits put him under a continuous threat of death. Imagine that he is quite calm and clear-minded about the dangerous life he leads. Indeed, our hero describes himself as committed to a set of values radically different from ours. When asked, he contends in all seriousness that longevity is less important for him than the sheer thrill he derives from driving the way he does. You might insist that the motorcyclist has a deep desire to stay alive. His behavior, you might claim, is not completely consistent with what he *really* wants. But if you are willing to acknowledge the existence of a "coherent" nonbourgeois value system so alien to your own conception of the good life, then you will have to conclude that the motorcyclist's conative state reflects this value system and is hence free from any practical inconsistencies.

To see how this concession to Normative Diversity (conjoined to some plausible auxiliary presumptions) supports externalism, imagine that at some point our biker decides to change his ways. He may have fallen in love, read a moving novel, or undergone a religious experience. He now claims that he has come to realize the importance of life and trades in his Harley-Davidson (no pun intended) for a sensible Camry. Life, he claims, is sacred—a notion he did not use during his biking days. He describes the dramatic change (as many converts do) as a correction of a grave normative error on his part. The point is that an internalist cannot grant the reformed biker this point. If his current and former lifestyles represent radically different conceptions of the good life, then there could be nothing in his former set of desires and values to support his new judgment that that set of desires and values harbored a problem. From an internalist perspective, there can be no (internal) reason for replacing one fully fledged coherent normative outlook by another. The motorcyclist's description of his change of heart can only be justified with reference to external reasons. If his original conception of the good life is indeed a false one, he would have had reason, external reason, to change it *regardless of his conative state at the time.* Put differently, it is only with reference to external reasons that the two conflicting normative outlooks can be compared and ranked.

Now, Davidson rejects the externalist option and in doing so, we claim, more than implies the type of Normative Irrealism of which we speak. The following passage strongly suggests that Davidson is committed to Normative Diversity, and yet he would assert that the biker could not have had any reason to change his conception of the good life.

> The agent has reasons for changing his own habits and character, but those reasons come from the domain of values necessarily extrinsic to the contents of the views or values to undergo change. *The cause of the change, if it comes, can therefore not be a reason for what it causes.*[3]

We suggest, in other words, that this statement stems from a commitment to Normative Irrealism. Neither the motorcyclist's earlier self nor his later self are systematically mistaken with regard to what they take to be important for themselves. Rather, each of them uses the thin evaluative term *important* to express a different concept, which each applies truly. Cast in Davidson's coherentist idiom, it is the claim that internally coherent conceptions of the good life are true even if they are in conflict, and therefore truthfulness cannot be considered a reason to shift from one to another. And since something evidently prompted him to do so, Davidson concludes that whatever *caused* the change cannot be considered its *reason.*[4]

In what follows, we first sketch a Davidsonian approach to normative discourse that allows for normative factuality and diversity. Such an account, we argue, suggests an analogy between the descriptive and the normative. On the basis of this analogy we show that interpretable creatures share a substantial body of basic descriptive and normative concepts, yet nonetheless they are liable to create radically different theoretical conceptions of the world, and radically different conceptions of the good life. We then go on to show how Davidson's idiolect-based conception of meaning leads to Normative Irrealism.

Theoretical and Normative Diversity in Davidsonian Theories of Meaning

The basic thought that grounds the Davidsonian project is that natural languages are essentially learnable: intelligent people can acquire a previously unknown language by observing the overt behavior of its speakers. The process of learning can be presented as a process of building "a theory of interpretation," the theorems of which are of the type, "Q in L means that p" (Q is the name of a sentence, L is the name of the speaker's language, and p is a sentence in the language the interpreter uses to state his theory). We call such claims *meaning theorems*.[5] We take it that the presumptions adopted in building the theory that yields true meaning theorems are true, if communication, meaning, and thought are possible. Call this thesis *Davidsonian Interpretivism*.[6]

Before getting down to business, we have to reemphasize an introductory remark we made previously. We outline a Davidsonian approach rather than attribute it to Davidson. Most important, we completely ignore the crucial question that burdens Davidson's theory of meaning, namely, how radical is its holism. We assume, for example, that lay members of two different communities use the same color concepts even if the physics they utilize is different. We are hence fully committed to the distinction between observational and theoretical concepts and beliefs.

Interpreting Descriptive Discourse: The Unity of the Observational and the Plurality of the Theoretical

Here, then, is an outline of what we take to be a Davidsonian theory of interpretation with regard to descriptive discourse. The data for the interpretation theory is the set of sentences the speaker holds true.[7] The interpreter is assumed to be capable of detecting that the speaker holds true a certain sentence Q, before knowing what Q means. Given such a set of *sentential attitudes,* the interpreter's first task is to identify the building blocks of the speaker's language—the semantic items from which the more complex sentences are composed. In doing so, she has to distinguish composite sentences from simple ones. And this involves singling out the machinery for composing sentences. Since complexity is, at least in part, a matter of logical structure, the interpreter will start by locating the logical words used by the speaker. In doing so, she will reveal the speaker's "logical patterns of behavior." Notice, though, that a pattern of behavior is "logical" in virtue of being explained by rules of inference with which the *interpreter* complies. The patterns of inference of the speaker and the interpreter are presumed to overlap (again, at least in part). The question is not, What are the speaker's rules of inference? but rather, What is the *vocabulary* of logical constants that govern the already known rules of inference?

Singling out the logical constants makes the simple semantic units of the speaker's language (more) visible. At this stage,

> [p]rogress depends on attending . . . to the events and objects in the world that cause him to hold the sentences true. The circumstances, observable by speaker and interpreter alike, under which an agent is caused to accept as true sentences like "It is raining", "That is a horse"[,] . . . provide the most obvious evidence for the interpretation of these sentences and the predicates in them.[8]

Hence, observational sentences possess an ineliminable element of methodological primacy because their meaning can often be guessed by generalizations based on direct empirical observation.[9] To take one of Davidson's examples, suppose that the interpreter observes that the speaker holds true Q1, whenever it is raining. This generalization would lead her to hypothesize that every utterance of Q1 by the speaker means that it is raining.

Such a move is packed with metaphysical presumptions. We shall not unpack them all. The most apparent of them is the one central to our argument, namely, that the interpreter *must* presume that the speaker and she share enough of their observational concepts and enough of their observational beliefs about the world in which they both live. After all, for the hypothesis that an utterance of *Q1* means that it is raining to be justified, it must be presumed that the speaker *believes* that it is raining when it is raining in his vicinity. The interpreter must take it that the speaker's belief that it is raining is caused by the fact that it is raining. (To see even more vividly why this is so, imagine that the fact that it is raining causes a certain speaker to believe that a certain prayer has been answered, and that his utterance of *Q1** means just that. In this case, with no further information to go by, the correct interpretation of *Q1** would be impossible.)[10]

A weaker version of Davidson's famous argument against the very idea of a conceptual scheme can be developed.[11] It is impossible to attribute to other speakers radically different systems of logical inferences and/or radically different sets of observational concepts and beliefs. Put roughly, the argument runs as follows: attributing a radically different conceptual scheme must be the result of an interpretive process. But for a process of interpretation to get on the road, the speaker is presumed to share most of the interpreter's inference rules and a large body of the interpreter's observational concepts and beliefs. It is therefore self-contradictory for an interpreter to conclude, on the basis of such a process, that a speaker's rules of inference and observational concepts and beliefs are radically different from his own.

Having completed the first two stages—that of identifying the logical constants and that of matching some of the speaker's utterances with prevailing states of affairs—the interpreter still has much work to do, work that requires more sophisticated tools. How, for instance, is she to go about interpreting a sentence *Q2* that means that it will rain *tomorrow?* In order to answer this question, we have to develop a brief account of "theoretical" beliefs. Generally, they are explained not by "objects and events in the world" so much as by inferences from some of the speaker's relatively more observational beliefs. That is, the speaker believes that it will probably rain tomorrow by reasoning inductively from the fact that the wind is picking up, temperatures are dropping, and the sky is overcast to the west. The agent, in other words, was not caused to believe that it will probably rain tomorrow by the *fact* that it will probably rain tomorrow but rather by other beliefs he has.[12] After all, the fact that it will probably rain tomorrow is not observable in the sense that rain itself is observable.

This notion of theoretical belief as prompted by other more observational beliefs strongly suggests a notion of subjective probability. In our case, in addition to his beliefs about the observable world, the speaker believes that the wind picking up, the temperatures dropping, and the sky becoming overcast to the west render probable that it will rain tomorrow. This belief together with the belief that the wind is indeed picking up, the temperature is indeed dropping, and the sky is indeed overcast to the west are what cause the speaker to believe that there is good chance of rain tomorrow.

Back, then to our question, how does the interpreter make sense of *Q2?* Davidson envisages the need for a new sentential attitude. The mutual relationships between beliefs that support each other "are in general holistic and probabilistic. We can therefore spot them only if we can detect the *degree* to which an agent holds a sentence true. . . . Simple assent and dissent are at extreme and opposite ends of the scale; we need to locate attitudes intermediate in strength. Degree of belief, however, cannot be directly diagnosed by the interpreter."[13]

As noted, a speaker normally does not firmly hold *Q2* true but only to some degree. The partiality of the assent can be explained by the nature of the inductive relationship between beliefs: in most cases they support each other *to some extent.* Hence, the empirical generalization that supports the meaning theorem for *Q2* would be as follows. Whenever the speaker believes that the wind is picking up and the sky is overcast to the west, he holds *Q2* true *to some extent* (unless there is other evidence available to him from which he infers that it is nonetheless unlikely to rain tomorrow). On the basis of this interpretive knowledge about the agent's observational belief, and the (defeasible) conjecture that the speaker believes that such facts support the belief that it will rain tomorrow, it would be a reasonable guess that *Q2* means that it will rain tomorrow.

Note that the partial assent to *Q2* might express full belief that it will *probably* rain tomorrow. Indeed, most developed languages contain certain notions of probability that characterize (among other things) states of uncertainty with respect to what is not directly observable. In order to find the term that expresses this notion, an interpreter would look for a sentence $Q2^*$ that the agent holds fully true when he partially assents to $Q2$. That is, the meaning of "probable" is detectable through the speaker's partial assents. Note, however, that his full assent to $Q2^*$ is not directly observable, because a component of the proposition it expresses is theoretical.

The example of probability regarding such phenomena as the weather is only the beginning. The evidential relations between beliefs generate a very rich realm of other theoretical concepts. Think of such terms as *atom* or *field* in physics and *culture* or *population* in the social sciences. The meaning of these terms is "proximal" rather than "distal": it is determined by the set of truths *viewed by the speaker* as the main and most certain body of *evidence* for the claims in which they appear. This is the distinction on which we rely in what follows, namely, that between the *distal* determination of the meaning of observational terms on the basis of direct observation and the *proximal* determination of the meaning of theoretical terms on the basis of the speaker's other beliefs.[14] Regarding the concepts expressed by terms whose meaning is proximally determined, Davidson says:

> [W]hat counts as evidence for the application of a concept helps define the concept, or at least places constraints on its identification. If two concepts regularly depend for their application on different criteria or ranges of evidential support, they must be different concepts.[15]

A mark of the theoretical is a freedom, spontaneity, and open-endedness that has three main sources. First, one set of competing considerations might inspire different people to arrive at different theoretical conclusions. Two analysts might come up with different predictions of the weather or of political developments on the basis of exactly the same data. Second, theoretical concepts are for the most part a matter of invention rather than discovery. And third, once a theoretical framework is chosen, its adherents are motivated to expand and test it further, such that different theoretical frameworks are liable to expand the observable in different respects and directions. The distance between the observable and the theoretical becomes so great as to generate a level of theoretical underdetermination that renders a plurality of theoretical conceptual schemes almost inevitable. Conceptual schemes will be different but, on a Davidsonian showing, never radically so. In a Davidsonian world, all such schemes will have in common a substantial body of shared belief concerning small and mid-sized objects and events that have some specific causally relevant properties. Still, the levels of underdetermination in *choosing* theoretical concepts and entities will remain considerable.

Davidson's famous argument against the very idea of a conceptual scheme, we insist, cannot exclude radical theoretical diversity: different communities might adopt radically different *theoretical* approaches to the world despite sharing a substantial body of observational belief. The existence of radically different theoretical conceptual schemes is a fact of life that is hard to deny, even from an avid Davidsonian perspective. Theoretical conceptions of the world might be in conflict in many respects. They might yield contradictory predictions, and thus be given to adjudication, and yet they might not. They might also be in disagreement as to what requires explanation, or what should count as an interesting problem. Yet in making no set of theoretical beliefs or concepts necessary for interpretation, Davidsonian theories of meaning remain fully compatible with the existence as well as the factual grounding of radical theoretical diversity.

The point to stress is that the idea that theoretical conceptions of the world might be radically different to the point of contradiction remains fully compatible with the idea that they are nonetheless factual (i.e., truth apt).

We shall claim that a plausible Davidsonian approach to normative discourse has the very same structure. Normative judgments are factual—in the sense that they are truth apt as any descriptive judgment. Furthermore, any interpretable conception of the good life must contain basic normative concepts that are both action guiding and world guided (concepts such as pain, tasty, pleasing, suffering, damage, cruelty). Yet, here too radically different conceptions of the good life are liable to emerge due to people's tendency to impose higher-level cohering structures on their first-order normative judgments—a process that yields an array of abstract normative terms whose meaning can only be proximally determined.

The Factuality of Normative Discourse

A complete semantic theory of a well-developed language would need to deal with the terms and phrases that express the notions of importance, good, right, rational, and so on, that is, the predicates that express the most general normative concepts. In an important sense, such purely normative concepts are part of any system of concepts attributed to *persons* (as opposed to, say, wanton humans)[16] whose language reflects the richness of their thought. After all, in general, persons act under the guise of the good. Typically, therefore, self-conscious action reflects implicit or explicit normative judgments such as that the action is desirable, worthwhile, and the like.[17]

Should value judgments be interpreted as factual, or are they just expressions of a conative attitude? We believe that, within the Davidsonian framework, the truth-aptness of the purely normative is simple and straightforward. In the present subsection we confine ourselves to pointing to the elements in Davidson's theory of action that are responsible for Factuality ((iii) above).

The first element is the way the Davidsonian interpreter treats phrases that express "concrete reason-giving concepts": pain, suffering, pleasure, enjoyment, danger, hunger, cruelty, and so on. The task of interpreting such phrases requires an enrichment of the set of conceptual tools used by the interpreter in building her semantic account of the language she explores. Apart from the "cognitive" sentential attitude ("holds true," for example), there are conative attitudes of the type "*X* desires (or prefers) *Q* to be false," to which the interpreter would have to appeal in building a theory of interpretation. This is because singling out the facts that cause the speaker to want sentences to be true or false is the most natural way to interpret the phrases that express such concepts as listed above. Or so we argue. True, these concepts have a clear descriptive import; in fact, they are traditionally conceived as descriptive concepts. Yet they typically function in explanations of the speaker's desires, attitudes, and actions. In other words, despite being world guided (descriptive) these concepts are, at least typically, action guiding (normative) as well. In order to account for their action-guidingness, the interpreter will let them play a conceptual role in explaining conative sentential attitudes.

Here is an example of the interpretive strategy we have in mind: if an interpreter notices that whenever a speaker is in pain he *desires Q3 to be false,* she will reasonably guess that what causes the speaker to want Q3 to be false is his pain. Hence, she will reasonably infer that Q3 means (in the speaker's language) that the speaker is suffering pain. Is it necessary to stipulate conative sentential attitudes and explain them in this way in order to interpret concrete reason-giving concepts? To see why the answer to this question is positive, all you have to do is to consider a case in which whenever the speaker is in pain and shows obvious discomfort he holds true a sentence, Q3*, which he desires *not* to be false. Then, clearly, the hypothesis that Q3* means that the speaker is in pain would be unreasonable.[18] Hence, in order to find out how the speaker refers to pain, the interpreter must find how he expresses the appropriate conative attitude to pain. This can be generalized. Predicates in the speaker's language that express concrete reason-giving concepts like enjoyable, hurtful, offensive, or tasty are most naturally interpreted with the help of the conative sentential attitudes that, just like the cognitive sentential attitudes, constitute the data of the interpretation theory.

According to the theory of practical reasoning Davidson develops in "How Is Weakness of the Will Possible?" this feature of concrete reasons implicates the factuality of purely normative statements. To see this, let us explicate the assumptions the interpreter takes for granted in inferring that Q3 means that the speaker is suffering pain.

By opting for the interpretive strategy we have described, the interpreter tacitly assumes that facts about how things are rationally explain preferences in the way "objects and events in the world" rationally explain beliefs. As noted, this is to say that in assuming that facts about the speaker's aches and pains justify his conative sentential attitudes, the interpreter takes it that concepts like pain or pleasure are action guiding. Now, Davidson suggests analyzing the action-guidingness of concrete reasons thus: first, if "enjoyable," "painful," and so on, express action-guiding concepts, then, for all x, pf (x is enjoyable/useful, x is desirable for the agent) and for all x, pf (x is offensive/painful, x is undesirable for the agent), where pf(p,q) means that p is a prima facie reason for (the *truthfulness* of) q. Second, if the speaker is interpretable, he is presumed to know basic normative truths; he knows that for him his own pain is prima facie undesirable. Third, one's preferences are expressions of purely normative judgments. Hence, to say of the speaker that he believes that his own pain is undesirable for him is to say of him that, other things being equal, he prefers not to be in pain. These three assumptions legitimize the interpretive strategy described above: if every time the speaker is in pain he wants $Q3$ to be false, plausibly, $Q3$ means that the speaker is in pain.

The connective pf(p,q) applies to truth-apt sentences. Thus, the action-guidingness of the concrete reason-giving concepts exposes the factual nature of the normative: if purely normative predicates express concepts that function in such pf-judgments, then purely normative judgments are factual. Hence, according to Davidsonian Interpretativism, we get

Factuality: Normative discourse is factual (truth apt).

Of course, we do not claim to have deduced Factuality; we are claiming only that, given the character of concrete reasons and the theory of practical reasoning Davidson develops in "How Is Weakness of the Will Possible?" pure normative statements of the type "x is desirable for the agent" are truth apt. Supposedly, philosophers who deny the truth-aptness of value judgments would be able to redescribe the action-guidingness of concrete reason-giving concepts without being committed to the factuality of purely normative statements. An expressivist might argue that the interpreter assumes that, being much like herself, the agent interpreted approves of pleasure and disapproves of pain and uses value judgments to express these attitudes. Conversely, the expressivist might argue that concepts such as pain and pleasure are thick concepts and that, as such, they are not simple concepts but are compounded of purely normative and purely descriptive elements. And he would go on to argue that only the normative element is not truth apt. Both expressivist lines of arguments contradict Davidson's own construction of practical judgments. On a Davidsonian showing, pf-judgments are constituted by two truth-apt sentences. We do not take sides in the matter. Writing from the start from a Davidsonian perspective, we have no need to take issue with expressivism or to defend Davidson's treatment of prima facie reasons.

Normative Diversity

Treating concrete reason-giving concepts in the way described has another important implication. The theory of interpretation is built not only on the basis of the set of sentences the speaker holds true but also on the basis of those he *wants* to be true. And for these latter attitudes to be interpretable, the speaker must share some of the concrete reason-giving concepts the interpreter possesses and (because of the action-guidingness of these concepts) some of her basic beliefs about goodness and desirability. Otherwise, the interpretation of the set of sentences they want to be false (or true) would be impossible. In deducing that Q3 means that the speaker is in pain, the speaker is presumed to know the basic normative truth that for him to be in pain is prima facie undesirable. Hurley is thus right with regard to the *basic* normative concepts: to be a basic reason for action is just to be one of our basic reasons. Both speaker and interpreter strive to avoid pain, bad eggs, and going hungry; neither will kill babies for fun. In other words, both judge that desirability is such that for all x, pf(x is enjoyable/pleasing, x is desirable) and for all x, pf(x is offensive/painful, x is undesirable).[19] Every conception of the good life is presumed to contain (trivial) value judgments about the tasty, the painful, the deadly, and so on. In other words, as with regard to the empirical, persons who act under the guise of the good are taken by Davidsonians to agree on basic features of what it is to be good. Otherwise, they would not be interpretable.

Normative conflicts arise from another aspect of normative facts, which relates them to theoretical facts in an important way. Indeed, a limited analogy between the normative and the descriptive will enable us to argue for Normative Diversity. To properly establish the analogy, we have to briefly present some additional themes from Davidson's theory of action and practical reasoning.

Consider a vital yet painful medical procedure. The speaker wants the procedure to be performed more than he wants to avoid it, since he believes that uncomfortable as it may be, it is crucial to his well-being. Typically, the value judgment that the operation is all-things-considered desirable explains (or is an expression of) the above preference. All-things-considered judgments result from deliberations that take place because different *concrete* reasons frequently pull in opposite directions. Hence, most conative attitudes resemble cognitive attitudes in not being all-or-nothing states of affairs. And many actions are the product of considering the joint effect of a number of conflicting concrete considerations. Davidson thus suggests that weighing the considerations for and against two "incompatible" actions *a* and *b* ends with a judgment of the type pf(E, *a* is better than *b*) or pf(E, *b* is better than *a*) where E is a conjunction of *all* the relevant considerations.[20]

Given that this is a correct description of practical deliberation, the interpreter would find the sentences that express all-things-considered judgments in the following way. Suppose that Q5 means that this medical procedure will be performed and that the agent desires (to a significant degree) Q5 to be true. Just like cognitive attitudes to theoretical sentences, so the conative sentential attitude to Q5 is also not directly observable. The interpreter has to be able to discern degrees of desires. She cannot directly diagnose them, however, so the interpretive hypothesis that the agent desires (to a significant degree) Q5 to be true can be confirmed only on the basis of more basic beliefs and desires attributed to the speaker in earlier stages of the interpretation.[21]

Now, suppose that the interpreter successfully identified the speaker's sentential conative attitude to Q5. According to the Davidsonian picture, the complex preference that Q5 be true is typically accompanied by an all-things-considered judgment expressed by Q6: "the operation is (all things considered) important for the agent." Hence, there is a sentence (call it Q6) such that the speaker holds true whenever he desires (to a significant degree) Q5 to be true. A reasonable guess would be that Q6 means that, all things considered, undergoing the medical procedure is important to or in the interest of the agent. Thus, the complex conative attitude to Q5 is expressed by a purely normative all-things-considered judgment expressed by Q6. The analogy to the descriptive discourse is striking: the partial assent to Q2 ("it will rain tomorrow") might be expressed by full assent to Q2* ("it will probably rain tomorrow").

The crucial difference between concrete reason-giving concepts and the less basic normative concepts is analogous to the difference between the observational and the theoretical in descriptive discourse. Theoretical and purely normative all-things-considered beliefs are explained with reference to the (more observational) beliefs that ground them, whereas observational beliefs are interpreted on the basis of their causal relations to objects and events in the world.

But the analogy between the normative and the descriptive extends even further; both are realms of freedom and spontaneity. For although abstract normative predicates are necessary in order to balance out conflicting first-order reasons, their necessity runs deeper. Take the theoretical realm first. The scientific picture of the world is more than the mere sum of the scientists' observational beliefs. It is generated by virtue of a constitutive ambition for a layered, coherent, and objective description of reality. Similarly, *a general conception of the good life* (or *a normative outlook*) amounts to more than the mere juxtaposition of simple facts about the tasty, the smelly, the painful, the pleasant, the damaging, and so on. A conception of the good life is a connected system of value judgments about what is important in life, what gives life meaning, what final ends should be pursued, and what means are permissible to achieve them.[22] To form such a conception of the good life, a person is required to take a step back and to form and articulate a general and systematic attitude toward the raw materials of his psychic life, which is directly affected by the basic normative facts that are expressed by basic reason-giving concepts.

One's conception of the good life is achieved by structuring one's motivational set with the help of *relatively abstract* normative concepts like duty, moral imperative, rights, law, sin, guilt, responsibility, self-fulfillment, autonomy, sacredness, and God. And as with the theoretical conceptual schemes of a science, the freedom we enjoy in adopting reason-giving concepts of this sort renders different conceptions of the good life inevitable; one normative outlook might contain concepts wholly lacking in another. In light of the expected conceptual differences in the normative realm, despite the Davidsonian bias against the very idea of conceptual schemes, Normative Diversity seems more than plausible:

> *Normative Diversity:* There are fully informed and internally coherent conflicting conceptions of the good life.

Normative conceptual differences between normative outlooks generate the conflicts of the type described at the beginning of the chapter. Recall the reformed biker. Cast in Davidsonian terms, before the biker's great change of heart, regarding almost any instance of a breathtaking ride that he had considered, *a,* he had believed that pf(E, *a* is more important than avoiding *a*), where E is a conjunction of the relevant facts about *a.* This pattern of concrete value judgments is the basis of the more general value judgment attributed to him: he values the thrill of the wild ride more than longevity. Now he has come to denounce these beliefs. He claims that the former value judgement was false. His change of heart might be explained by the change in his reason-giving concepts—life, he now believes, is sacred, and endangering it unnecessarily, as by continuing to ride the way he does, is wrong. He is thus led to judge pf(E, *a* is more important than avoiding *a*) as false.

We shall argue in the next section for Comparative Normative Irrealism. In other words, we shall argue that both of the motorcyclist's consecutive outlooks are true. But, as we have already noted, Factuality without realism faces obvious difficulties. *Taken by itself,* Factuality suggests that normative realism is true, that is, that at least one of two conflicting normative outlooks is false. Moreover, the analogy between the theoretical and the normative is further reason to believe in normative realism. For at least on the face of it, conflicting theoretical conceptions of the world *are* contradictory. So, why can't the motorcyclist defend his explanation for changing his lifestyle on the grounds of the Davidsonian theory proposed above? A weather forecaster might discover that the evidence he had been relying on supports the opposite hypothesis; an astronomer might change his mind, by virtue of new theoretical concepts that generate a different conception of the data. Why should there be any difference between accounting for the motorcyclist's radical normative reevaluation and the kind of theoretical reevaluation so common in the sciences?

Thus, at first blush, it seems that from the Davidsonian perspective we have presented, our motorcyclist is justified in describing his newly found way of life as a correction of a serious and systematic error on his part. Again, at first blush, it seems that he came to "realize" that longevity is more important to him than the thrills and rushes of even the best of his rides.

But according to the normative irrealist position we shall be defending below, the motorcyclist does not *realize* anything; he simply forms a new view. At best, he realizes that his new/different concept of what is important or worthwhile applies in such-and-such a way—not that his old opinion was false. This, we shall argue, is because, unlike the scientist's change of heart,[23] the motorcyclist ceases to employ the concepts that had figured in the formulation of his old outlook. Our task in the next section is to show how and why the Davidsonian theory of meaning we are constructing leads to this surprising view of normativity.[24]

Factuality without Realism

Let us now look at another typical difference between the normative and the descriptive, which, in the framework of Davidsonian Interpretivism, makes a crucial difference.

Consider a change of view in the theoretical realm that would seem to resemble that of the motorcyclist as closely as possible. As is well known, Israeli intelligence failed to predict the October 1973 war. Several junior officers within the intelligence community attempted unsuccessfully to draw attention to the preparations for attack conducted by both Syria and Egypt only to have their reports and evaluations suppressed by their superiors. War eventually broke out as they had predicted. Suppose now that after the event, in an attempt to explain their position at the time, the senior staff claimed that they had been blinded by a biased conception of the political situation in the Middle East and, as a result, had failed to see the obvious. Their explanation of the error seems straightforward and plausible.

In the theoretical realm, it is generally the case that once the data and the conceptual resources are made available, there will be little disagreement among clear-minded and rational discussants as to what, given the data, are the probable outcomes. Theoretical shifts typically occur when new data or new theoretical concepts become available. Indeed, had the new data and the new theoretical definitions put forward by Einstein been available to Newton and his generation, a Davidsonian might confidently assume that they would have happily accepted Einstein's revolutionary proposals.[25]

It follows that from a Davidsonian standpoint, cognitive changes of mind of the type described are predictable *on the basis of the speaker's ac-*

tual linguistic behavior. Had the officers not been biased, they would have made different judgments about what was in fact probable. The mistake we attribute to them is explainable as a local failure that owed to special conditions, that had they not obtained would not have occurred. According to Normative Diversity, changes of heart like that of the motorcyclist are a different matter entirely: *if there was a normative fact that the motorcyclist missed, his error would be systematic.* But there is not. He is a person who knowingly and consistently preferred the thrill of a wild ride to the security of playing safe. He had no illusions and made no (factual) mistakes concerning the facts of the matter and the nature of the risks he was taking. No preknowledge of future events could have convinced him otherwise. His use of the thin predicate "important to me" is not unusual or inconsistent, for he applies the concept it expresses just as he applied it up until now. Of course, the biker's case might be thought to be of the bizarre yet consistently irrational variety of which we spoke briefly above. But in light of the possibility of radically different conceptions of the good life, this would be an implausible description. The biker's initially endorsed conception of the good life was radically different from ours, one we completely understand but do not share. Normative Diversity is the claim that in the normative realm this might well be the case; some differences and conflicts cannot be explained as *local* failures of one of the sides.

True, he now claims not merely to have changed his mind, but to have been systematically mistaken all along. But, quite unlike the senior Israeli intelligence officers, this judgment is clearly retrospective. It cannot be confirmed by any counterfactual with regard to the behavior or knowledge of his former self. Looking back, he cannot point to any bias, ignorance of relevant facts, failure to reason something through, or defect or disorder that might have led him astray. His past set of motivations reflected a different set of values. Hence, from his earlier standpoint, he would have resented the bourgeois preferences of his later choices and vice versa. Put somewhat differently, there is nothing in the biker's behavior that would motivate the interpreter not to employ his initial value judgment in interpreting his use of the phrase, " . . . is more important to me than . . ."

So why is this difference crucial? The answer is rooted in the Idiolect-Based Conception of Meaning, which denies the possibility of systematic errors.

The Idiolect-Based Conception of Meaning: Possessing a concept implies having the capacity to apply it correctly. Errors in applying a concept are failures to apply it in the way the agent *usually* applies it. This failure is due to ignorance of the facts that the speaker takes to be relevant, an exceptional failure to reason something through, or some sort of defect or disorder such as irrationality, stupidity, confusion, or illness. These failures can be identified as *unusual* uses of the term by individual agents. Coherence of the individual speaker—applying the concept as he used to up until now—guarantees the truth of the application.

Now, suppose that the judgment to which the senior officers were committed was that in all probablity there will not be a war in the near future. The interpreter *would not* consider this initial judgment pertinent to the meaning of the phrase "probable" coming from the officers. After all, their judgment is the result of their failure to reason adequately. That is, the officers' prediction was not coherent with the data to which they were exposed, as it reflects weakness of the will, wishful thinking, or a failure to reason something through.[26] On the other hand, there is nothing in the biker's story that would motivate a Davidsonian interpreter *not* to employ the motorcyclist's initial value judgment in interpreting his use of the phrase, " . . . is more important for me than . . . " He continues to use the phrase "important to me" in the way he always did. The failure cannot be attributed to lack of information or abnormal conditions.

The expression "important" as it comes from the motorcyclist on either side of his change of heart exemplifies the following general statement. "[I]f what is apparently the same expression is sometimes correctly employed on the basis of a certain range of evidential support, and sometimes on the basis of another range of evidential support (or none), the obvious conclusion would seem to be that the expression is ambiguous."[27] In particular, "different people are attaching different meanings to evaluative words like 'generous' . . . and even 'good' and 'bad.'"[28]

Once we follow Davidson's lead in saying that people are—and should be—interpreted individually, the right question to ask is not what terms like "good," "right," and "rational" mean in general but what they mean *coming specifically from them.* In order to be interpreted, people are to be considered in the richness of their specific contexts but (almost) in isolation of other users of their vocabulary. An adequate account of communication and interpretation involves no more than a speaker, a hearer (the interpreter), and a largely shared external environment. From this stark Davidsonian perspective, a more substantial notion of a linguistic community or of linguistic conventions is neither necessary for attributing meaning nor, as we shall see, *possible*. Meaning is attached to individual uses of "good," "rational," "important," and so on, on the basis of *each agent's* linguistic and other behavior.

This, we believe, is enough for deducing Comparative Irrealism. Based on the three principles discussed,

(i)   *Factuality:* Normative discourse is factual (i.e., truth apt).
(ii) *Normative Diversity:* There are fully informed and internally coherent conflicting conceptions of the good life.
(iii) *Idiolect-Based Conception of Meaning:* Coherence and full information guarantee truth.

we can infer that both conceptions of the good life held by the motorcyclists are true, although their normative concepts are different. Or more generally,

(iv) *Normative Irrealism:* A person's normative outlook is true if fully informed and internally coherent. Therefore, if fully informed and internally coherent, then conflicting conceptions of the good life are all true.

It might be objected that the argument begs the question. Normative realists would not grant that the biker, though an enthusiastic and reckless rider prior to his change of heart, had "no illusions and made no (factual) mistakes concerning the risks he was taking." They would deny the normative/descriptive distinction in the stories we told. For them "important" and "probable" behave in exactly the same way. Indeed, given that normative discourse is factual, why couldn't the realist say that during his biking days the agent was ignorant of (or not sufficiently "clearminded" with regard to) the high value of leading a safe and responsible life? One may *assume*, of course, that there is no fact of the matter valid *for all* about what the value of a safe life is, but then, so the objection would go, one is simply begging the question by assuming Normative Irrealism.

The objection misses the point. We argue that the interpreter *cannot* attribute a mistake to the motorcyclist, unless she rejects either Normative Diversity or the Idiolect-Based Conception of Meaning. To see why let us look again at the latter. The idiolect-based conception of meaning maintains that understanding a speaker (or attributing a concept to a speaker) is fundamentally based on a successful prediction of that speaker's behavior. Specifically, an interpreter is justified in inferring that an utterance u produced by a speaker means that p if the speaker would hold true a u-like utterance whenever he realizes that p is the case. Testing such a generalization adds up to nothing more than testing the hypothesis that a lion jumps as a result of hearing a bell ring or a whip crack.[29]

> The longer we interpret a speaker with apparent success as speaking a particular language, the greater our legitimate confidence that the speaker is speaking that language. . . . To the extent that we are right about what is in someone's head, and therefore are right about what he would mean by the endless things he does not say, we are right about 'the' language he speaks. . . . The point of the answer is that there are not two questions, one about reasons for believing that a speaker is speaking one language rather than another, and a second question about how we naturally form expectations; the first question is simply a case of the second.[30]

In particular, once the interpreter knows how the motorcyclist would apply the phrase "important to me" in the future, she would know its meaning. She would know, in other words, the property expressed by the motorcyclist who uses this phrase, on the basis of this prediction alone. Hence, a mistake in applying a concept must be an exception, a local failure of the individual speaker. The poor epistemic conditions of the circumstances in which the speaker made the mistake would explain *why* the speaker made it. And the interpreter would be able (on the basis of his interpretive knowledge) to identify the unusual epistemic features responsible for the mistake. Normative Diversity implies that conversions of the type the motorcyclist underwent might be *un*predictable from the interpretive standpoint.

The Idiolect-Based Conception of Meaning

Most conceptions of meaning join Davidson in denying the possibility of basic or massive error in applying a concept. Should a person, well acquainted with a mode of behavior (or object) that is deemed paradigmatically cruel (or red), fail systematically to pronounce it cruel (or red), he would not be held to have been mistaken but as not having the concept of cruel (or red) at his disposal. This is, of course, true, unless we can explain his mistake as a local failure.[31] As noted, within the Idiolect-Based Conception of Meaning, not only is the possibility of a basic error denied, but also the possibility of a systematic error. The distinction is subtle but very important: systematic errors in the application of concepts are errors that cannot be identified on the basis of a speaker's actual linguistic behavior; they are not exceptions from the regular behavior of the speaker. On a Davidsonian showing, the only counterfactuals that allow the interpreter to attribute a mistake to the speaker refer to the regularity observed in the speaker's behavior: "had the speaker been better informed, clearer-minded, and mentally healthy, he would have judged the situation *as he usually does.*" The conceptual impossibility of systematic errors follows immediately. And if this is so, we are doomed to irrealism.

As noted, realists argue that the motorcyclist is more like a Newtonian scientist who (under a naively realist construal of scientific framework transitions), faced by the conceptual innovations of relativity theory, changed his conception of the data. But (even under such a construal) this comparison is baseless from the interpreter's point of view, for she infers the property expressed by "important to me" from the motorcyclist's uses of this term. In the case at hand, she cannot argue that he misses the fact he would express by the sentence "Life is more important to me than wild riding" on the basis of his actual behavior. There is no further information that can support counterfactuals of the type, "had he known . . . he would have judged the situation differently."

In sum, the argument can be put thus: were there a normative fact the motorcyclist missed, his error in applying the concept he expresses by "important to me" would be systematic (this follows from Normative Diversity). But there are no systematic errors (this follows from the Idiolect-Based Conception of Meaning). Hence, there is no normative fact that he missed (this follows from Irrealism). No question-begging assumptions are involved: Normative Diversity does not make any claim about the individuation of normative facts.

But there is another worry that merits attention.[32] On our reconstruction of Davidson's view, there are two determinants of meaning: causal connections between words and the world (or, relatedly, the set of things to which we do in fact apply the word); and inferential connections among different uses of the word. The inferential connections could be regarded as a simple theory of what it is for something to be *F*—which works alongside our actual practice of applying the term *F* to such-and-such things. Of course we have to strive to maximize truth. But the meaning-determining role of the inferential connections may be in tension with the meaning-determining role of the actual applications of the term. In such a case, there is surely room in Davidson's framework for us to regard the inferential connections as defeating the assumption that most of the actual applications of the word are correct.[33] The more theoretical a word or concept, the easier it is to make sense of a speaker broadly misapplying it *by his own standards.* Thus, for words whose meaning depends on causal relations to the world, widespread truth is guaranteed. But there are more complex and theoretical words for which grosser errors are possible.

Why, the objection goes, should we see the motorcyclist's value judgments as belonging to the first rather than to the latter kind? By committing ourselves to the view that different people attach different meanings to such evaluative words as "good," we presume that the *dominant* meaning determinant of "good" or "important" are the set of things to which the word is in fact applied. The objector's complaint is that we neglect the role of the inferential connections in determining the meaning of these words: if some of the inferences partly determine the meaning of "important," the motorcyclist's two selves can be said to employ the same concept. In fact, some of the implications of the value judgments the motorcyclist expresses by "important to me" *are* preserved in his later uses of this expression. Furthermore, what are we to make of the motorcyclist's retrospective conviction that what he now means by "important" is just the same as what he earlier meant by it—that he had simply changed his view of the sorts of things that are worthwhile? Of course, the motorcyclist's conviction has a better chance to be respected once the the role of the inferential connections is taken into account.

We believe, however, that in the motorcyclist case the inferential connections to which the objector points cannot determine the meaning of "important." The reason is this. The two meaning determinants described above are deeply related. A speaker who employs a *theoretical* term F might indeed make grosser errors: he believes in a simple theory (call this theory T_F) of what it is for something to be F but fails to apply the term in accordance with T_F. Thus, a speaker might believe that items of a certain type are F while T_F implies that they are not. In such a case the following counterfactual would be true. Had the speaker known that T_F implies that o is not F, he would avoid the judgment that it is. This "grosser" error is still a *local* (framework-dependent) failure; it can be identified by the interpreter on the basis of the linguistic behavior of the speaker.

Consider the following counterfactual: Had the motorcyclist's earlier self known that $T_{important}$ (in which he believes) implies that his exhilarating rides were not important to him, he would have ceased claiming that they were. If this counterfactual were true, the interpreter could have realized it was true on the basis of the motorcyclist's linguistic behavior *prior to his change of heart*. But then the conception of the good life attributed to him would be internally incoherent—and this goes against one of our assumptions, namely, that the motorcyclist's earlier normative outlook is fully informed and internally coherent.

Needless to say, the Idiolect-Based Conception of Meaning is controversial, and it is not our intention here to defend or decide the issue. Let us, however, isolate that element of it responsible for the version of Normative Irrealism we are defending.

Many philosophers (most notably Dummett and Burge)[34] argue insistently that language is an essentially social phenomenon. In their view, the biker shares the language he speaks and the concepts he applies with the community to which he belongs. We never study individual linguistic behavior in isolation but always as exemplifying conventions shared by members of a larger community of speakers. Language, these philosophers insist, is to be attributed first and foremost to a community, and concepts should be individuated, at least to some extent, independently of the linguistic behavior of particular individuals. Hence, there is no need to appeal merely to the *biker's* actual or counterfactual behavior in order to interpret the words he uses. Appeal must be made to the behavior of *other* members of his community. Within such a framework systematic errors are clearly possible: a person might confuse gold with fool's gold on a regular basis, even if he has all the information he takes to be relevant.

An aspect of the debate between Burge and Davidson exemplifies the element of the Idiolect-Based Conception of Meaning relevant to the restricted form of Normative Irrealism we have deduced. According to Davidson, "there is a conflict between Burge's social externalism, which ties a speaker's meaning to an elite usage he may not be aware of, and first person authority."[35]

> The presumption [that speakers, but not their interpreters, are not wrong about what their words mean] is essential to the nature of interpretation—the process by which we understand the utterances of a speaker. This process cannot be the same for the utterer and for his hearers.[36]

A sufficient condition for first-person authority is the Idiolect-Based Conception of Meaning, which implies that the coherence, full information, and mental health of the individual speaker guarantee truth. This promises that the speaker knows the extension of the terms he uses. But if the concepts he employs are individuated at the level of the community, as Burge believes, he might fail to know their extension.

The importance Davidson attaches to first-person authority is evident in his skepticism regarding the prospects of constructing a notion of conventional meaning. In what respect, he asks, is the fact that language is shared central for communication? The answer, presumably, is that in order to communicate, people have to comply with a shared set of conventions. According to the community-based conception of meaning, linguistic competence is associated with the acquisition of a set of social conventions, and communication is explained by the fact that, when speaking to each other, the speakers comply with the same set of rules.[37] But, Davidson claims, "[the] myth of two speakers picking the same book . . . reveals the question begging assumption; for how do we or they know the speaker and interpreter will interpret the book in the same way?"[38] If a speaker uses a shared book, he must first interpret it. Otherwise, he will not be able to use it. The fact that speaker and interpreter share a book cannot guarantee that they interpret it in the same way. They will only be able to find this out by face-to-face communication, for the success of which their sharing the book is itself irrelevant.

Davidson's revolutionary suggestion is to do without rules, conventions, or shared languages. On his view, claims of the sort "*s* speaks a language *L*" play no role in interpreting *s*'s utterance: speakers do not necessarily intend to use a language (not even implicitly)—and communicating thoughts is possible with no intention to comply with any shared convention. A theory of interpretation has, therefore, always to deal with particular speakers and should not commit itself to such theoretical entities as a shared language. As Goldfarb puts it, a theory of meaning of this sort should "draw on actual, face-to-face occasions of acquiescence of persons to each other."[39]

As we have seen, the conceptual impossibility of systematic error follows immediately. And thus, despite its firm rejection of the community-based approaches to meaning and opposition to the very idea of a too radical diversity of reason-giving conceptual schemes, the Davidsonian approach fares no better with regard to normativity. Here too normative outlooks taken whole, though factual, remain immune to rational evaluation, to the kind of critical appraisal capable of finding them mistaken by comparison.

PART II

Rationality from Within

Introduction

We have sought in Part I to establish how acknowledgment of the fact of normative diversity commits the two main approaches to meaning to a restricted yet significant form of normative relativism. The arguments we offered were detailed yet, we believe, sufficiently general to enable us to ignore the otherwise substantial differences between various variants of each approach. Thus, in the case of the community-based approach, for example, it makes little difference if one formulates the argument from the very different point of view of Bernard Williams or Michael Dummett. In either case Rorty's basic intuition was fleshed out, properly grounded, and found to hold. On both showings normative discourse between subscribers to a shared normative vocabulary can remain fully factual—world guided and action guiding—and yet incapable, in principle, of applying meaningfully between sufficiently different outlooks. Two different outlooks, we argued, cannot be normatively ranked in a manner acceptable to both. Put somewhat differently, while the positive, thin concepts of a normative outlook can always be consistently *self-*applied both comparatively and noncomparatively (if vacuously, since hailing a form of life better than another by its own lights is flatly circular), there seems to be no sense in which a *negative* thin concept can be self-applied without contradiction, unless it can be done comparatively. In what sense and with respect to what property can a normative outlook be deemed *by those whose outlook it is* wrong, evil, or systematically mistaken if not in comparison to another? But Comparative Irrealism rules out such comparisons. It seems to follow, therefore, that a normative outlook cannot be criticized by its practitioners, in which case it cannot be deemed the outcome or the subject matter of rational appraisal and reasoned revision.

In so arguing, we may have made the point more generally perhaps than it has been made before, and in differentiating as we do between the thick and the thin, perhaps more carefully than it has been previously presented. Other than that there is not anything very new or controversial in what we have said so far. Only few if any have explicitly raised and discussed the question of the constraints placed by latter-day accounts of normativity on criticism from within a normative outlook, but then only few, it seems, would object to our conclusions so far, which are not merely entailed but in the works of many clearly implied.[1]

John McDowell is an exception. Although he too associates rationality, for the large part, with justificationary reason giving, he does occasionally point quite explicitly to the "standing obligation [of each generation of speakers of a language] to engage in critical reflection" as part of "being at home in the space of reasons."[2] At one point he explicitly addresses, if very briefly, the very issue of normativity and rationality: the need for our self-subjection to norms to be responsive to reasons. Talking of "the central image in the German idealist tradition" of "legislating for ourselves," McDowell explains:

> The point of the image is that the subjection to norms should not be an infringement on freedom; we are authentically subject only to norms whose authority we acknowledge. Thus the norms that bind us are our own dictates to ourselves, not alien impositions. But any intelligible case of agency, legislative or any other[,] . . . must be responsive to reasons. It makes no sense to picture an act that brings norms into existence out of a normative void. So the insistence on freedom must cohere with the fact that we always find ourselves subject to norms. Our freedom, which figures in the image as our legislative power, must include a moment of receptivity.[3]

The remaining six chapters purport to substantiate McDowell's desideratum, while remaining fully committed both to Normative Diversity and Comparative Irrealism. We seek to make a case for the idea that a person may come rationally to deem elements of her normative outlook to be normatively wanting to the point of motivating her to seek an alternative. But in firmly conceding Comparative Irrealism we commit ourselves to seeking a notion of normative self-criticism that is *not* comparative. When, in chapter 6, we take a closer look at McDowell's suggestions, it will become apparent that it is doubtful whether the notion of normative self-criticism of which he speaks ventures beyond troubleshooting one's normative outlook merely for consistency, coherence, or clarity. We shall be aiming higher, namely, at the possibility of deeming them wrong, bad, inappropriate, or undesirable, not merely vague, incoherent, self-contradictory, or mutually inconsistent. The problem is that lacking an external normative footing (on which we shall have more to say in chapter 4), conceding Comparative Irrealism seems frustratingly to render the problem unsolvable. For what is it to deem a normative outlook undesirable or wrong if not in relation to a better, less problematic alternative? But Comparative Irrealism renders such comparisons meaningless.

The first two chapters of Part II look closely at two seemingly unrelated major philosophical contributions—one to ethics and one to the philosophy of science—that would appear highly relevant to the project we have set ourselves. Both explicitly concede Normative Diversity, both firmly imply commitment to Comparative Irrealism, and both would appear not only sympathetic to the undertakings of this book but also to contribute to them significantly. We are referring to the so-called interpretive account of ethics that builds on Michael Walzer's *Interpretation and Social Criticism,* to which we devote chapter 4, and the account of rational scientific framework replacement late of Carnap and Kuhn developed in Michael Friedman's *Dynamics of Reason* and subsequent publications dealt with in chapter 5.

The existence of Normative Diversity, the incomparability in principle of different normative outlooks, and the idea of normative improvement motivated by normative criticism from within are the principles on which the interpretive account builds its entire approach. Our aim in chapter 4 is twofold. First, we seek to substantiate as far as possible the interpretive account along with the noncomparative notion of internal normative criticism it advocates, and in a manner not restricted to ethics. Rearticulated to apply to normativity in general, the interpretive approach will serve to partly ground the account of normative self-criticism we shall eventually propose. Once properly substantiated, the second and more critical objective of chapter 4 is to expose and explore the limits the interpretive account imposes in principle on the type of normative criticism from within it purports to promote.

Although we endorse much of the interpretivist approach to normativity—which in chapter 6 we argue receives powerful articulation in Brandom's inferentialist brand of pragmatist expressivism[4]—we find it, as it stands, incapable of supporting the full range of connected social criticism of which Walzer speaks. Under an interpretivist construal, normative criticism can venture no further than to challenge other *articulations* of a given way of life but can never challenge the form of life itself. As it stands, Brandom's account of normativity suffers from the same drawback. Explication, like interpretation, we argue, lacks any critical bite with respect to its *explicandum*.

The main thrust and point of departure of Friedman's *Dynamics of Reason* would seem to approximate our own to a greater extent than any other thinker we engage. His view (late of Reichenbach, Carnap, and Kuhn) of science's changing linguistic frameworks, not merely as viable interpretations, but also as *constitutive* of scientific thought and practice, would appear to concede both Normative Diversity and Comparative Irrealism. And in devoting his work (unlike Reichenbach, Carnap, or Kuhn) to the possible rationality of such transitions "despite the fact . . . that from the point of view of the old framework, [the new] is not even possible," he seems to share our concern with rationality of normative revision, at least with respect to the exact sciences. Finally, in combining acknowledgment of the constitutive role of scientific frameworks with the possibility of their rational replacement, Friedman undertakes to accommodate transitions of far greater magnitude than interpretivists are capable and, more important, to engage transitions in scientific thought and practice, not merely in their articulation. To an extent, Friedman is and remains an important ally, but a closer look at his project reveals three major areas of disagreement. First, *Dynamics of Reason* limits itself exclusively to inquiring into the rationality of transitions to well-formed alternatives, to explaining the conditions under which a new framework can be rationally considered "a live option" from the perspective of the old. It leaves wholly unattended questions concerning the rational motivation for developing such alternatives in the first place.[5]

Second, for the new to be portrayable as a live option for practitioners of the old, Friedman feels forced to play down the radicality of the transitions he studies, rendering paradigm shifts far gentler and more natural than Kuhn would have us believe—a step we firmly contest. The upshot is an account of rational framework transitions that, quite contrary to our own, seems not to require maintaining a critical stance with respect to the norms constitutive of one's work and thinking.[6]

Third, by fashioning a special case for the framework transitions of mathematical physics, Friedman's work more than implies that in his opinion transitions between constitutive normative frameworks in other areas cannot be considered rational. Needless to say, we part company with Friedman on all three counts.[7]

There is much we concede and much that we value in both the interpretivist approach to ethics and Friedman's approach to science, but their treatment of social criticism and scientific framework transitions fail, respectively, to account for the rationality of significant shifts in normative commitment. If schemes of values stand merely as *interpretations* to practice, rather than as *constitutive* of normative commitment, then normative criticism is necessarily limited to challenging how normative commitment is *understood* rather than what it should *be*. Friedman, who does view linguistic frameworks as constitutive of scientific practice, offers, by contrast, no account of the reasons practitioners might have for desiring to replace them.

Robert Brandom's work, to which we devote chapter 6, presents the deepest and most detailed treatment of discursivity and rationality to date whose neo-Kantian and neo-pragmatist setting we fully concede. Focusing on discursivity and sapience in general, and in the nature of conceptual norms as such, it has extremely little to say about the rationality of becoming and ceasing to be committed to a particular conceptual framework. Unlike Walzer or Friedman, we read Brandom not for the way we believe his work engages the problems we have set ourselves—it does not—but for what we believe it implies that is relevant to doing so. In other words, ours could well be described as a *de re* reading of Brandom,[8] not unlike the way he himself reads many of the philosophers before him. We read him (i) as addressing conceptual norms but in a manner easily and naturally extendable to all manner of normative commitment (as Jeffery Stout reads his earlier work, and his more recent work more clearly implies);[9] (ii) as implicitly premising a distinctly self-critical dimension we make explicit, as it were, in his portrayal both of the "determinate critical integrative task-responsibility" we have for managing our own commitments[10] and of how we keep track of the ways others manage theirs; and (iii) calling him to task for concentrating exclusively on the management of given, up-and-running commitments while omitting any account of how new commitments come to be endorsed in place of others.

We locate the dormant critical element in the way Brandom moves, late of Sellars, between intra- and intersubjective definitions of rationality: defining rational beings repeatedly once as beings who "*ought* to have reasons for what they do, and *ought* to act as they have reason to,"[11] and once as capable and willing participants in the game of giving and asking for reasons, without ever explaining why commitment to *acting* for reasons commits one to engage in the intersubjective inquisitive, communicative game of mutually exposing and examining *each other's* reasons. What rational motivation might one have to be at all interested in other people's reasoning and in getting them interested in one's own? Do we play the game and keep its score merely to be able to predict and help second-guess what other people might do, or, as we suggest, are we motivated self-critically with a view to learning something from how other people think, and exposing our own reasoning to the scrutiny of fellow reasoners? In Brandom's identification of rationality's commitment not merely to *act* for reasons, but to engage in the inquisitive, intersubjective *discourse of* reasons lies dormant, we argue, a central, motivational element of self-doubt we seek in chapter 6 to make explicit.

CHAPTER FOUR

The Limits of Connectiveness

Criticism from Within and the Interpretive

Account of Normativity

Introduction

According to "the interpretive account of normativity,"[1] normative argumentation and rational disagreement make sense only within the assembly of institutions and practices that constitute a communal normative outlook. Normative reasoning is an interpretation of the existing practice of a particular community. So a normative claim is true by virtue of it being an adequate interpretation of that practice, namely, a value-laden or thick description of the concrete conception of the good life accepted by the community.[2]

A direct consequence of such an account of normativity is a form of relativism with regard to normative disagreement: "If we disagree . . . there is nothing else to do but go back to the 'text'—the values, principles, codes and conventions that constitute the moral world,"[3] writes Michael Walzer, a major proponent of the interpretive account, in the spirit of Bernard Williams's well-known claim that since sets of values are the product of historically contingent cultural and historical forces, comparing them is pointless.[4] A shared "text" is a precondition for genuine disagreement. To sustain the type of cross-cultural reasoning capable of rationally resolving cross-cultural normative disagreement, people must occupy sufficiently close "normative worlds." It is easy to see that the interpretive approach sits well with Comparative Irrealism. But it is not as straightforward as it might seem.

In what follows we first present our version of the interpretive account of normativity in some detail, demonstrate how Comparative Irrealism follows, and show, by arguing for the possibility of a shared universal minimal code, that the interpretive account is invulnerable to the objection most commonly raised against it. We then go on to address one of the most powerful and compelling objections to the interpretive account, in which it is accused of reversing the order of normative evaluation. Morality, the objection goes, constitutes an enduring challenge to the rules and conventions with which all human communities comply. The function of a community's scheme of values is to explain and critically assess its practice, not merely interpret it, and can do so because some central moral truths are not gleaned from practice but explain it. In this sense the interpretive account is accused of mistaking the order of explanation. Addressing this objection will allow us in the final sections of the chapter to begin to elaborate an account of normative criticism from within, whose striking feature is that, though prompted by cross-cultural disagreement between alien normative outlooks, even when effective, it is *not* committed to their normative ranking. The interpretive approach, in other words, makes room for a modest (yet, as we shall argue, overly modest) form of externally *motivated* internal normative criticism, that is not in violation of Comparative Irrealism. Although we ultimately find interpretivism insufficient as it stands for satisfactorily accounting for the kind of normative self-criticism we (and even they) seek to articulate, we do remain in sympathy and agreement with the basic pragmatism that characterizes its approach to normativity, on which we continue to build in much of the remainder of the book.

Truth by Interpretation

The interpretive view defines normative truth by the notion of an ideal interpretation. The basic claim advanced by its proponents is that (in the usual case) a normative statement made by a person is true relative to the context in which it is stated,[5] if and only if it follows from the ideal interpretation of the practice of that person's community. Moreover, it is true because (or by virtue) of being an implication of the ideal interpretation of the practice. To substantiate this thesis, and explain the notion of an ideal interpretation, we have first to analyze the basic notion employed by the interpretivists, namely, that of a normative outlook.[6]

There are two constitutive elements of a normative outlook: the community's practice and its scheme of values. The first comprises the complex of practices that make up the community's normative life, including the customs, codes, conventions, and norms abided by its members and institutions. The second is seen as a kind of institutionalized theory of what is good about such a normative life. A community's scheme of values plays three different yet related roles. First, it identifies the particular goods found to inform certain practices or institutions; it tells us, for example, that a certain code of dress is modest. Second, it explicates the precise nature of modesty and lays bare its relations to those practices and institutions; it articulates what it is to be modest and explains why it is worthy to conduct oneself modestly and how various practices achieve modesty. Finally, a community's scheme of values portrays the priorities and interrelations that obtain between the different goods that constitute the "building blocks" of its normative life.[7] For example, it articulates the relationship between modesty and holiness and how they are ranked and connected. In Brandomian terminology, the community's scheme of values serves to *make explicit* the values and norms implicitly embedded in its practices and institutions.

What renders the view we present specifically "interpretive" is its insistence that the second, theoretical element—the community's scheme of values—is, in essence, an interpretation of the first: its practice. The community's theory (scheme of values, normative worldview) interprets, rather than dictates, its practice. And its practice is the sole target of its interpretive efforts. This is not a merely sociological description of what we do but a thesis about the nature of the propositions that normative statements express. In fact, in the interpretive view, our normative judgments are best conceived as statements about the value of our practices and the values they implicitly embed. Hence, in evaluating the truth of these statements, we appeal to the moral world we live in. The first interpretive thesis, then, is that an atomic normative statement is true by interpretation: it is true in the context in which it is uttered, if it follows from an ideal interpretation of the practice in this context.[8]

Walzer's position was initially forged in explicit opposition to the normative universalism of the so-called Kantian liberals,[9] whose most prominent representatives are John Rawls and Ronald Dworkin.[10] When addressing epistemological questions, Rawls insists that the data on which it builds do not extend beyond human intuition. It is just that reasonable persons share as such intuitions as to what is just.[11] These intuitions transcend all manner of particular local practice. According to Rawls, we are endowed with a sense of justice whose existence is independent of the historical contingencies of any particular form of life in which human beings happen to find themselves. We possess it by virtue of being persons. This epistemology allows for a noninterpretive metaphysics of justice. Justice acts as an external normative constraint on all concrete sets of communal practice and, hence, of any attempt to make sense of them. As such, it dictates (or is constitutive of), rather than interprets, those practices.[12]

Interpretivists disagree: "the value of concretely conceived goods," argues Sreenivasan, "cannot be deduced from any set of independently valid principles."[13] Despite impressions to the contrary, our shared intuitions— the data that Rawls's theory attempts to systematize—are not about the right or the just, conceived in ahistorical abstraction, but reflect the value of our shared practice viewed as understood by those *whose practice it is.* Indeed, for the interpretivist, the question who "we" are is crucial to evaluating the truth of our claims about justice: "the notions of community and shared values mark the limits of practical reason," not (as in Rawls's theory) its point of departure.[14] With regard to justice, the interpretivist thesis comes down to this: a community's theory of justice is true (in a particular context) by virtue of its principles being the best interpretations of that community's existing practices (in that context).

One major qualification is in order. According to our construal, normative truth depends fully and exclusively on the "practice of the community of which a person is a member." What about resident aliens in communities that are not their own (a conservative, say, among the liberals of our contrived example) who are critical of those communities, and they of them? On reflection, this problem can be easily dissolved by a simple analogy. Consider the referent of "we" in phrases like "we all agree that. . . ." In the usual case, in uttering the singular term "we" in context, a speaker refers to the group comprising himself and his audience. Still, we can easily imagine a speaker referring to all Americans, for example, and by so doing *excluding* the non-Americans in the audience he happens to be addressing. Likewise, given the speaker's manifest intentions, a normative statement uttered by him might be evaluated relative to a remote context, pertaining to whom the speaker takes to be his social point of normative reference.

This move provides a partial answer to a related difficulty: deprived of Rawls's universalistic conception of justice, how are interpretivists to account for their intuitions regarding the justice or injustice of another community's social practices? The answer is simple: the practices of other communities may be evaluated internally, relative to one's own notions of justice (in which case, one will not be disputing or approving those whose practices they are, so much as explaining why one's own community abides or refrains from abiding by those practices). On the other hand, one might be interested in understanding other people's practices from *their* community's point of view, or (if the two normative outlooks are close enough) from that of the combined community.[15] We shall take this question up in detail farther down, when discussing the nature of interpretive normative reasoning and dispute.

The Thick and the True

The idea that value judgments are true by interpretation must come accompanied by a more or less explicit idea of an ideal interpretation. Our account relies heavily on Sreenivasan's characterization of the notion of *adequate* interpretation. Sreenivasan exploits the notion of "a criterion of fit":

> An interpretation fits an ethical practice to the extent that the requirements of the good it identifies as informing the practice coincide with the requirements of the practice that are valued by the community. . . .

[T]he consideration of fit also serves as a criterion of comparative interpretive adequacy. . . . Consider two accounts of the good informing a
given practice, *A* and *B*. . . . [I]t is perfectly comprehensible for a community to judge that *A* is superior to *B* as an interpretation of the practice *if*, other things being equal, *A* fits the practice better than *B* does.[16]

Note that the "ideal" interpretation—the one that best fits the practice—
is not to be defined as the interpretation actually accepted by the community. The accepted interpretation might be unwarranted; it may fail
to be attentive to the "text" that constitutes their moral world.[17]

In other words, although interpretations articulate, and thereby lend
meaning to practice, the arrow of *viability* and *warrant* points in the opposite direction: interpretation in an important sense *answers to* practice rather than vice versa. Hence, although Sreenivasan seems to have no
need for the term, for us the primacy of practice in this respect centrally
implies that an interpretation of practice will be considered adequate
only if it constitutes a "thick," value-laden, and explicit description of the
practice it purports to interpret. Thus, the interpretive conception of normativity, as we construct it, overcomes the fact/value distinction by appeal to the notion of thickness Williams borrows from Geertz, discussed
at length in chapter 2 above.[18] An adequate (let alone ideal) interpretation
of a religious dress code, for example, must include such thick notions as
modesty, and of a religious ritual, such notions of holiness. What renders
them minimally viable is, in part, that they are value-laden: the concepts
of modesty and holiness are "thick," reason-giving concepts.

The thesis that normative statements are true by interpretation is
built on the action-guidingness of the thick concepts. Suppose the concept of *Tk*-ness is a thick concept that denotes a specific value. Suppose
that this value is part of the ideally interpreted ethical outlook of the community to which *S* belongs. The thesis is that under such conditions, if *x*
is *Tk*, the sentence "*x* is prima facie good" is true (relative to the context
in which *S* would utter it). Put negatively, if *x* is immodest, it does *not*
necessarily follow that *S*'s assertion of "*x* is prima facie bad" is true. For it
might well turn out that in the context in question the value of modesty
does not survive scrutiny; it might fail to be a value in the *ideally* interpreted ethical outlook of the community to which *S* belongs.[19]

It follows, as we have already noted, that central to the interpretive approach is the idea that normative disagreement necessarily presupposes a shared "text." To this an objection can be raised that we shall address in greater detail below. Imagine coming across a community whose members torture any alien they can lay hands on just for fun; you need to know nothing else about them to disagree with them profoundly. All you need to know is that they are human to know that what they do is wrong. What is the shared text, or practice, that, according to interpretivists, you differently interpret? The answer, as we shall explain in greater detail below, is that Normative Diversity in general and its interpretivist version in particular do not deny the existence of a commonly shared minimal code that pertains to what human beings share qua humans. Their shared biological nature, for instance, renders all humans vulnerable to pain and hunger. Hence, the concepts of pain and hunger will be part of any human scheme of values. And it is, therefore, analytically true that hunger and painful states of affairs will be for all human societies prima facie undesirable. If "pain and hunger are prima facie bad" is true relative to all imaginable human contexts, so is "torturing or starving people for fun is bad." The shared thickness of the concepts of pain and hunger dissolves the above worry but *not* because the universal immorality of frivolous torture or starvation cannot be considered true by interpretation for lack of a shared text. On the contrary, their universality does not prove their *non-dependence* on culture but, quite the opposite, that they are *part of* every imaginable culture. They are, therefore, true by interpretation of an embodied "text" that happens to be shared by all conceivable discursive human societies—which cannot be said of justice. But more on this below.

The Thin and the Void

The final thesis of the interpretive account of normativity thus construed aims consequently to empty thin concepts of independent normative content: in contexts in which, for example, "*x* is good" is true, the proposition it expresses is of the type:

(G)—There is a specific (thick) value (in the speaker's [S's] ideally interpreted normative outlook) that is instantiated by x.

The bracketed addendum is the contribution of the extralinguistic context to the semantic content expressed by "x is good" in this context. Note that (G) contains a quantifier, and the domain of quantifiers are in general restricted by context. For example, the sentence "All the bottles are empty" uttered by someone holding up three empty bottles is in all likeliness shorthand for "All *these* bottles are empty"[20]—the three bottles he is holding being his assertion's contextually relevant domain. Likewise, in the typical case, if adherents of one normative outlook *N1* say of *y* that it is bad, and *N2* adherents say of it that it is good, both parties may well be speaking the truth, *without* expressing contradictory propositions. This is simply because, due to the different, thick concepts employed in their respective normative vocabularies, the different contexts in which the two judgments are uttered render their domains of quantification nonoverlapping.

And if (G) indeed captures the propositions expressed by truly asserting "x is good," the same should apply to all true assertions that employ thin concepts. (G) should be generalized to claim that all statements about the bad, the good, the rational, (etc) are true only if they satisfy the condition we call "the Essentiality of the Thick." Let *Tn* and *Tk* denote thin and thick concepts respectively.

The Essentiality of the Thick (ET)—x is *Tn* (for *S* at time *t*) only if there is a specific value denoted by *Tk* such that: (i) "x is *Tn*," uttered in a context, follows analytically from "x is *Tk*" conjoined to a set of non-normative sentences; and (ii) the fact that x is *Tn* (for *S* at *t*) is fully explained by the fact that x is *Tk*, and some other non-normative facts.[21]

We shall say of a property *Tn* that it is *irreducibly* thin if the fact that x is *Tn* (for *S* at *t*) fails to satisfy clause (ii), namely, that there exists no thick property *Tk* such that (together with some other non-normative facts) explains *Tn*.

To illustrate ET, suppose that "b is prima facie bad" is true relative to the context of the conservative outlook introduced in chapter 2. According to ET, it is true due to (i) the fact that there exists a thick concept—modesty (in our story)—such that the sentence "b is (prima facie) bad" follows analytically from "b is immodest," and (ii) the fact that b is prima facie bad is fully explained by the fact that b is immodest. Of course, explaining why *b* is, *all things considered,* bad requires a far more complex set of normative and descriptive facts (for even diehard conservatives can envisage situations in which modesty should be sacrificed for a higher good).

Our construal of the interpretive view leaves many questions open. First and foremost, we have not provided necessary and sufficient conditions for interpretation, not to speak of "ideal interpretation." All we have presented is one necessary condition, namely, that every adequate interpretation be a true, thick, value-laden description of the practice.

Second, our construal purposefully blurs the distinction between interpreting, articulating, evaluating, and making a community's practice explicit. We adopt an approach to interpretation according to which understanding is not that different from explicating and evaluating.[22]

Comparative Irrealism and the Limits of Normative Comparison

Let us now look at how interpretivism can account for the prospect of normatively ranking different and conflicting outlooks. To recall, on an interpretive showing, a normative outlook comprises a scheme of values and a practice or way of life it purports to best interpret. Given the Essentiality of the Thick, Comparative Irrealism can easily be seen to follow from two additional assumptions that interpretivists are most likely (indeed, would seem compelled) to concede. The first is Normative Diversity, the possibility of there existing normative outlooks sufficiently alien for the ideal interpretation of one to substantially conflict with that of the other. It is the kind of diversity our (overly) schematic example of the conservative and liberal communities sought to capture. Let their normative outlooks be *N1* and *N2,* respectively. From an interpretivist perspective, their normative diversity is captured by the fact that the notions of holiness and modesty, for example, that are central in *N1* are absent from *N2* and cannot contribute to the interpretation of liberal practice, while notions such as gender discrimination, self-determination, and equality, central to *N2,* are wholly missing from *N1* and play no role in the interpretation of conservative practice. Normative Diversity is the claim that concrete conceptions of the good life might be diverse and in conflict, even if ideally interpreted.

The second assumption is that in the typical context in which liberals *(N2)* and conservatives *(N1)* disagree as to whose way of life is normatively preferable, each presumes an irreducibly thin property that orders their normative outlooks. This is so especially where the parties are aware of the fact that their normative outlooks are alien. Consider the sentential component "*b* is good" as it appears in sentences like "For liberals, *b* is good, but they are wrong" or "Those liberals believe falsely that *b* is good." It can easily be seen that in most cases the proposition expressed by "*b* is good" in such linguistic contexts is *not* captured by (G). Conservatives do not want to say that there is a "conservative disvalue" instantiated by *b*; liberals would not disagree with that. After all, conservatives employ such sentences exactly to deny a proposition that the liberals *would* affirm, so it cannot be relativized to their own scheme of values. In other words, in the case of such disagreement, an irreducibly thin normative ordering must be said to be presumed. But according to the Essentiality of the Thick, such irreducibly thin comparative properties do not exist. Each community can, of course, full well deem the other normatively inferior *from its own* perspective. But relative to contexts of (attempted) *real* cross-cultural disagreement, in which such assertions purport to make sense across communal boundary lines, the comparative judgment "*N2* is normatively preferable to *N1*" is either false or suffers from a truth-value gap.

Hence, with regard to sufficiently diverse normative outlooks, interpretivism too entails Comparative Irrealism. However, given the specific set of assumptions that ground the interpretive approach, some normative comparative leeway remains that a purely semantic analysis, of the type presented in the previous two chapters, fails to disclose. To put it simply, sufficiently diverse outlooks—that is, couplets of practice and practice articulation, *interpretandum* and *interpretance*—are normatively incomparable, but very different normative outlooks *can* be normatively compared if and when they share one of their two components. A normative outlook *N1* can be deemed normatively superior to another, *N2* (relative to their respective contexts, and in a manner adherents of *N2* are capable of appreciating), if it comprises a scheme of values that better interprets the practice it shares with *N2*, or if it is composed of a practice that better fits the scheme of values it shares with *N2*. If one of these conditions obtains, normative ranking among considerably diverse outlooks is possible, and can serve to facilitate keen internal normative criticism. Here are two illustrative stories, both borrowed from Sreenivasan.

In Locke's view, forcing people to convert from one religion to another is not only wrong, but irrational. Religion, as Locke understands it, aims at personal salvation, and salvation cannot be forced. On a Lockean showing, if a society purports to be truly religious it must practice religious tolerance. Let $L1$ be the nontolerant religious outlook criticized by Locke and $L2$ the one he promoted on the grounds that practicing toleration better embodies the institutional good of salvation central to the scheme of religious values shared by $L1$ and $L2$. On an interpretivist construal, Locke claims that $L2$ is morally preferable to $L1$ because the practice it advocates is better articulated by the scheme of religious values it shares with $L1$.[23]

Now imagine a tolerant religious community prudently conducting and interpreting itself along Lockean lines *(L2)* that comes into contact with a similarly tolerant, yet liberal, secular community, whose normative outlook is of a "Rousseauian" rather than a Lockean nature. In a Rousseauian society, rational self-determination is taken to be a basic political good. Imagine further a religious social critic attempting to import into his home community the recently discovered value of autonomy he encountered among the liberals. He urges his fellow religionists to reconsider their customary Lockean interpretation of their tolerant practice, and reinterpret what is religiously good in their institutions by adopting autonomy as a value, arguing that the concept of autonomy better interprets their community's actual practices. Thus, a new normative outlook $L3$, normatively superior to $L2$, might be generated—"superior" in that its scheme of values is deemed a better interpretation of the practice it shares with $L2$.[24]

Two Objections

Understood thus in its interpretivist construal, Comparative Irrealism can now be shown to be immune to two of the most popular objections raised against the idea that sufficiently diverse forms of life are normatively incomparable.

First is the accusation that such a position constitutes a counterintuitive form of anything-goes normative or cultural relativism. If two normative outlooks are far enough apart, the interpretive view cannot rank them, for there is no standpoint from which one can be said to be inferior to the other, where "inferior" means the same from either perspective. This is why, we have argued, interpretivism implies Comparative Irrealism. And if this is not anything-goes-relativism, what is, claims the opposition? As noted at the outset, we believe this objection to be unfounded exactly because the interpretive approach fully acknowledges the existence of universal normative constraints on the normative outlook of any human society—though not of the kind advocated by such Kantian liberals as Rawls, Dworkin, and Kymlicka.[25] As we have seen, there is nothing in the interpretive approach to deny, for example, that it is in all probability a universal truth (i.e., true relative to all imaginable contexts) that torturing for pleasure is morally wrong—a claim whose universality interpretivists can account for *without* admitting irreducibly thin properties or practice-independent moral facts.

As we have already argued, the notion of physical pain is one shared by any scheme of values developed by corporeal sapiens by virtue of their shared corporeality. Furthermore, pain is a thick concept in the sense that, for the agents who use it, it is both descriptive and prescriptive. Facts about pain speak directly in favor of some actions and in favor of avoiding others; pain is a world-guided and action-guiding concept for all communities just like modesty, spontaneity, and holiness are for some. For any imaginable human scheme of values, the fact that something is physically painful entails that it is prima facie undesirable.[26]

It might be objected that if the normative is as interpretivists conceive it, namely, wholly contingent on communal practice, it is possible for there to be an (ideally interpreted) outlook in which causing pain does not count against actions. Intepretivists can and should deny that by arguing that an (ideally interpreted) outlook in which causing pain does not count against actions is impossible for human beings qua human beings, and that if the notion of pain appears to have no normative content in the practice of some community, it cannot be *our* notion of pain.[27] Because sensations such as pain, hunger, and pleasure and their associated desires *happen to be* experienced by all humans, concepts such as pain, hunger, and pleasure are *necessarily* shared by all humanly employed schemes of values—from which follows that an outlook such as the one described is inconceivable.

But then can we not imagine a "double standard" normative outlook the ideal interpretation of which implies only that the unnecessary pain inflicted on its members is bad while pain inflicted on other people is not? (Genghis Khan obviously cared about avoiding pain and not inflicting it on those he cared for but didn't think twice about inflicting pain on those he attacked.) We join such philosophers as Thomas Nagel, Derek Parfit, Christine Korsgaard, and others in insisting that the answer is negative on the grounds that such a view is simply incoherent.[28] Conceptually speaking, it is impossible that mỳ pain could be coherently considered prima facie bad while yours is not. Genghis Khan may well not have cared about causing pain to others, but this was because he was morally bad (and this statement is true relative to our own contexts as well as to to his). Unnecessary pain is (prima facie) undesirable; Genghis Khan either missed this truth or, more likely, chose immorally to ignore it.

A different, subtler objection merits closer attention, however. We have defended the universality of a minimal moral code[29] on the basis of the partial overlap of all imaginable human schemes of values due to what human beings share as a species. Now, if all there is to being true in a context amounts to being *an implication of an ideal interpretation* of the community's practices in this context, what accounts for the minimal overlap between the ideal interpretations of different practices? Why, for instance, should we take it that the same concept of pain, or hunger, or sexual desire is present in all schemes of values? When it comes to a community's normative attitudes, even the most natural and base of our bodily endowments will always be thickly mediated by our culture-bound second nature. And, conversely, if indeed the requirement not to torture for fun does follow from all possible schemes of values, why then is the Kantian top-down explanation not preferable to the interpretive account? Why does whatever is responsible for this uniform interpretation not count as a "practice-independent moral fact"?

In light of what has been said of the interpretive approach so far, the answer to both questions seems to us to be straightforward. First, human biological nature is rich enough; it explains the uniformity the objector finds ungrounded. Despite cultural differences, we share several basic concrete values, such as our deep resentment toward pain and hunger and the pleasure we take in sex, to which different cultures respond, of course, in different ways but basically leave intact. Second, for interpretivists, the Kantian top-down explanation is inferior, for obvious metaethical reasons; metaphysically necessary moral truths seem to be queer and suspicious. So, rooting universal truths in human nature is a way to understand Kantian intuitions regarding the status of these truths in a more modest way. Indeed, the universal truth of a moral statement is nothing more than its truth relative to all imaginable contexts.

Needless to say, the interpretive theory of universal normative concepts envisaged here is still underdeveloped. For our needs, however, the very possibility of such a theory is enough; with it the road is open for interpretivists to defend the universality of certain moral truths about basic universal thick concepts along lines similar to those we have sketched and, in doing so, to make a first and important step toward an interpretivist account of a minimal code, to which any imaginable (and ideally interpreted) human way of life should be committed. If such a project is feasible, accusations of unchecked relativism, as if interpretivism is incapable of ever deeming an outlook normatively wanting, prove unfounded. A worldview such as the Nazis' is very easily criticized on interpretive grounds. It has no respect for the minimal code; and hence, relative to its own normative outlook (or rather, to what it necessarily shares with those of the rest of humankind) is deemable normatively inferior. Indeed, Comparative Irrealism, understood as an aspect of the interpretive account, is fully compatible with our belief in the moral inferiority of the Nazi moral world.

In sum, there is enough normative consensus or similarity between collectives or cultures—whether or not their explicated, actively employed vocabularies show it—to render the minimal-code thesis plausible. Of course, one could imagine an extraterrestrial, intelligent species with a biology very different from ours, in whose normative outlook even the minimal code fails to hold. But that, we believe, would no longer count as a nonintuitive form of moral relativism. There is no a priori true principle that commits any sapient community to *make* the notion of physical pain part of its scheme of (dis)values. When we say that, from the perspective of any normative outlook, causing unnecessary physical pain is prima facie wrong, all we mean is that, by virtue of their shared biology, causing physical pain to others will be condemned by every normative outlook adhered to by human beings. Needless to say, nothing of this applies to societies of intelligent creatures who do not feel pain as we do, or do not know what pain is—should they exist.

The Challenge of Moorian Realism

The most extreme opposition to the interpretive account is Donald Regan's Moorean realism. For a person to be an agent, Regan says, "she must be thinking about the goods her action achieves qua 'good.'"[30] There is, in Regan's view, no more basic articulation of this thought. That is to say, agents as such try to track goodness per se—where "good" is not shorthand for a set of local, culture-determined thick concepts but an irreducible, transcultural,[31] nonnatural,[32] thin,[33] yet substantially evaluative,[34] concept in its own right. Hence, if deliberation is not an illusion, the metaphysical component of the Essentiality of the Thick is flatly denied. The fact that something is good explains events (i.e., deliberations) that cannot be explained by any other fact; it follows that the fact that *x* is good is not fully explained by any other fact because no other fact can fully explain the deliberations that facts about goodness explain. Hence, according to Regan's Moorean realism, if deliberation is not an illusion, goodness is an irreducible normative property. It seems that the semantic part of the Essentiality of the Thick is also denied by Regan's insistence on the deliberative primacy of the thin. The sentence "*x* is good" uttered in a context, conjoined to other sentences about *x* and *S*, analytically implies that "*S* has a reason to do *x*." According to the Moorean realists, there are no descriptive sentences that have this logical feature.[35] In fact, Moorean realism reduces the thick to the thin; facts expressed by thick concepts can explain deliberations only because they are partly explained by facts composed of irreducibly thin moral properties.

The interpretive account, however, has a simple response to Regan's Moorean realism (not to the viability of his reading of Moore's views, of course, but to his attempt to give them contemporary "philosophical life").[36] From an interpretivist perspective, answering "the desire transcending question" indeed requires that norms be *real* but not that they be absolute or universal. The world-guidedness and action-guidingness of the thick suffices to keep all levels of personal desire in meaningfully normative, deliberative check without having to grant similar status to the thin. Thus construed, interpretivists can indeed be tagged as "substantial realists," for they do view agents as capable of spotting, not normative entities, but value-laden states of affairs "wafting by." But their realism owes exclusively to their communities' framework- and culture-dependent vocabularies of thick concepts rather than to an absolutist concept of the good. To Regan we say, paraphrasing Jay Wallace: why do moral agents require a shared, absolute, and irreducibly substantive concept of the good for meaningfully deliberating about what to do?

> Won't it suffice to apply our general procedures of critical normative reflection to such concrete values (and disvalues) as loyalty, suffering, betrayal, need, dependence, autonomy, and choice, deriving conclusions about our reasons for action by clarifying the proper way of understanding and responding to these values?[37]

The difference between a trained rescue dog and a moral agent who rescues a stranger from a burning house, writes Regan, is that the latter, as we quoted him above, "must be thinking about the goods her action achieves qua 'good'" rather than "to have responded reflexively to the *descriptive* facts *purely* as such."[38] What Regan fails to acknowledge, and interpretivists make central, is the value-ladenness of thick descriptions. As Frank Jackson puts it in a passage cited by Regan: "What we should aim at is not doing what is right *qua* what is right. I should rescue someone from a fire, because if I don't they will die, not because that is the right thing to do."[39] From an interpretive perspective, it is the right thing to do (for me now), because if I do not they will die—rather than vice versa—and my deliberation is fully explained by this latter fact. True, in deliberating we do look for the "good" thing to do: but this, for us, is a mere generalization. In one context, the search for the good is for the more pleasing thing to do; in another, for what is fair, and so on. Of itself, "goodness" is an empty expression used as a placeholder.

But acknowledging the deliberative primacy of the thick is not enough in itself. The interpretive account of ethics remains inconsistent with weaker and less ambitious moral theories than Regan's, which, unlike him, do not deny the deliberative primacy of the thick. For lack of a better term we dub them collectively "Weak Absolutism."[40] Weak absolutists do not deny the deliberative primacy of the thick, but they do deny the thick's metaphysical essentiality (according to which every moral fact is explained by facts expressed by thick concepts). Specifically, weak absolutists agree that facts expressed by thick concepts speak directly in favor of some actions. Nonetheless, some moral properties, they believe, are irreducibly thin. And practices can be criticized on practice-independent grounds, that is, by facts composed of irreducibly thin moral properties.

A Weak Absolutist position might be formed, for example, on the basis of Scanlon's contractualism. According to Scanlon, wrong- or right-making properties are analyzed in terms of rational agreement. In this view, what makes a set of principles just is that no person can reasonably reject it. This definition presents justice as practice-independent: whatever the practice of the community, it would be unjust in case someone can rationally reject it. Having said that, the earlier Scanlon concedes that "there are also right- and wrong-making properties which are themselves independent of the contractualist notion of agreement."[41] Thus, for example, the obligation to keep promises can be explained on contractarian grounds. Yet, in some societies, the obligation to keep one's word is not a matter of justice but of honor—and, in the relevant context, it serves as a cogent justification. Thus, as far as Scanlon's contractualism is concerned, the properties that are independent of the contractualist idea might be specific values denoted by thick concepts. As we shall see in the following section, Weak Absolutism is the most serious alternative to the interpretive account of normativity by virtue of the so-called open question argument, which we shall address after a brief summary of our argument so far.

The version we have presented of the interpretive account (generalized from an account of ethics to an account of normativity as such) comprises three main theses that were stated, explained, but not really argued for: (I) Normative statements are *true* relative to a context if they follow from the community's ideal interpretation of its practice in this context; (II) an *adequate* or *viable* interpretation is a thick, value-laden description of the practice; and (III) thin normative concepts are "empty" of intrinsic, nonderivative meaning, and this implies the metaphysical and semantical essentiality of the thick. We then went on to argue that, conjoined to two further assumptions interpretivists are most likely to accept—namely, Normative Diversity and the way agents employ thin normative concepts to rank their normative outlooks with respect to others—the Essentiality of the Thick implies Comparative Irrealism. Still, as we then showed, Comparative Irrealism is fully compatible with the existence of what we intuitively take to be universal moral truths and commitments that comprise the minimal code.

The case we here make for the interpretive approach is not polemical. We do not seek to *defend* interpretivism as preferable to certain approaches to normativity (as does Walzer) or as preferable to certain approaches to the study of humankind (as does Taylor). Our advocacy on behalf of interpretivism derives from the aim of our study, which is to explore and articulate the possibility of normative self-criticism, firmly committed to Normative Diversity, to a broadly conceived neo-Kantian, neopragmatist account of language, and to the Comparative Irrealism we have argued they jointly entail. As noted in the introduction to Part II, we find the interpretive account of normativity attractive for the powerful theoretical grounding it provides for Comparative Irrealism, to which we shall remain firmly committed while still making room for some measure of comparative normative criticism. But before exploring the virtues and limitations of interpretivism any further, we must first meet the serious challenge of Weak Absolutism.

The Interpretive Account and the Open Question Argument

This most basic of challenges to the interpretive account can be put very simply thus: when we ask ourselves first-order normative questions in deliberating what to do, we do not normally ask ourselves, "What do we usually do in situations like this?" or "What are the ways of my tribe or community?" Rather, we ask ourselves, "What is the right, or the best, or the preferable, or the appropriate, or the moral thing to do?" When we do consult traditions and collective expectations, we do so for instrumental reasons. It is true that some people do proceed in a manner much akin to the interpretive route, and address their first order normative deliberations to a kind of imagined communal tribunal. But then it is seriously doubtful whether such people ask themselves a moral question at all!

Walzer poses a similar objection:

> But the question commonly posed to ordinary men and women arguing about morality has [this] form: what is the right thing to do? . . . It does not appear that the question is about the interpretation of an existing and particular morality, for it is possible that that morality, however interpreted, does not tell us the right thing to do.

His answer is very illuminating:

> But if we follow the course of the argument, listen to it, study its phenomenology, we will see that its real subject is the meaning of the particular moral life shared by the protagonists. The general question about the right thing to do is quickly turned into some more specific question[,] . . . ["W]hat is the right thing *for us* to do?"[42]

This is the sense in which *normative* disagreement presumes a shared "text": "If we disagree," argues Walzer, "there is nothing else to do but go back to the 'text'—the values, principles, codes and conventions that constitute *our* moral world—and to the 'readers' of the text."[43] Thus, in Walzer's opinion, the above objection fails to perceive one basic fact—that the disagreement about the correct interpretation of, say, the law, the custom, or the constitution is normative as much as it is descriptive. Thus, the sharp distinction between the moral and the interpretive is deeply misguided. Walzer's own first-order ethical works verify this claim.

But our defense of the interpretive view will focus on a metaphysical difficulty that Walzer does not consider, a difficulty that concerns second-order, rather than first-order, deliberations and, therefore, one that goes to the heart of normative self-criticism. A fully rational and clear-minded member of a community might know every relevant fact about his community's ideally interpreted normative outlook, yet still meaningfully wonder whether it is right or good. Hence, being the ideal interpretation of the existing practice has a property that the property expressed in this community by the term *right* or *good* does not, namely, that it is an open question whether it is "right" or "good." Thus, what *S* expresses by "right" relative to a context cannot be what best interprets the practice of the community to which *S* belongs. If this is so, the community's "text" cannot be considered the ultimate normative stopping point Walzer claims it is.

We propose facing this challenge by conceding that (even) members of the community whose normative outlook *is* ideally interpreted might challenge its rightness. This concession, we shall argue, nonetheless remains consistent with the claim that normative statements are true by interpretation. In order to do so, however, we need to supplement our so far purely communal account of the interpretive view with a plausible theory of personal goodness, and to make a crucial point about it.[44]

A Digression on Personal Goodness

The theory of personal well-being we shall use is James Griffin's. In his view,[45] personal goodness is seen as fixed in terms of what, given a person's current motivational system, he would want himself to want under conditions of full information. In this view, what is good for a person (= what is important to him) is the satisfaction of his informed (= rational) desires. The most salient feature of this theory is that despite being a "desire-based" account of well-being, it is anti-Humean. Desires are not brute forces for which the only role played by reason is to combine and order. Reason, in other words, is not merely the slave of passion. On the contrary, a desire might be deemed to be intrinsically irrational. To take Frankfurt's well-known example, a person who dedicates himself to avoiding stepping on the cracks on the sidewalk sustains an intrinsically irrational desire.[46] Contra Hume and others, Griffin assumes that under conditions of full information a rational person could not (or, in Frankfurt's view, should not) want to obsessively avoid the cracks; likewise, it would be wrong for people to prefer certain pains to others just because they happen to occur on Tuesdays.

Now, suppose that the desire for social status is reasonable—or at least not intrinsically irrational—and that satisfying it in a respectable manner is considered a real accomplishment. Suppose further that, at a certain point in her life, a fully informed person who desired and strove reasonably to achieve social status gradually loses interest and begins to find the whole thing pointless. This suggests that a person might know everything about her set of informed desires up to the point of deliberation and find herself a moment later painfully hesitant with regard to the projects she had always felt obliged to undertake. In other words, it is possible that all the facts about a person's set of desires up to the moment of deliberation will prove insufficient for determining what is good for her. Volitional discontinuities are not uncommon, so that it could well be that at the moment she asks herself the Socratic questions about how she should live or what she finds or should find important, the set of her informed desires of a moment ago will no longer be relevant. "Rosati's observation":[47] a fully informed person can come to care about things, which were previously unimportant to him, and by caring about them *make* them important to him.

At first glance Rosati's observation seems to be inconsistent with the informed-desires account of well-being. On such an account, to say that a person who knows every knowable fact about his informed desires could fail to know what is good for him would seem a contradiction in terms. Our point is that, in fact, this is so only if one ignores the time dimension and the very effect of asking such Socratic questions. At any time *t*, a person can reopen the question of how he should live, even if he is privy to everything about his set of informed desires prior to asking. This is because, by the very act of raising the question, *I make my set of desires less* than fully coherent and, hence, *less than fully informed;* in asking the Socratic question, it is reopened.[48] Now, in the final analysis, what is good for a person *is* what satisfies his informed desires. Since caring is a mode of desiring (a desire that is sustained by other higher-level desires), it is still the case that every fact about individual goodness is a fact about the satisfaction of informed desires. Still, what one wholeheartedly cares for or loves at one moment (we here use Frankfurt's terminology without embracing his conception of rationality)[49] may be found to wane and wither at another, so that what might be good to him *now,* just before deliberation, might not be identical to what he *will* rationally care about after his deliberations get under way.[50]

It follows that deliberation is not unreasonable, even when it cannot be explained by other informed desires (i.e., reasons). Even if the social climber has no informed desire capable of explaining why she gradually came to stop caring about her social status, such a change of heart would not be unreasonable, at least in the minimal sense of not being irrational or insane.[51] People, we conclude, enjoy the freedom of questioning, re-articulating, and revaluating their volitional nature. We have not argued for Griffin's conception of personal goodness. What we have established is a consistency claim: Griffin's informed-desires theory of well-being allows that a fully informed person may stop caring about things that were important to him (= good for him), and start caring about things that were previously unimportant to him, thus leaving the Socratic question forever open.

The Essentiality of the Thick and the Normative Question

Bearing all this in mind, let us return to the difficulty with which we began, namely, that despite everything we have said about Comparative Irrealism, from an interpretive perspective, goodness *is* an irreducibly thin property. For a member of any community might know every relevant fact about his community's ideally interpreted normative outlook, yet still wonder whether it is good or just. Our strategy will be analogous to what we have said in the previous section about personal goodness: we shall imagine a world in which the Essentiality of the Thick and Comparative Irrealism both hold. In this world, we submit, there is a sense in which at every point, the question whether a normative outlook is right can be opened without violating either principle.

Imagine, then, such a world. Suppose, further, that in this world the various normative outlooks are ideally interpreted, and the diversity of historical and cultural contexts is so great as to render all differences between normative outlooks incomparable. Hence, in the world we imagine, since $N1$ and $N2$ are both ideally interpreted and conflicting, in all contexts, neither "$N1$ is morally superior to $N2$" nor "$N2$ is morally superior to $N1$" are true. More precisely, in the polemical context in which people try to express a proposition that $N1$ adherents affirm and $N2$ adherents deny, the comparative judgment to the effect that $N1$ is righter or better than $N2$ is either false or gappy. There is no irreducible thin comparative property expressed by "better than" in such a context.

The gist of the argument is this: even if *N1* was ideally interpreted, its practice may have since changed as a result of what might be called a "real confrontation" with *N2*.[52] Consider again the Lockean tolerant religious society of Sreenivasan's example. And suppose that its normative outlook is ideally interpreted. Imagine that its committed members are confronted with the value of self-determination as a result of an encounter with the similarly tolerant, yet differently interpreted Rousseauians. Following Frankfurt, we argued that fully rational people who are currently committed to a religious outlook are able to care about autonomy once this value becomes available to them. Such an attitude to the foreign value can be generated because a fully informed person can make things important to himself by coming to care about them. And such a person's new informed desire for self-determination might be rationally unrelated to his previous set of informed desires.

In Frankfurt's rich picture of individual identity, no role is given to community practice and community values. Frankfurtian individuals are not envisaged as members of communities, committed to, or informed by communal values, or engaging them in any way. Viewed in isolation, what a person ultimately cares about and makes important — which for Frankfurt form the sole basis for normative commitment — can be found to have changed, even abruptly, from one moment to the next, in a manner wholly arbitrary from the point of view of his former informed desires, and, therefore, in a way that leaves the Socratic question forever open.[53]

When cast in interpretive terms, and viewed as an intersubjective group phenomenon, the potential discrepancy, or delay between coming to care for something and (becoming aware [informed?] of one's caring,[54] and hence) making it important, are precisely the discrepancies between something a group has come to *practice* and making that practice explicitly endorsed in its scheme of values.

To return to our example, the fact that the value of self-determination begins to acquire a measure of cultural presence in the religious society's way of life should count as a change of *the practice* of the community. The structures of families and of rituals change somewhat; women become more active in both family and religious contexts. These changes gradually become visible in the public sphere and demand articulation. It is at this point that individuals and small groups begin to act as Walzerian social critics, challenging their community's concrete conception of the good life by appeal to the newly emerging ways it is now lived. And these individuals are free, as we have seen, to care about values that have had no presence in the current scheme of values that comprises their own moral world, even if these values are alien to the existing ideal interpretation of their way of life. If the attitude of the members committed to the ideal of self-determination is institutionalized—that is, if it comes to be present in the public sphere—the attitude and its behavioral expressions become part of the conventions, discourse, and way of life of the community. Its "text" will have changed. And at this point, a collective, social Socratic question is meaningfully reopened as the community as a whole may well ask how it should live. And different interpretations, some wholly alien to its existing scheme of values, will be meaningfully pitted against each other, and eventually adjudicated meaningfully as some are deemed better interpretations than others.

In the world we imagine, if *N1* and *N2* are indeed ideally interpreted, there is no irreducibly thin normative property that can order them. Comparative Irrealism strictly obtains. But in the event of "real confrontation" between the two societies, a change in practice may result in one of them that renders its normative outlook no longer ideally interpreted, and open to reinterpretation. The basic conviction that animates the interpretive account is reaffirmed; the partial moral order ("*x* is better than *y*") among different normative outlooks *that purport to interpret the same set of practices* can be articulated by thick interpretive concepts only.

To summarize, any true statement about the rightness of a normative outlook, made by members of the community, follows analytically from other statements about the ideal interpretation of the practice of the relevant community. In particular, facts about the normative superiority of a normative outlook are fully explained by interpretive facts about specific values (denoted by thick concepts). The normatively superior of the two outlooks is either the one whose scheme of values better interprets their shared practice or the one whose practice is better fitted by their shared scheme of values. Still, at any time *t*, a community can open the question of whether its normative outlook is the best. The question would be meaningful even if the normative outlook had been, up until now, ideally interpreted. For, once the question is asked, the interpretation ceases, if only potentially, to be ideal. But the main point is that the normative rankings involved in such deliberations remain forever reducible to the thick without (thin) remainder.

The interpretive account thus reverses the absolutist order of explanation, according to which the question of goodness is similarly rationally open, even for normative outlooks ideally interpreted, but not because goodness functions independently as an external yardstick. According to the interpretive account, the question is open because members of the community ask it, for by the very act of meaningfully asking it, the interpretation of their normative outlook is rendered *interpretively* questionable. It is in this way that the question of goodness can remain in principle open, in a manner consistent with the Essentiality of the Thick and Comparative Irrealism.

Furthermore, Rosati's observation suggests that reflective individuals are in fact unable to close themselves to newly available challenging values, even if their sets of desires are maximally informed. Because of this, normative outlooks are bound to be kept open to confrontations from within (in the light of newly available values) and from without (in the light of newly considered values originating in other cultural contexts). Openness to confrontation with alien values is what distinguishes a community's attitude to its normative outlook from what it considers to be mere rules of etiquette. It is the very difference between norm and custom. To undertake reflectively to consider the question, how we—as a community—should live, or what we should care about, is to take the measure of our existing normative outlook in comparison to its meaningful alternatives. Yet whether an alternative is meaningful is indeterminate; it is wholly dependent on the changing practice, which in turn is dependent on what members of the community come to care about.[55] An interpretive slogan we formulated earlier was that the thin without the thick is empty; we now realize that the thick without openness to real confrontations is, in a clear sense, blind.

Comparative Irrealism in the world we imagine still runs deep. Religious people are free not to care about autonomy, and to resist any impact of any liberal notion on their conception of the good life. If autonomy remains unimportant to them, then their concrete conception of the good life, steeped in notions like holiness, modesty, charity, need, spirituality, moderation, and humbleness, will remain incomparable to the liberals' conception of the good life. In other words, significantly different normative outlooks may become comparable to each other only if people *make them* comparable. But to make them viably comparable to other members of the community, for their social criticism to be *hearable,* something needs to have already shifted at the level of communal practice in the now-desired direction.

Taking Stock

Studying the interpretivist approach in terms of the thick/thin distinction and against the backdrop of the two approaches to meaning discussed in Part I, renders far more explicit the profound pragmatism that underlies all three. A community's normative vocabulary, its scheme of values, is fashioned from within, on the interpretive account, by an ongoing and critical (almost Davidsonian) process of self-interpretation that is thoroughly practice directed—a process very different from the aimless casting around for alternatives by which Rorty's ironist seeks to revitalize her final vocabulary. As we have seen, from an interpretivist point of view, a community may deem its scheme of values wrong or problematic and replace it with what it takes to be a better-suited alternative. In this respect, a normative outlook can be made subject to rational scrutiny and modification in ways that Rorty fails to acknowledge.

But, and this is the crucial point, although *an* interpretation may be found wanting and replaced by another, interpretation is an activity that, in and of itself, lacks normative thrust. On an interpretivist showing, interpretations may be found wanting but not the practices of which they purport to make sense. The resulting articulated scheme of values will be action guiding, and as such constitutive of the way members of the community will conduct themselves. But, barring confrontations from within and from without, interpretation can do no more than unquestioningly make explicit and render consistent what is essentially already there. The community's practice, though open to change by confrontation, remains immune to criticism from within that goes beyond troubleshooting for coherence, fit, and clarity. From an interpretive point of view, a community, prompted by its trusted and "connected" critics, is liable to find its conduct untrue to itself but not more. As we have seen, as a result of confrontation, a community's practice may undergo significant changes, which upon reflection may be deemed by hindsight progressive. But, as noted above, these changes, even when found to be reasonable by hindsight, cannot be *introduced* rationally. Practice may be found to have been modified but never to be in need of modification! In this important sense, a community's normative outlook remains as worryingly immune to rational scrutiny as Rorty describes.

CHAPTER FIVE

Rationality as Agreement

Friedman's Special Case for Science

Introduction

Taken together, chapters 2 and 3 have argued that the very assumption of Normative Diversity commits one to a bounded, yet crucially significant form of normative relativism almost regardless of one's approach to meaning. If normative diversity exists, or is even possible, then, we have argued, two sufficiently diverse normative outlooks are, in principle, humanly unrankable in ways acceptable to both. Here we are less concerned with the extent to which different normative outlooks can be compared or ranked than with the extent to which single outlooks are susceptible to critical, normative appraisal from within. Denying the former, however, seems clearly to entail denial of the latter. The logic is simple: if for lack of suitable thin normative concepts, an outlook cannot be deemed by its adherents normatively inferior to another, then, for the very same reason, it would seem, neither can they find it *normatively* wanting. For the question would always be: wanting in comparison to what? From within, a normative outlook may be judged to be inconsistent, incoherent, or unacceptably inexplicit but not wrong, false, unjust, or unworthy; from within, an outlook cannot be deemed *normatively* problematic by its own lights. And if a normative outlook cannot be normatively criticized from within, its present state cannot be deemed to be the outcome, or the subject matter, of rational scrutiny as defined at the outset of this study, except in the very limited sense of being troubleshot for consistency, coherence, explicity, or clarity.

Chapter 4 then argued that the interpretivist approach to normativity is capable nonetheless of accommodating a modest level of reasoned normative modification from within a normative outlook but only after suitable modifications of the community's practice are already in place. Social criticism proceeds, on the interpretivist view, by attempting to make good normative sense of the community's *existing* texts and practices. Interpretivism is a form of pragmatism, in the sense that practice drives conceptual articulation rather than vice versa.[1] Interpretive modifications of a community's normative outlook can be reasoned for only after the event, only after its practice is found to have changed. Much like Brandom, interpretivists view the process of formulating and developing a normative outlook in expressivist terms: as one of rendering explicit norms embodied implicitly in social institutions and community practice. But the picture they paint goes an importantly dynamic step beyond Brandom in allowing for changes in practice to prompt a rethinking of the normative.

Still, despite its inherent lack of critical bite, the interpretivists' pragmatist approach to normativity does succeed in enriching the scope of internal social criticism to include, in addition to testing the community's normative outlook for consistency, coherence, and clarity, questioning its *authenticity* to the community's changing way of life. However, this, as we noted in our conclusion to chapter 4, though a modest beginning, is still far from enough.

Michael Friedman's neo-Kantian "idea of a scientific philosophy"[2] would seem to have much in common with the interpretive approach to normativity. Similar to the interpretivists, Friedman views science as a practice constituted at any one time by a normative conceptual framework developed by its practitioners that is the job of philosophy of science to make explicit. And yet Friedman's position differs from that of the interpretivists in important respects. First, in endorsing Kuhn's theory of scientific revolutions, Friedman seems perfectly willing to entertain changes in a science's normative conceptual framework far more radical than anything the interpretive approach is capable of admitting. But what renders Friedman's undertaking especially relevant to the concerns of the present study is the centrality he assigns to combating what he describes as the "explicitly relativistic philosophical agenda [that] now informs a significant segment of research in the history, sociology and philosophy of science"(57) by presenting as rational even the "radical transitions between incommensurable or non-intertranslatable conceptual frameworks" (56), and to do so without presupposing an external even modestly absolutist foothold.

Friedman's *Dynamics of Reason* and subsequent work along its lines certainly constitutes the most informed attempt in recent years to confront the problem of the rationality of framework transitions in science from an explicitly neo-Kantian perspective in a manner fully aware of the relativistic tendencies of latter-day Anglophone philosophy of language and mind. But we find the price he ends up willing to pay for the special case he pleads for the sciences he studies unjustifiably high, and his understanding of rationality so different from our own as to leave the problems we purport to address largely unattended. Still, although we contest his conclusions, Friedman's project merits close and serious attention both for the light it sheds on the gravity and urgency of the problems at hand and for two important departures from Kuhn that we shall note in due course and return to in the final chapter of the book. These concern (a) the relevant discursive contexts in which science functions and develops, which in Kuhn's well-known account are given no role to play; and (b) the role played in scientific revolutions by intermediate figures whose work straddled the great divides they helped eventually to create, for whom, again, Kuhn's account has no room.

Limiting his project to science, Friedman refrains from casting his analysis in general philosophical terms, purporting to make a special case for "the scientific enterprise" by attempting to mark it off from other communal forms of normative endeavor. In addition, Friedman tends at crucial points to make his case historically rather than philosophically. He explores and explains the rationality of science apropos a rich and detailed picture of the actual developing content and structure of mathematical physics that he describes from an explicitly neo-Kantian perspective akin to the approaches we have discussed. But alert as Friedman is to

the neo-Kantian roots and aspirations of much current work in philosophy of mind and language,[3] his *Dynamics of Reason* steers wide, for the
reasons stated, of the challenge they pose to rationality outside the narrow confines of the best of the physical sciences. In order to bring Friedman's analysis to bear on the more general philosophical concerns of the
present study, we are required in what follows to adopt a far more expository approach than in previous chapters.

From Kant to Kuhn

Friedman traces the idea of a scientific philosophy back to Kant's distinction between first-level scientific inquiry and the second-level "distinctively philosophical 'transcendental' inquiry" (8–9) into the conditions
of its possibility. For Kant, the task of philosophy had ceased to be that of
justifying the success of Newton's physics, or of proposing ways to improve or replace it. The excellence of Newton's scientific achievement was
for Kant beyond dispute. Philosophy's task was to account for its success:
to explain "whether and how . . . [it] actually made rational sense" (8–9).

Kant's scientific philosophy, as described and endorsed by Friedman,
thus stands to the practice of science as, for interpretivists, ethics stands
to communal practice. But Kant's First Critique, and with it Friedman, go
a significant step further. The former's interpretation of Newtonian physics yields a vocabulary of a priori concepts that are not merely deployed
in, and do not merely articulate, but are *constitutive of* the ways in which
that physics is practiced. Philosophical sense is made of the practice of
science by exposing by interpretation the second-order normative vocabulary of concepts and principles that determines and governs it. However,
the profound changes that mathematical physics has undergone since
Kant have thrown into stark relief the notion of the synthetic a priori in
Kant's original form. The idea of scientific frameworks comprising "absolutely fixed and unrevisable a priori principles built, once and for all,
into our fundamental cognitive capacities" (30) had to be rejected. Rather
than dispense with the Kantian approach altogether (in favor, say, of
Quine's "radically opposed form of epistemological holism" [32]), Friedman follows Schlick, Reichenbach, and the later Carnap[4] in opting for

a relativized and dynamical conception of a priori mathematical-physical principles, which change and develop along with the development of the mathematical and physical sciences themselves, but which nevertheless retain the characteristically Kantian constitutive function of making the empirical natural knowledge thereby structured and framed by such principles first possible.[5]

In Carnap's *Logical Syntax of Language* (1934), Friedman finds this view's "most mature expression," according to which "all standards of 'correctness', 'validity' and 'truth' . . . are relative to the logical rules or principles definitive of one or another formal language or linguistic framework" (31). Such rules are firmly constitutive of all standards, yet relative to— that is, contingent on—one or another choice of linguistic framework.

This is the foundation on which Friedman builds his own neo-Kantian picture. Siding with Carnap against Quine, he knowingly endorses the former's two basic and related distinctions between (a) the *L*-rules of a science's linguistic framework, and the empirical *P*-rules of which they are constitutive, and (b) "internal" questions decidable within the system in accord with its *L*-rules and "external" questions to do with choosing which linguistic framework to adopt.[6]

The case Friedman mounts in favor of the first distinction against Quine's famous "Two Dogmas" argument[7] is wisely constructed along historical rather than analytical lines.[8] Friedman admits that Carnap's construal of the nature of the *L*-rules and especially of the fundamental distinction between them and the system's *P*-rules as purely formal or logical are indeed seriously undermined by Quine's famous argument (41). Nonetheless, even if they cannot be distinguished formally, it is not the case, he argues, that Carnap's distinction can be reduced to a continuum of mere relative entrenchment and relative resistance to revision. Friedman's historical arguments pertain both to the specific function played by certain elements within mathematical physics at a given time and to the ways in which mathematical physics was as a whole transformed *over time*. The way in which the calculus stands to the laws of motion in Newtonian mechanics, for example, cannot be plausibly described as being merely a matter of relative resilience to empirical disconfirmation, subject merely to "a maxim of minimum mutilation."[9] The function of the calculus in

Newtonian physics is constitutive. Without the calculus, "[Newton's] second law of motion could not even be formulated or written down, let alone function to describe empirical phenomena" (35). Moreover, when Newton wrote the *Principia,* the calculus, while centrally constitutive of its entire project, was still so controversial that Newton saw fit to conceal its use "in favor of traditional synthetic geometry" (39). And the same goes for the mathematical theory of Reimannian manifolds and the principle of equivalence, which, while constitutive of Einstein's theory, were hardly well-entrenched parts of the mathematics of their day. It is during such revolutionary moments, argues Friedman, that the inappropriateness of Quine's attempt to reduce the apriority of such elements to mere relative entrenchment becomes most apparent, despite the fact that Carnap's attempt to demarcate them formally was indeed proved groundless by Quine.

It is in Kuhn's theory of scientific paradigms, rather than in Carnap's overly formalized theory of linguistic frameworks, that Friedman finds "an informal counterpart, in effect, of the relativized conception of constitutive a priori principles developed by the logical empiricists" that by virtue of its informality remains untouched by Quine's attack. And in Kuhn's distinction between revolutionary and normal science, he finds a close "parallel [to] the Carnapian distinction between change of . . . linguistic framework and rule-governed operations carried out within such a framework" (39).[10]

Yet, while generally endorsing the stratified and dynamic picture of scientific knowledge formalized by Carnap and historicized by Kuhn, Friedman takes serious issue with both their accounts of framework replacement. For lack of a higher-level framework, a framework as a whole, Carnap argued in typical formal idiom, "cannot be judged as being either true or false because it is not an assertion. It can only be judged as being more or less expedient, fruitful, conducive to the aim for which the language is intended."[11] "[W]e post-Kuhnians," cautions Friedman, cannot contend with "the relativistic predicament arising in the wake of Kuhn's work on scientific revolutions," to which Carnap remained oblivious, and which he "nowhere considers seriously" (57).

Friedman's response to Kuhn's treatment of external questions is equally negative but more complex, oscillating between the gestalt-switch rhetoric of some of Kuhn's original formulations and the more nuanced, language-bound, and less relativistic account of paradigm change found in his later work. In the first two of the three lectures making up the first part of *Dynamics of Reason* what Earman calls Kuhn's "purple passages"[12] set the tone. "Just as, for Carnap," writes Friedman, so "changes of paradigms in revolutionary science, for Kuhn, do not proceed in accordance with generally agreed upon rules as in normal science, but rather require something more akin to a conversion experience."[13] Kuhn is here described as advocating an account of framework replacement even less reasoned and rational than Carnap's. Elsewhere, however, especially in the course of Lecture 3, Friedman brings a very different Kuhn to the fore: the Kuhn of the "Afterwords" to Horwich's *World Changes* (1993), in which he reflected anew and in keener linguistic idiom upon "the nature of . . . what I once called 'scientific revolutions.'"[14] What Friedman here brings to the fore is precisely the most significant departure one finds in the later Kuhn from the "conversion experience" account of paradigm shifts advocated in *Structure*, namely, the idea that scientific revolutions (now described as replacements of a science's "structured lexicon" of kind-concepts) are governed by a set of criteria that remain "necessarily permanent" between paradigms: accuracy, precision, scope, simplicity, fruitfulness, consistency, and so on. "These criteria," writes Kuhn in the last paragraph but one of this last of his published works, "whose rejection would be irrational, are the basis for the evaluation of work done during periods of lexical stability, and they are basic also to the response mechanisms that, at times of stress, produce speciation and lexical change."[15]

Friedman, as we shall see in greater detail below, is as firmly opposed to the later Kuhn's "universalistic" conception of scientific rationality as he is to the "conversion experience" relativism of *Structure*. If the latter would seem to concede conceptual relativism its point, the former seems, conversely, to rob Friedman's commitment to a relativized yet still constitutive conception of the apriority of its radical dynamism.

The Problem of Rationality: Carnap, Kuhn, and Conceptual Relativism

Dynamics of Reason builds on and away from Carnap and Kuhn but does not purport systematically to expose, or to trace, the development of their thinking. It is the first of Friedman's books that is not primarily expository, and its interpretive choices of emphasis are eclectic and geared in the main to the development of its author's own position, whose commitment to their radical neo-Kantianism runs deep but whose commitment to the rationality of science runs deeper. In this respect, it is the Kuhn of *Structure* that he finds most problematic.

> The most fundamental problem raised by the Kuhnian account of scientific revolutions is to explain how it can be rational to move to a new constitutive framework, ... despite the fact that this new framework, from the point of view of the old framework, is not even possible. What rational motivations can there be—and how can it be rationally intelligible—to make such a radical shift? (99–100)

But as the argument shifts from the task of establishing the neo-Kantian idea of the relativized a priori to that of deliberating the rationality of scientific framework replacement, so do the philosophical adversaries Friedman sees fit to engage. While he locates the central threat to the former in Quine's epistemological holism, he detects the threat most pertinent to the latter in "sociological conceptual relativism," which receives its "most explicit and provocative defense ... in the 'sociology of scientific knowledge' of the so-called Edinburgh School" (48–50).

Here, however, a different and disturbing note creeps into Friedman's reasoning. Underlying the work of the Edinburgh relativists, he cautions, "is the idea that the traditional notions of rationality, objectivity, and truth reduce, in the end, to local socio-cultural norms conventionally adopted and enforced by particular socio-cultural groups," an idea, he charges quoting extensively from the works of Barry Barnes and David Bloor, that is supposedly "derived from Kuhn," to the effect—and this is the point to notice—"that there are no '*universal standards*' of human reason, no '*context-free* or *super-cultural* norms of rationality.'"[16] This sudden universalist turn of phrase of Friedman's is surprising, since from the neo-Kantian position he claims to endorse, no such norms, one would think, are *in principle* forthcoming. Friedman obviously opposes the Edinburgh relativists' contention that the standards of rationality, objectivity, and truth reduce to local norms that are "*conventually* adopted and enforced," as he does Carnap's conventionalism. But from Friedman's neo-Kantian perspective, neither can the universalism he accuses the Edinburghians of denying be a viable option. Or can it? One wonders if something has come undone in the "notion of a relativized yet still constitutive a priori" he is "attempting to articulate"(71).[17] And as if to confuse the issue even further, it is at this point that he introduces, in the disjointed double role of both asset and foil, the universalism of the later Kuhn to combat Edinburghian relativism.

Curiously, however, apart from the above-cited disapproving dismissal of the relativists' renunciation of all universal, supracultural, interparadigm standards of human reason, Friedman makes no attempt to engage their claims and arguments. He limits his criticism to the left, as it were, to quoting extensively from Kuhn's "Afterwords" with a view to proving that Kuhn himself rejected their relativistic reading of his work. (Notwithstanding the fact that "Afterwords" was written more than a decade after Barnes published his study of Kuhn.) Kuhn is cited, then, to prove that Barnes and Bloor were wrong in taking him for a relativist but not to disprove Edinburghian relativism for what it is. Nor, as it turns out, is Kuhn cited in *Dynamics of Reason* to prove that *he* had got it right! For Friedman goes on immediately to argue long and hard against Kuhn's latter-day universalist turn (51–53, 83–85, 93–103). The Edinburgh relativists believed Kuhn was an ally, and are chided for denying there being universal standards of reason. Kuhn is then cited to prove he was a universalist, and therefore no friend of social relativism, but only to have the universalism he proposed firmly rejected.

Now, being the neo-Kantian he purports to be, Friedman is *necessarily* a relativist, though, he insists, not of the Edinburghian, starkly conventionalist brand. Rationality, at least in science, he argues against Carnap and the Edinburgh school, cannot be made to rest on the mere convention of local standards. On the other hand, he objects to Kuhn's universalism partly because he firmly believes that standards of human reason are (again, at least in the sciences) thoroughly framework-relative. Is there a third option for science that is not conventionalist but at the same time not universalist in the manner suggested by Kuhn? Friedman believes there is. To see how, let us first look briefly at the threefold argument he mounts in *Dynamics of Reason* against the later Kuhn's universalism.

First, he argues, "there are powerful reasons arising from Kuhn's own historiography for doubting whether any such puzzle-solving criteria are really permanent across revolutionary scientific change" (51). This is not merely a matter of fact, but one of principle. Due to the notorious diversity of human ends, he argues, "there *can be no* ground for a truly universal rationality within purely instrumental reason. This . . . is why Kuhn's attempt to find permanent criteria or values held constant throughout the development of science *necessarily* fails" (55; emphasis added).

Second, even if one concedes the existence of permanent criteria definitive of scientific success, "it remains entirely obscure how there can be an 'uncommitted' or paradigm-independent standpoint for rationally assessing the satisfaction of such criteria" (52).[18]

Third, and most important for Friedman, even if one takes Kuhn's instrumentalist puzzle-solving account of interframework scientific rationality as unproblematic (the possibility of which in *Dynamics of Reason* he seriously doubts), it is still one thing to conceive scientific theories as mere devices for maximizing quantitative accuracy, precision, simplicity, and so forth (53) but quite another, he argues elegantly, to view them, as Friedman does (and believes Kuhn [supplementing Carnap] implies) as contentful and testable attempts to formulate laws that are empirically *true* by virtue of the a priori constitutive framework that secures them as such.[19]

> Both a Newtonian and an Einsteinian physicist, for example, can and must agree that general relativity yields more accurate predictions for the advance of the perihelion of Mercury. From the Newtonian physicist's point of view, however, general relativity can *only* be accepted as a pragmatically acceptable device for prediction; it *cannot* be a true description of empirical reality. For, from the Newtonian point of view, the constitutive framework of general relativity is not even possible or coherent, and there is thus no sense in which Einstein's field equations can actually be empirically true. (83–84; original emphasis)

In previous chapters we have argued quite generally that the fact that normative vocabularies or outlooks are diverse and replaceable is *not* an argument against the essential factuality (world-guidedness and action-guidingness) of the thick concepts they employ when viewed from within.

In other words, Friedman's is an argument against scientific *instrumentalism,* not against scientific conceptual relativism—or normative irrealism, to use the phraseology we have introduced.[20] As noted, neither does Kuhn deny the essential factuality of normal science. Each of a science's successive linguistic frameworks, he states in marked Wittgensteinian idiom, "makes possible a corresponding form of life within which the truth or falsity of propositions may be both claimed and rationally justified."[21] From what we have seen so far, Friedman is in no position to contest the conceptual relativism of the conceptual relativists, especially if it is construed in the limited form we have termed Comparative Irrealism. In conceding the contingency of the constitutive a priori, he wears his relativism on his sleeve. The real point of contention between Friedman and the Edinburghians, we suggest, is (a) their implied denial of the two-tier, normatively constituted nature of scientific knowledge and practice and (b) their implied, and, in Friedman's opinion, all too easy Rortian denial of the very idea of scientific framework replacement being rational. Friedman's dismissive treatment of the conceptual relativists is confusing because he seems unaware of how unique and radical his own project is. No one before him had undertaken to account philosophically for the rationality of paradigm replacement in science while endorsing, as he does, both their contingency and their thoroughly constitutive normative role. As preceding chapters have amply proven, among those who take the constitutive role of normative vocabularies seriously, conceptual relativism has been the unchallenged norm.

Friedman's question would seem to nicely accord with our own. How, he asks, is it possible to view the replacement of one constitutive framework by another as rational, if the framework one is reasoning *for* is normatively incomprehensible from the point of view of the framework one is reasoning *from?* He appears to be raising for science the very problem raised by the present study for normative outlooks in general.

But the affinity is only apparent, for he frames the question very differently. We ask how members of a community can be said to rationally deem their linguistic framework to be *in need* of replacement, while Friedman asks how a framework different from their own can be rationally deemed a worthy alternative. The difference might seem inconsequential, but it is not. Friedman ponders the problem of the rationality of *shifting allegiance* between *given* frameworks; we ponder that of the rational *motivation* for *developing* an alternative framework in the first place. Rationality for Friedman does not function as a prospective evaluative category of scientific *inquiring* but as a retrospective evaluative category of scientific *choice*. Friedman nowhere asks what could have rationally prompted Einstein to initially seek to replace the framework constitutive of his work and thinking, but only how, given his fellow practitioners' commitment to the old, could the new framework he had proposed have earned their rational approval? The fundamental problem of rationality becomes for Friedman that of explaining the grounds for granting expert *imprimatur* in cases where the very framework by which such imprimaturs are granted is itself being replaced. For us, by contrast, the fundamental problem of rationality is to explain how a functioning constitutive framework can come to be considered deficient to the point of despair by those whose work it constitutes. Where we seek to articulate the possibility of rationally faulting a framework from its own perspective, Friedman seeks to articulate the possibility of approving the worth of one framework from the perspective of another.[22]

But are these differences as significant as we make out? Surely a responsible scientific community would not undertake to modify or replace an existing framework unless firmly convinced that it was seriously flawed, and it would never approve and endorse a different framework unless convinced that the new was significantly superior to the old. In which case, it could be argued, the problem of approving the new and that of criticizing the old are in the last analysis one and the same. Could Friedman deny this? His text may lay greater stress than ours on the problem of approval, but that in itself does not make him a Rortian ironist. Friedman clearly does not concede Rorty's contention that a new framework can "have its utility explained only retrospectively,"[23] and that only after it is endorsed does it "make possible for the first time a formulation of its own purpose."[24] Friedman explicitly presents the problem as that of justifying the endorsement of the new from the normative vantage point of the still-functioning old. And what kind of justification would satisfy Friedman, the objection would go, if *not* some sort of reasoned self-critical argument rendered from within the old pronouncing it deficient in ways that render it normatively inferior to the new? If that is the case, Friedman's project would seem to nicely dovetail with our own. But it is not, and it does not. A closer examination of Friedman's solution reveals that he in no way associates the rational approval and endorsement of the new framework with critique of the old. Friedman is indeed no Rortian ironist; nonetheless, the notion of scientific rationality developed in *Dynamics of Reason*, as we shall see, is not made to turn on critical reflection at all.

Science in Context

Locating the rationality of scientific framework replacement in the act of *approving* and *endorsing* the new (while still committed to the old)— as opposed to locating it in the critical *pondering* of the old (prior to formulating the new)—commits Friedman to a tripartite agenda. First, locating the rational thus, minimally requires him to fashion a notion of communal or specialist rational consent, which he purports to find in Jürgen Habermas's well-known idea of "communicative rationality."

Second, not all consent is rational. To be considered (communicatively) rational, evaluative acts of approval must be *reasoned*. Interframework reasoning requires interframework *mediation*, which is made possible in science, Friedman argues, by virtue of a "higher-level, straddling meta-framework . . . capable of mediating the transmission of (communicative) rationality" from the old to the new (105).

Third, and pace Kuhn, Carnap, and much of his own rhetoric, to be meaningfully bestrided by a "meta-paradigm" capable of facilitating "agreement or consensus across different paradigms" (58), paradigm shifts in science, Friedman insists, cannot be allowed to be too drastic. Although he continues to describe scientific revolutions as "transitions between radically different conceptual frameworks" (105), he posits, as Alan Richardson observes, exceedingly "kinder, gentler revolutions in the realm of science" than Kuhn ever did.[25] Friedman's account of successive scientific frameworks thus differs considerably from Galison's portrayal of Kuhnian paradigms as isolated "island empires."[26] In Friedman's picture,

successive scientific revolutions come to resemble series of nested, con-
verging developments in which, looking back, earlier frameworks "are
exhibited as limiting cases" of their successors, while, looking forward,
"the concepts and principles of later paradigms" are seen to "evolve continuously, by a series of natural transformations from those of earlier
ones" (63).

A Kuhnian Dilemma

To better appreciate Friedman's Habermasian account of interparadigm
rationality, let us briefly look again at Kuhn's last work. Responding to
Ernan McMullin's criticism of his "curiously divided" heritage—namely,
his insistence on maintaining "the rational character of theory choice in
science while denying the epistemic character of the theory chosen"[27]—
Kuhn takes the opportunity to restate the full extent of his neo-Kantian
commitments, this time in decidedly semantic terms. He is a realist, he
insists, but of Kantian rather than of naive representationalist stock.

> My goal is double. On the one hand, I aim to justify claims that science
> is cognitive, that its product is knowledge of nature, and that the criteria
> it uses in evaluating beliefs are in that sense epistemic. But on the other,
> I aim to deny all meaning to claims that successive scientific beliefs be-
> come more and more probable or better and better approximations to
> the truth and simultaneously to suggest that the subject of truth claims
> cannot be a relation between beliefs and a putatively mind-independent
> or "external" world.[28]

Scientific truth can be spoken of, and progress toward it achieved, according to the later Kuhn, only in the context of a shared and fixed "structured
lexicon" of kind-terms.[29] It is a form of realism that Kuhn explicitly aligns
with the second of Reichenbach's two meanings of the Kantian a priori (as
described in Friedman's contribution to the same volume).[30] Scientists
operating with different taxonomic structures describe the world differently and make different generalizations about it. Such differences can be
resolved by importing concepts from one to the other. However, cautions
Kuhn, importation is an option only in cases of pure supplementation,
cases in which the host lexicon remains fully intact.

But if the terms to be imported are kind-terms that overlap kind-terms already in place, no importation is possible, at least no importation which allows both terms to retain their meaning, their projectibility, their status as kind-terms. Some of the kinds that populate the worlds of the two communities are then irreducibly different, and the difference is no longer between descriptions but between the populations described. Is it, in these circumstances, inappropriate to say that the members of the two communities live in different worlds?[31]

Cast in our terminology, Kuhn is claiming (a) that irreducibly different scientific lexicons exist and (b) that such lexicons do not share a set of thin normative concepts capable of normatively ranking them in a manner acceptable to both (unless, of course, one replicates or is wholly contained within the other). This is the sense in which in "Afterwords" Kuhn deems estranged lexicons incommensurable.[32] Kuhn's text thus implies that since overlapping lexicons cannot be ranked, a single functioning lexicon cannot be deemed sufficiently problematic or wanting to motivate its practitioners to seek a better alternative. Lexical replacement (as opposed to lexical *enrichment*), in other words, cannot be reasoned for prospectively, only rationalized retrospectively:

There is, for example, no way, even in an enriched Newtonian vocabulary, to convey the Aristotelian propositions regularly misconstrued as asserting the proportionality of force and motion or the impossibility of a void. Using our conceptual lexicon, these Aristotelian propositions cannot be expressed—they are simply ineffable—and we are barred by the no-overlap principle from access to the concepts required to express them. It follows that no shared metric is available to compare our assertions about force and motion with Aristotle's and thus to provide a basis for a claim that ours (or, for that matter, his) are closer to the truth. We may, of course, conclude that our lexicon permits a more powerful and precise way than his of dealing with what are *for us* the problems of dynamics, but these were not his problems, and lexicons are not, in any case, the sorts of thing that can be true or false.[33]

And it is at this point that Kuhn makes the deliberately Wittgensteinian observation noted above that "each lexicon makes possible a corresponding form of life within which the truth or falsity of propositions may be both claimed and rationally justified, but the justification of lexicons or of lexical change can only be pragmatic."[34]

Friedman's criticism of Kuhn's conclusion is well founded. If lexicons are not treated as mere instruments by their practitioners but are thought of as constitutive of their "phenomenal world," of their scientific form of life, of their very professional identity, then there is no sense at all in attributing the rationality of their replacement to mere pragmatic, instrumental considerations. If the theories generated by a community's lexicon purport to be true and are tested for truth, lexicons will not be replaced for, and their replacements will not be justified by, reference to instrumental criteria. Neo-Kantian realism (or world-directedness) and instrumentalism are incompatible philosophical positions.[35]

Undetected by Friedman, however, Kuhn's "Afterwords" harbors a deeper tension. Despite his clarity and confidence of tone, Kuhn seems considerably ill at ease with the radicality of his relativized Kantianism. Alongside his firm denial of "all meaning to claims that successive scientific beliefs become more and more probable or better and better approximations to the truth," his vivid description of different lexical communities living in "different worlds," and his insistence that acquiring a different lexicon, is, in principle, not a matter of translation but of "bilingualism,"[36] Kuhn, in an attempt to mark off his project from Carnap's, sees fit nonetheless to declare the following:

> Concerned from the start with the *development* of knowledge, I have seen each stage in the evolution of a given field as built—not quite squarely— upon its predecessor, the earlier stage providing the problems, the data, and most of the concepts prerequisite to the emergence of the stage that followed. In addition, I have insisted that some changes in conceptual vocabulary are required for the assimilation and development of the observations, laws, and theories deployed in the later stage (whence the phrase, "not quite squarely" above).[37]

"The transition to a new lexical structure, to a revised set of kinds," he adds further down, "permits the resolution of problems with which the previous structure was unable to deal."[38] These declarations are extremely problematic. In what sense can two overlapping, truly incommensurable lexicons be said to be even partially built on one another? Conversely, if a lexicon can be said to provide its successor with the problems, data, and most of the concepts prerequisite for its emergence, in what sense can it be said to represent a language so different as to resist translation and to generate a different world? If one lexicon successfully builds on another with a view to resolving pending problems, why can the transition only be justified "pragmatically"? More seriously, if incommensurable lexicons are supposed to be constitutive of different worlds, in what sense can one at all talk of the pending problems of one being solved by another? Finally, and most significantly from the point of view of the present study, in what sense can a constitutive framework be said to admit of problems it is unable to solve?

Kuhn offers no relief to these tensions. Indeed, nowhere does he as much as acknowledge that in the context of his theory of scientific lexicons they are problematic. The horns of the dilemma are stated clearly enough but not as horns of a dilemma. He seems clearly to maintain that a constitutive lexicon can admit of problems with which it is incapable of dealing, but he nowhere discusses how such deep-reaching normative self-criticism is possible. He seems to believe that two successive, truly constitutive, yet unintertranslatable lexicons could represent meaningful and distinct steps in a developmental progression toward ever better science, while declaring that they constitute genuinely different worlds. But we know that they cannot, for truly different lexicons are normatively unrankable, even in retrospect. Kuhn evidently thought they could be ranked, and that the set of thin instrumentalist concepts he listed—"accuracy, precision, scope, simplicity, fruitfulness, consistency, and so on"[39]—suffice to do the job. But, as Friedman argues,[40] he was wrong on this count too.

The Dual Normativity of Scientific Frameworks

Friedman seems aware of all this for he treads more carefully than Kuhn, both in framing the problem and in the way he purports to solve it. Friedman refrains throughout from characterizing a new constitutive framework as building on its predecessor—evolving out of it, yes, but not building on it—or as capable of resolving problems and difficulties with which its predecessor was unable to deal.[41] This is because Friedman's notion of a scientific constitutive framework amounts to much more than that of a taxonomy of kind-terms. Tsou's differentiation between the incommensurability of meaning and of values is pertinent here.[42] Friedman's frameworks are normative in ways that the later Kuhn's lexicons are not. A science's constitutive a priori, Friedman submits, steering closer to the Kuhn of *Structure* than the Kuhn of "Afterwords," is definitive of

> the fundamental spatio-temporal framework within which alone the rigorous formulation and empirical testing of first or base level principles is then possible. These relativized a priori principles constitute . . . at least relatively stable sets of rules of the game, as it were, that define or make possible the problem solving activities of normal science— including, in particular, the rigorous formulation and testing of properly empirical laws. (45)

In part 2 of Friedman's book the normative force of the constitutive a priori is further accentuated by appeal to what he terms an "empirical space of reasons," a concept he coins in explicit analogy to "the Sellarsian notion of the 'space of reasons' . . . recently . . . given prominence in Mc-Dowell (1994)."[43]

A science's constitutive framework determines and normatively regulates *both* levels of scientific work and deliberation. At the "first or base level," on which Friedman mainly concentrates, it determines and regulates the scientific work of forming, elaborating, and testing empirical hypotheses. This is what Friedman dubs late of Kant the realm of "real (as opposed to merely logical) possibility" (84–85).[44] But intensive scientific work is also required and constantly performed at the second level: on that of the framework itself. It is the kind of expressivist undertaking Brandom describes as making explicit the norms implicit in the practices they govern. In science, this is the theoretical task of formulating and expanding the complex inferential network of logical, mathematical, and conceptual relations that constitute the sciences' *logical* space of reasons, along with what Friedman calls the "coordinating principles" of the theory (which determine which logical possibilities become real possibilities).[45] It is a task that, though performed *on* the framework, is determined and normatively regulated—that is, constituted—*by* the framework.

Such an account of the role and function of a science's constitutive a priori is a far cry from those of the taxonomies of kind-terms sketched in Kuhn's "Afterwords."[46] A framework may be further elaborated and expanded, its network of inferential relations traced through and extended from within. And yet Friedman seems to presuppose that it nonetheless cannot be *reformed* by its own lights. A framework, he implies, though constitutive of the process of its self-exploration and self-elaboration, cannot be said to be constitutive of the process of its own normative self-critique. Nowhere is any of this stated openly, however. But it is clear from the way Friedman frames the problem of scientific rationality, and more so by the way he purports to solve it, that he gives up in advance on the entire question of the rationality of framework critique, and on that of subsequent framework construction, and consequently makes no attempt to engage the problem of the rational motivation for replacing a functioning framework, nor that of accounting for the rationality of the creative work invested in crafting and developing alternatives to it.

Nonetheless, Friedman's approach, at least as presented at the outset, is unique in clearly conceding both the normative diversity and the constitutive role of successive scientific frameworks while insisting on the rationality of their replacement; an approach that steers close to the type of community-based approaches to meaning and normativity discussed in previous chapters. What lends a scientific framework its force and status, according to Friedman, is not its instrumental uility but the factuality—the world-guidedness—the community attributes to its "thick" normative vocabulary. Such frameworks are constitutive of their communities' scientific endeavor exactly because they are definitive of what their members take true.[47] This is the background to Friedman's claim to have found a viable concept of interframework rationality in Habermas's well-known notion of communicative rationality.

Friedman's Habermasian Turn

Interesting in itself, the extent to which Friedman's borrowings from Habermas remain true to the original is a question we cannot fully address within the confines of the present study. Our interest here lies primarily

in the view of rationality put forward by Friedman, not in the accuracy
of its ascription to Habermas. Nonetheless, certain of the differences, both
of emphasis and of philosophical premise, between what Friedman claims
to derive from Habermas and the way Habermas and the vast literature
devoted to his ideas present and argue for them are centrally relevant to
our understanding and critique of Friedman's project.

Unlike Carnap and the later Kuhn, Friedman refrains from casting
his account of scientific frameworks in linguistic terms. His book displays no interest at all in exploring the constitutive role, or the dynamics
of change of normative frameworks *in general*. Apart from the one brief
mention-in-passing of Sellars's and McDowell's general notion of a "space
of reasons" noted above, there is nothing in Friedman's text to indicate
that he even acknowledges the existence of normatively constitutive,
yet changeable synthetic a priori principles in realms of human cognition and judgment other than in science—which, as noted, is a lesson he
learns from Reichenbach's and Schlick's neo-Kantian studies of relativity
rather than from engaging the work of philosophers of language, society,
and mind similarly inclined. Nowhere is Friedman's account of the dynamics of scientific frameworks presented as deriving from, or as possibly bearing on the rationality of, *language* acquisition, use, or replacement in general. On the contrary, Friedman invokes Habermas's idea in
order to argue that in science alone "we are . . . able to achieve a situation
of communicative rationality far exceeding that possible in other areas of
intellectual and cultural life" (58).

Habermas himself makes no such distinctions. Communicative rationality is for him a collective facet of any language-sharing "communication community" whose members strive to secure and especially to
expand their "rationally motivated agreement" as to their "intersubjectively shared *lebenswelt* or lifeworld."[48] The assumption of a shared lifeworld, states Habermas citing the sociologist Melvin Pollner,

> does not function for [the members of the community] as a descriptive
> assertion. It is not falsifiable. Rather, it functions as an incorrigible speci-
> fication of the relations which exist in principle among a community of
> perceivers' experiences of what is purported to be the same world (objec-
> tive world).[49]

As if responding to Friedman's remark concerning the special status of science, Habermas states explicitly that "[a] greater degree of communicative rationality expands . . . the scope of unconstrained coordination of actions and consensual resolution of conflicts,"[50] in all manner of normative, world-guided and world-guiding discourse, all discourses—theoretical, practical, moral, aesthetic, therapeutic, and explicative—in which speech-acts display "the character of meaningful expressions, understandable in their context, which are connected with criticizable validity claims."[51]

And yet, although communicative rationality is treated by Habermas, quite generally as "a disposition of speaking and acting subjects,"[52] and despite the fact that the entire project of his *The Theory of Communicative Action* is, as Charles Taylor notes, an attempt "to understand society from the vantage point of language,"[53] it is ultimately *not* a project rooted in the type of neo-Kantian considerations that stimulate the works of Carnap, Kuhn, and Friedman in the philosophy of science (or, for that matter, those of the philosophies of language and society examined in previous chapters). The "vantage point of language" responsible for Habermas's "universal pragmatics" is provided, on his own admission, by "the paradigm change in philosophy of language" that was introduced by J. L. Austin and refined by Searle[54]—namely, by the pragmatics of speech-act theory rather than by the pragmatism of the later Wittgenstein, Sellars, Rorty, or Davidson.[55]

> With the illocutionary force of an utterance a speaker can motivate a hearer to accept the offer contained in his speech act and thereby to accede to a *rationally motivated binding* (or bonding, *Bindung*) *force*. This conception presupposes that acting and speaking subjects can relate to more than only one world, and that when they come to an understanding with one another about something in one world, they base their communication on a commonly supposed system of worlds.[56]

For Habermas, language functions primarily as "a means of communication which serves mutual understanding" between speakers capable and willing to engage in critical dialogue, thereby creating for them "an intersubjectively shared lifeworld." Habermas claims that his central notion of a shared "lifeworld" "owes much" to Wittgenstein,[57] but, unlike a Wittgensteinian form of life, Habermas's lifeworlds are presented throughout far more as the shifting and changing outcomes and fruits of rational communicative discourse than as *constitutive* of those discourses.[58] Habermas either denies the possibility of, or is unconcerned with discrepancies between, lifeworlds so great as to render them normatively incomparable, and hence communicatively unbridgeable. He clearly distinguishes between "the use of language oriented toward agreement" and its use "oriented toward reaching understanding,"[59] but, to the best of our knowledge, nowhere does he discuss the limits in principle (or if at all) of the former. By the end of the day, Habermas leaves the distinct impression that reasoned communication is capable of surmounting any cultural difference.[60] As Rorty notes, Habermas shares with him and Davidson Sellars's "anti-foundationalist coherentism" but "is dubious of the move I [Rorty] want[s] to make from coherentism to anti-representationalism."[61]

At the level of individual instrumental action, Habermas's formulations seem to steer close to the neo-Kantian, framework-dependent representationalism of Friedman and the later Kuhn. "Because acting subjects have to cope with 'the' world," he writes, "they cannot avoid being realists in the contexts of their lifeworlds. Moreover, they are allowed to be realists because their language games and practices . . . 'prove their truth' *(sich bewähren)* in being carried on."[62] Substituting "scientific framework" or "paradigm" for "lifeworld," Habermas would thus seem to endorse Kuhn's and Friedman's realist world-guided account of normal science. But at higher levels of discourse, those in which the lifeworld itself is scrutinized, Habermas insists, contrary to Kuhn and supposedly also to Friedman, that context can be somehow rationally transcended.

> This pragmatic authority responsible for certainty—interpreted in a realist way with the help of the supposition of an objective world—is suspended on the reflexive level of discourses, which are relieved of the burdens of action, and where only arguments count. Here our gaze turns away from the objective world . . . to focus exclusively on our conflicting interpretations of the world. In this intersubjective dimension of contested interpretations, . . . the fallibilist consciousness that we can err

even in the case of well-justified beliefs depends on an orientation to-ward truth whose roots extend into the realism of everyday practices—a realism no longer in force within discourse. The orientation toward *un-conditional truth* . . . reacts back upon everyday practices without thereby destroying the dogmatism of the lifeworld.[63]

The "dogmatic" realism, which, according to Habermas, is carried over from the built-in, lifeworld-determined, first-order "orientation toward" (conditional) truth to the second-order realm of reflexive discourses *of* lifeworlds is more, much more than a merely lingering habit of thought. On the contrary:

> The entwining of the two different pragmatic roles played by the Janus-faced concept of truth in action-contexts and in rational discourses re-spectively can explain why a justification successful in a local context points in favor of the *context-independent* truth of the justified belief.[64]

This is because Habermas believes that a philosophical "idealization of the justificatory conditions" of rational discourse "does not in any way have to take the thick characteristics of one's own culture as its point of departure."[65] According to Habermas, rational intersubjective discourse can start with, and be sustained by

> the formal processual characteristics of justificatory practices in general that, after all, are to be found in all cultures—even if not by any means always in institutionalized form. . . . Whoever enters into discussion with the serious intention of becoming convinced of something through dialogue with others has to presume performatively that the partici-pants allow their "yes" or "no" to be determined solely by the force of the *better* argument. . . . What we hold to be true has to be defendable on the basis of *good* reasons, not merely in a different context, but in all possible contexts.[66]

Now, it is not our intention to discuss the viability of Habermas's posi-tion other than in the context of Friedman's account of scientific frame-work replacement.[67] From Friedman's declared perspective, there seems no clear (noninstrumentalist, nonconventionalist) sense in which arguments and reasons generated by different frameworks could at all be ranked "better" or "good" in this respect, and no sense at all in which interframework discourse can be said to "point to" or be "oriented toward" unconditional context-independent truth. Indeed, the very notion of unconditional and context-independent truth, one would think, is incoherent from Friedman's professed neo-Kantian point of view.

Friedman, as noted, shows no intention of applying the insights and findings of *Dynamics of Reason* beyond the narrow confines of scientific discourse and practice. This may explain why, uncomfortable perhaps with the Wittgensteinian ring of "lifeworld," he chooses to depart from the standard 1984 English translation and in his one direct quote from Habermas to render *lebenswelt* "context of life."[68] Apart from that, Friedman would appear to endorse Habermas's concept of communicative rationality without reservation. But a closer look reveals a more complicated picture. First, Friedman draws the line between intraframework and interframework rationality very differently from the way Habermas draws the line between subjective, intralifeworld and intersubjective, interlifeworld rational action. Second, as already noted, Friedman's avowed neo-Kantianism would seem incompatible with the very universalist premise on which the Habermasian discourse of "contested interpretations" is made to turn, along with the distinctly comparative normative realism it entails. Third, and most important, Friedman's attempt to present the rationality of scientific framework replacement as a case of communicative rationality, we shall argue, ends up lacking the latter's most defining feature: its deliberative, reason-giving basis.

Scientific Revolutions—An Evolutionary Approach

Communicative rationality, Friedman writes in true Habermasian idiom, "refers to our capacity to engage in argumentative deliberation or reasoning with one another aimed at bringing about an agreement or consensus of opinion," and must, therefore, "appeal to patterns of argument or reasoning acceptable to all parties in the dispute"(54). But while for Habermas the *realm* of such rational reflexive discourse is, by definition, that of *interlifeworld* deliberation, for Friedman it falls, again by definition, paradigmatically on the other side of the intra/interframework divide. Communicative rationality, he states explicitly, "is [therefore] the kind of rationality *underwritten by a given scientific paradigm or conceptual framework,* whose function is precisely to secure an agreement on fundamental constitutive principles" (55)—to which he adds in an accompanying footnote, alluding again to Sellars and McDowell:

> communicative rationality—as opposed to merely instrumental "black box" predictive success—places us within a shared public language or linguistic framework, and thus within a shared "space of reasons," where theoretical propositions can be meaningfully subject to evidential evaluation. (55 n. 66)

Kuhnian normal science, he notes, "is entirely based" on this kind of second-order consensus. That being the case, one would have expected Friedman to declare communicative rationality inadequate in principle as grounds for the rationality of framework replacement. Friedman, however, chooses to turn the discrepancy on its head, declaring Kuhn's account of scientific revolutions a threat to Habermasian rationality rather than the other way around! This is the first major turning point in Friedman's argument. Here is how Kuhnian science is now presented:

> Normal science, for Kuhn, is then entirely based on this kind of 'firm research consensus.' But it is precisely because there is also revolutionary science—radical transitions between incommensurable or nontranslatable conceptual frameworks—*that the idea of a truly universal rationality (that is, a truly universal communicative rationality) is now threatened.* (55–56; emphasis added)

In order to maintain the communicative rationality of science *in the face of* Kuhnian revolutions, Friedman sets forth to show that in science even the most revolutionary transitions preserve a measure of continuity sufficient to support rational discourse across the divide. Interframework scientific disputes, he argues from this point onward, are communicatively rational and capable of agreed resolution, because they are *not* incommensurable and nontranslatable in the full Kuhnian sense of the term.

Just as the scientific enterprise aims for, and successfully achieves, agreement or consensus *within* particular paradigms, there is also an important sense in which it aims for, and successfully achieves, agreement or
consensus *across* different paradigms. (58; original emphasis)

To speak of "the scientific enterprise" as the agent supposedly aiming for
and achieving reasoned agreement in the sciences is unhelpfully vague
and hopelessly impersonal. Habermasian communicative rationality is
not a category of "enterprises" but of human agents in dialogue. What
Friedman needs to show is how the scientific *community*, when split between flesh-and-blood adherents to two different constitutive frameworks, succeeds in doing so. For people whose professional work and discourse owe to nontrivially different constitutive frameworks to be able
rationally to forge a consensus around one of them, they need to share
enough of a common linguistic framework, and hence a shared "space of
reasons," capable of mediating the two camps' estranged perspectives.[69]
Friedman's suggestion to this effect marks an interesting first major departure from Habermas's approach in having no use for the veridical universalism so central to the latter. Unlike Habermas, Friedman appears quite
comfortable within the confines of his initial neo-Kantian, intraparadig-
matic, essentially relativist notion of empirical truth, which he gives no
sign of radically modifying. He achieves this by remaining wholly indifferent to the prospects of rational dialogue between practitioners of *any* two
conceptual frameworks—the question central to the Rorty-Habermas debate on truth and justification—and limiting his interest in rationality
and in the dynamics of reason to the only type of interparadigm discourse
engaged in practice by scientific practitioners, namely, that between *successive* paradigms. Friedman thus creates an interestingly localized vari-
ant of Habermas's communicative rationality,[70] such as is maintained between members of speech communities whose differences, he goes on to
argue, are forever kept within well-controlled limits.

Science, argues Friedman, "differs fundamentally" from other intellectual and cultural enterprises "in the way in which it treats transitions
between such stages" (58). This is because scientific revolutions are significantly less "revolutionary" than Kuhn led us to believe. Scientific revolutions are communicatively rational because they represent transitions
that are never too radical to be reasoned through. According to Fried-

man, they do not resemble irrational or a-rational acts of conversion or inexplicable gestalt switches, nor are they undertaken for merely conventional purposes. They are rational because practitioners of the old framework are won over by the arguments leveled against them by those of the new.[71] This is the basic strategy of Friedman's game plan.

It is in this sense that the problem of the rationality of scientific framework replacement reduces for Friedman to that of the rationality of choosing between fully functional, well-formed alternatives for which members of the community are both capable and willing to argue. Before a reasonably developed alternative framework that has won the support of well-standing members of the community[72] is in place, the question of the rationality of all but normal science seems not at all to arise for Friedman. Above all, as noted above, his account omits all mention of the most creative realm of scientific research—that with which the present study is most concerned—namely, such processes of reflexive, self-critical reasoning responsible for stimulating the initial *search for* and *creation of* alternatives to functioning frameworks deemed by some to be wanting. We shall return in the final sections of the chapter to this important point, on which, it is easy to see, communicative rationality can have little bearing.

Friedman's inevitable first step is to tone down the Kuhnian picture from which he initially set forth. Kuhn's comparison of interparadigm discourse to "a communication breakdown . . . [between] members of different language communities,"[73] he insists, is unduly exaggerated.

> Practitioners of succeeding paradigms are not helpfully viewed as members of radically disconnected speech communities. . . . On the contrary, successive paradigms emerge precisely from one another, as succeeding stages in a common tradition of cultural change. In this sense they are better viewed as different evolutionary stages of a single language rather than as entirely separate and disconnected languages. (60)

He justifies his retreat from a revolutionary to an essentially *evolutionary* account of scientific paradigm succession "despite . . . our commitment to a relativised yet still constitutive conception of the a priori" (95–96) by arguing that transitions between successive scientific paradigms typically meet two related conditions that set them apart from paradigm changes in other areas of intellectual and cultural life.

(a) They can be shown to make sense, and are, therefore, capable of being reasoned for and against from either side of the divide.
(b) Owing to the fact that successive scientific frameworks are mediated by a third, straddling meta-framework, such reasoning can be said to comprise genuine dialogue.[74]

Friedman argues for (a) by distinguishing between "retrospective" and "prospective" communicative rationality,[75] between looking at the interframework divide first, retrospectively from the vantage point of the new, and then, more interestingly if more problematically, prospectively from that of the old.

Science differs from other areas of intellectual and cultural life, he urges, because in new scientific frameworks a real effort is made to preserve the preceding framework as far as possible, exhibiting it "as an approximate special case . . . of the succeeding paradigm" (58). This allows practitioners of the new to toe the tricky line between depicting themselves "as extensively agreeing with the practitioners of the preceding paradigm" and "disagreeing fundamentally on the concepts and principles of the paradigm itself" (59). More important, it allows practitioners of the old, to some extent, to make minimal sense of the transition by reasoning that although they cannot appreciate what is *gained* by adopting the new, they can appreciate that nothing vital is lost.[76] Though a necessary (if far from sufficient) condition for the communicative rationality of the transition, the point goes unnoticed by Friedman.

Moreover, rare are the cases of scientific revolutions in which this is at all the case. In many cases, the new framework does not preserve the old as a limiting or special case at all, such as in the transition from corpuscular to wave optics, or the transition to plate tectonics in geology. But even in cases in which the old is to an extent preserved in the new, much more is needed in order to render such transitions meaningfully debatable across the interframework divide. The fact that practitioners of the old are able to identify, preserved within an otherwise alien system of concepts and principles, an approximation of their own scientific world does not provide even minimal grounds for eventually winning them over (for reasons other than instrumental utility or mere convention). Alien as it is, Friedman rightly argues, supporters of the old must be able to view the new as "a live option" from their own perspective (100). But in what sense, he asks, can a framework based on a radically new set of mathematical and coordinating principles become for them a live option if from their point of view it "is not even (empirically) possible? What rational motivations can there be—and how can it even be rationally intelligible—to make such a radical shift?" (99).

As noted, the one answer Friedman does not consider is the one to which the present study is dedicated: that for creative people, especially in positions of responsibility, radically different options become "rational possibilities" when the systems to which they are committed and for which they feel responsible are believed to *fail* in significant respects and to significant degrees. If it is possible for a functioning framework to be found normatively wanting, then, serious consideration of different, even radically different possibilities becomes for its practitioners not merely a live and rational option, but a rational *necessity*. If a functioning framework can be thought to fail, the very search for and willingness to experiment with alternatives is both the natural and rational response. This is not an option Friedman discusses and dismisses but one he fails to even mention. He seems to be in silent agreement with Rorty, Davidson, and others in assuming that it is impossible for a functioning constitutive framework to be self-criticized (and, therefore, with Carnap and Kuhn, that Popperian criticism is irrelevant to "external questions").[77]

And yet, quite unlike those who deny or imply denial of normative framework self-criticism, Friedman stands alone in insisting that scientific framework replacement *is nonetheless* a rational process, that practitioners of a functioning framework can find rational reason, a là Habermas, to replace it. But what is it to be rationally persuaded in this respect if not to be capable of realizing that the proposed framework is in important respects *superior* to one's own? And what is that if not to be capable of realizing that one's own framework is comparatively flawed? And if that is the case, isn't Friedman then forced to address the problem explored here of somehow overcoming, at least for science, the barrier of Comparative Irrealism, which, as we have so far shown, appears to plague all relevant accounts of normative semantics?

But this is *not* the route Friedman takes. He seems clearly to accept, as we do, the idea that sufficiently different frameworks are indeed normatively incomparable. Practitioners of the old, he argues explicitly, are incapable from their own perspective of even envisaging the new as an empirical possibility, and, therefore, are unable to compare it favorably to their own. Friedman is thus left no choice but to attempt to formulate an account of the rationality of framework replacement wholly *devoid* of normative self-criticism, which nonetheless does not fall prey to Comparative Irrealism. He does so by arguing that framework replacement in science is rational, not because practitioners of the old are able to deem the new to be in some way *better* than their own, but because they are able to see it as *"a natural continuation"* of their own. This is what he terms "prospective" communicative rationality. Scientific revolutions form a class of their own because in science "the concepts and principles of the new constitutive framework do not only yield the concepts and principles of the old framework as a special case (whether exact or approximate), but they also develop out of, and as a natural continuation of, the old concepts and principles." Practitioners of the old framework perceive the new as "a quite deliberate modification or transformation of the old constitutive framework, developed against the backdrop of *a common set of problems, conceptualizations and concerns*" (101; emphasis added).

This represents the second major turning point in Friedman's argument, one that also marks its most significant departure from Habermas. Practitioners of the old framework are capable of reasoning their way into rationally accepting the new because, in addition to realizing that much of their scientific world remains preserved as a special case in the new, they are able to appreciate the new as having been developed, framed, and elaborated in a process emanating naturally from the old, by colleagues originally committed to it, just like them—colleagues who continue to share with them "a common set of problems, conceptualizations and concerns" (101). Thus, he concludes, bordering on the oxymoron:

> Despite the fact that practitioners of the new framework indeed speak a language incommensurable or non-translatable with the old, they are nonetheless in a position rationally to appeal to practitioners of the older framework, and to do this, moreover, using empirical and conceptual resources that are available at precisely this earlier stage. (101)

The air of paradox is real, for Friedman does not explain how it is possible for successive paradigms to be genuinely "incommensurable or non-translatable" and yet for their practitioners to share "a common set of problems, conceptualizations and concerns" that are (not merely conventional or instrumental, but) sufficiently broad and contentful to rationally motivate those faithful to one to shift allegiance to the other. He seems to realize that he cannot have it both ways, that by definition two frameworks cannot be seriously deemed incommensurable while pertaining to such a common basis without doing violence to at least one of the terms. Nor can such discrepancies be a matter of degree (as he seems to imply toward the end of the book).[78] If, as he himself puts it, successive frameworks are conceived of as constitutive of "essentially different and even incommensurable 'logical spaces'" (95), then, as the later Kuhn argues with respect to transitions between any two noninclusive lexical structures, the *degree* of their noninclusiveness is beside the point. Incommensurability (in Friedman's own sense of the term) entails contentful and normative discontinuity and vice versa.

Reasonable Motives

Friedman's way around the problem is to argue that while new frameworks develop "out of," and as "natural continuation[s] of, the old," they do not do so by exclusive appeal to resources available *within* the old. Such transitions are neither self-sufficient nor conducted in vacuo. According to Friedman, scientific revolutions relate and draw on a broader and less regimented intellectual realm of essentially philosophical meta-scientific deliberation and dispute of which the practitioners of both the old and the new are aware, and with reference to which the latter are able to justify to themselves and to their adversaries their radical departures from the ways of old, at least as reasonable possibilities. Thus:

> Einstein was able rationally to appeal to practitioners of the preceding paradigm in (classical) mathematical physics partly by placing his articulation of fundamentally new coordinating principles within the long tradition of reflection on the question of absolute versus relative motion going back to the seventeenth century. (105)

It is a tradition of reflection that stretches back to the "sharply divergent" opinions of Descartes, Huygens, and Leibniz regarding the nature of motion "which, at least in part, fueled Newton's . . . articulation of both a radically different first-level scientific paradigm . . . and a radically different answer to the question of absolute versus relative motion" (106). Despite the former's "unequivocal and uncontroversial triumph" during the eighteenth century, problems and disagreements about the latter persisted, first in the works of Samuel Clarke and Euler and eventually Kant and later in those of Mach. And it is with reference to this background of ongoing dispute that Einstein was able to present to his unconvinced fellow physicists his two new "striking and unexpected" coordinating principles (the light principle and the principle of equivalence) as recognizably "live options" (106).

Even if one grants the point (which many would contest) that the radical elements of scientific revolutions are never new to philosophy, it remains quite unclear *why* familiarity with a position taken, or a move made in philosophical or mathematical dispute, even one of long standing, should count toward considering its adoption as a constitutive framework radically different from one's own. What lies at the heart of communicative rationality is not the relative strangeness, or even the relative philosophical respectability of the opposition but one's ability, in principle, to *rationally justify its endorsement,* to formulate, or at least to appreciate arguments in favor of its relative superiority to one's own. But how is that ever possible when one's own constitutive framework is being questioned? For a new and radically different framework to become a live *scientific* option for practitioners of the old, long-standing familiarity and philosophic respectability will simply not suffice—unless, of course, the old is in some sense *doubted,* but this, as we have seen, nowhere becomes a live option for Friedman. Had he purported to present the "common set of problems, conceptualizations and concerns," against which, he claims, the new constitutive framework is developed, as a set of *scientific* problems, conceptualizations, and concerns, a case for communicative interframework rationality could have been made. Practitioners of the old and new frameworks would then be described as deliberating different viable solutions to a set of shared scientific problems. But he does not. The shared "problems, conceptualizations and concerns" of which Friedman speaks are philosophical and mathematical,[79] not scientific—belonging wholly to the meta-framework, the only common ground he maintains is shared by the two groups of scientific practitioners.

Friedman's very choice of the terms *meta-paradigm* and *meta-framework* (e.g., 105) and talk of them as comprising a third level supplementing Kuhn's original two (e.g., 44 ff.), creates the misleading impression that the realm of "philosophical articulation of . . . meta-paradigms or meta-frameworks for revolutionary science" (44) is capable of sustaining communicative rationality across the scientific divide. But the impression is false. Friedman's meta-frameworks have unhelpfully little in common with the self-sufficient, consensual, and most of all constitutive neo-Kantian frameworks of science proper. What he calls meta-frameworks are neither constitutive of the scientific frameworks situated "below" them (as the latter are of the level of first-order scientific research situated below *them*) nor rational in Friedman's required, communicative sense of the term.[80] As he readily admits, the philosophical, mathematical, and other discourses of which he speaks "necessarily fail to reach the (communicatively) rational consensus achieved" in science (107). Certain philosophical suggestions may well end up enriching scientific discourse if and when scientists seek such enrichment, but in and of themselves neither philosophy nor any other discipline holds a normative grip on the two levels of scientific practice.[81] Even if *all* the key elements of a new scientific framework have their origin beyond the ken of science proper, it makes no sense to equate their *scientific* relevance with their (disputed) nonscientific viability. The fact that philosophers of standing had long debated the relativity of motion, and others (primarily Helmholtz and Poincaré) were debating the foundations of geometry,[82] does not, of itself, begin to explain why certain of their views rather than others suddenly became a live option for Einstein's dramatic revolution of classical physics and why the strikingly new constitutive framework he subsequently produced became at once a live and relevant option for his incredulous colleagues to the extent that they "would have been irrational, unreasonable and irresponsible"—in their "own terms"—"to fail to consider it as a live alternative" (108).

The only question Friedman does address in this respect, and does so forcefully, is that of the bearing of philosophy on the communicative rationality (rather than the specific content) of science. If the rationality of scientific framework replacement is to be communicative, he asks, how can a realm of philosophical discourse "inevitably and permanently fraught with unresolved intellectual disagreements" possibly "help in mediating and (re)fashioning such rational consensus during scientific revolutions?" (107). As it is the culminating point of the entire enterprise of *Dynamics of Reason*, Friedman's threefold answer merits close attention.

First, to be considered communicatively rational, we require of scientists only that the new constitutive framework be for them a "reasonable and responsible live option" (107). Second, although "a stable consensus" is never attained regarding "the *results* of distinctively philosophical debate," a relatively stable consensus does normally exist on "what are the important contributions to the debate and, accordingly, on what moves and arguments must be taken seriously" (107). Friedman's first point is certainly valid. For interframework debate to be considered communicatively rational, consensus with respect to the new paradigm is not required to be *reached* but only to be *reachable*. It is the demand that the new be a reasonable live option for all involved, which for Friedman would be to show how practitioners of the old are able to engage supporters of the new in reasoned deliberation of the possible scientific value of the new from, and relevant to, their radically different old perspective. But this Friedman does *not* show. Nothing in his account constitutes a *scientific* argument in favor of the new from either point of view. As we have argued, the fact that the new framework indeed comprised elements deemed respectable elsewhere, and indeed preserved the old as a limiting case, which, as noted, is hardly always the case, is not enough to motivate dedicated practitioners of the old to seriously consider it as a viable normative alternative.

His second point is also obviously true. Respectability does not entail acceptance, and the philosophical moves to which he refers are paradigms of philosophic respectability. But the way he frames the point is worrying. The fact that a field is "inevitably and permanently fraught with unresolved intellectual disagreements" does not mitigate against its communicative rationality. The achievement of reasoned consensus is indeed *proof of* communicative rationality but is not a criterion of adequacy or a necessary condition for communicative rationality. Again, communicative rationality is primarily a category of dispute. Communicatively rational disputes are *reasoned* disputes whose participants strive for (though may not necessarily achieve) *reasoned* agreement. The philosophical disputes comprising Friedman's meta-framework thus squarely fall within the category of the rational à la Habermas, despite hardly ever achieving closure. What Friedman does not show is how disputes between parties committed to radically different scientific constitutive frameworks can be *reasoned* in ways comprehensive to all when the frameworks themselves are in dispute.

Although this is the culmination point of Friedman's argument, where the case for the rationality of framework replacement in science is supposedly clinched by appeal to the philosophical context and the forward- and backward-looking dimensions of such transitions, he chooses to make it by arguing from precedent, by appealing to fine-grained and extended example rather than to general argument. His detailed and largely compelling accounts of how the revolutionary frameworks introduced by Galileo, Newton, and Einstein all contained the frameworks they were replacing as limiting cases, and all incorporated certain philosophically respectable moves and arguments, fail, however, in their main objective. They bear out Friedman's *description* of how successive scientific frameworks of the past stood to each other and to their philosophical settings, but they do not begin to chart how and certainly do not explain *why* at each of these junctures practitioners of a well-entrenched, functioning framework felt *obliged* to seriously consider replacing it by a radically different one.

The element crucially missing from Friedman's analysis is that of rational agency, or rational incentive. Even if the containment of the old as a limiting case ("retrospective communicative rationality") and the philosophical or mathematical pedigree of the new's key components are deemed *necessary* conditions for framework replacement, in and of themselves they are incapable of rationally *motivating* researchers to seriously consider giving up the framework that gives life and meaning to their scientific world and lifework. Even if deemed to be criteria of adequacy for framework replacement, Friedman's descriptive criteria do not begin to constitute reasons for working scientists to seriously explore new alternatives to their scientific form of life. It all comes back to the same thing: for a working scientist to feel compelled to seriously respond to arguments in favor of a constitutive framework significantly different from her own—let alone feel compelled to accept them—they must be shown to pose, or to respond to, what she is able to perceive as real and acknowledgable *challenges* to her lived scientific lifeworld. Friedman's descriptive conditions remain ineffective in this respect.

As we have seen, the option explored here, to identify the rational incentive to take a new framework seriously with the old being recognized as sufficiently wanting to merit replacement, is one Friedman not only seems resolute not to consider, but to which his analysis seems largely irrelevant. For if the old has in some way come to be considered defective by its practitioners, and a new framework is in the making, the arguments mounted for and against the new would focus naturally on its ability to do better than its predecessor *regardless* of whether it somehow preserved it as a special case, and of its career and standing among nonscientists. But Friedman seems determined to render interframework dialogue wholly *un*critical.

This brings us to the third and final component of his argument. To recall, according to Friedman, the third requirement of framework replacement in science is that the new not only regularly include the old as an approximate limiting case, but that it "evolve continuously out of the old . . . by a series of natural transformations" (66). Rather than view the new framework as a reasoned attempt to overcome normative difficulties perceived to plague the old, he describes the transition from one set of constitutive principles to the next in decidedly evolutionary, rather than revolutionary, terms—as evolving smoothly while interacting with independently cultivated discourses external to it. And it is to the latter that all significantly critical and reformative elements of the discourse are supposedly relegated.[83] This is the third and final point he makes in attempting to explain the role played by other disciplines, in this case philosophy, in achieving rational consensus in science.

[C]haracteristically philosophical reflection interacts with properly scientific reflection in such a way that *controversial and conceptually problematic philosophical themes become productively intertwined with relatively uncontroversial and unproblematic areas of scientific accomplishments;* as

a result, philosophical reflection can facilitate interaction between different (relatively uncontroversial and unproblematic) areas of scientific
reflection, so as, in particular, to facilitate the introduction and communication of a new scientific paradigm at the same time. (107; emphasis added)

Friedman agrees that the radically new constitutive principles introduced by Galileo, Newton, and Einstein were indeed initially forged in
the face of deep conceptual problems. But he insists that the problems
that prompted their formulation were not scientific ones. Such bold alternatives take form elsewhere, he insists, and are introduced into science
ready-made, as it were, not as means to replace or modify a faulty scientific framework, but as natural extensions of a well-functioning one perceived to be "uncontroversial and unproblematic." As a result, in the history of the great upheavals of mathematical physics charted by *Dynamics
of Reason* in considerable detail, the highly creative problem-seeking and
problem-solving elements of the discourse end up being written out of
the story altogether. Friedman continues to pay lip service to Kuhn's picture of revolutionary scientific development, but his rhetoric sounds less
and less convincing as his argument develops, bordering more and more
on the oxymoron. Viewed prospectively, "from a properly historical point
of view," he writes toward the end of part 1,

> we see . . . that, although there is indeed an important sense in which suc-
> ceeding paradigms are incommensurable or non-intertranslatable, the
> concepts and principles of later paradigms still evolve continuously, by a
> series of natural transformations from those of earlier ones. . . . [W]e can
> thus view the evolution of succeeding paradigms or frameworks as a
> convergent series, as it were, in which we successively refine our constitu-
> tive principles in the direction of greater generality and adequacy. (63)

He gives no account of what he means by "greater adequacy" in this context. Had he done so, he may well have found ways to locate the rationality of framework replacement in the felt *inadequacies* of the old. But
he leaves the phrase philosophically unaccounted for. Needless to say,
troubleshooting for mere generality lacks the critical bite of doing so for

scientific inappropriateness. And so the most unsettled and exciting moments of creative scientific innovation are redescribed by Friedman in extraordinarily placid, almost phlegmatic terms. "When we move from the Aristotelian framework to that of classical physics," he writes as if ticking a checklist,

> we retain Euclidean geometry intact, discard the hierarchical and teleological organized spherical universe, and modify the Aristotelian theory of natural motion—in such a way that we retain the idea, in particular, that there is a fundamental state of natural motion following privileged paths of the underlying geometry. (63)

Similarly:

> When we move from classical physics to special relativity, we again retain Euclidian geometry, and also, of course, the law of inertia, but we now move from a three-plus-one dimensional to an essentially four dimensional spatio-temporal structure—which, however, yields the older three-plus-one dimensional structure as a limiting case. (63)

And the same goes for the subsequent move to general relativity (63–64).

In order to render these moments of momentous conceptual upheaval rational, in his sense of the term, Friedman is compelled to retell them in the form of retrospective acts of stock-taking that succeed in remaining astonishingly indifferent to the anxious processes of self-critical deliberation and critical dialogue—within the physics community!—by which the elements retained were judged suitable, those discarded deemed to be wrong, and those modified deemed to be wanting, as if they were irrelevant to the rationality of science.

An "Is" for an "Ought"

Friedman's strategy of addressing the philosophical problem of scientific rationality by appealing to the history of science—to glean the "ought" off the "is," as it were—would seem to bring him in line with the interpretivist approaches to normativity and subsequently with Brandom's expressivist normative pragmatics. Why, then, unlike other neopragmatist undertakings, reversing the order of explanation ends up in Friedman's case impoverishing the *explanans* instead of enriching the *explanandum?* It is because Friedman's is ultimately not an argument from the *practice* of science. The history of physics on which his philosophy is made to rest is not a history of how physics was practiced or performed, but, in the last analysis, an account of the stratified structure and "the conceptual evolution" (xii) of physical *theory;* not a history of the ways physicists worked and reasoned during periods of conceptual upheaval, but of the theories they subsequently produced. *Dynamics of Reason* is thus beset by a fundamental discrepancy between the subject matter of its philosophical undertaking—namely, scientific *reasoning*—and that of the historiography from which it is meant to derive—namely, that of the *fruits* of that reasoning. A descriptive account of the changing produce of scientific activity is expected to yield a normative assessment of the rationality of that activity. Adopting Habermas's communicative rationality enables Friedman (mistakenly, we have argued) to limit the purview of the latter not only to the *deliberation* of ready-made alternative constitutive frameworks (to the exclusion of their creation), but to the rationality of forging an *agreement* on the matter. As we have seen, even under such severe restrictions, rationality remains for Habermas a normative category of reasoned *action* that is not easily reducible to descriptive accounts of its eventual *outcomes* without begging the very question it is meant to answer.

In the last analysis, the most problematic aspect of Friedman's account of the rationality of scientific framework replacement is less its inattention to the entire realm of scientific framework *construction* than its systematic skirting of the entire realm of scientific reasoning about frameworks. Both oversights are related, we believe. They are also related to the other aspect of *Dynamics of Reason* that we find worrying: its insistence on making a special case for the rationality of scientific framework replacement, to the implied exclusion as irrational or nonrational of comparably significant upheavals in all other areas of intellectual and cultural endeavor.

Nonetheless, from the point of view of the present study, *Dynamics of Reason* remains a crucially important work, for the way it poses and aspires to solve the problem of the rationality of framework transition.

Friedman's undertaking for science, we have noted, is, in principle, inter-pretivist, seeking to formulate a normative account of scientific change that is warranted by the good interpretive sense it makes of how the best of science evolved in practice. The problem with interpretivism in ethics, we have argued, is its failure to appreciate how limited the scope of rea-soned normative change it is capable of yielding. As if responding to this critique, Friedman drives a solid wedge, as it were, between the rational-ity of scientific framework replacement and the reasoned critical dia-logue conducted by scientists. As a result, his scientific philosophy (pace Habermas) ceases at that point to be an interpretation of scientific *prac-tice* and morphs into an interpretation of scientific *produce*. The upshot, as we have seen, is a "rational reconstruction" of scientific development sufficiently impoverished to constitute a reductio ad absurdum of his efforts—certainly for those thinkers from within the camp, like McDow-ell, Brandom, and the present authors, who identify "the rationality that qualifies us as sapient," as Brandom aptly puts it, "with being a player in the normative game of offering and assessing, producing and consuming reasons."[84]

What is the lesson to be learned from Friedman's failure to address rational agency? If (a) Normative Diversity is taken to entail Comparative Irrealism, and if (b) Comparative Irrealism is taken to entail that nor-mative outlooks (final vocabularies, constitutive linguistic frameworks) are immune to internal criticism, then, if (c) rationality is identified with normative self-criticism, one is forced to conclude that (d) transitions between significantly diverse normative outlooks (final vocabularies, linguistic frameworks) are, by definition, nonrational (i.e., a-rational at the very least). For those who concede all the above, Friedman's failure constitutes an exceptionally vivid demonstration of their point. It proves that even if successive scientific paradigms are only as alien as Friedman claims they are, they remain sufficiently alien to rule transitions from one to another nonrational even in mathematical physics, the most rational of human undertakings, according to Friedman.

But can the impasse be broken? Friedman (if indeed he is taken to concede (a) and (b)) can be read as contesting (d) by surreptitiously deny-ing (c)—pace Habermas, of course. For us this is not an option. In the re-mainder of the book we propose to take a route that has so far nowhere been seriously explored, namely, to contest (d) by denying (b) while fully conceding (a) and (c). Unlike Friedman, we attempt to drive a wedge between Comparative Irrealism and a normative outlook's insusceptibility to normative criticism from within. In other words, we shall argue along broadly pragmatist lines for a notion of normative self-criticism sufficiently robust to enable deeming a normative outlook to be normatively wanting from within, despite being normatively incomparable to other, sufficiently dissimilar outlooks.

▮

CHAPTER SIX

Toward a Critical Pragmatism

A Brandomian Beginning

Friedman, McDowell, and Beyond

Friedman's understanding of science and its development draws heavily on Kant, while his account of the rationality of scientific change draws on Habermas. The latter account, however, suppresses the implied disputational and deliberational nature of Habermas's communicative rationality. Still, if our reading of *Dynamics of Reason* is not entirely off the mark, then there is much in Friedman's approach with which we agree: its explicit endorsement of Normative Diversity, its implied acceptance of Comparative Irrealism, its broadly interpretivist approach, and, most of all, its central concern for the rationality of constitutive framework replacement.[1] But, as we have argued in detail, we also part company with Friedman on major issues.

First, although many would agree that the mathematical sciences present a paradigm case of rational development, few would agree that their claim for rationality is as exclusive as Friedman implies. (Habermas certainly believed that the scope of the form of rationality Friedman adopts for the sciences extended far beyond that of the *lebenswelten* of mathematical physics.) The special case Friedman fashions for science against the "threat of conceptual relativism" strongly suggests that corresponding

upheavals in the constitutive linguistic frameworks of all but the most developed and exact sciences display a relativism that, in his opinion, defies
rationality. We firmly disagree. Contrary to Friedman, the case the present
study seeks to make for the rationality of framework modification and replacement extends in principle to normativity in general.

Second, we disagree completely with Friedman's contention (late of
Habermas) that the ultimate motivating objective of the sort of rational
endeavor invested in framework replacement is the achievement of consensus.[2] It is true that successful normative upheavals normally result
in communal consent—certainly under an interpretivist construal—
but what makes such transitions *rational*, we insist, is not that they end
up commanding wide agreement but that they do so rationally. A *rational* transition from one normative outlook to another is a transition
undertaken for a reason; a *justified* transition; a transition deemed to
be acceptable because it is considered *arguably preferable* to the outlook
abandoned. Indeed, if consensus per se was the defining aim of scientific
rationality, the very proposal of alternative frameworks would be frowned
on as undermining the rationality of science. Yet Friedman writes explicitly as if the high level of agreement achieved in science in the wake
of such transitions is itself the measure of their very (communicative)
rationality.[3] Arguing along these lines wrongly conflates the prospective
appraisal of reasoned action with the retrospective evaluation of its outcome. While the former is essential to assessments of rationality, the latter,
we shall argue, is arguably largely irrelevant.[4]

For such transitions to be reasoned through rationally (as opposed
to rationalized after the event) practitioners must be able to argue against
the framework to which they are currently committed. Hence our third
major disagreement with Friedman who treats the problem of internal
normative criticism as unsolvable. For Friedman insists (contra Habermas)[5] that scientific revolutions owe their communicative rationality ultimately to the formal relations successive scientific frameworks typically
bear to each other rather than to the self-critical reasoning responsible in
the first place for stimulating the search for alternative frameworks and
for subsequent deliberation of their relative shortcomings and merits.

The special case Friedman makes for science serves at best as the
exception that proves the rule. Truly diverse constitutive frameworks, it

presupposes, cannot be ranked or compared. It is impossible, therefore, for practitioners of the one to argue self-critically in favor of the other. Transitions between truly diverse frameworks can, therefore, not be conducted rationally. The reason why transitions between successive scientific frameworks *are* rational is, according to Friedman, not because Comparative Irrealism is overcome in science but because in science Comparative Irrealism does not (fully) apply. Successive scientific frameworks are not truly diverse. They remain sufficiently of a cloth to allow their mutual replacement to be rational.

But Friedman wants to have it both ways. His commendable insistence on the rationality of scientific development ends up caught between discordant Kuhnian and Kantian commitments. On the one hand, he considers successive scientific conceptual frameworks à la Kuhn to be too "radically different," too diverse to be properly debatable across the divide. Yet at the same time he considers them sufficiently related (in ways boasted by no other realm of intellectual or cultural endeavor)—the old framework sufficiently preserved, nested within the new, the two sufficiently accommodated by different sides of higher-level sufficiently respectable philosophical disputes—to somehow render the new "a reasonable and responsible live option" for practitioners of the old. Despite its confident tone, Friedman's account of the rationality of scientific paradigm shifts remains uneasily suspended between the irreconcilable extremes of normative continuity and rupture—acknowledging the fundamental "sense in which the Kuhnian claims of incommensurability and non-intertranslatability between successive frameworks in a scientific revolution are correct"[6] while maintaining at the same time that they form "a convergent sequence" approximating "an ideal limit of scientific progress," "governed by what Kant called the regulative use of reason."[7] And thus, in effect, rather than solve the problem of the rationality of framework replacement, Friedman's account forcefully restates it.

But can it be solved? Can one remain firmly committed to Normative Diversity and Comparative Irrealism, as well as to a basically interpretivist approach to normativity and meaning, and at the same time salvage a notion of normative self-criticism sufficiently robust to enable rationally assessing the normative merits of the very normative outlook by which it is governed?

Among the thinkers whose work we have discussed, McDowell stands alone in formulating precisely thus the desiderata for what he terms, late of Aristotle, "practical wisdom"[8]—namely, "the kind of intelligibility that is a matter of placement in the space of reasons."[9] One's ethical outlook is constitutive both of how one conceives reality and of how one elects to act in response. However, the ethical outlook to which one's reasoning is subject, he goes on to claim, should be included in the space of reasons it generates and not be treated smugly as an unquestioned given belonging merely to "the realm of law." In chapter 1 we alluded briefly to the following passage in *Mind and World* that we now cite more fully.

> Like any thinking, ethical thinking is under a standing obligation to reflect about and criticize the standards by which, at any time, it takes itself to be governed. . . . Now it is a key point that for such reflective criticism, the appropriate image is Neurath's, in which a sailor overhauls his ship while it is afloat. This does not mean such reflection cannot be radical. One can find oneself called on to jettison parts of one's inherited ways of thinking; and though this is harder to place in Neurath's image, weaknesses that reflection discloses in inherited ways of thinking can dictate the formation of new concepts and conceptions. But the essential thing is that one can reflect only from the midst of the way of thinking one is reflecting about. So if one entertains the thought that bringing one's current ethical outlook to bear on a situation alerts one to demands that are real, one need not be envisaging any sort of validation other than a Neurathian one. The thought is that this application of one's ethical outlook would stand up to the outlook's own reflective scrutiny.

"The idea of getting things right in one's ethical thinking," adds McDowell, "has a certain autonomy; we need not conceive it as pointing outside the sphere of ethical thinking itself."[10]

Substitute "normative" for "ethical," and McDowell's limpid text would seem the present study's perfect motto. Clearly conceding both Normative Diversity and the constitutive role of normative outlooks, McDowell conceives acting rationally as action not only deliberated in accord with a normative outlook, but as deliberated in accord with a *deliberated* normative outlook—an outlook subjected to "reflective criticism" from within. Friedman's case for science shares McDowell's premise that the rationality of addressing internal, intraframework questions is incomplete unless external, interframework questions can also be said to be dealt with rationally. But unlike Friedman, McDowell seems to have no qualms identifying the latter form of rationality with internal, even radical internal criticism leveled "from the midst of the way of thinking one is reflecting about." And unlike Friedman, McDowell does not at all limit the reflective scrutinizing of outlooks to acts of decision between developed alternatives. On the contrary, for McDowell, rationality's "standing obligation" is to hold one's normative outlook in constant review of its "own reflective scrutiny." And thus, while for Friedman it is in response to the proposal of a better-suited alternative that practitioners of a functioning framework may find it wanting, for McDowell it is the other way around; for him criticism prompts creativity rather than vice versa. It is the "weaknesses that reflection discloses in inherited ways of thinking" that supposedly "dictate the formation of new concepts and conceptions." And needless to say, unlike Friedman, McDowell by no means limits any of this to science.

But although McDowell appears confidently to suggest that a case can be made for deeming an operative ethical outlook normatively deficient from within without violating Comparative Irrealism, he nowhere actually makes it. Nowhere does he show how internal, noncomparative reflection can get us much beyond merely troubleshooting for coherence, consistency, or clarity. He seems to recoil almost immediately from the strong language of "radical" reflection and being called on to "jettison" "inherited ways of thinking," cautioning far more modestly in the next paragraph but one that "[t]he best we can achieve is always to some extent provisional and inconclusive."[11] McDowell is clear in rejecting as fantasy the idea that these doubts are somehow capable of "external validation," but he leaves the distinct impression that although we lack access to an external or comparative foothold, by persistently troubleshooting for deviations from the existing order the existing order itself can be brought under reflective scrutiny. But the gulf between the two categories of critique cannot be bridged that easily. If, as Davidson and Rorty famously argue, it takes a norm to reason against a norm,[12] and if one's space of normative reasoning is indeed fully determined by one's normative outlook, then normative self-criticism cannot, in principle, extend beyond adjudicating first-order discrepancies between values in the light of a second-order normative ranking or prioritizing *internal* to the system—in which case the second-order ranking is reaffirmed. In what he has to say about ethical outlooks, McDowell offers no reason to assume that a notion of normative self-criticism more radical than that is available, and that his valorization of second-order critical normative reflection ventures in effect any further than Rorty's.

With regard to ethics, McDowell thus remains disappointingly declarative, but what of the question of *empirical* accountability, to which he devotes the lion's share of his recent work in this area?[13] How can our worldview be rationally adjustable in response to our experience, he asks promisingly, if it is constitutive of our experience?[14] "Bald naturalists," such as Quine, untenably conceive the preconceptualized impressions the world makes on us as the tribunal of our empirical thinking "even while he understands experience in terms of irritations of sensory nerve-endings."[15] At the other extreme, equally untenable for McDowell, "Rampant platonists"[16] like Davidson deny that such purely natural happenings can impart any content, and advocate a thorough coherentism that views our connected system of concepts and conceptions as "spinning frictionlessly in the void" of a space of reasons of its own device.[17] The middle Kantian ground McDowell purports to locate between the two extremes is a view of perceptual experience as the passive, involuntary "actualization, together, of conceptual capacities whose active exercise, with the same togetherness, would be the making of a judgment."[18] Unlike Kant, McDowell usefully locates our conceptual capacities as coming "with being initiated into language,"[19] and their specific content, by virtue of that initiation, as belonging to our second nature.[20]

The problem is that what McDowell ultimately offers is not answerability to the world per se, but to the world we habitually/instinctively experience by virtue of the conceptual content we *actualize* involuntarily in perceiving. And, therefore, it is not at all clear how he can be said to transcend pure coherentism. For perceptual experience to constitute a meaningful tribunal, it is not enough that it be of sufficient conceptual content to merit placement in the space of reasons. The conceptual content it carries cannot be of our own device. As McDowell has it, empirical accountability boils down to subjecting our *considered* judgments to the tribunal of those we make unthinkingly. Under these conditions it is not clear at all why we should normatively privilege the latter. Unless we are missing something crucial, this is party-line coherentism with a reverse interpretivist twist. If any real critical space is opened by McDowell's very limited notion of empirical accountability, it is between what we take our concepts to be and those tacitly operative in perceptual experience. That is not the critical space needed for the kind of framework replacement witnessed in science.[21]

Interpretivism Revisited: Enter Brandom

Interpretivist construals of normativity allow a little more critical space in this regard. For them the internal/external divide is mediated by the conception of the good life manifest and embedded in community practice, and is, therefore, less starkly dichotomous. Schemes of values are liable to be found deficient in terms of their inner coherence and consistency, but they are also liable, even when found perfectly coherent and consistent, to be deemed untrue of their community's way of life. This is because they play a double role. On the one hand, they determine, as McDowell has it, how a person "conceives her practical situation" and present her with "apparent reasons for acting" and with the means to evaluate and adjudicate between different courses of action. This is their constitutive role. But schemes of values also serve individuals and communities to make normative sense of their particular form of life, to articulate and justify the norms that tacitly inform it, and in this respect can be found lacking in a quite different sense.[22] In their first capacity, as constitutive of a person's space of reasons, schemes of values evaluate and determine action. Agents are deemed to have acted rationally when what they do, or contemplate doing, meets the standards of their scheme of values. Schemes of values function here as the means, not as the subject matter, of criticism; as providing the premises of critical arguments, not as their conclusions. But in their second, explicatory capacity, interpretivists reverse the arrow of determination and adjudication. Here it is the community's way of life, its practice, that rationally determines its normative vocabulary, the latter standing in judgment before the former rather than the other way around. Considered in their role as valid interpretations of their community's practice, schemes of values thus become the subject matter of critical scrutiny that goes beyond the purely internal.

Moreover, for interpretivists, the two functions performed by schemes of values, and the two subsequent modes of normative critique they engender are not only different but are logically *ordered*. Interpretivism credits schemes of values with constitutive and adjudicative authority not in addition to, but *by virtue of* them being considered valid interpretations of communal practice. It is in this sense that for them normative criticism *of* a scheme of values (as opposed to normative criticism *by means of* a scheme of values) can well exceed troubleshooting for consistency and coherence. Michael Walzer's entire theory of social criticism is made to turn on the potential (and in his view, the inevitable)[23] disparity between a community's scheme of values and the set of embedded norms tacitly formative of its particular way of life. Social critics call communities to task not by confronting them with alien forms of life they deem ethically superior by objective standards, but by confronting them with schemes of values they believe *better correspond* to their *own* form of life. Social criticism thus remains internal to the form of life in question, yet external to the scheme of values under review. Social criticism remains comparative, but without violating Comparative Irrealism.

Still, as argued in chapter 4, normative criticism remains on an interpretivist showing, in principle, severely limited in *scope*—restricted to discrepancies between a community's articulation of its norms and values and its practice's ideal interpretation, and dependent on its members' sense of a better interpretation. Thus, while schemes of values can be criticized and improved upon, the corresponding ethical outlooks remain immune to criticism, and, therefore, although apt to surreptitious change, are not subject to *rational* scrutiny.

Should this be taken as an argument against interpretivism as such, or as a flaw, or oversight capable of being dealt with and overcome *within* an interpretivist framework? In what follows we take the latter course, and explain why. To this end we first need to take a closer look at the interpretivist account of norms and normative conduct.

Our discussion of interpretivism has addressed normativity in general but has concentrated so far on the interpretivist approach in ethics — on the works of Walzer and Sreenivasan in particular — mainly because of its major concern with internal normative (social) criticism and its role in normative change, so central to the concerns of the present study. Theirs, however, is not the most philosophically developed form of interpretivism. As indicated in passing in former chapters, we find in Robert Brandom's expressivist normative pragmatism an account of normativity akin to that of the interpretivist approach to ethics that is not only more richly and systematically developed but more richly embedded in the neo-Kantian and neopragmatist premises shared by the present study. Brandom's inferential semantics rests on a general account of norms and normative commitment. However, unlike Walzer and Sreenivasan, he does not venture explicitly into ethics, and, with the exception of his most recent work, limits his discussion to *discursive* commitment.[24] The upshot is an account of the set of norms jointly shared by all members of all communities who engage in "the social practices that distinguish us as rational . . . concept mongering creatures — knowers and agents."[25] Because his analysis is devoted to the most fundamental and universally shared normative component of the minimal code, it is not surprising that it remains indifferent to questions pertaining to the diversity of specific forms of life, the possibility of cross-cultural deliberation, and that of the rational critique and amelioration of local normative outlooks that so animate Walzer, Sreenivasan, Friedman, and the authors of the present study.

As noted at the outset of Part II, we turn to Brandom not because his work in any way directly addresses the concerns of the present study, or for his account of discursive commitment per se, but for the manner in which in general it conceives the normative and its grounding in practice, and for the place it implicitly makes for normative criticism.[26] Ours, as we put it, is a *de re* reading of his account, similar to his own Hegelian readings of the "mighty dead" of generations past as anticipating his own interests and positions.[27] It purports to read him generously, as writing specifically (in *Making It Explicit*) about conceptual norms in a manner naturally expandable to all forms of normativity, and as identifying rationality (as sapience) late of Sellars with the capacity for engaging in the game of giving and asking for reasons.[28]

In the following pages Brandom's work is made to bear on our own by (a) teasing out (making explicit) the self-critical element implicit in his account of the "determinate critical integrative task-responsibility" people have for managing their commitments, and for keeping track of the ways others manage theirs,[29] and (b) calling him to task for focusing exclusively on the management of given, up-and-running commitments while omitting all mention of how new commitments are rationally forged and old commitments rationally modified or replaced.

Between Normative Status and Normative Attitude

According to Kant, to be considered *normatively* bound by a rule or law, as opposed to being merely subject to it, one has to some extent conceive of and acknowledge it as such. Brandom emphasizes the necessary linguistic presupposition of Kant's position. To be motivated by *acknowledging* the law requires that it be *conceptualized*. As merely natural beings we act according to rules, as *rational* beings "we act according to our *conceptions* of rules."[30]

Such a Kantian "government by norms" is, therefore, compatible with the possibility of *mistake*, "of those subject to the norms going *wrong, failing* to do what they are obliged by those norms to do, or doing what they are not entitled to do."[31] The sense of "ought" involved in saying that a physical object, or even one of our "sentient and purposive," yet nonsapient "mammalian cousins, primate ancestors, or neonatal offspring," *ought* in certain circumstances to act in a certain way entails that it will so act. But in the case of a failed prediction, it would be absurd to claim that the stone, for instance, was *wrong* not to fall as predicted, or that the tomcat was *mistaken* not to respond to the kitty in heat or *right* to lick itself dry after coming in from the rain. According to Kant, to be normatively compelled is to knowingly undertake an obligation or commitment to comply with a rule aware of the possibility not to. Brandom terms this view "*regulism* about norms."[32]

Regulism raises the question of the *origin* of the rules and, more important, faces the problem posed by Wittgenstein's and Sellars's regress-of-rules arguments. Because rules specify the right thing to do in certain circumstances, they may themselves be applied correctly or incorrectly. Norms explicated as rules, therefore, necessarily presuppose other rules, which, to avoid infinite regress, must be said at some point to reside implicit in practice. The nature of that residing, central to Brandom's position, is a point in dispute. If for a norm to be in force presupposes the possibility of it being mistakenly applied or wrongly conceived, then talk of norms implicitly embedded in practice requires there being room for a distinction between what Brandom dubs an agent's normative *attitude* toward a performance and its normative *status;* between what *is* and what is *taken to be* correct according to the norm in question.[33] Following Wittgenstein, Brandom takes this as a criterion of adequacy for any account of "norms being in force." Here lies the key to Brandom's interpretivism. The point is worth quoting at length.

> The thought here is that the distinction between status and assessment . . . is essential to the notion of genuinely normative status. It is motivated by the idea that assessing is itself something that can be done correctly or incorrectly, and furthermore that it is the norm according to which performances are being assessed that determines which assessments are correct or incorrect. If there is no distinction to be made between correct and incorrect assessments, then there is no sense in which the performances being assessed are governed by a norm *according to which* they are being assessed.[34]

As noted, Brandom limits his concern to "conceptual norms"—norms that govern taking or treating various applications of concepts as correct or incorrect. The view he opposes, attributed to Wittgenstein by Crispin Wright, identifies the normative status of being a correct application of a concept with it being taken as such by the entire community. On such a showing, although individual performances and individual assessments of performances can both be correct or incorrect, no such distinctions apply to communal performances or assessments. As Wright puts it: "for the community itself there is no authority, so no standard to meet."[35] Brandom agrees that every society boasts many socially instituted norms and rules of this kind. Kwakiutl traditions are his example: "it makes no sense to suppose that they could collectively be wrong about" what they "treat as an appropriate greeting gesture for their tribe, or a correctly constructed ceremonial hut."[36] But *conceptual* norms, he insists, are different. Contrary to "normative statuses about which the community's all-inclusive practical assessment cannot be mistaken, such as who is really married or what obligations are incurred by spitting in front of the chief,"[37] we would like to think that

> our use of the term 'mass' is such that the facts settle whether the mass of the universe is large enough that it will eventually suffer gravitational collapse, independently of what we, even all of us and forever, take those facts to be. We could all be wrong in our assessment of this claim, could all be treating as a correct application of the concepts involved what is *objectively* an incorrect application of them.[38]

Brandom's point is general and is not confined to norms governing empirical or scientific concepts. He concedes Wright's contention late of Wittgenstein that in order to keep normative status distinct from normative attitude, the practices of concept application and their assessment must be understood as *social* practices but insists, contrary to Wright, that to do so does not entail relinquishing the idea that conceptual norms are objective. "The primary explanatory challenge to a social practice theory of discursive commitments," he declares, is to hold on to the former while denying the latter.[39]

Two related yet different distinctions are at work here—one explicit, one implied. The former is between the kind of norms of convention of which Wright speaks, and about which even Brandom agrees the community as a whole cannot be mistaken, and objective conceptual norms, about which he insists it can. The second distinction at work, though nowhere made explicit by Brandom, concerns the notion of a normative *mistake*. The kind of normative mistakes of which Brandom speaks remains fully confined to mistaken applications (and mistaken assessments of applications) of conceptual norms. Objective as he takes such norms to be, Brandom's notion of a mistake, a problem, or a flaw, even in the realm of the conceptual, does *not* extend to the norms themselves. A norm can be wrongly applied or its application wrongly assessed—in the case of conceptual norms, even by the entire community—but even a conceptual norm, his argument implies, cannot of itself be deemed wrong or problematic.

Making Brandom Explicit I: The Constitutive Role
of Conceptual Norms

Or can they? Let us first return to Brandom's disagreement with Wright, for it is not at all clear what it is about. It goes without saying that the community as a whole, or for that matter, the relevant communal authorities, cannot be mistaken about the rules and regulations they have exclusive power to make or to change. But it seems equally obvious that even with respect to the *application* and assessment of those kinds of rules—for example, rules of ceremonial greeting, rules of marriage—even the community as a whole *can* be mistaken! Jeffrey Stout captures this nicely in his baseball and soccer examples, on which his entire system of ethics is made to stand.[40] Before human beings invented the game of soccer and instituted its rules, "there was no such thing as the normative status that soccer people refer to as 'having committed a foul.'" In major league soccer, something akin to a divine-command model obtains. Goals are awarded and fouls acted upon only when the designated referee says so. And yet, just as with Brandom's "mass" example, the normative claims made by soccer players, designated referees, the sport's commissioners and officials, or for that matter the entire soccer community, as to who fouled whom can clearly be mistaken. "Whether it is true that Beckenbauer fouled Charlton in the fifty-third minute of the 1966 World Cup Final," explains Stout in an attempt to explain Brandom, is clearly "not a question about our subjective states," or those of the designated officials, or of the entire soccer community.

And if this is true of soccer and baseball, argues Stout, "then there is no reason to suppose that the adoption of [Brandom's] form of pragmatism deprives ethical discourse of its title of objectivity."[41] If Stout's account of Brandom is correct, then Brandom's disagreement with Wright is primarily *not* a disagreement about the objectivity of *certain* socially instituted norms (those governing the correct application of concepts about which even the entire community can err) as opposed to others (such as the rules of soccer and marriage, about which it cannot), but a disagreement about the nature of the norms governing the application of *any* socially instituted norm. Whether Brandom believes contrary to Wright that *all* first-order socially instituted norms are of the sort of which the community as a whole cannot be mistaken is a question we can leave open. But if Stout's analysis is correct, then Brandom should be taken as arguing that all *second*-order rules and assessments of *all manner* of norm *application* pertain to norms of the non-Wrightian variety that can be mistakenly applied by all and everyone now and forever. It is in this sense that it is "norms all the way down," as Brandom describes the grounding of norms in practice.[42]

Does this mean that in limiting *Making It Explicit* to discursive commitment Brandom misrepresents his own project? On the face of it, yes, but in principle, not necessarily. To assess whether the foul called (or failed to be called) was in fact committed, or the ceremonial greeting properly extended, or for the marriage registered deemed rightly so is to assess whether in the cases in question the *concepts* 'foul', 'greeting', and 'marriage' were correctly applied. Experienced referees blow their whistles as instinctively and unthinkingly as seasoned noncoms throw their salutes. But when for some reason their playing by the rules comes under review, and the appropriateness of their actions questioned (or self-questioned), their performances will be scrutinized in accord with what are taken as the correct applications of "foul" and "salute" in the circumstances in question.

According to this reading, which we adopt, Brandom's account of discursive commitment, his theory of inferential semantics, and its grounding in normative pragmatics are rendered not only the defining minimal code for all communities of sapient, concept-mongering humans, but the shared normative core necessarily common to *all forms of human normativity*. Brandom's identification of sapience (rationality) with normativity, and normativity, not only with the possibility of *being* mistaken, but of being *proven* mistaken, the Sellarsian inferential semantics he argues for and its expressivist-cum-interpretivist grounding in discursive practice render Stout's account of *Making It Explicit* highly relevant to the concerns and premises of the present study.

But is Brandom himself privy to Stout's interpretation of his work? Nowhere in *Making It Explicit* is the point made by Brandom that conceptual norms are not merely one important form of normativity, but necessarily partake in all normative assessment—even the most ceremonial, conventional, and contrived. That work describes conceptual norms as forming a subcategory of normative statuses, but nowhere are they presented there as the linguistive framework *constitutive* of *all* forms of normative commitment, as Stout takes them to be. But this changes quite distinctly in Brandom's most recent work, especially his Woodbridge Lectures published in 2009. Here too he remains exclusively focused on conceptual norms, making, as before, no reference to ethics or to questions of normative diversity. But by locating his point of departure in Kant's Second Critique more markedly than ever before, conceptual norms are all but explicitly attributed constitutive authority over all of "normative space."

> Judging and acting—endorsing claims and maxims, committing ourselves to what is or shall be true—is binding ourselves by norms. It is making ourselves subject to assessment according to rules that articulate the *contents* of those commitments. Those norms, those rules, [Kant] calls 'concepts.' In a strict sense, all a Kantian subject can do *is* apply concepts, *either theoretically in judging or practically, in acting.* Discursive, that is to say, concept-mongering, creatures are normative creatures—creatures who live and move and have their being in normative space.[43]

He then goes on to explain the nature of "the responsibility undertaken in judging" (which he describes at length as "the responsibility to *integrate* one's judgments into a *unity of apperception,*" comprising a consistent, coherent, and explicated unity in all of one's commitments),[44] noting in a telling aside that "there is a parallel story about endorsing a practical maxim."[45] Finally, in summarizing the Kantian chapter of his "Semantic Sonata in Kant and Hegel,"[46] judging and willing are effortlessly run together is such statements as, "The rules that settle [the relations of material incompatibility and inferential consequence] are the *concepts* one counts as applying in *judging or willing,* which activities then become visible as endorsing specifically discursive (that is, *conceptual*) contents."[47]

These later texts firmly corroborate Stout's extension of Brandom's inferential semantics to normativity in general. And yet, in view of the opposition, Brandom's concentration on assertion, to the near-exclusion of other forms of commitment, is understandable. Brandom's style of philosophizing is not polemical. He argues his case systematically, at times historically, but never as the remedy to the failings of his rivals. Nonetheless, as he is clearly aware,[48] his inferentialism's most natural and challenging rival is what he dubs "the master concept of Enlightenment epistemology and semantics": the understanding of meaning in *representational* terms,[49] whose intuitive correspondist semantics of assertion poses the gravest challenge to Brandom's coherentist alternative. If Brandom cannot meet the representationalist challenge by making viable coherentist sense of committing oneself to the assertion that things *are* thus-and-so, he will have failed regardless of the sense he is capable of making of committing to acting so that things *shall* or *should be* thus-and-so.[50]

Making Brandom Explicit II: The Normative and the Critical

In view of all this, Stout's account of *Making It Explicit* seems less in disagreement with Brandom's understanding of his project than in making explicit an important unacknowledged aspect of it with which Brandom should (and in fact later seems to) agree.[51] Cast in interpretivist terms, Stout's rendition of Brandom rings truer than the original because it sets up his normative theory of linguistic practice as a general meta-theory of normativity *by virtue of it being* a normative theory of linguistic practice.

However, the centrality of conceptual norms to all forms of normative assessment is not the only "master idea" of *Making It Explicit* that Brandom "does not make . . . as explicit as one would like."[52] Brandom's two most basic commitments—to Kant's understanding of normativity and to Sellars's inferential account of the game of giving and asking for reasons—tacitly presuppose a notion of skeptical self-awareness that goes, unacknowledged by Brandom, to the heart of his project. Hence the central relevance of his work to the present study.

In one of the several intermediate summaries generously scattered throughout *Making It Explicit*, Brandom takes helpful stock of the "five strategic explanatory commitments" that inform the twin—normative and inferentialist—components of his system (which he also takes the opportunity to duly credit).

(i)   The strategic commitment to treating what is expressed by the use of *sentences* (rather than what is expressed by the use of singular terms or predicates) as the fundamental sort of semantic content is an element . . . taken over from Kant.

(ii) The pragmatic strategic commitment to understanding semantics in terms of pragmatics (the *contents* associated with expressions in terms of the practices governing their *use*) is an element . . . taken over from Wittgenstein.[53]

(iii) The strategic commitment to specifying such a pragmatics in the first instance in normative terms is an element . . . taken over from Kant, Frege, Wittgenstein, and Sellars.

(iv) The inferentialist strategic commitment to treating the public linguistic practice of asserting involving such contents, rather than the private mental practice of judgment, is an element . . . taken over from Dummett.

(v)   The strategic commitment to understanding asserting a sentence as a significance a performance acquires in virtue of its role in a practice of giving and asking for *reasons,* of justifying and communicating justifications, is an element . . . taken over from Sellars.[54]

This seemingly linear set of argumentative links comes full circle in the final chapter of *Making It Explicit* where the "idea that is followed out in the deontic score-keeping pragmatics" from (ii) and (v) is restated in the idiom of, and as deriving from, the Kantian view of normativity that grounds (i) and (iii). Here the normative attitudes that drive the former are set side by side with the Kantian notions of responsibility, obligation, disobedience, and normative error that comprise the latter. But the way Brandom understands their connection is marred by a related yet different oversight.

This is how the links of the chain are presented there: Kant's "realm of responsibility" is the realm of rules followed by virtue of being explicitly acknowledged. Only such rules can be both binding and disobeyed. It is the capacity for such explicit acknowledgment that, therefore, "institutes distinctively normative statuses such as duty and responsibility,"[55] and marks us sapiens off as capable of adopting explicitly normative attitudes and, most important for Brandom, as capable of *taking* ourselves and others to be "bound by the norms that are our concepts." The twin normative attitudes of undertaking commitments and attributing commitment to others manifest themselves in the linguistic "practice of giving and asking for reasons, of justifying and communicating justifications," that Brandom thoroughly and systematically follows through. What Brandom fails to explain, however, is how the one gives rise to the other; why a capacity for taking ourselves and others to be bound by norms *should* manifest itself in insistent reasoning and mutual interrogation about them.

The pragmatist order of explanation he adopts (to which we concede as interpretivists) does an impressive and convincing job of grounding "an inferential semantics on a normative pragmatics," to quote one of his chapter subheads,[56] but it leaves the pragmatic *explanans* largely unexplained. Working back from semantics to pragmatics, the question that exercises *Making It Explicit* is:

> What features *must* one's interpretation of a community exhibit *in order properly to be said to be an interpretation of them* as engaging in practices sufficient to confer genuinely propositional content on the performances, statuses, attitudes, and expressions caught up in those practices? (61; emphasis added)

The order of the chapters of the book notwithstanding,[57] the scorekeeping model of linguistic practice, the heart and culmination point of Brandom's entire system, is argued for by reasoning "upstream" from the inferential semantics it purports to explain rather than "downstream" from the Kantian account of the normative and its Wittgensteinian-cum-Hegelian embeddedness in social practice. But why should the game of giving and asking for reasons be at all played? It is clear what playing the game can *explain*, and to what notion of rationality being able to play it gives rise.[58] But what might rationally *motivate*, or socially or cognitively *explain*, undertaking to play it in the first place? Brandom's text insinuates, though nowhere actually argues, that it has to do with us being normative creatures in Kant's sense of the term; that the self-aware, explicit acknowledgment of the rules we undertake to follow somehow compels us to not only to commit ourselves to following them, but to justify them for ourselves, and not only that, but to take keen interest in the normative choices of our fellow sapiens, to the point of prompting them to disclose their reasons for making them, and to keep close score of what we take our and their commitments and entitlements to be. But in truth, nothing in what Brandom has to say of Kantian normativity as applied to concepts seems capable of motivating or explaining why a capacity, a need, or a will to engage in this type of game should arise.

The route from Kantian conceptual normativity—(i) and (iii)—to the deontic scorekeeping model of linguistic social practices—(ii) and (v)—is established by Brandom, not by rendering explicit something implicit in the former, but by supplementing them with Sellars's inferentialist theory of meaning. While the Kantian approach to conceptual norms nicely *accommodates* Sellars's account of "conceptual understanding," it is clear that Brandom does not think it *commits* one to it. All agree that "the difference that makes the difference" between a parrot "trained to respond to the presence of red things by uttering the noise 'that's red' . . . and a genuine observer of red things . . . is that the sapient being responsively classifies the stimuli as falling under concepts, as being of some conceptually articulated kind." But there are more ways than one to understand "what makes something a use of a word in the sense relevant to the application of concepts" and the formation of judgments—all of which, one would think (and Brandom implies), are equally accommodated by Kant's account of the normative. "Sellars's answer," he writes, is that for something

> to be characterized as . . . a coming to believe that such-and-such is the case, is for it to be the making of a certain kind of move or the taking of a certain kind of position in a game of giving and asking for reasons. It must be committing oneself to a content that can both serve as and stand in need of *reasons,* that is, that can play the role both of premise and of conclusion in *inferences.* The observer's response is conceptually contentfull just insofar as it occupies a node in a web of inferential relations.[59]

Thus while the arrow of *explanation* runs in Brandom's theory from the pragmatics of deontic scorekeeping to Sellarsian semantics, the arrow of *reasoning* and *commitment* points in the opposite direction (and in doing so, provides a fascinating example of a noninferential yet commitment-preserving act of transcendental reasoning that works by working in the opposite direction, as it were). Brandom's commitment to the latter determines the search for the former and is the *reason* and justification for its development. His commitment to the Kantian picture of normativity runs deep, of course, and is deepened in his later work, but as it stands it is given no *inferential* role—explanatory or justificationary—to play in his system. Kant's picture, we have said, nicely accommodates deontic scorekeeping but does not, and seemingly cannot, *explain* it, Brandom's text implies. This, we believe, is a grave oversight on Brandom's part—an oversight all the more evident by the omission of any mention of deontic scorekeeping in his most recent publications.

A Brandomian Doubter

The difference Brandom rightly insists on between normative attitude and normative status ensures the objectivity of norms in his system, and hence the persistent possibility of error in norm application and application assessment. The difference between normative attitude and status, coupled to the grounding of the normative in practice, we have argued, is what, in addition, renders his system of a cloth with the interpretivist approach to ethics. What the Brandomian picture might benefit from at this juncture is the imaginary perspective of a fictive character similar to Rorty's ironist, a smart, fully fledged, make-believe *practicing* Brandomian who conducts herself in recognition and awareness of all that Brandom late of Kant, Hegel, and Wittgenstein assumes of norm-bound agents. Among other things, such a person will act in knowing self-awareness of the two-tiered structure of her normative behavior: when knowingly compelled to follow a rule or abide by a norm she will be knowingly committing herself not only to doing *what is* right, but to doing *it* right.[60]

Alert to the complexity of her situation, the diversity of normative attitudes, and to the discrepancies between them and the normative statuses they aspire to emulate, she will also be constantly aware of the real possibility of being called to task by other members of her community for the quality of her understanding and her performances. She, therefore, shares with Rorty's ironist a healthy self-doubting wariness. But that is about all she shares with her. Unlike Rorty's ironist, her skepticism is not directed holistically against her "final vocabulary" in general, against the possibility of having been born into the wrong tribe ("wrong" in what sense exactly?). What she has doubts about are her specific normative choices and performances. She will do her best to justify them, but aware of being judged to be wrong, will at the same time be attentive to the way others respond in similar circumstances, and curious of their reasons for so doing, and she will be even more attentive to their reaction to her responses. This is true of all but the most banal and automatic normative choices, including conceptual ones. In other words, such a Brandomian doubter will be apt to engage in the game of giving and asking for reasons not because of her partiality to Sellars's inferential semantics but by virtue of her neo-Kantian self-understanding of the norms that bind her and the nature of their binding.

A more significant difference between Rorty's ironist and our Brandomian doubter has to do with whom they represent. Rorty's ironist represents a philosophical ideal, a model for a new and desired creative elite capable of distancing itself from itself, as, even they admit, few of us can. Rorty's ironist represents a new breed of strong, new self-describing poets, philosophically motivated, restlessly self-experimenting, aware of the deep and disturbing implications of latter-day developments in the sciences and the humanities. Our Brandomian doubter, by contrast, can be easily seen to represent almost anybody. There is nothing avant-garde about her, nothing especially intellectual, certainly nothing radical. She is exceptional only in the sense that she holds explicitly to the normative attitudes to which most of us hold tacitly. She is, therefore, perhaps more open to criticism than some, more curious about other people's choices and performances than others, less defensive perhaps in the face of criticism than many, maybe even more conscientious than most. But that is only because she strikes us as a slightly idealized version of ourselves, not as someone who has come to realize something that most of us do not or to have attained a level of informed self-awareness few of us can. The force of her example owes to her recognizable *ordinariness* rather than to a unique insight or disposition. She is we made explicit, Brandom might say.

The example of our Brandomian doubter suggests a solid explanatory route from the Kantian view of normativity that grounds theses (i) and (iii) to all the main elements comprising the deontic score-keeping pragmatics of (v). One is thus able to set forth from an independently established normative pragmatics from which a full-blooded Sellarsian inferentialist semantics can then be genuinely *made* explicit. The way the master argument of *Making It Explicit* is set up, one has the uneasy feeling that the pragmatist target rings are drawn after the event to accommodate a previously shot inferentialist arrow. This can now be put right. But the advantages of our little thought experiment far transcend merely streamlining Brandom's argument.

First, the explanatory route from (i) and (iii) to (v) is rendered at once quite general. It applies to all forms of normative assessment and is not confined to conceptual norms per se. In this sense it bears out what we have referred to as Stout's understanding of Brandom's argument, but it does so for different reasons. According to the view we attribute to Stout, Brandom's deontic score-keeping model applies to all forms of normative assessment *by virtue of applying to conceptual norms*, because conceptual norms are necessarily involved in all forms of normative assessment. According to the argument we propose, the reasoning is reversed: the practices of deontic scorekeeping apply to conceptual norms *because* they apply to all forms of normative assessment. It is true that only assertions can be reasons and can stand in need of reasons. It is also true that conceptual norms are necessarily involved in all forms of normative assessment and that its essentially assertional nature is indeed what *enables* engaging in deontic scorekeeping about it. But the *motivation* to engage in such scorekeeping, and hence its *explanation*, is a matter quite different from the discursive conditions necessary for doing so. What motivates, and hence explains, our Brandomian doubter's engagement in the game of giving and asking for reasons, we insist, is her Kantian-cum-Wittgensteinian understanding of normative awareness in general and its embeddedness in the social, which applies equally to all forms of normative assessment.

Second, and more important, inquiring into the motivations of our Brandomian doubter suggests going beyond Brandom's understanding of sapience and rationality in ways centrally relevant to the concerns of the present study. Sapience, according to Brandom, consists in us being "the ones on whom reasons are binding, who are subject to the peculiar force of the better reason. . . . Being rational is . . . placing ourselves and each other in the space of reasons, by giving and asking for reasons for our attitudes and performances."[61] Characteristically, Brandom identifies sapience and rationality pragmatically, defining them in terms of what rational sapient creatures *do* and are capable of doing. Those who engage in the deontic practices of giving and asking for reasons are rational *by virtue of* their very engagement. Reflecting on his project in later work Brandom formulates his strategy explicitly:

> The overall idea is that the rationality that qualifies us as sapiens (and not merely sentients) *can be identified with* being a player in the social, implicitly normative game of offering and assessing, producing and consuming, reasons.[62]

"On this view," he writes in *Tales of the Mighty Dead*, summarizing the inferentialist "model of rationality . . . I elaborate in *Making It Explicit*," "to be rational is to play the game of giving and asking for reasons. . . . To be rational is to be a producer and consumer of reasons: things that can play the role of both premises and conclusions of *inferences*."[63] However, if we are right in assuming that our Brandomian doubter places herself in the space of reasons and partakes in deontic scorekeeping *for a reason*, then the foothold for identifying sapience and rationality must be pushed further back. Rationality may *assert itself* in, and may even be *warranted* by, participation in the game of giving and asking for reasons, but if the game is played for a reason, rationality must be *identified* with *that* reasoning rather than with its practical consequence. In a word, if for Brandom a person is rational because she plays the game, we view her as playing the game because she is rational. Again, this is not to deny that because all and only rational creatures are producers and consumers of reasons, being a player is a definite *sign* of sapience and a dependable *indication* of rationality. But we insist that her playing the game is but a *symptom* of her rationality, not to be confused with what it *consists in*. To paraphrase Brandom's critical appraisal of the logical and instrumental conceptions of rationality in comparison to his own, we could say that he "mistakes the shadow of rationality for its substance."[64]

This brings us to the most significant difference between Rorty's ironist and our Brandomian doubter. Rorty's ironist, we have noted, is wary of her scheme of values, our Brandomian doubter is not. She does not doubt the norms to which she is committed and the rules by which she is compelled—at least not in the first instance (more on this in later chapters)—but she is worried about getting them right, of applying them properly. Knowingly committed to abiding fittingly by the norms that bind her, she is wary as to how to go about it. Her doubts do not breed irony with regard to her norms. She is not motivated by recognizing the *contingency* of her normative commitments but by recognizing the complexity of her situation and the possibility of erring despite being fully committed. Her doubts, therefore, reflect determination to taking her commitments seriously. In a sense, her commitment and her wariness reinforce each other. And it is because she is both committed and wary of performing correctly that she is motivated to justify her judgments and actions to herself and to her critics, to interrogate those who in similar circumstances chose to respond differently, and to keep track of their reasoning. Her rationality certainly *manifests itself* in doing all this, but its substance resides not in *what* she does so much as in *why* she does it.

Arguing from within (Stout's understanding of) Brandom's neo-Kantian, inferential, and interpretivist account of normativity, we thus arrive back at something closely akin to McDowell's Aristotelian identification of rationality with self-doubting critical reflection from which this study set forth. One advantage of the Brandomian setting—if largely unacknowledged by Brandom himself—is that the sort of reflective normative criticism it identifies with rationality does not remain confined, as in McDowell, to wishful thinking or to Neurathian housekeeping. More important, though interpretivist in substance, from what we have so far seen of the Brandomian picture, it locates the elbow room for normative criticism differently from the interpretivists in ethics. Cast in Brandom's idiom, the latter limit their discussion to the distinction between normative statuses and attitudes regarding the norms themselves—that is, between the community's articulated scheme of values and its practice's ideal interpretation. The Brandomian picture, by contrast, locates the critical tension responsible for deontic scorekeeping in the space of possibilities of mistakes of performance and especially mistakes of assessment, that is, in the gap between normative statuses and attitudes toward norm application.

Neither, however, suffice as they stand, since according to both accounts, normative self-reflective criticism remains confined to the community's existing normative outlook. Our Brandomian doubter remains knowingly committed to (what she takes to be) the norms that bind her, just as the interpretivists' social critic remains knowingly faithful to (what he takes to be) the community's practices' true interpretation. But if normative reflection cannot get beyond making explicit the norms already implicitly at work in the community's changing way of life, in what sense can it be said to change rationally? In discussing the normative force of our scientific concepts, Korsgaard makes the point forcefully:

> The normative question is a question about the status of the concepts, not about whether they have been correctly applied. Is our conceptual scheme adequate? Is it the correct one, or the best one, or the one that captures the most, or the one that captures what is "really" true about the world? Philosophers will of course disagree on whether any of these questions are coherent and, if so, which one is the right one to ask. But since science leads us to modify our conceptual scheme, and we think of these modifications as improvements, it does appear that some such question is in order.[65]

The key to moving forward is to realize that we have unfinished business with the Brandomian picture, that the commonplace pedestrian self-criticism of our rational Brandomian doubter cannot be taken to stand for the entire realm of possible normative rethinking. She epitomizes rational *conformity*. She is not a social critic. In order to move from her anxious conformism to a more fully fledged Brandomian picture of normative reform, we need to return for a moment to Walzer's social critics.

Walzer's Prophets

Central to Walzer's theory of social criticism is the way it not only allows for, but privileges the view from within. If the aim of social criticism is to stimulate people to rethink the right thing *for them* to do by confronting them with a recognizably superior interpretation of *their* way of life,[66] the advantage of membership, Walzer argues, is enormous. The second-person moral rebuke of a fellow citizen carries with it the intimacy and solidarity of the shared responsibility of us- and we-talk; always conveying true concern, always conveying self-rebuke to some extent. It also carries the authority and plausibility of firsthand, lived, intimate acquaintance with the moral culture it aspires to correct. Walzer's vivid comparison of the prophecies of Jonah and Amos brings the point home forcefully. "When Jonah prophesies doom in Nineveh," he notes,

> he cannot refer to a religious tradition or a moral law embodied in covenantal form. Whatever the religion of the inhabitants of Nineveh, Jonah appears to know nothing about it and to take no interest in it. He is a detached critic of Ninevean society. . . . Nineveh has its own moral and religious history, its own creed, its own code. . . . But it is not Jonah's purpose to remind the people of what is their own; only a local prophet (a connected critic) could do that.[67]

Amos's "judgment" of the nations presented in the first two chapters are similarly universalist, detached, and remote. But when the prophet turns to address Israel, his prophecy, Walzer submits, becomes social criticism

> because it challenges the leaders, the conventions, the ritual practices of a particular society and because it does so in the name of values recognized and shared in that same society. . . . What makes the difference is Amos's membership. His criticism goes deeper than Jonah's because he knows the fundamental values of the men and women he criticizes. . . . [A]nd since he in turn is recognized as one of them, he can call them back to their one "true" path.[68]

Walzer's distinction between detached and connected normative criticism, especially in its "prophetic" setting, brings to the forefront three major issues Brandom leaves unattended, the third of which even Walzer himself falls short of properly acknowledging: (a) The idea of a diversity of norms sufficient for Comparative Irrealism to apply; (b) the special significance and additional normative force of the inside critic; and (c) the potentially radical scope of normative self-criticism.

First let us turn to Normative Diversity. As noted above, the "we" Brandom is interested in comprises sapien kingdom in its entirety. The ability to assert, conceptualize, be committed to a norm, be bound by a rule knowing one can break, and to offer and to ask for reasons are capacities shared by "the one great Community comprising members of particular communities" of "reasoning beings."[69] Those who say "we" in such a way distinguish by their scorekeeping "a 'we' of rational agents and knowers, inhabiting a normative space of giving and asking for reasons, from an 'it' that comprises what does not live and move and have its being in such a space."[70] The only question remotely related to Normative Diversity that he raises is how radically different the noises members of an alien community can utter, the marks they make (or, for all that it matters to the abstract score-keeping model of discursive practice, the colors they turn, the odors they emit, or the voltages they shift) for the conceptual contents they express to be no longer *understood*.[71] The interpretive answer he offers is broadly Davidsonian, the details of which need not concern us here.[72] Because we can only keep score of the commitments and entitlements of those we understand, the question of *interpretable* diversity is important.

Comparative Irrealism is, of course, a thesis not about the limits of *understanding* but about those of normatively *comparing* and *ranking* sufficiently alien normative outlooks. Brandom does not raise the question of ranking different outlooks but is certainly aware that "members of one speech community may be divided into competing schools of thought on various topics" to the extent that they "may not recognize the entitlements [and] therefore the challenges of those from other groups, as regards claims concerning those topics."[73] With respect to such topics assertional authority will, therefore, not enjoy the universality of the normative pragmatics of scorekeeping per se, or of the inferential semantics that grounds it. Brandom thus clearly recognizes not only the existence of normative diversity, but its bearing on the extent to which members of different groups are capable of challenging one another. But the point is not developed further. *Making It Explicit* is dedicated to explicating what we share as members of any kind of norm-bound discursive culture, not to what we fail to share by virtue of the specific cultures to which we belong.

Still, the point is not so easily set aside. Much of the incentive and vitality of Brandomian scorekeeping depends on its prima facie normative bearing. The critical impact assertions have on the track competent discussants keep of their own and each other's commitments and entitlements is of the essence of Brandom's deontic scorekeeping.[74] If our analysis of the Brandomian doubter is not completely off the mark, then deontic scorekeeping is not an idle exercise. Her motivation to engage in giving and asking for reasons turns decisively on the thought that she is liable to be obliged to rethink, adjust, and even modify her commitments and entitlements in the light of moves made by other players. Therefore, if a person's commitments and reasoning are so remote as to render them irrelevant to one's own, Brandomian scorekeeping loses much of its *normative* grip and incentive. But if they are deemed irrelevant to the normative system to which one is committed, why keep track of them? Rorty's ironist's approach is different. She does so out of curiosity, with a view to enriching her knowledge of and to experimenting with the exotic and the alien. But this is because she is motivated very differently from our Brandomian doubter—not by commitment to her normative outlook so much as by a desire to try on others for size.

Simply listening to members of an alien culture, doing one's best to understand what they are saying, what they believe, and why they do what they do, requires keeping Brandomian score. But if there is nothing normative to be learned from them—no commitments to acknowledge and possibly endorse, no entitlements to inherit—playing the game becomes a largely academic exercise lacking normative bite and motivation. Unless, of course, one is normatively driven to cast around for alternative systems in the light of *problems* one perceives in one's own. Rorty's ironist is constantly casting around for supplements and alternatives, but she is not normatively driven to do so. Neither is our Brandomian doubter, whose doubts remain confined to the application of the norms to which she is uncritically committed. We shall return to this point shortly. But first more must be said of the critical aspects of her straightforward scorekeeping.

As shall be argued in some detail in the next chapter, playing the game of giving, asking for, and being presented with other people's reasons is a necessary but not a sufficient condition for being normatively challenged by them. For *A*'s reasoning to prompt *B* to reconsider his, it must be both relevant to and critical of *B*'s own reasoning. *Relevance* in this respect is a function of the commitments *A* and *B* share. The *challenge* it may pose to *B*, on the other hand, is a function of those they do *not*. And the two are usually intimately related: the more significant the one, the more profound the other. The more two players have in common, the greater will be the potential challenge of their differences, and vice versa: the less they share, the less their differences are felt to matter.

To put this in the somewhat more structured idiom of the next chapter, to criticize an opinion, belief, or action (as opposed to merely voicing a doubt about them) is to *argue against* them. Criticism is a form of reasoned questioning by which a person is confronted (or self-confronted) by an argument whose premises he or she are thought to accept and whose conclusion implies retracting, modifying, or replacing currently held commitments. It is an addressed (or self-addressed) act of reasoned questioning that always takes the form of an argument—at least tacitly. For their criticism to be at all relevant, critics must argue from premises their addressees hold true. It is useful, especially with Brandom's deontic scorekeeping model in mind, to distinguish, therefore, between direct and indirect criticism, depending on who initially formulates and levels the critical argument. A direct critical argument is an argument addressed by a critic with a view to proving its addressee wrong or in some other way at fault. Direct criticism is not itself a move in the game of giving or asking for reasons, but it necessarily presupposes it having been played—at least to the extent that it presupposes second-guessing those of its addressees' commitments it employs as premises and those it argues against. Direct critical discourse thus goes far beyond giving and asking for reasons. It is a different game altogether, one in which reasons are not merely laid bare, but are deliberated, interrogated, and challenged by argument. To play it effectively requires at the very least being reasonably well acquainted with the relevant beliefs and commitments of those criticized.

Walzer argues, however, that being well acquainted in this respect is often not enough. However well intended, criticism is always to some extent a disturbing and disruptive act. And the deeper it purports to hit, the more people instinctively tend to ignore or defensively dismiss it. The *validity* or *soundness* of a critical argument may be a matter of formal logic, but its force and impact owe to it being taken to heart. For a direct critical argument to be effective, for its addressee to take it seriously, formal validity alone, we shall argue in detail in the following chapters, will most often not suffice. The most effective direct criticism, according to Walzer, is that leveled on the basis of *shared* commitments and premises. Walzer's whole point about connected, as opposed to detached, criticism is that to be effective direct criticism most often requires a significant level of intimacy and trust, and nothing compares in this respect to the intimacy and the trust of a shared culture.

But people are frequently and effectively challenged by what other people think, say, and do without being directly criticized by them. These are cases in which the assertions or actions of others prompt self-criticism. Here the critical argument is *self*-formulated and *self*-directed, and it is here that deontic scorekeeping is of crucial importance, for it is here that by attending closely to the commitments and entitlements of others one is alerted to new possibilities one finds relevant to one's own. Such moments of self-critique inspired by what one encounters away from home, as it were, are, again, not moves in the game of giving and asking for reasons but the direct outcomes of playing it. They lack the confrontational aspects of direct criticism and are, therefore, less disturbing and disruptive, and hence relatively less liable to be dismissed defensively. They allow one to consider, weigh, and reflect on normative choices different from one's own from a safe distance, to hesitantly try them on for size without the embarrassment and insult of direct condemnation. Here too relevance will still be a matter of normative closeness, for one will find other people's choices normatively meaningful only to the extent that certain of their commitments and entitlements are deemed compatible with, and containable within, one's own inferentially structured system. However, the type of untroubled, inquiring curiosity from which indirect criticism usually arises tends to expose people to new ideas farther afield than the ones they would normally encounter when effectively confronted directly.

Still, and this is the important point, indirect criticism is *not* primarily problem driven. It arises from being exposed to modes of thought and conduct one initially suspects may in some sense be superior to one's own. Indirect criticism is, therefore, necessarily subject to the limitations of Comparative Irrealism. And if the reaches of indirect criticism are the broadest we can envisage, we seem to be back at square one.

From the point of view of what Brandom leaves us with, we have really been at square one all the time. For if criticism is limited to the *application* of norms, to the assessment of normative *performance*, the norms themselves, one would think, are never questioned. Our Brandomian doubter, who is the embodiment of Brandom's project, does not question the norms she applies, only the quality of her performance. Walzer, we have argued, in insisting on connected criticism from within, appears to follow suit. And yet there is something about Walzer's examples of social criticism at its best that seems to fly in the face of Comparative Irrealism. On the one hand, they ring true and convincing; on the other, they seem far too radical for the limits of Comparative Irrealism to apply. The fiercely transformative criticism of Amos is leveled from within, yet at the same time far transcends the conservative, conforming questioning of norm application. Amos, it seems, challenges the very norms of his audience, and does so from within. But then he is no Brandomian doubter either. The target of his outrage and ridicule is not the quality of norm application in Israel but the norms themselves Israel has come to abide by. Are we to conclude, therefore, that similar to the other approaches we have examined, Brandom's system (even when enriched by Stout's reading) is also incapable of accommodating normative criticism from within? We think not. Although Brandom's system as it stands does not go beyond the critique of norm application, we believe it can. To explain how, however, we shall need to take a closer look at the type of speech act we have begun examining, namely, the critical argument, which is the subject of the next chapter.

PART III

Normative Self-Criticism

Introduction

The key to moving forward requires going a crucial step beyond both Brandom and Walzer. In later work, as we show at the outset of chapter 7, Brandom addresses the problem of norm determination but nowhere raises the question central to our concerns here of normative modification or replacement. He offers interesting accounts of the way, analogous to a common-law judge, precedent is rendered normatively binding by individuals and how normativity is conferred by reciprocal group recognition. But he shows no interest in accounting for the critical processes of norm reconsideration and revision, except for the uninteresting (and as we shall argue, underdeveloped) case of troubleshooting for incompatibility.

Walzer's work on social criticism, by contrast, focuses centrally on processes of normative realignment as the result of criticism. But he gives no account at all of its transformative impact. In order to get a better grip on the potentially rational, compelling effect of normative criticism, we need to take a much closer look, first, at criticism in general and normative criticism in particular and the precise nature of their transformative purport; and second, at the nature of the binding hold of personal normative conviction such criticism aspires to dislodge. Both are needed in order to assess the possibility of the former rationally transforming the latter. This is our aim in what follows.

Following a brief analysis of Brandom's later work, the second, and main part, of chapter 7 presents a relatively detailed phenomenology of criticizing as an addressed speech-act, with special emphasis on normative criticism. Building on Harry Frankfurt's well-known work on normativity and personal identity, the first part of chapter 8 then presents an account of personal normative commitment. Our solution to the problem this study set out to solve, of accounting for the possibility of rational normative revision, is achieved by looking closely at the dynamics of intrasubjective deliberation when exposed to the keen yet trusted normative criticism of others—a possibility that has formerly not been explored in the literature. Such criticism is powerless to convince, we argue, but is capable, nonetheless, of destabilizing commitment to the norms it questions sufficiently to motivate rational reconsideration.

By way of concluding this study, chapter 9 takes a second look at the rationality of scientific framework transitions in the light of the findings of chapter 8. Building on and away from Friedman's *Dynamics of Reason* by substantially extending Peter Galison's suggestive notion of the scientific trading zone, we show in brief outline how these transitions should be studied from the point of view of the ambivalated yet creative individuals who set them in motion.

CHAPTER SEVEN

The Critical Stance

Brandom on the Rationality of Norm Making

For those who concede both Normative Diversity and Comparative Ir-realism, the problem of rationality boils down in the first instance to whether norms can be found normatively wanting by those they bind— not merely vague, incoherent, self-contradictory, or mutually inconsistent, but wrong, bad, inappropriate, or undesirable. Normative Diversity renders it a question crucial for those who insist, as Friedman does for science and McDowell does for all forms of normativity, that transitions between frameworks or schemes of values can be undertaken rationally. Comparative Irrealism, on the other hand, seems frustratingly to cast the question as unsolvable. For what is it to deem a normative outlook undesirable or wrong, if not in relation to a better, less problematic alternative? And yet Comparative Irrealism renders such comparisons meaningless. This, we have argued, explains perhaps why Friedman ends up significantly toning down the levels of normative diversity that exist between successive scientific frameworks, and why Mc-Dowell refrains from developing further his notion of normative criticism. Not all accept Normative Diversity, of course, but those who do cannot deny Comparative Irrealism. It follows, therefore, that if it is at all solvable, the problem of normative rationality must reduce further to that of being able to find *noncomparative* fault with one's own normative outlook; to finding it problematic per se rather than relatively so in comparison to different and recognizably superior alternatives. In other words, normative rationality, if possible within the constraints of Normative Diversity and (consequently) Comparative Irrealism, consists in the ability to troubleshoot one's normative outlook for the kind of problems that can motivate and justify the search for alternatives, as opposed to those that the recognized presence of an alternative calls forth retrospectively.

But by what standards is this feat to be performed? In the light of what can one expose one's own norms as normatively lacking, if not in the light of a better alternative? By what standard can one judge one's standards, if not by comparison? (Except, of course, to be circularly judged favorably!) If to criticize one's norms is to form an argument proving their faults, what could serve as its premises? What notion of normative failing is available to such an account, if the existence of external normative yardsticks is denied—both absolute and relative?

Interpretivism allows for some measure of nonrelational normative criticism. From an interpretivist perspective, a scheme of values can be found normatively deficient but not in comparison to a different *form of life,* only in comparison to different *schemes of values* that purport to better make explicit one's own form of life. This form of criticism clearly places the critique of norms in a genuinely normative context that transcends troubleshooting merely for consistency or clarity, in which normative choices are judged correct or incorrect, good or bad, proper or improper according to how they rank as plausible interpretations of the community's "text." But similar to the way our Brandomian doubter confines her self-criticism to understanding and applying the norms that bind her, interpretivism limits social criticism to the task of best explicating their community's form of life. The community's form of life, the *interpretandum* of its scheme of values, just like the norms that bind Brandomian doubters, remain, on these accounts, immune to criticism, and hence beyond the pale of rational reflection in the strong sense in which we use the term. They are modified over time, of course, at times even significantly, but not as the result of subjection to rational scrutiny. Rationality (as critical reflection), these accounts imply, does not apply (because it cannot apply) to the normative outlooks to whose very normativity we owe our capacity for placing our beliefs and actions in the space of reasons—although Brandom makes a convincing case not only for the claim that it is "norms all the way down," but that our rationality owes to this normative pervasiveness. Still, it is not and cannot be "*rationality all the way down*" (in the sense of critical reflection), his texts and the example of our Brandomian doubter imply, because one's norms, even when made explicit, act as given entry moves into the game of giving and asking for reasons, to coin anew a Brandomian phrase—moves that ground and constrain thought, speech, and action but serve as their normative stopping points, at least in the picture painted in *Making It Explicit*. The game of producing and consuming reasons, he writes, "takes for granted a set of inferentially articulated norms as an already up-and-running enterprise."[1]

Brandom does not leave the question of the rationality of norm making unattended, however. *Tales of the Mighty Dead* (2002), published eight years after *Making It Explicit,* is a work devoted exclusively to explaining, in theory and by extended example, how we can be said to attribute normative meaning to actualities of social practice *rationally*—a position worked out in detail seven years later along Hegelian lines in his *Reason in Philosophy* (2009).

Of the five interestingly nested "Conceptions of Rationality" Brandom discusses in the opening chapter of *Tales,* the last two—the "inferentialist view of rationality" and the "historicist" view—jointly represent his own position. The inferentialist view identifies rationality with playing the game of giving and asking for reasons with reference to a given set of norms, while the historicist view, ranked fifth, purports to explain the sense in which we subject ourselves rationally to the determinate norms whose prior existence the inferentialist view takes for granted. Aware that the question of rationally making one's norms one's own strikes deep, Brandom deems the historicist view the culmination point of the "series of ever more radical critical questionings of the semantic presuppositions of theories of rationality" (13). But even here, rationality remains articulated for Brandom in a manner wholly devoid of critical reflection. By 2009 this is remedied in two important respects, both of which, however, fall short, as we shall see, of addressing the problem of normative self-criticism.

Taking his lead from Hegel, Brandom, in both these works, likens this form of rationality to that of a judge in a common law tradition who

> justifies her decision in a particular case by rationalizing it in the light of a reading of that tradition, by so selecting and emphasizing particular prior decisions as precedential that a norm emerges as an implicit lesson. And it is that norm that is then appealed to in deciding the present case, and is implicitly taken to be binding in future ones. In order to find such a norm, the judge must make the tradition cohere, must exhibit the decisions that have actually been made as rational and correct, given that the norm she finds is what has implicitly governed the process all along. Thus each of the prior decisions selected as precedential emerges as making explicit some aspect of that implicit norm. (13–14)[2]

"The rationality of the current decision, its justifiability as a correct application of a [norm]" (14), is hence secured by the sort of rational reconstruction of the past Imre Lakatos advocated for philosophy of science.[3] Similar to Lakatos's work, *Tales of the Mighty Dead* purports not only to elaborate such a view in theory, but to "sketch the outlines of such a history" in rational support of its author's latter-day philosophical position. But the scale of Brandom's historical undertakings far exceeds that of Lakatos's, who backs his polemical paper with very few historical examples. *Tales*, by contrast, offers substantial reconstructions of various strands in the works of Spinoza, Leibniz, Hegel, Frege, Heidegger, and Sellars, and, more recently, Kant,[4] all of whom, Brandom argues, anticipate major aspects of the inferentialist position systematically set forth in *Making It Explicit*. More important, unlike Lakatos, who notoriously presented his rational reconstructions as history of science and mathematics proper, Brandom wears the tendentiousness of his readings on his sleeve. The eight historical chapters of part 2 of *Tales* are candidly described as a series of self-serving exercises of "genealogical, historical, expressively progressive reconstructive rationality," devoted, in one sense, to "rewriting the history of philosophy to make the present day a safe and congenial environment for views that are in any case going to be recommended" (15–16).[5]

What marks Brandom's historical project off from other philosophically and ideologically tainted histories is its reflexive, *dialectical* nature.

Similarly to the common law judge, but unlike most *X*-ist histories of *Y*, Brandom's *Tales* aspires to justify his philosophy not by applying it successfully outside philosophy but by using it to rationally reconstruct the very philosophical tradition to which it belongs. Quite unlike Brandom, Lakatos purports to prove polemically that his methodology makes better sense of more episodes in the history of science (as opposed to episodes in the history of philosophy of science) than its three main rivals (inductivism, instrumentalism, and Popperian fallibilism). Lakatos does not purport to locate anticipations of his position in the texts of former philosophers but to better account for the norms of scientific conduct he finds *implicit* in the practices of exemplary past scientists. Contrary to Brandom, Lakatos presents his methodology as a great philosophical innovation. Brandom, by contrast, reconstructs a philosophical tradition in which the work of earlier fellow philosophers is shown to have anticipated his own by making *explicit* various of its central aspects. He "takes the tradition to be rational by a Whiggish rewriting of its history," and in that way "makes the tradition be and have been rational" (14),[6] as he puts it. For Lakatos's argument to work, the scientific episodes he reconstructs must be held rational *prior to and independently of* being found reconstructable by his philosophy. His philosophy is deemed rational not by making the tradition it belongs to "to be and have been rational" but by successfully applying itself to a tradition held to be rational already. But for Brandom, it is by rereading former philosophy in the light of his own, by now fully developed philosophical position that "a distinctively valuable sort of prospective guidance is afforded by a special kind of retrospective insight" (15).

As noted, Brandom's fourth and fifth conceptions of rationality pertain to the two levels of normativity: the inferentialist model, to agents offering and asking for reasons with reference to a given "up-and-running" set of norms or normative framework; the historicist model, to the way the framework to which they are committed rationally supposedly acquires for them its normative force. The kind of reasoning Brandom advocates at the second level is clearly far more contrived and dialectical than the giving and asking for reasons typical of the first level. The reciprocal dependency of the fruits of one's rational reconstructions and the normative statuses they are meant to establish does not map easily onto the strictly linear inferential ordering of commitment and entitlement constitutive of level 1 rational discourse. Brandom admits this in not so many words. The sense in which his own historical essays claim to be correct, "the sense of endorsement for which [they] petition," cannot be "an exclusive one," he explains, because, "it is the thinker who has only one such idiom in which to express and develop his self-understanding who is in thrall." And since thinkers will presumably stand by their self-serving exercises, rather than criticize their tendentiousness, "the best philosophical response to such a narrative," he concludes, is "the telling of *more* such stories . . . motivating other contemporary philosophical undertakings" (16).

All of this is further and more systematically developed in the tripartite reformulation of his entire position offered in his Woodbridge Lectures delivered in 2007 and published in 2009, which is nicely summarized in the closing pages of Lecture 3.[7] It also makes more explicit than in earlier works the self-critical attitude we found implicit in the way our Brandomian doubter conducts herself.

The base level is provided by Kant's account of knowers and agents as freely self-constrained by discursive norms, "as beings who live and move and have [their] being in the normative space of commitments and responsibilities, and so . . . reasons."[8] Responsibility here amounts to "obliging oneself" to rationally integrate one's "new commitments into a unified whole comprising all the other commitments one acknowledges," while undertaking to resolve any material incompatibilities, and acknowledge commitment to any material inferential consequences of one's commitments.[9] As noted at the outset, in order to ensure that normative status is not circularly reduced to normative attitude, that one be genuinely *constrained* by the content of the norms by which one binds oneself, the Kantian "autonomy model of normative bindingness"[10] must presuppose the prior availability of a fully determined conceptual vocabulary that *stands above* normative attitude. As it stands, therefore, this model is incapable of accounting for the determination of normative statuses; they are simply taken as given.

The second level, which Brandom attributes to Hegel, locates normative status socially, in the form of "reciprocal recognition" among knowers and agents. "Someone becomes responsible only when others *hold* him responsible, and exercises authority only when others *acknowledge* one's authority." Hence, the process by which individuals synthesize their rational unities of apperception is "a social process of reciprocal recognition that at the same time synthesizes a normative recognitive community . . . bound together by reciprocal relations of authority over and responsibility to each other."[11] The only forces at play are individual attitudes, and yet "together, the attitudes of myself and my fellows in the recognitive community, of those I recognize and who recognize me, are sufficient to institute normative statuses that are *not* subjective in the same way that the normative attitudes that institute them are."[12]

The third, historical level is introduced with a view to squaring off the perfect symmetry of mutual recognition at the second level, with a similarly symmetrical account of conceptual application and determination. This is achieved, as anticipated in *Tales,* by viewing individual decisions to *apply* concepts in judgment and action while rationally integrating them by "extracting consequences and extruding incompatibilities,"[13] as constitutive of the process of determining the contents of those concepts, analogous to the way in which ongoing process of individual applications of norms by common law judges, when set in a model of mutual recognition, serves to determine the content of those norms for future generation to apply or to reject.

The problem is that, for all its sophistication, Brandom's account of rational norm determination shows no interest at all in processes of norm *changing.* The elaborate grafting of Kant's picture of intrasubjective normative commitment onto Hegel's historicized picture of intersubjective recognition, anticipated in *Tales of the Mighty Dead* and fully worked out in *Reason in Philosophy,* leaves wholly unaddressed the problem of framework *replacement* that so animates Friedman's *Dynamics of Reason,* for example.[14] Subsequently, his account does not involve a comparative element. One does not justify one's normative choices by comparing them to others. But then his is really not an account of norm making at all. Brandom's "historicist rationality" is not about creating or modifying norms but about bestowing explicit normative meaning (or perhaps status) on the endorsement of norms *already held*—at least implicitly. It is not an accident that Brandom's inferentialism had to be fully articulated and endorsed before embarking on *Tales.* In other words, even here, at level 2, the norms in question must be in an important sense an up-and-running (if only implicit) enterprise in order to be rationally justified. Brandom's historicist rationality is not about rationally creating or modifying norms. It is not even about rationally subjecting oneself to an existing norm. People do not become inferentialists by reconstructing an inferentialist tradition. At most they justify being inferentialists by doing so.

Since "historicist rationality" is not about the process of deliberating or even evaluating the choice of norms, it is not surprising that the notion of justification that grounds Brandom's historicist conception of rationality is as wholly devoid of normative reflective self-criticism as his account of inferentialist rationality. As ingenious and compelling a common law judge's account of past rulings or a Brandomian tale of the mighty dead might seem, they are in both cases knowingly construed and crafted to justify, never to challenge, their author's normative commitments. Even in Brandomian retrospect, one does not justify one's normative choices by arguing that they survive the implied *critique* of the mighty dead but by showing that they are to a significant extent partly and positively anticipated in their writings. Brandom's historicist rationality thus remains, as it stands, quite at odds with what McDowell and the present authors consider its very essence. If, as Brandom's text seems to imply, the historicist view of rationality is meant to exhaust the realm of the rational at the level of norm endorsement, one wonders how, from a Brandomian perspective, a person could ever be called upon *rationally* to rethink, let alone jettison, parts of his normative outlook.

In the previous chapter we suggested that Brandom's failure to acknowledge a role for reflective normative self-criticism in the game of producing and consuming reasons—that is, at the level of inferential rationality—attests less to an inherent shortcoming of his system than to a failure on his part fully to appreciate the Kantian view of normativity on which it builds. If there is any truth to the thought experiment concerning our imaginary Brandomian, then acknowledging the place of normative self-criticism in inferential rationality, we have argued, does not require us to modify or even supplement Brandom's philosophy so much as to make explicit something implicitly present at its core. The same, however, cannot as easily be said of level 2. The Kantian approach to agency central to Brandom's thinking entails a healthy measure of awareness both of the freedom involved in explicit normative conduct and, with it, of the possibility of disobeying a norm and erring in its application. The problem is that of itself, the Kantian notion of normative autonomy offers no clear sense of how to articulate rational discontent with a norm. The very freedom to subject oneself, defy, ignore, and even reject a norm does not suffice in and of itself to explain the sense in which doing so can be undertaken for a reason. In relation to what can one even be wary of being *wrong* in one's normative choices or being right in endorsing or rejecting them? Unlike the first-level realm of norm application, here there are no socially embedded (meta-)normative statuses to speak of. With regard to the rationality of norm making and norm changing, Brandom's system, it seems, needs to be supplemented rather than further explicated.

Making Criticism Explicit

To see how this might be possible we shall need to get down to Brandomian basics. By this we mean, to follow his pragmatist lead first in distinguishing between the two sides of what Sellars called "the notorious 'ing'/'ed' ambiguity"—between criticism as the act of criticizing and as the content, the critical uptake, it delivers—and, second, in giving explanatory primacy to the former. Taking our cue from the two basic ideas that ground Brandom's project, we attempt in what follows to understand and explain the limits of what can be achieved by criticism, by appealing to a careful analysis or phenomenology of the *activity* of criticizing, understood normatively á la Brandom as a form of judgment.

Prudent criticism is a particular kind of speech act: a reasoned call aimed at motivating its addressees to acknowledge and to respond to the problems or failings it purports to expose. On a Popperian showing acts of criticism amount to exposing what he calls "problem situations," which he envisages as objective, freestanding features of an agent's circumstances. What harbor problems, we might say abstracting from Popper, are *things* such as theories, instruments, institutions, artifacts, plans, procedures, and strategies, the kind of objects Fisch has characterized in former work as "goal-directed systems."[15] A problem is a system's failure to adequately serve its purpose, a malfunction, if you wish, like a predictive theory's failed prediction. Popper treats problems as facts, facts of a system's substandard performance. And criticism reduces for him to a fact-finding test report, the mere exposure of which is expected to move all involved to action. Heeding criticism becomes for him paradigmatic of rationality exactly because it is conceived as a simple matter of instrumental reason. For what is it to act rationally, if not to ensure that the means we employ adequately serve the goals or interests they are employed to achieve, and when they do not, to act to replace them or to put them right?

What Popper wholly overlooks are criticism's *discursive, personal,* and, most important, *normative* dimensions, each of which renders the picture of rational exchange exceedingly more complex than he and his followers have tended to paint. To begin to see this one needs to distinguish criticizing from a number of kindred concepts.

Between Criticism and Doubt

Criticism sets forth from doubt, it expresses and presupposes doubt, but as activities, as expressive speech acts, criticizing has little in common with doubting. To voice a doubt requires little more than to apply a question mark or to raise an eyebrow. Doubt is a form of wariness, of suspicion due to lack of proof to the contrary. One doubts an assertion or claim not because one has compelling reasons to believe it is false but because one lacks compelling reason to believe it is true. To doubt is to *suggest* the possibility of a better alternative without actually having one. Doubt becomes a problem only where absolute certainty is the norm. In casting doubt, one commits oneself to nothing.

Criticizing is a different matter entirely. If to doubt is to suspect something might be wrong, to criticize is to *argue* that it is. In this sense criticizing consists in more than suspecting, or asserting that, or attesting to there being a problem. It consists in presenting one's reasons for thinking so. To criticize requires one to fashion an argument, to make a case for there being a problem. If to prudently assert is in general to pronounce judgment knowingly prepared to be prompted for one's reasons for doing so, to prudently criticize is to present one's reasons in advance for a particular type of judgment—namely, to the effect that something is amiss.[16] Criticism is an act of *reasoned questioning*. Rorty's ironist doubts her final vocabulary but is allegedly incapable of criticizing it.

In formulating a viable theory of criticism along these lines, the following points are pertinent and shall be variably elaborated in what follows.

Problems Large and Small

To criticize is to argue for the existence of problems. But not every such argument will count as criticism. Arguments knowingly aimed at exposing insignificantly minor, trivial, or inconsequential problems, or problems about which all agree nothing can or should be done, do not count as criticism. To criticize is to argue for the existence of *such problems that should and can be dealt with* either by attending to them directly or by abandoning the systems they plague. But even within the realm of significant problems, criticism is not of a cloth. Criticizing can be more or less serious, more or less devastating, more or less poignant, according to the gravity and urgency of the problems it purports to expose. Hence a theory of criticizing requires a theory of problems rich enough to distinguish between problems relevant and irrelevant, significant and insignificant, large and small, pressing and less pressing, and solutions full and partial. We know of no philosophical account of problems published to date that addresses these issues adequately, let alone treats them as conditions of adequacy for an account of criticizing.[17] We shall have more to say about problems after saying something more about criticizing.

Criticism's Essential Boundedness

Because criticizing requires framing an argument, a critic can only proceed to question by taking true much without question. Presupposing hypothetically will not suffice. Critical arguments are not hypothetical. Rather, they resemble existence proofs. They argue not only that the shortcomings, flaws, or problems they describe follow logically from their premises, but that they exist (and demand attention). Arguing critically purports, then, to be not merely valid, but sound, boasting premises it takes to be (regarded as) true. (This cumbersome qualification is explained below.) To criticize is not to argue that "*if* these premises are (held) true, *then* the system in question must be (deemed) defective" but that "*because* they *are* (held) true, the system in question *is* defective." Because criticizing is a form of questioning that can only be undertaken on the basis of unquestioned true premises (and much background knowledge), criticism can only be undertaken piecemeal.

Popper too, of course, famously speaks of the need to proceed piecemeal in reformative social engineering, but he does so for a different reason entirely. His arguments in favor of piecemeal, as opposed to wholesale, utopian social engineering are moral and have nothing in principle to do with the nature of criticizing as such. Apropos Popper, the system criticized may well be itself hypothetical—a conjectured theory, an entertained plan, an industrial prototype, an experimental institution—but that does not render criticizing it hypothetical. Even when leveled against a tentatively held system, to be effective, a critical argument has to proceed from premises *held true*—even if they are only held true of the system. There is no such thing, we insist, as a critical argument that is not argued from firm commitment.

Criticism as Speech Act

But criticizing amounts to more than merely articulating or pronouncing such an argument. Criticism is what J. L. Austin called a "performative utterance." It is an *addressed* speech act leveled at concrete addressees with a view to prompting them to acknowledge and to attend to a mistake, shortcoming, or problem within the domain of their responsibility. Criticizing can be indirect, such as when arguing against a position with a view to contesting its supporters' loyalty, or to justifying one's opposing it, rather than to inspiring efforts to putting it right. However, if and when such forms of criticizing do end up inspiring acknowledgment of the problems exposed and motivating responding to them, it will be because they are taken as direct criticism at the receiving end. In the paradigmatic case, on which we shall focus, the critical argument is not exploited rhetorically for ulterior motives but is leveled directly with a view prudently to motivating its addressees to take it to heart, that is, to acknowledge and attend to the problems for which it argues. From this simple observation much follows.

Criticism and Self-Criticism

One might think that because it is self-addressed, self-criticism forms but a tiny subset of critical discourse. In a limited sense this is true, but in a different sense, an illusion. Even if self-criticizing does initially form but a tiny subset of prudent criticizing, self-criticizing lies at the very heart of all forms of critical discourse, because stimulating self-criticism is in an important sense the single most important aim of *all* prudent attempts to criticize. For what is the point of direct criticism if not to motivate one's addressee to endorse and take to heart the critical arguments by which one confronts him? The ultimate purpose of prudent critics is to convince their addressees to adopt their arguments and endorse them as acts of self-criticizing.[18]

It follows that when criticizing others, one need not be committed to the truth of one's argument's premises, only to make sure that they proceed from premises one's addressees hold true. The notions of veracity, validity, and gravity involved in fashioning and assessing (prudent) critical reasoning are hence *necessarily* relative — relative, that is, to its addressees' world of discourse.[19] For those who endorse Normative Diversity, it follows that to prudently and effectively criticize requires an ability and willingness to argue from within one's addressees' normative outlook, with a view to motivating them to follow suit[20] — which in turn requires keeping score of one's addressees' relevant commitments and entitlements in precisely Brandom's sense of the term. Prudent criticism thus necessarily brings us squarely up against the problem of internal criticism — whether imagined (by the critic) or real (when successful, by her addressee).

The sort of self-questioning that all direct, prudent criticizing purports to motivate can be thought of as a form of inner reasoning by which one exploits some of one's own commitments and entitlements to examine others, and which proceeds by feats of personal self-scorekeeping within one's personal space of reasons, of a cloth with one's "critical responsibility," as Brandom puts it in later work.[21]

The problem arises, of course, exactly at the point that Brandom leaves off. It is easy to say that one has a critical obligation to "weed out materially incompatible commitments" by "rejecting candidate judgments that are incompatible with what one is already committed to and responsible for, or relinquishing the offending prior commitments." Inconsistent commitments pose a problem that certainly requires attention. And solving it indeed consists in weeding out or modifying those one deems "offending"—be they new or old. However, consistency can be restored in any number of ways. To do so *rationally* is to do so by relinquishing those commitments one has *reason* to deem "offending." The mere fact that two commitments are found incongruous will not suffice to decide which of them be hailed sufficiently normatively problematic to justify dismissal. To do so requires the application of higher-order normative considerations, which in many cases are readily available but in some can pose serious dilemmas. Such higher-level commitments stand to the lower-level commitments in question as framework considerations. And it is in this sense that to rationally synthesize what Brandom calls "a unity of apperception" requires more an obligation to integrate "all of one's commitments in the light of the relations of material inferential consequence and incompatibility they stand in to one another."[22] To be able do so rationally requires, pace Brandom, that one's body of commitments be normatively stratified in a manner wholly unaffected by the reciprocal recognitive Hegelian social context in which it operates.

The problem of normative self-criticism arises, of course, when one's higher-order framework commitments are challenged. Brandom's account does not begin to address this question, because it wholly lacks a dynamic account of rationally becoming, being, and ceasing to be committed. Lacking such an account, he can speak of a responsibility to weed out normative inconsistencies but not of a responsibility to do so *rationally.*

To move forward we need to delve deeper into the pragmatics of criticizing. For it is only by criticism—leveled by ourselves or by others—that commitment can rationally be dislodged and relinquished.

Like all forms of reasoning, the critical argument purports to commit its addressee to endorsing its conclusion. In the case of critical arguments the conclusion is without exception an assertion that a problem exists that requires attention—namely, that it be solved, or that the system it plagues be abandoned—which brings us up against another grossly understudied concept in recent analytical philosophy: that of problemhood.[23] Here too we propose to proceed pragmatically.

The Teleology of Problemhood

What is a problem? In general, problems are not independent, freestanding entities but features, unwanted features of something else, features that stand in the way of that something else being or becoming what we would have wanted or expected it to be or to become. As noted, to capture this essentially teleological aspect of problemhood, we find it useful to think and talk about how we think and talk about problems by means of the idea of a *goal-directed system*—by which we mean any structure, theoretical, institutional, or material, designed or adopted by agents as means to specific ends. A concept, a theory, a plan, a speech act, one's car, a person's German, even works of art are all goal-directed systems. Such systems will be deemed problematic when they fail to live up to their promise. In the broadest possible sense of the term, a problem— any problem—we propose, is defined as the apparent failure of a goal-directed system to fully achieve its intended goals. A problem is an undesired malfunction, dysfunction, defect, inadequacy, or other form of imperfection harbored by such a system—an unwanted *discrepancy,* that is, between what the system is capable of achieving and what it is meant or expected to achieve. We find the teleological dimension of problemhood inescapable, because we cannot think of anything we would be prepared to view as a problem other than in relation to the frustration or partial frustration of some desired objective. Of course, not every such discrepancy will be considered a problem. Imperfection per se is not necessarily problematic. As noted, to criticize is to attempt to give one's addressees reason to believe not only that such a discrepancy exists, but that it should not exist.

A problem is thus construed as an objective feature of a goal-directed system, not as an epistemological category; as a fact of the matter, not as a cognitive state of perplexity or a part of speech, such as a question.[24] And since problems are, by definition, *undesired* features of systems, they are, therefore, *normative* entities. Problems, Brandom would say, are normative statuses of a system, as opposed to the normative attitudes of those who perceive them. A problem may go unnoticed. Problems can be discovered, guessed at, misconceived, overlooked, or misjudged like any other matter of fact. Russell, it seems reasonable to claim, discovered (rather than created) the inconsistency that plagued set theory long before he formulated the paradox associated with his name.

A goal-directed system may be born problematic or be rendered problematic in time due to deteriorating performance, a revision of its goals, or a change of external circumstance (or any combination of the three). Problems of the latter kind can arise intentionally or unintentionally. A social institution, fully capable of doing its job, may become problematic in the event of unforeseen demographic or political changes, just as a formerly successful scientific theory may be rendered problematic by new findings. But systems may be rendered problematic when applied deliberately outside their formerly envisioned domains, as when appliances are intentionally applied to tasks they were not initially designed to perform, or when scientific theories are knowingly applied to phenomena different from those they were originally meant to accommodate. Such a distinction has no bearing on the analysis of problems or problem-solving as such. However, since we are arguing for a theory of rational thinking and acting as thought and action in the face of problems, cases of the latter kind, where action seems to be deliberately taken with a view to raising rather than to resolving problems, will demand special attention.

Problems Solved and Resolved

Taken as unwanted discrepancies between the actual and intended achievements of goal-directed systems, problems will be said to have been fully resolved if the discrepancy is effectively obliterated and partially resolved if effectively reduced. The criterion is qualitative, relative, and local, of course. There cannot be anything like a general shared "metric" of goal frustration that is valid across systems, except in extremely limited and controlled settings, as when the cost-effectiveness of dealing with problems in different products of the same firm is compared.

The weight and urgency of a problem and the viability, effectiveness, and value of the different ways of treating it will ultimately turn on more than the schematic difference between intended and actual performance. Still there is much to be gained by looking at the schematics of problemhood and problem resolution.

Weight aside, not every resolution of a problem can be regarded a *solution*. Problems may be fully or partly resolved by either modifying the system to improve its performance or modifying its goals. The gap between a system's actual and intended objectives can be closed by enhancing the former or lowering the latter. But a problem will be said to have been *solved* or partly solved only when resolved in the former sense, when by suitable modification the system is rendered better capable of achieving its *original* objectives. When dysfunction is eliminated or diminished by an ad hoc reformulation of the faulty system's goals, the problem may be said to have been fully or partly *dissolved* or *mitigated* but not solved. A scientific theory found incapable of accommodating the full range of phenomena to which it was originally meant to apply may be rendered less problematic, or even unproblematic, by an appropriate restriction of its domain of application. But we would not consider this a solution to the problem of accounting for the kinds of phenomena excluded by such a move. When, for example, the representation of the sun, planets, and moons by mass points was replaced in Newtonian astrophysics by solid spheres that better approximated their true dimensions, certain of the problems that beset the original theory were solved. But when, following the advent of relativity theory, classical mechanics was restricted to inertial systems moving relatively to each other at low velocities, it was rendered unproblematic without solving any of the problems it was known to harbor. A medication may be rendered less problematic by restricting its prescription to populations in which it proved safely effective, but in doing so the goal of effectively combating the malady for which it was originally designed is on no count better achieved.

Readjusting goals, and lowering standards in the face of problems, is often done cynically and arbitrarily (as when, some years ago, the Ministry of Education in our country set easier national exams so that the system could boast higher levels of success), but it often represents an agent's candid, sober awakening to the inappropriateness, portentousness, or simple wrongheadedness of the objectives or standards with which he originally set forth. Such cases are highly significant to the concerns of the present study because of the way the critical process of exposing and awakening to problems is seen to prompt normative reassessment. The point to notice is that in cases like these the critical argument is not initially leveled against the norms that are eventually reassessed but against the means for attaining them. Here, standards end up being called into question, not because they are directly perceived to be flawed, but because their *realization, attainment,* or *implementation* prove to be persistently problematic. What critical reflection initially discloses in such cases are not direct *normative* failings but what we shall term below "failures of practice." And it is when they persist that the norms that govern those practices are liable gradually to become suspect.[25]

A Frankfurtian Caveat

But we need to tread more cautiously. As Harry Frankfurt argues, while "the notion of an arrangement of ends and means comprehends both the purposefulness and the rationality that are essential features of our active nature," our understanding of the relationship between means and ends "has to be more spacious and more supple"[26] than it is normally conceived. The target of Frankfurt's perceptive critique is the twofold "fundamental asymmetry" late of Aristotle in the attribution of value to means and ends, according to which (a):

> A means derives its instrumental value from the relationship in which it stands to its end, but an end derives no value from the relationship between itself and the means to it.

And (b):

> A means acquires no terminal value from being useful. The relationship in which it stands to its end can endow a means only with instrumental value. Of course, what has instrumental value may have terminal value as well. But it cannot have the latter by virtue of the fact that it has the former. . . . The fact that something is desirable *for its own sake* cannot possibly be explained, on an Aristotelian account, by its desirability *as a means* to something other than itself.[27]

Frankfurt contests both (a) and (b), blaming them on the undue imper-sonality of the Aristotelian approach, as a result of which attention is diverted from the fact that it is not means that have ends or aims; it is *agents*. For a person to live meaningfully, argues Frankfurt, is for him to live purposefully, to engage "to some considerable extent, in activity that is important to him"; in activity "devoted to something that he cares about."[28] Frankfurt lays the stress on the person's activity rather than on the end to which it is devoted.

> It is not essential that the activity he devotes to the things he cares about be successful. The extent to which a life is meaningful depends less upon how much it accomplishes than upon how it is lived. What counts pri-marily is the extent to which the person cares about the final ends at which he aims.[29]

When placed thus, in the normative, value-laden context of specific agency and volitional preference, the roles of means and ends can be-come subtly reversed. One's final ends are what gives the means adopted to pursue them their direction and purpose, but it is often the case that one selects ends *for the sake of engaging in their pursuit* rather than vice versa. What lends meaningfulness to a person's life might well be the gar-dening rather than the garden, the painting rather than the picture, the deliberation rather than its outcome, playing rather than winning.[30] In such cases, a person's final ends cease in a sense to be final, by functioning as the means or the incentive for engaging in the activity she *really* cares about, namely, the means for achieving them. The means-ends distinc-tion remains, in principle, intact but is indeed rendered "more spacious and more supple," as Frankfurt puts it, and with it so are the notions of problem and problem-solving, criticism and rationality it underlies in our analysis. In cases where means are granted terminal value by virtue of their instrumental value, the system they comprise may be deemed problematic not because they prove ineffective in achieving the systems goals, or because the goals prove unachievable, but because working to-ward those goals in some way loses its appeal. A means can lose its *value* for a person, even when highly successful in achieving its ends. Indeed, paradoxically, a means may lose its appeal because it proves too effective.

An end achieved, or too easily achieved, may be abandoned for no longer posing a creative challenge or for losing its novelty. This essentially normative deficiency is of a kind different from the sort of malfunctions we have so far considered.

Frankfurt's subtle extension of the normative from what a person takes as the norms and duties that bind him to the things he cares about,[31] and from them to caring about them (thus reversing the means-end distinction),[32] requires special attention in the present context. For it is easy to see how a goal or an activity may be rendered normatively problematic in the above sense but less clear as to how realizing such deficiencies can be the outcome of rational, self-critical reflection. Remaining true to one's volitional commitments and preferences, and attentive and (retrospectively) responsive to how they shift and change, is a matter very different from making them the objects of critical scrutiny. It is the difference between being candidly responsive to what one *finds* one cares about and modifying what one cares about *in the face of problems*. In Frankfurt's opinion, the volitional necessities of wholehearted caring are basic. They ground practical reason and are therefore unsusceptible to rational review. "In my judgment," he writes at the outset of his 2004 Tanner Lectures,

> the authority of practical reason is less fundamental than that of love. In fact, I believe, its authority is grounded in and derives from the authority of love. Now love is . . . essentially—at least as I construe it—a volitional matter. In my view, then, the ultimate source of practical normative authority lies not in reason but in will.[33]

However, as we shall argue in some detail in the following chapter, Frankfurt construes rationality somewhat differently than we do. The extent to which volitional preferences of this sort can be scrutinized rationally (i.e., critically) will be discussed there after a richer picture of Frankfurt's account and our own is in place. In the present context suffice it to note that in the light of the original twist Frankfurt adds to the means-ends distinction regarding cases in which the normative roles of means and ends are to an extent reversed, solving a problem may well require modifying or replacing the ends rather than the means.

Problems and Progress

Thus understood, problem-solving gives rise to a system-related understanding of progressive change. In changing from state *A* to state *B*, a goal-directed system will be said to have *progressed* (or to have been upgraded or ameliorated) exactly if problems it harbored in *A* are wholly or partly solved in *B*. Conversely, a system will be said to have *deteriorated* or *regressed* in changing from state *A* to state *B* exactly if it is more problematic in the latter state. In other words, a progressive change is one in which the system's performance is enhanced. To be said to have progressed, it is not enough for a system to be merely less problematic now than it was before. If progress is to represent improved performance, it must involve the (at least partial) solution, not merely the resolution of problems.

These are the straightforward cases in which a modified system's performance is enhanced or impaired. But system performance can be enhanced or impaired in a different way: when the object of modification are its *goals* rather than the means to attain them. Much innovation comes as a result of creatively applying old means to new tasks. Language is constantly expanded by redeploying concepts to new purposes. Current meanings are stretched and supplemented and old words reinvigorated.[34] William Whewell viewed the surprising success of a scientific theory outside its original domain of application as a rare and special virtue, even as a sign of its truth.[35] Conversely, perfectly well-functioning systems are frequently rendered problematic when applied to new and strange domains and purposes. In cases of the former kind something new and positive is obviously accomplished; in the latter, more problems than before now challenge those involved. And yet it seems rather forced to describe the former as cases of *system* enhancement and flatly wrong to deem the latter cases of system mutilation. The discovery that Newton's theory of universal gravity or Fresnel's undulatory theory of light (to take Whewell's two prime examples) enable us, without further adjustment, "to explain and determine cases of a kind different from those which were contemplated in [their] formation"[36] (the tides, for example, in the first case, and double refraction in the second) certainly represents scientific advancement, and arguably lends additional support to the theories in question (though doubtfully the "stamp of truth" Whewell claimed it did).[37] There is nothing in principle to stop one from defining progress in these terms. However, in view of our special focus on reflective action taken in response to problems, it makes better sense to articulate the key terms of the discussion along those lines—as long as nothing vital is lost, of course.

Redeploying a system in the manner described, applying it to a broader set of objectives than before, is a move very rarely taken in response to problems harbored *by that system*.[38] It is normally not considered a corrective move.[39] On the contrary, the deliberate application of a system to new tasks is usually an indication of former successes, a vote of confidence in the light of prior performance, not a sign of weakness, worry, or disappointment.

Bracketing cases of accidental or unwitting redeployment, we may distinguish between two types of deliberate goal extension—deliberated and undeliberated. In deliberated cases a system's goals are extended *for a reason*. Such reasoning will take the form of a twofold argument purporting to explain (a) why the extension to G is desirable and (b) why the system S in question should be considered a viable option for the job. Reasoning thus necessarily presupposes, if tacitly, an essentially critical subargument. To deem G a desired or required objective while seeking means to (better, or more easily) achieve it, clearly implies dissatisfaction with former attempts to do so. In this sense deliberated redeployment *is* a form of action taken in the face of problems, and as such, when successful, represents progress in the sense proposed. However, it is not the system S that is ameliorated, for it is not S that is deemed problematic and hence not S that is criticized. The problem(s) S's redeployment purports to solve reside in the system or systems formerly considered in the pursuit of G—as when methodologies, instruments, procedures, even certain skills are imported from one field to another for specific purposes.[40] Deliberated goal extension is an attempt to apply one system to the solution of a problem found in another. Viewed from the perspective of the system replaced by S, such moves bring to the fore the interesting topic of rational despair and surrender, where the difficulties encountered in deploying a system to the eventuation of a goal are perceived as sufficiently grave to justify radically rethinking the entire project.

Undeliberated goal extension is equally intentional but unlike the deliberated case is prompted, as a rule, by little more than idle, at times playful, curiosity. It is not reasoned action in the usual sense of the term but action motivated merely by a desire to see what happens. This is not as outlandish as it may sound, for it often amounts to much more than mere doodling. In mathematics, for instance, work is not always undertaken in response to or in search of problems. Much mathematics is far more playfully experimental, as when testing modified sets of axioms for coherence and consistency, or searching for symmetries. In the course of such "fishing expeditions," where experts, not driven by problems, cast around creatively in search of interesting results and findings, much is often achieved that is recognized in retrospect as progress in the sense proposed. In the normative realm, Rorty's ironist is playfully experimental in precisely this respect.

The Twofold Neutrality of Problems

Brandom's account of "reasoning, representing and discursive commitment," to quote the subtitle of *Making It Explicit,* rightly boasts neutrality with respect to the diversity of discursive communities and normative forms of life to which it purports equally to apply. His account transcends the particularities of any specific normative framework by resting on what all "concept-mongering creatures" share by virtue of their very discursiveness. Different communities exhibit different vocabularies of conceptual norms differently integrated into different inferentially structured networks that carve up the world and the self differently. These communities combine jointly to constitute the "we" of which his book speaks: the community of sapient creatures who display their rationality by their reasoning and attentiveness to the reasoning of others. The complete generality, and hence universality, boasted by Brandom's theory owes to its grounding in perfectly general notions of concept, assertion, normativity, and reasoning, perfectly distilled of all manner of specific content.

The articulation of problemhood and problem resolution by means of the perfectly general notion of a goal-directed system proposed here lays claim to comparable levels of generality and universality, as do the articulations of progress, criticism, and rationality they entail. There is no such thing as a culture-neutral goal-directed system, just as there is no such thing as a culture-neutral human language or normative framework. Considered, as they are here, as the objects of human reflection and means of human endeavor, all arrangements of means and ends here termed goal-directed systems are, by definition, culture- and context-dependent. And by implication, so are the problems that beset them, the solutions they are given, and the measure of progress they represent. Their essential culture- and context-dependence does not mitigate their objectivity, however. They are at once both as objective and as community-specific as are Brandom's normative statuses. Nonetheless, talk of goal-directed systems in general, the definition of problemhood, and the typology and dynamics of problem resolution in the manner proposed constitutes a meta-language for the discussion of criticism, progress, and rationality that remains as neutral to Normative Diversity[41] as does Brandom's talk of concepts, assertion, and normativity (and is, therefore, capable of supplementing Brandom's system as long as the two are not found to be incompatible).

Such an account of system amelioration renders assessments of progress normatively neutral in yet a different sense. The articulation of problem-solving and progress evaluation here outlined turns exclusively on assessments of the discrepancy between a system's intended and actual achievements. Progress is achieved if, when modified, a goal-directed system is found better capable of accomplishing its intended objectives *whatever they are*—and not, as sometimes urged, when rendered better capable of accomplishing only what are thought to be commendable, virtuous, or fitting goals. Grounding the evaluative appraisal of system enhancement in the value-neutral, means-end logic of problem-solving renders such judgments neutral with respect to *the evaluator's* particular normative outlook. Progress, as we use the term, is an evaluative criterion of system performance in relation to its goals (that is to say, those set by the agent in question), and not an evaluation of them. No contradiction in terms is involved in speaking of problems encountered and overcome and progress achieved in the service of deplorable objectives. And the same applies to rationality—not because it is rational to pursue deplorable goals, but because a deplorable goal can be pursued rationally (as opposed, say, to pursuing it impulsively, or unwittingly). This requires distinguishing between rationally selecting a goal and rationally pursuing it, which in turn requires a better differentiated and less holistic approach to rationality than Brandom's. More on this shortly.

Nonetheless, assessments of problemhood and progress remain value-laden with respect to the norms governing the thought and action of the agents whose treatment or lack of treatment of the system in question is being evaluated. The fact that those working on or with a system take notice of certain problems that they intentionally undertake to solve clearly attests to the value they ascribe to the goals they purport to achieve (deplorable as they are liable to seem to others), which in turn determine the weight and significance they attribute to those problems and the merit they see in their solution.[42] In cases of deliberate troubleshooting our construal of progress retains (if tacitly) the value judgments of the agents under consideration. What remain value-neutral are the evaluator's second-order erotetic assessments of the measure of progress thereby accomplished. These, we insist, premise no more than the abstract logic of problem-solving. Progress assessment does not, of course, necessarily premise prior intent. Problems are frequently solved accidentally, and may well go unnoticed, as when a loose cog is jolted back into place by a bump on the road. Automatic cybernetic devices, to take another example, detect and right malfunctions as a matter of course wholly devoid of human intervention or awareness (although their programming reflects the value-laden intent of whoever employs them). Nonetheless, any retrospective depiction of such accomplishments will invariably involve *someone's* particular context-dependent perspective—be it that of the original designer-user or that of a latter-day narrator. And in all such cases the logic of assessment will remain the same.

Matters are complicated, of course, when progress with respect to one set of objectives entails regress with respect to another. Modifications of a system designed to solve one set of problems may at the same time inevitably give rise to others. Systems may, and usually are, designed simultaneously to achieve a variety of objectives while subject to a variety of constraints, with respect to which modifications may very well be at cross-purposes. Problems of this kind arise all the time, as when balancing the effectiveness of a drug against its side effects, or attempting to improve a product without overstepping budgetary limits. In some cases they are resolved by appeal to a hierarchy of goals determined in advance as part of a higher-level system. Scientific theories, for example, are supposed, among other things, to be both simple and comprehensive, but simplicity is usually sacrificed readily for the sake of comprehensiveness. However, such dilemmas rarely resolve themselves so readily, as, for example, when meeting a deadline, lowering the cost, and guaranteeing the adequate performance of a product are at cross-purposes. What seems to be called for, in such cases, are quantitative rather than qualitative criteria of progress. That is to say, ways of somehow weighing the progress achieved with reference to one set of objectives against the appropriately factored necessary regress it involves with reference to others. Considerations of this kind will always be system- and context-specific.

The Critical Stance

As we have insisted from the start, the kind of activity we consider deemable as rational is the kind undertaken for a reason, consciously and deliberately. In this way we eliminate the obviously nonrational and a-rational, such as the unconscious, unintended, or purely accidental eventuation of desired goals. On the other hand, it would be equally wrong to consider rational all conscious deliberation invoked in the pursuit of goals. For as Polanyi famously argues, conscious deliberation can at times be seriously detrimental.

> Subsidiary awareness and focal awareness are mutually exclusive. If a pianist shifts his attention from the piece he is playing to the observation of what he is doing with his fingers while playing it, he gets confused and may have to stop. This happens generally if we switch our focal attention to particulars of which we had previously been aware only in their subsidiary role.[43]

It is simply not the case that action reflected upon is always preferable to acting unthinkingly. Situations abound in which to reflect on what one's doing is decidedly *not* the rational thing to do. And there are certainly

situations in which, though not detrimental, doing so is blatantly superfluous or inappropriate, as when questioning the application of a perfectly well-functioning system, or pondering a failing one while (knowingly) lacking the minimal qualifications to do so. Gray areas abound.
But in the first instance it makes sense to limit our focus to cases in which
a conscious appeal to reason is justified, where the pursuit or consideration of a goal *requires* it. These will typically be cases in which more than
one viable line of pursuit is available or in which one suspects that the
one selected is liable to prove insufficient. In the former case, the agent
will be required to assess, compare, and subsequently choose between alternative lines of approach;[44] in the latter, to deal with a possibly problematic one. In both, reflective attention is required. In the former, to act
rationally is to assess the relative suitability of each system in order to select the least problematic; in the latter, in the absence of alternatives, to
critically assess the system in hand, with a view to attending to the problems exposed. Hence, again, the inherent and defining relationship between rationality and criticism.[45]

Criticizing versus Testing

Back, then, to criticism. We have so far exposed some of the discursive
and personal dimensions of criticizing. We now turn to what we take to
be criticism's most distinctive feature, at least from the perspective of the
present study, namely, its inherently *normative* dimension. One way to see
this is by distinguishing between the criticizing and the act most closely
related to it, that of testing—a distinction that, to the best of our knowledge, is nowhere made in the literature and that some readers may find
a little forced at first.

   Testing is, of course, part and parcel of the critical process, but not all
testing is performed with a view to criticize, and not all test results, grave
as they may be, amount to criticism. When subjecting one's car to an an-
nual checkup, or when a pilot runs through her preflight checklist, criticism simply does not seem the right term to use, even when something is
revealed to be seriously amiss. Test results amount to criticism, we suggest, not when used to prove *something* wrong but only when used, in addition, to prove *someone* wrong or to warn *someone* off. When a physi-

cian calls a person's eating habits to task in the light of his blood work, she will be criticizing, but if she diagnoses his condition and recommends a new course of medication or a change of lifestyle, she will have been testing and mending, not criticizing. Systems are tested, but it is agents who are criticized.

Criticism as a speech act amounts, then, to more than an attempt to stimulate someone to attend to a problem by merely pointing it out and advising or even pleading with him to do so—as when one is urged by one's accountant to cut one's overhead. Criticism, we submit, aims at provoking a person to do so by proving him to have been in some sense *wrong:* irresponsible, neglectful. In addition to exposing a system's malfunction, criticism purports to *accuse its addressee* of substandard performance. Hereby lies criticism's essentially *normative* import; its inherent element of blame or reproach, its implicit demand for self-reckoning. When called upon to attend to a system in response to worrying test results, one is being made responsible for putting them right. But when called upon to do so in response to criticism, one is being held in some way responsible for it going wrong.

In other words, all criticism, even the most technical, involves an inherent and defining element of rebuke, an element of *normative* criticism, if you wish; a call, not merely to mend or abandon the system in question but also to *mend or abandon one's ways.*

Criticism's normative element comes in two importantly different varieties, however. Much of the time one is chided for being inattentive, careless, or neglectful of what one knows to be right. What critics find problematic in these cases is the *application* of one's norms, not the norms themselves. "Given the standards you abide by, this shouldn't have been allowed to happen," they argue; "given those standards, it would be wrong of you to even consider this an option"; "given what you stand for, how could you remain silent?"; and so forth. Here the normative component of criticism amounts to holding us unproblematically to our standards and calling us to task for not properly living up to them. Cast in Brandom's terms, such criticism reduces to questioning a person's *entitlement* to act or refrain from acting in certain ways *in the light of* his prior (normative) commitments. We say "unproblematically," not because such criticism is always easy—it is certainly not—but because framing and self-framing such an argument poses no philosophical problem. In such cases, one is not criticized for the norms one purports to abide by but for failing adequately to abide by them. Such criticism straddles the space between normative status and attitude, valued practice and its interpretation, scientific paradigm and science as practiced, and so on, and as such is articulable in terms fully acceptable by its addressee.

But at times what we are criticized for are not deviations from the order we are supposedly committed to but for being committed to it in the first place; not the substandard use to which we put the norms we adhere to, but our very adherence to them. Accounting for this form of normative criticism goes to the heart of the connection between rationality and normativity, reason and commitment. If our basic commitments ultimately determine our reasons, how can *they* be held accountable to reason? If all criticism is inherently normative, and if to be normative, it must hold its addressees to *their* standards, in what sense can those standards be deemed self-criticizable? By what standards? We shall return to a detailed analysis of this form of normative criticism in the course of chapter 8.

To recapitulate: criticism is a part of speech, a speech act that always has some system *S* as its subject matter, and is always addressed to or directed at some person or people *P*. When leveled prudently, criticism purports schematically to make a fourfold claim:

to argue:	(i)	that <u>S is flawed,</u>
and that given	(ii)	<u>S's importance to P, or P's caring for S,</u>
and	(iii)	<u>the gravity of the problems allegedly exposed from P's perspective,</u>
	(iv)	<u>P should have done something about it.</u>

To be effective, all four elements must make their mark. Unless *P* can argue convincingly that his critics' diagnosis of *S* is wrong, that *S*'s condition is no concern of his, that *S*'s shortcomings are known and are inconsequential, or that *S* is simply not his responsibility, not heeding their criticism will be deemed irrational by his critics.

To be effective, a critic must be considered *right* in all these respects, at least to a meaningful extent, at least by *P*. But there is yet another side to her being effective, a side that will bring us closer to the heart of the matter—namely, cases in which *S* represents *P*'s very standards.

Comrades, Critics, and Strangers

Aphorism 1:6 of *Pirkei Avot*, the Mishna's Book of Principles, states, "Choose yourself a master; acquire yourself a friend." In commenting on the aphorism, *Avot de-Rabbi Nathan* A, 8, presents a touching account of friendship much in the spirit of Walzer's theory of the member critic:

> What is meant by "Acquire yourself a friend"? It teaches us that one should acquire a friend with whom one can eat and drink, with whom to read and reread, with whom to sleep, and with whom one can candidly share one's hidden thoughts—one's secrets of Torah, as well as one's worldly secrets.

And the reason a person needs such close and intimate friends, the text goes on to explain, is not for the cozy solace of companionship, but because

> when two such comrades study Torah together, if one of them should err regarding a matter of law, or a premise; wrongly pronouncing the pure impure, or the impure pure, permitting the forbidden, or forbidding the permitted, his comrade will mend his mistake—as it is said: "Two are better than one.... For if they fall the one will lift up his fellow." (Eccl. 4:9)

To which Version B adds:

> But a student who sits and studies alone, if he errs on a matter of law—wrongly pronouncing the pure impure, or the impure pure—if he has no friend to mend his mistake, of him it is said: "Woe to him who is alone when he falls; for he has not another to help him up." (Eccl. 4:10)

Self-criticism, this remarkable passage implies, is something that people are not very good at. Serious, informed, objective criticism is what real friends are for. It is the greatest gift a person can give to another, precisely because it is something people cannot effectively perform alone. But the text suggests more than that, namely, that effective criticism requires considerable levels of intimacy and trust, that it can *only* come from someone close. (Version B, by the way, speaks of marriage in this context, and in the very same terms.) As we have already seen, to be effective, critics have to be privy to the way those they criticize think, to have a good sense of what they hold true and what they consider a problem, what they deem important, and what they care about (the allusion to Frankfurt is indeed deliberate). But the kind of intimacy and closeness the rabbinic text implies far exceeds being merely well informed. The text offers what might be described as a personal, one-on-one version of Walzer's theory of social criticism. Walzer focuses on social criticism. His interest lies in forms of criticism capable of motivating entire communities to reconsider their ways and on the kind of critic capable of inspiring significant social change. The rabbinic text, by contrast, draws attention to the most personal level of critical discourse, at which individual agents are confronted and urged to take responsibility for their mistakes and oversights. At this level, the rabbinic text implies, one needs to be close, sympathetic, and trusted in order to be heard.

True friendship, it also implies, is a tricky business, because the intimacy of such a close relationship is easily spoiled by too much criticism; and effective criticizing, by too much intimacy. Insofar as the point of acquiring a friend is to acquire an effective critic, friendship, the rabbis teach, is a delicate line to toe. It is an observation at once both psychological and cognitive. The well-placed critic always dithers delicately between getting too close and maintaining her distance, between standing near and stepping back, between the ability to scrutinize a system through the eyes of her friend and retaining her own voice and perspective.

But Walzer and Rabbi Nathan both seem to fail to fully appreciate the most important aspect of the closeness prudent criticizing must achieve. They emphasize the intimacy, the solidarity, and the trust it requires, and stress the importance of membership and comradeship respectively. But the really tricky and less natural part of getting close in criticizing is the self-distancing involved in attempting to assess a system's performance from someone else's perspective—someone with whom one disagrees, for criticism always involves some measure of disagreement. It is a self-distancing born of the sort of empathetic understanding R. G. Collingwood viewed as central to the historian's ability to appreciate the "logic of question and answer" that motivated those he studies;[46] the straddling sort of understanding Gadamer so deftly problematized and articulated. The real achievement of effective criticizing is a "fusion of horizons," but in a sense somewhat different from Gadamer's—namely, the ability to think and reason like somebody else, not in order to identify with, to interpret, or to understand that other person's world, but in order to stand back and call it to task.

But is the kind of social and personal comradeship of which Walzer and Rabbi Nathan speak as indispensable to the effectiveness of prudent critics as they maintain? Prudent criticizing is never an end in itself. As noted previously, the whole point of prudent criticism is to provoke self-criticism. If it does not succeed in doing so, if its addressees remain unmoved, it will have achieved nothing. It is important, therefore, to consider criticizing from the point of view of its receiving end, for it is in normative self-criticism that the challenge addressed by the present study truly lies.

Walzer and Rabbi Nathan strongly suggest that, at both the social and personal levels, the intimacy of members and close friends is essential for criticism to be effectively leveled, endorsed, and interiorized. Needless to say, a critical argument will not be endorsed and adopted as self-criticism if not deemed sound—and if not deemed *truthful,* its soundness will not even be considered. It is also true that members and friends are usually considered more trustworthy in this respect than most. Nonetheless, friends and members, sincere and well meaning as they may be, are often too blinkered to be effective critics, especially with respect to foundational problems. Their closeness normally ensures better acquaintance than most with the world, work, and standards of their colleagues, which better places them to notice certain, usually minor failings in the way their addressees proceed. But with regard to basics, the more standards and norms she *shares* with those she criticizes, a critic's closeness and involvement is a real disadvantage. Friends and fellow members may be better situated than most for effectively criticizing *deviations from* the existing shared order, but for criticizing the existing *order itself,* their very closeness is a serious impediment.

Indeed, much of the most effective criticism of the latter kind is leveled not by comrades and friends at all. The sharp, devastating critiques of the religious, social, and political orders offered by the likes of Feuerbach,

Marx, and Nietzsche are not, and do not even pose as, leveled in friendly solidarity from within those orders. On the contrary, they are outspokenly antagonistic and aim openly to overthrow them. Yet, despite their obvious animosity, they have proven significantly effective with regard to many, even to the point of igniting rebellion.

Walzer realizes this but refuses to consider such effective-though-unconnected critiques as social criticism at all. "In a sense," he writes, "Marxists are not properly called critics of bourgeois society, for the point of their politics is not to criticize but to overthrow the bourgeoisie."[47] Social criticism, he states, requires distance, a stepping back from certain aspects of one's society but not from society as a whole. Stepping too far back, to the point where a critic's undercommitment to his own society morphs into abstract "philosophical detachment" or a "treasonous" over-commitment to a "some theoretical or practical other," claims Walzer, transforms critics into enemies, and "an enemy is not recognizable as a social critic; he lacks standing."[48] Arguments purporting to prove the existence of *fatal* problems, he thinks, do not count as *critical* arguments at all but as assaults on the system from without. He considers connected fatal criticism a contradiction in terms. Fatal critics are by definition enemies, who by arguing as they do locate themselves beyond the pale of viable argument from within.

In one sense Walzer and Rabbi Nathan are obviously right: for criticism to be effectively endorsed, it must strike an authentic chord. Even if the demand for personal nearness, solidarity, and intimacy is rejected, and effective yet socially or personally unconnected criticism is allowed, the unconnected critic's picture of the system criticized cannot afford to be *uninformed*—which is all the more true, the more radical the critique. Outsiders are often more readily heeded than friends, colleagues, and members because of their ability to notice failings to which insiders are blinkered. Socially connected critics are ill-placed for the type of out-of-the-box thinking typical of the more radical forms of criticizing. Despite their decided nonmembership, Feuerbach, Marx, and Nietzsche were deeply informed critics who took an enormous interest in the systems and societies they criticized and knew them through and through. Their effectiveness as critics owes to the perceived intimacy of their knowledge and the penetrating diagnoses, an intimacy that has nothing to do with the *solidarity* of membership or friendship. Walzer's and Rabbi Nathan's mistake is to conflate the two, or at least view the latter as a precondition for the former. To be effective, critics must be perceived as close, but their closeness, in this context, we insist, pace Walzer and Rabbi Nathan, is primarily an epistemological rather than a social or psychological category. What they say must be perceived as trustworthy, reliable, and knowledgeable, where they stand, especially in the case of radical criticism, is, we submit, largely beside the point.

Walzer's reluctance to treat radical criticism as criticism runs deeper, however, than questions of trust, standing, and credibility. It has to do with what they have to offer. Radical criticism deviates too sharply from Walzer's interpretivist construal of the critical *argument*. From an interpretivist perspective, the sort of problems normative criticism professes to expose are discrepancies between a society's scheme of values and the concrete conception of the good life embodied in its texts, practices, and institutions. Since the former purports faithfully to interpret the latter, normative problems reduce to failures of interpretation. Walzer understands the radical critiques of Marx and Sartre not to be interpretive challenges at all but challenges to their addressees' conception of the good life itself. Theirs are not demands to live up to the norms embodied in their addressees' practiced form of life, but to keenly question them. As such, their critiques lack the "standing" necessary to be heeded. To normatively question the interpretive subject matter of a community's scheme of values is, for Walzer, not a critical act of reasoned, grounded questioning but an aggressive act of ungrounded dismissal.

Although we cast our lot, to a significant degree, with the interpretivists in ethics (along with its Brandomian equivalent in normativity and semantics), we insist that normative criticism not be confined to the interpretive (or, in Brandom's case, the expressivist) project of making a form of life explicit, and that it be applicable from within, in noncomparative fashion, to the form of life itself. If framework replacement can be rational, room must be made for effective radical normative criticism.

But the important point is that to place the onus of rationality on criticism, as we do, is to ultimately locate the transformative drama of rational deliberation in the realm of intrapersonal rather than interpersonal discourse. Indispensable as the public participation in the game of giving and asking for reasons is to rationality, it is in the processes of *self-scrutinizing* that rationality properly resides and asserts itself. If the making and changing of norms can be undertaken rationally, then the space it occupies is that of reasoned normative self-questioning. Such questioning can be, and often is, undertaken directly. But for reasons implied above and elaborated below, we are not very good at self-criticism, and wholly incapable of normative self-criticism, unless, as we shall argue, we are questioned by others.

None of the thinkers we have so far considered, goes beyond the interpersonal. But then, none of them identify the rational with the critical as centrally as we do. Whether the problem of normative rationality can at all be solved along the lines and within the boundaries we have set ourselves can only be determined by taking a closer look at the nature and limitations of the self-reflecting single agent. To this end we turn to one of the most influential writers on normativity, rationality, personal identity, and agency in recent years, Harry Frankfurt.

CHAPTER EIGHT

The Achievement of Self-Criticism

The Critical Moment

The final end of all rational discourse is the transformative moment of successful self-criticism, which reaches its high point, we would like to think, when self-applied to one's very standards of thought and action. Normative self-criticism is also the ultimate form of criticism from within, the should-be culmination point of Walzer's project (and for that matter, also of Brandom's) that interpretivists have yet to take beyond the social (and Brandom and Taylor,[1] beyond the interpersonal). In self-criticizing too, a certain balance between closeness and remoteness must be struck, but it is the reverse, mirror image of the sort of such balance characteristic of prudently criticizing others. Here too a measure of self-distancing and self-detachment is centrally involved but to a profoundly different end from when criticizing someone else. When criticizing another person, the critic creates distance from herself in an attempt to *emulate* the other person's perspective and way of thinking. Second-guessing others is not always easy, but it is something we do habitually, and not only to criticize. "Deontic scorekeeping," Brandom's term for the check we regularly keep on our fellow discussants' commitments and entitlements, forms the cornerstone practice that grounds his entire picture of "mind, meaning and rationality." One does not have to be a Brandomian inferentialist to acknowledge this, or a Walzerian interpretivist to realize that the better informed people are of their addressees' culture and scheme of values, the easier such feats of self-distancing as required in criticizing others are.

The self-distancing required in self-criticism, however, is a different matter entirely. Here one aims not at second-guessing and emulating someone else's way of thinking but at gaining a detached perspective on one's own. This cannot be achieved, as in ordinary criticism, by purporting to adopt someone else's perspective. All that would entail is the realization that that other person sees things differently. Self-criticizing requires being of two minds, literally—both of which are one's own!

We can now begin to better appreciate how important trustworthy critics can be. If we deem our critics sincere, even if we do not accept their criticism, we will be deeming *their* account of how *we* think an honest portrayal. We may judge them to be wrong perhaps, to have mistaken us for someone we are not, but, if we deem them sincere, we shall have to admit that others see us differently than we see ourselves. And the better acquainted those others are perceived by us to be, the more disturbing and humbling the discrepancy. Criticism becomes effective when a person's critics' portrayal of him is at least partly endorsed to the at least partial rejection of his own self-portrayal. That is the *transformative* critical moment, we shall be arguing in detail in what follows, the moment in which a person's mind is changed about itself by internalizing someone else's picture of it.

But first to self-reflection. We self-reflect constantly, acquainting ourselves with what we deem true and right by making explicit and then applying the norms and standards that underlie and underwrite our self-assessment. Many stress the inherently self-critical dimension of self-reflection, but most limit it, as does Brandom in his recent work, to troubleshooting the unity of one's commitments for clarity, coherence, consistency, and priority.[2] But, as Harry Frankfurt argues, normative self-criticism can extend much further, in ways that involve unsettling levels of self-detachment, self-estrangement, and even self-alienation. Frankfurt's much-discussed "mesh" account of free will, especially his grounding of personal identity, rationality, and normativity on a firm distinction between first- and higher-order desires, sets forth from an insightful account of both the threatening and prized features of self-reflection.

Normative self-criticism, if not in the full sense sought for in the present study, is central to Frankfurt's picture of agency and rationality, although he leaves it a largely unanalyzed phenomenon of self-management. In what follows we take Frankfurt's influential picture as our point of departure, not only because of the major role it plays in so much recent discussion of questions of agency and normativity,[3] but, as will become apparent, because of the way it interestingly reflects and extends to the intrapersonal major themes of the collectivist, interpersonal accounts of normativity with which we have so far been dealing.

Here is how Frankfurt introduces the profits and perils of "our peculiar knack of separating from the immediate content and flow of our own consciousness . . . which enables us to focus our attention directly upon ourselves."[4]

> When we divide our consciousness in this way, we objectify to ourselves the ingredient items of our ongoing mental life. . . . We are then in a position to form reflexive or higher-order responses to [our conscious mind].[5]

According to Frankfurt, our higher-order responses enable us far more than self-awareness. They render us keenly self-critical, and normatively so.

> We may approve of what we notice ourselves feeling, or we may disapprove; we may want to remain the sort of person we observe ourselves to be, or we may want to be different. Our division of ourselves situates us to come up with a variety of supervisory desires, intentions and interventions that pertain to the several constituents and aspects of our conscious life.[6]

However, our capacity "to divide and objectify ourselves" is both a blessing and a curse. On the one hand:

> It accounts for the very fact that we possess such a thing as practical reason; it equips us to enjoy a significant freedom in the exercise of our will; and it creates for us the possibility of going beyond simply wanting various things, and coming instead to care about them, to regard them as important to ourselves, and to love them.[7]

But at the same time, the very same "division within our minds . . . generates a profound threat to our well-being."

> The inner division that we introduce impairs our capacity for untroubled spontaneity. . . . It exposes us to psychological and spiritual disorders that are nearly impossible to avoid . . . [and] can be seriously disabling. Facing ourselves, in the way that internal separation enables us to do, frequently leaves us chagrined and distressed by what we see, as well as bewildered and insecure concerning who we are. Self-objectification facilitates both an inhibiting uncertainty or ambivalence, and a nagging general dissatisfaction with ourselves.[8]

Both forms of self-alienation—our frequent uncertainty or ambivalence "about whether we really ought to care as we do about what we care about," on the one hand, and the "nagging" similarly frequent realization "that we have desires and inclinations, that we really would prefer *not* to have," on the other, as Buss and Overton note[9]—preoccupy much of Frankfurt's extensive writing on moral responsibility, human agency, and love. Discerning who we really are and deliberating who we want or ought to be, jointly define his Janus-face project of "Taking Ourselves Seriously" and "Getting It Right," to quote the titles of his two recent Tanner Lectures. As noted, both are decidedly self-critical, normative undertakings. However, in all Frankfurt has written on these issues, both undertakings—that of discerning who we are and who we want and do not want to be—are depicted as purely personal and private, belonging wholly within the confines of a person's inner dialogue. Nowhere does he address the possible bearing on them of the person's critical interaction with others.[10]

Cast in Brandom's language, Frankfurt, we might say, advocates a sort of insulated, inner, two-tiered process of volitional self-scorekeeping, which is not part of, or a continuation of, a wider, intersubjective give-and-take. At one level, the shape of the will and the limits of our autonomy are determined by taking volitional stock of our feelings and desires, attitudes and motives, and dispositions to act in certain ways. Then, the foundations of normativity are laid down by a similar process of volitional selection determined by what we find we care about.[11] We take responsibility for our "psychic raw material" by "developing higher-order attitudes and responses" by which "we disrupt ourselves from an uncritical immersion in our current primary experience, take a look at what is going on in it, and arrive at some resolution concerning what we think about it or how it makes us feel."[12]

"Resolutions" of this kind consist in selectively identifying with certain of our attitudes, desires, and dispositions, and making them our own, while rejecting and externalizing those with which we refuse to identify. To identify with the former is to "recognize them as grounds for deciding what to think or what to do," while externalizing the latter is, by contrast, to "deny them any entitlement to supply us with motives or with reasons."[13] Formulating the last clause positively, identification is what constitutes us as agents, or as Frankfurt puts it in response to Moran: "It is Identification that indispensably constitutes the source and the ground of reasons."[14]

The analogy to Brandom's score-keeping model of intersubjective discourse is not perfect, but neither is it as forced or far-fetched as it might seem. Frankfurtian identification is an ongoing twofold process that brings to the fore both senses of the word. A person first identifies *what* his attitudes and inclinations are—a process akin to *making them explicit*—and then identifies *with* some and alienates himself from others—that is to say, endorses some and rejects others. Frankfurt thus describes a vibrant, hierarchical, reflective self working self-critically to draw its volitional boundaries in a manner that interestingly bears at least a structural resemblance to Brandomian discourse. As will become apparent, the way he analyzes normativity and (volitional) rationality in terms of means and final ends bears a suggestive affinity, as well as poses an interesting challenge, to our similar use of goal-directed systems. However, the problems Frankfurt's work addresses are different from the concerns of the present study. He is not centrally concerned with articulating rationality,[15] and his interest in normativity touches only very briefly (and negatively, as we shall see) on the question of normative criticism.[16] In fact, although his account of agency is centrally critical, and normatively so,[17] he seems largely uninterested in the problem of normative self-criticism per se and quite indifferent to the relations it might bear to criticism from without. His system will therefore serve us in what follows less as a resource than a template.

Toward a Frankfurtian Analysis of Normative Criticism

In addition to first-order desires to perform certain actions to achieve certain goals, people are depicted by Frankfurt as possessing higher-order desires that determine which first-order desires they want, along with higher-order volitions that decide which first-order desires they want to be their will.[18] Incoherence can be experienced in two ways: in cases of conflict between a person's first-order and higher-order desires and in cases of ambivalence within the latter. Bad habits typify the first kind of incoherence. A person whose second-order desire is to lose weight or to stop smoking, who wants those desires to be what effectively motivate his behavior, may find himself in the grip of an irrepressible first-order desire too strong to control to indulge in dessert or take a cigarette. It becomes his will, as it were, but *against* his will. In such cases his "will is not under his own control. It is not the will he really wants, but one that is imposed on him by a force with which he does not identify and which is in that sense external to him."[19]

A goal-directed system found wanting in this respect is one whose goals and/or means are at odds with the higher-order normative commitments of those responsible. Criticism along such lines, however, is of little interest in the present context. For at most it calls into question the agent's inability to implement her wholehearted normative choices, not their normative worth. What is exposed are difficulties in *norm application,* not the presence of defective norms. And bracketing the natural embarrassment of having one's weaknesses exposed, it is a form of criticism that does not pose a problem, for it is easily acknowledged and easily endorsed (even if not always as easily acted upon).

Nonetheless, though not directly indicative of a normative failing, persisting "failures of practice," enduring difficulties in applying norms, can often lead, as frustration mounts, to doubts regarding the norms themselves. Repeated failure to achieve a goal, to realize one's love, or to implement a norm often leads to a weakening of commitment and even to its abandonment. The question, of course, is how to distinguish between mere rationalizing, that is, unwillingly giving in to a weakness and rationally cutting one's losses. Most situations are not as clean-cut as addiction. In both cases, identification with a higher-order volition is repealed by first-order considerations. Indeed, the truest of loves—Frankfurt's paradigm of wholehearted normative commitment—is always liable to lose its appeal and even turn sour as a result of first-order failures of practice. And since Frankfurt is reluctant to treat such internal conflicts as *reasoned* deliberations (explicitly rejecting his critics' suggestions to do so),[20] we shall need in what follows to go a step beyond him. However, whether rationally, irrationally, or a-rationally, a higher-order volition repealed is a higher-order volition rendered (at least) ambivalent, which brings us to Frankfurt's second category of volitional conflict, and with it to his important notion of volitional wholeheartedness.

This second kind of incoherence occurs within "the volitional complex with which the person identifies and wants his behavior to be determined,"

> when there is a lack of coherence within the realm of the person's higher-order volitions themselves. . . . It is not a matter of volitional strength but of whether the highest-order preferences concerning some volitional issue are *wholehearted*. It has to do with the possibility that there is no unequivocal answer to the question of what the person really wants . . . because the person is *ambivalent* with respect to the object he comes closest to really wanting. . . . In the absence of wholeheartedness, the person is not merely in conflict with forces "outside" him; rather, he himself is divided.[21]

In Frankfurt's view, volitional ambivalence poses a graver threat to the self than conflicts of the first kind. They indicate ruptures in the self's "inner cohesion or unity."[22] Care and love lie at the core of Frankfurt's account and define at any moment the self's stable hard core of wholehearted commitment. They do so not by virtue of the approval of yet higher-order volitions but because caring and love signal in and of themselves the very boundaries of the will.[23]

> What people cannot help caring about . . . is not mandated by logic. It is not primarily a constraint upon belief. It is a volitional necessity, which consists essentially in a limitation on the will.
>
> There are certain things that people cannot do, despite possessing the relevant natural capacities or skills, because they cannot muster the will to do them. Loving is circumscribed by necessity of this kind: what we love

and what we fail to love is not up to us. Now the necessity that is characteristic of love does not constrain the movements of the will through an im-
perious surge of passion or compulsion by which the will is defeated or
subdued. On the contrary, the constraint operates from within our own
will itself. It is by our own will, and not by any external or alien force, that
we are constrained.[24]

Or as he puts it in mildly (if typical) oxymoronic fashion elsewhere: The
difficulty for someone thus constrained "is that he cannot organize himself
volitionally in the necessary way. In attempting to do so, he runs up against
the limits of his will. . . . For him willing to perform it is unthinkable."[25]

Normativity and "the Contingent Necessities of Love"

Most important for the present context, according to Frankfurt, the
volitional necessities manifest in caring and loving are the sources of
normativity.

> The origins of normativity do not lie . . . either in the transient incite-
> ments of personal feeling and desire, or in the severely anonymous re-
> quirements of eternal reason. They lie in the *contingent necessities* of love.
> These move us as feelings and desires do; but the motivations that love
> engenders are not merely adventitious or (to use Kant's term) heterony-
> mous. Rather, like the universal laws of pure reason, they express some-
> thing that belongs to our most intimate and most fundamental nature.
> Unlike the necessities of reason, however, those of love are not imper-
> sonal. They are constituted by and embedded in structures of the will
> through which the specific identity of the individual is most particularly
> defined.[26]

Frankfurt's grounding of normativity in necessities that are volitional
in both senses of the term—namely, *willed* necessities *of* the will (or
in Bratman's words, "necessities in the sense that involves wholehearted
support")[27] powerfully captures the way "reflective endorsement"—to
use Korsgaard's suggestive phrase—grounds normativity for Kant.[28]

Frankfurt does not share what Brandom terms Kant's "regulism about norms,"[29] although he is yet to respond to Korsgaard's interesting suggestion that the very logic of caring and loving "commits us to universal shared values, and so to morality," and hence to the Kantian extension of Kant she argues for in *The Sources of Normativity*.[30] Frankfurt agrees that the objectivity and authority of the principles of morality derive from the fact "that they elaborate and elucidate universal and categorical necessities that constrain the human will." However, in all he has written to date, he insists, contrary to Korsgaard's suggestion, that they do so (when they do so), not because they are necessarily implied by or presupposed in the logic of caring, but because they are wholeheartedly *endorsed*.[31]

However, the value of Frankfurt's account for the discussion of normative *criticism* is untouched by questions concerning the precise relationship the truths of morality bear to the necessities of the will. Our own commitment to Normative Diversity places us more on Frankfurt's than on Korsgaard's side of the debate in its present state—taking from Kant the grounding of normativity in free will, as do Brandom, Frankfurt, and Korsgaard, but stopping short of arguing further with Kant, as does Korsgaard, that such grounding suffices to establish our identity not only as individual agents, but universally as Citizens of the Kingdom of Ends.

The entire body of a person's beliefs, feelings, and desires, though all his own, fall, at any one time, according to Frankfurt, in one of three categories: (i) beliefs, feelings, and desires with which he identifies and which he views as authentic expressions of himself; (ii) those with which he does not identify, from which he dissociates himself and treats "as categorically unacceptable, and tries to suppress . . . or rid himself of [them] entirely";[32] (iii) and those to which he is ambivalent, indecisive as to whether he is for or against them. A person's norms and standards derive exclusively from items of the first category. In Frankfurtian terms, successful normative self-criticism can be thought of as an act or a process of *volitional demotion* by which a norm or standard wholeheartedly endorsed is rendered ambivalent or less. But what room can there be in Frankfurt's picture for such direct normative self-criticism? If a person's norms and standards mark the necessary limits of her will, what can it mean for her to find fault in those limits? In what sense can a necessary constraint be found problematic by the person whose constraint it is?

To see if there is any sense in which such a process could be considered rational on a Frankfurtian showing, we need to take a closer look at his reasoning. What a person cares about and loves are what lend his deliberations their direction and provide him with reasons to act. But how do people responsibly determine *what* they should care for and love (and more important from our perspective, what they should *stop* caring for and loving)? Frankfurt devotes the second of his Tanner Lectures to this question. His opening move sounds promising:

> In designing and committing our lives we cannot rely on casual impulse. Our deliberations and our actions must be guided by procedures and standards in which it is *appropriate for us* to have mature confidence. The final ends by which we govern ourselves require authentication by some *decisive rational warrant.*[33]

The problem is that the procedures, standards, and decisive rational warrants that supposedly decide what we *should* care about are determined exclusively by what we *do* care about. They provide powerful normative strictures, but their bootstrapped grounding (to use Barbara Herman's term)[34] would seem to render them immune to criticism. Frankfurt, who warmly deems Herman's characterization of his views "extraordinarily comprehensive and accurate," states in response:

> In my view, there really is no authority for us other than the authority of what we care about—or, more particularly, the authority of love. What we love is what we care about in a way that is not up to us. It is its necessity, together with the fact that it defines our will, that provides it with authority. . . . This has very little to do with reasons or with a response to value.[35]

The point is elaborated further in the Tanner Lectures, where he also addresses most fully the question of the extent and limits of normative criticism.

Normativity is grounded, according to Frankfurt, in two related categories of volitional necessity: the necessary constraints of the *unwillable* and the necessary entailments of love; what we cannot will ourselves to do and what we cannot *but* will ourselves to do. The former entail the strictures of *volitional rationality*. Being volitionally rational "involves being incapable, under any circumstances, of making certain choices," not because we lack the capacity or skill, but because we are incapable of mobilizing the will to do so; because they are unthinkable.[36]

The dictates of wholehearted love, on the other hand, define the normative positively. They determine what we should care about, who we cannot help but being and wholeheartedly wanting to be. More particularly, Frankfurt explains, "love entails two related volitional necessities."

> First, a person cannot help loving what he loves; and second, he therefore cannot help taking the expectation that an action would benefit his beloved as a powerful and often decisively preemptive reason for performing that action. Through loving, then, we acquire *final ends* to which we cannot help being bound; and by virtue of having those ends we acquire *reasons for acting* that we cannot help but regard as particularly compelling.[37]

Taken together, the positive and negative categories of volitional necessity combine, for Frankfurt, wholly and exclusively, to define and ground the normative. To articulate the norms and standards that should guide our thought and action "requires a clear self-understanding and a wholehearted acceptance of the essential requirements and boundaries of our will. This amounts to finding a mature confidence . . . in which the authority of our norms of conduct are grounded[,] . . . a confidence in what we cannot help being."[38]

Getting Ourselves Wrong: Frankfurt on Normative Self-Criticism

Here lies the Frankfurtian intrasubjective analogue to the interpretivist component of Walzer's and Brandom's intersubjective accounts. Normative awareness is a matter of awakening to, articulating, and accepting the necessities implicitly entailed by our volitional makeup. Normative commitment is produced by a process of self-understanding in which the normative uptake of the necessities of will are made explicit. And not unlike Walzer and Brandom, Frankfurt also views it as a process capable of going "absolutely wrong."[39] And not unlike Walzer's picture of social critics disputing their community's normative self-understanding and Brandom's account of possible discrepancies between normative status and normative attitude, Frankfurt's own notion of normative failing is also discouragingly interpretive. When we deem ourselves to be normatively wrong or lacking, it is not our volitional necessities that are condemned but our *account* of them. The only kind of normative failing to which Frankfurt admits are the consequences of *self-misunderstanding*.

Frankfurt's exceedingly brief discussion of normative self-criticism acknowledges a limited and worryingly final repertoire of three classes of possible normative problems. All three derive from the daunting complexity of the "ground of normativity" that owes in part to our common nature as human beings and in part to our particular settings, circumstances, and character. The objects of love, and hence the sources of our volitional necessities, range, according to Frankfurt, from the universal love of living itself,[40] and the "love of being intact and healthy, being satisfied, and being in touch,"[41] to the more particular love of *a* life, *a* particular quality of experience, certain people, certain groups, certain ideals, a certain tradition, and so forth, that combine to give rise to a bewildering and inevitably conflicting array of final goals and motivations to act and refrain from acting. To get ourselves right first requires determining by keen introspection which of the conflicting objects of our love "arouses in us a more substantial interest and concern than the other."[42]

But prioritizing our final goals is not the only objective of normative criticism. We must always be "alert to the possibility that we do not understand the people, and the ideals, and the other things we love well enough. . . . Our loving may turn out to have been misguided because its objects are not what we thought they were."[43] Nor do we always understand ourselves very well. It is not easy for us to know what we really care about or what we really love. "Our motives and our dispositions are notoriously uncertain and opaque, and we often get ourselves wrong. It is hard to be sure what we can bring ourselves to do, or how we will behave when the chips are down."[44]

If this is the extent to which Frankfurt's account of normativity admits of self-criticism, we will not have made much progress. For on such a showing, a person cannot deem himself to be *wrong* in loving X. He may realize that his love for X was misplaced or merely apparent; realizing, after getting to know X a little better that he was mistaking X for something it was not, or realizing that he was mistaking mere infatuation for love. But if the love a person feels for the things he loves wholeheartedly is properly ranked and prioritized, fully informed and true, then, Frankfurt declares, there is no sense in which he can coherently deem himself to be wrong. "There is nothing else to get right," as he puts it.[45]

According to Frankfurt, a person's normative commitments may be found mistaken or misplaced but not normatively wanting; self-criticized for being inattentive to some of the relevant facts but not for being normatively unworthy. One's normative commitments do not remain constant, however. Different things may become important to us in time, and others may cease to be. Even the truest, wholehearted love may fade and dwindle, while other loves bloom and blossom. Yet if well informed, they do so, according to Frankfurt, in a manner uncontrolled and unmotivated by reason. Critical reflection can *disclose* our volitional makeup but cannot modify it at will. At any one time, it is a given, to be discerned, understood, interpreted, and the final ends and standards to which it gives rise, made explicit and prioritized, in much the same fashion as the given communal equivalents in the pictures painted by Walzer and Brandom. Or so it would seem.

But there is a significant difference. The Achilles' heel of Walzer's and Brandom's accounts of normativity is indeed the very givenness of the former's community texts and the latter's normative statuses. Being essentially social-communal realities, in the pictures they paint, individual agents do not produce or modify these givens. They form attitudes toward them, and act accordingly, but leave them untouched.[46] Normative agency is limited in these pictures, to interpreting (making them explicit) by, or with a view to, applying them to concrete situations. Frankfurt's picture of the normativity of reflective individuals is importantly different in this respect. The *interpretanda* of Frankfurtian normative commitment are not social realities (although their ultimate origin may well be social) but the necessities entailed by the inner reality of one's own nature. Although one's desires, dispositions, and tendencies are beyond one's immediate volitional control—in the sense that they cannot be willed in and out of existence by simple acts of will—one's agency with respect to them is not limited merely to understanding and making them explicit. A person is in far greater *normative* control of "the psychic raw materials with which nature and circumstance have provided" him in Frankfurt's account than he is with respect to their social analogues in the work of Walzer and Brandom. For he is able to exercise normative judgment on them by identifying with some and dissociating himself from others. These are acts of profound normative self-criticism. They are a far cry from Rorty's ironist's skepticism as well as from the mere awareness of being able to defy a norm or apply it wrongly, which Brandom so stresses late of Kant. And it goes without saying that troubleshooting desires, thoughts, or inclinations for "categorical unacceptability" is a form of passing normative judgment that far exceeds reviewing them for mere consistency or coherence.

But two distinct and different classes of normative disassociation need to be distinguished in Frankfurt's picture. The acts of identification that Frankfurt forcefully brings to the fore are those in which one rejects a desire or motivation to act by deeming it an external force that is not one's own. Strictly speaking, these are *not* acts of actual normative self-criticism. For although the desires rejected in this way are literally a person's own, they are not counted among the norms and values to which he is *committed*. Their rejection resembles more of a review process by which a "candidate" desire with which he has not yet identified is tested for inclusion among his normative obligations rather than one in which he deems a formerly endorsed value, norm, or standard he does consider his own to be normatively inappropriate. It is the latter cases of actual volitional *demotion*, about which Frankfurt has very little to say, that are of most interest in the present context. He clearly acknowledges their existence, for he considers identification as an ongoing dynamic process in which the volitional boundaries of the self are constantly drawn, reviewed, and redrawn again, and with them those of normative commitment.[47] However, his text strongly implies that volitional demotion, when it does occur, is reducible always to factual rather than normative considerations. According to Frankfurt, we select and rank our goals according to their importance to us, and their importance is gauged exclusively on what we care about.[48] Hence, *what* we care about is for Frankfurt the ultimate factual stopping point of normative self-questioning.

> The most fundamental question for anyone to raise concerning impor-
> tance cannot be the normative question of what he *should* care about.
> That question can be answered only on the basis of a prior answer to a
> question that is not normative at all, but straightforwardly factual—
> namely the question of what he actually does care about.[49]

In one sense, Frankfurt is obviously right. It is impossible to deem anything important that we do not care about (at least indirectly),[50] or unimportant if we do. In this sense the importance of *X* turns wholly and exclusively on whether or not we care about *X*, which *is* a straightforwardly
factual question. However, the passage cited goes a significant step beyond
exploring the relationship between caring and importance. Frankfurt
clearly rules out the very idea of *normatively questioning* what one cares
about; the very idea of a person asking himself, or of him reasoning and
arguing against himself, that he should be caring about something he
does not, or, more important, should cease caring about something he
does. Caring about something, Frankfurt more than implies, is a normative disposition a person simply discovers that he has or is gradually acquiring, a position he simply finds himself in, or is moving toward, but of
whose *formation* he has, and can have, no rational say. A person's first- and
higher-order desires and motivations constantly shift and change, and
with them the identity-defining line between those he desires, wants to
desire, and wants to want to desire. And these in turn generate subtle and
less subtle changes in the complex arrangement of his motivations to act,
in his final ends and the means necessary for achieving them, along with
their mutual dependencies and hierarchies.

But the active role we play in all of this ultimately reduces, according
to Frankfurt, to no more than keen *self-observation*, keen self-monitoring.
Frankfurt would have us believe that the volitional demotion of a desire
to which we are wholeheartedly committed is something we can only be
convinced has *happened to us*, never something we can become convinced
we should do because it is right to do. The transformative moment of normative self-criticism is a moment neither reasoned nor voluntary. It is one
responsible agents will do well to reflect upon and seriously consider. But
it is not a moment *of their doing* on which they can exercise their agency,
for which they can give reasons.

As several of his critics have noted,[51] Frankfurt's rich picture of human identity, agency, and normativity concentrates wholly and exclusively on the drama within. Frankfurt's persons emerge and evolve in a process of identification seemingly oblivious to the world without. The only dialogue he describes them as conducting is with themselves! They reflect, identify, and assess their desires and motivations, goals and limits, loves and obligations, in an intense and continuous process of intrapersonal deliberation, in which they are the sole participants. Frankfurt's persons are nowhere described as forming or questioning their identities and obligations *in conversation* with other people. They are nowhere depicted as doing so as members of communities, or as committed to a shared form of life. It is not as if Frankfurt imagines us as living in isolation, but he more than implies that the *import* of our external social and discursive encounters that is relevant to our inner normative discourse is wholly and ultimately *factual*, never normative.

In one sense Frankfurt's position is understandable, given the insistent opposition he (and we) shares with Korsgaard to what she describes as "the kind of normative realism which holds that 'volitional necessities are a response to an independent normative reality.'"[52] If self-consciousness is the exclusive source of normativity, then intersubjective discourse would seem incapable in principle of having any normative impact. And yet, how can it be denied that we are regularly convinced by critics of being wrong, even gravely wrong, not for failing to understand the situation, or for overlooking or miscalculating the significance of some fact of the matter, but for the quality of our norms and standards, evaluations and normative commitments, and that as a result we very often change our ways—not our descriptions of what we love or our understanding of what we really want, or what our volitional necessities really are.[53]

Frankfurt (like Korsgaard late of Kant) refuses to acknowledge the very coherence of the kind of normative self-criticism the present study seeks to articulate. Caring and loving, he insists, are not acts to which practical reasoning can be said to apply. What we care about and what we consider important provide us with motivations and reasons to act and refrain from acting. Our reasoning is governed and determined by our will, but the opposite is not true. To maintain that it is, that our will can be governed by reason, he argues, is to concede normative realism.

In previous chapters we have suggested (but, so far, have done little more than suggest) that the key to understanding the possibility of normative self-criticism is to be found in the protocritical self-distancing inherent in the element of self-subjection—or, to use Korsgaard's term, the element of "reflective endorsement"—central to the Kantian understanding of normativity. Korsgaard's pointed description of first-order reflection brings the point home vividly.

> [O]ur capacity to turn our attention on our own mental activities is also a capacity to distance ourselves from them, and to call them into question. I perceive, and I find myself with a powerful impulse to believe. But I back up and bring that impulse into view and then I have a certain distance. Now the impulse doesn't dominate me and now I have a problem. Shall I believe? Is this perception really a *reason* to believe? I desire and I find myself with a powerful impulse to act. But I back up and bring that impulse into view and then I have a certain distance. Now the impulse doesn't dominate me and now I have a problem. Shall I act? Is this desire really a *reason* to act? The reflective mind cannot settle for perception and desire, not just as such. It needs a *reason*. Otherwise, at least as long at it reflects, it cannot commit itself or go forward.[54]

Such decisions, writes Frankfurt in an earlier essay, are not only made on the strength of existing norms, but by making them a person's alignment of normative commitment is extended and refined.

> One thing a deliberate decision accomplishes, when it creates an intention, is to establish a constraint by which other preferences and decisions are to be guided. A person who decides what to believe provides himself with a criterion for other beliefs; namely, they must be coherent with the belief on which he has decided. And a person who makes a decision concerning what to do similarly adopts a rule for coordinating his activities to facilitate his eventual implementation for the decision he has made. It might be said, then, that a function of decision is to integrate the person both dynamically and statically. Dynamically insofar as it provides . . . for coherence and unity of purpose over time; statically insofar as it establishes . . . a reflective hierarchical structure by which the person's identity may be in part constituted.[55]

Both descriptions dovetail nicely with the critical dimension of Brandom's (2009) account of self as a rationally synthesized unity of apperception. However, the critical element exposed in our fictitious Brandomian thought experiment of chapter 6 extends beyond the kind of first-order deliberations of which Korsgaard and Frankfurt (and the later Brandom) here speak. Normative criticism is limited here to considering first-order impulses for normative status. Our discussion of Brandom brought to the fore a higher form of self-critical normative deliberation, where the issue is not to decide the normative status of a first-order impulse but to determine whether the norm employed in making such a decision *is properly applied.* Here (motivated with Brandom by Wittgenstein's private language argument) the example of our Brandomian doubter suggested that the context of intersubjective dialogue and mutual scorekeeping with others committed to the same norms is crucial. Reflective intrapersonal dialogue, keen as it may be, is powerless to ponder discrepancies between normative attitude and normative status. Only people engaged in interpersonal dialogue who have different normative attitudes to what they consider to be the same normative status can fruitfully question each other's performance. This is the first and obvious sense in which participating in the public, critical, interpersonal game of giving and asking for reasons can be seen to enhance and normatively enrich in ways that transcend the merely factual, the intrapersonal normative dialogue of self of which Korsgaard and Frankfurt speak.

But normative deliberation does not stop at questions of norm application. Apart from pondering the normative status of a perception or desire, and how to properly apply the norms that bind us in specific contexts, we frequently find ourselves entertaining doubts regarding the norms themselves. Like Rorty's ironist many of us do more than idly wonder whether we should be leading the life we are devoted to, or caring for the things we wholeheartedly deem important. Many of us know with certainty that in different circumstances the life we would be leading and the things we would deem most important would have been *decidedly* different; that the volitional necessities that determine our very identity are determined without remainder by contingent circumstance. Yet at the same time, it seems impossible from a Frankfurtian perspective for such doubts to acquire anything like a critical grip.

In mature reflection the division achieved within the mind is radically asymmetrical. One part, call it the *I*-part[56]—the part with which we are wholeheartedly identified, the seat of our second-order volitions, hence the seat of our norms and values—observes the rest, as it were from a distance, objectifying and evaluating, and acting upon what it "sees" as an inward-directed monitoring device. To an extent, it also monitors itself. But insofar as its own inner reasoning is all it has to go on—and, as already noted, such is Frankfurt's understanding—then the extent of its self-monitoring falls short of actual *normative* self-criticism. The *I*-part may discover that the volitional basis for its endorsing a norm or standard has waned, and no longer entails wholehearted commitment. It may find that although its volitional basis remains intact, it had misconstrued an object of its caring, or its feelings toward it. It may deliberate the placing and ranking of certain norms or standards within the prioritized complex of its normative preferences. But it cannot criticize a wholeheartedly endorsed norm or standard for being normatively *deficient.* On a Frankfurtian showing, in the absence of new *factual* information, when left to its own devices, a person's *I*-part cannot, on its own accord, further divide.

"Socializing Harry"

In the remainder of the chapter we propose going a crucial step beyond Frankfurt and Korsgaard, by considering the possible effect exposure to serious normative criticism from without might have on their accounts of intrasubjective normative reflection, with which we, in principle, agree.[57] We shall argue that the inner division induced by serious criticism does not necessarily respect the fault lines of the mind's self-reflective partitioning. When challenged by trusted critics, we shall argue, a person is liable to become estranged, at least momentarily, from some of his most cherished commitments, thus gaining a perspective on the challenged portions of his *I*-part that is quite unavailable in other circumstances.

Critical Feedback

The kind of self-distancing and inner separation that can be experienced as a result of hard-hitting normative criticism, we shall be arguing, is similar to the sense of self-estrangement we experience when watching or listening to recordings of ourselves perform. Such devices allow us to briefly experience, or imagine experiencing, seeing or hearing ourselves as others do; not quite recognizing ourselves, not always pleased with what we see or hear, very often critical. Such "out-of-body" experiences, even when powerful, do not usually run very deep, for they focus attention, for the most part, on the more outward, performative aspects of the case. They can help enormously in enhancing and correcting dramatic impact, and in improving the image and impression one hopes to create. The sort of self-reflection they motivate centers on the external, on the practical end-product, not on normative commitment. Viewing ourselves in this way can help correct technical errors but is near-powerless to delve much deeper. By watching a playback, a defense lawyer arguing a case, or a philosopher making a point, we can learn much about their demeanor, posture, and delivery, but little about the aptness of their norms or the quality of their reasoning; much about their rhetoric, but little about the real thing, in the sense Plato enlarges upon in the *Gorgias.*

Still, such devices can be enormously instructive exactly because they enable a perspective on ourselves that is wholly unavailable to us in "ordinary" self-reflection and self-consciousness. For a brief moment the tape recorder or closed-circuit camera allows the eye to see itself, as it were. The feeling that we are experiencing ourselves as others do is partly an illusion, of course, for it is us, not them, who perform the evaluation. Still, the self-estrangement can be very real, and the picture of ourselves, very different from what we take ourselves to be. The unique critical distance such playback devices allow is, therefore, undeniable, as is the real critical work they make possible.

The self-critical work proceeds in such cases as follows: discrepancies between the unflattering picture we receive from the recording device and the image we had had of our performance will be deemed problematic when considered trustworthy (i.e., not the fault of inadequate equipment or incompetent technicians), and too marked for comfort. When considered trustworthy, playback devices of this kind are capable of demonstrating that what our performance succeeds in achieving falls surprisingly and worryingly short of goals it was intended to achieve. In other words, the imagined impact of our performance is converted by the device from a set of objectives thought readily achievable into desired ends that our performance, as it stands, is now deemed incapable of accomplishing. In the first instance at least, it will usually not be the goals we set ourselves that are faulted, so much as our conceit in believing that our performance had succeeded in achieving them; not our objectives, but the means we employed to promote them. Eventually, after failing repeatedly to improve our performance, we may well sadly conclude that the task is beyond our reach, and that the goals we set ourselves and thought we could achieve, are in truth unrealistic. But even then, deeming an objective untenable, unrealistic, even overly pretentious is different from deeming it unworthy, undeserving, or contemptible. This is why this kind of feedback is a largely uninteresting form of normative criticism.

The kind of feedback one receives from a trusted normative critic is in some ways analogous, but in others not, and is not as easily analyzed. It is analogous, as we shall argue in detail, in the important sense that when normative criticism proves effective, its critical transformative force owes to what it enables its addressee to *experience* rather than to the perceived *validity* of its argument. In fact, it would be fair to say that insofar as trusted normative criticism can be effective, its impact will have little to do with the logical force of its argument. When our deepest convictions are challenged, our critics' logic will be of no avail, and of itself will tend to leave us unmoved. If an argument's conclusions are considered normatively unacceptable, it will be rejected even if its premises are deemed sound and its reasoning impeccable. Impeccably sound arguments to objectionable conclusions are at best deemed paradoxes and set aside for later consideration, and in the worse case, dismissed without further ado. This is the logic behind Kuhn's account of the way anomalies are set aside and ignored in the course of normal science.

From a Frankfurtian perspective, this is more than a descriptive claim about the way (lamentably, if understandably) many people react to normative criticism, but an outcome that for thoughtful, normative people is inevitable. For whenever an argument runs up against what he calls a volitional necessity or a wholehearted commitment, reasoning is rendered powerless, by definition. For Frankfurt, normative commitment runs deeper than the volitional rationality to which it gives rise, and certainly deeper than the force of the formal rules of inference. Volitional necessity marks the limits of what we are capable of thinking and of doing. It stands to reason that what we find unthinkable or undoable (despite being fully equipped to so thinking and doing), we will also find *unarguable.*

For the same reason that we are incapable of deeming the norms to which we are committed *normatively* lacking, we are incapable of being *convinced* by others to do so. But this, we insist, does not render us immune to normative criticism. Its transformative power, we shall explain below, lies not in the persuasiveness of its reasoning but in the disturbing *picture* it paints of us, and in this sense resembles the potentially transformative force of a recording device. By its special structure, normative criticism leveled at us by others allows us a glimpse, not merely of how we outwardly look or sound to them, but of how they think we think and should be thinking. The better informed and more trustworthy we deem them to be, the more profound the disorienting sense of self-estrangement they are capable of arousing. This is the sense in which we believe that normative criticism resembles a disturbing playback.

But in another sense it does not. The critical force of a recording device is a direct function of its conceived reliability. We are moved to reconsider and take action in the light of a disheartening recording exactly because we consider the picture it presents us as more authentic, closer to the truth, than our own self-image. We respond because we realize to our dismay that we had been gravely mistaken in our assessment of how we sound or look. But this is *not* the case with respect to the kind of normative criticism in which we are interested here. The critical impact of recording devices resembles cases of what we might term the "inner interpretivism," of which Frankfurt speaks; cases in which critics succeed in teaching us something about ourselves, in helping to get ourselves right in Frankfurt's sense of the term; when we realize, with their assistance, that we had not been thinking and acting *true to ourselves;* when their criticism helps us to realize what, in truth, we really are or really want. These are cases in which what is criticized, and subsequently transformed, is our *interpretation,* or *understanding,* of "the necessities of our own nature."[58] The type of normative criticism Frankfurt leaves unacknowledged (as everyone else we have studied) is the kind in which what are called to task and subsequently transformed are "the necessities of our nature" themselves; criticism that is offered and, most important, taken, if you wish, not as an insistent call to *get* ourselves right but to *put* ourselves right!

To reiterate a little more precisely a point made earlier. Frankfurt and Korsgaard, we have speculated, deny the possibility of such criticism hitting home, because for them the very idea of an external source of normative commitment or change of commitment would be to concede the form of externalism they term "normative realism." We certainly share their objection to this form of normative realism,[59] from which, we also agree, it follows that the kind of normative criticism of which we speak can never *convince*. However, contrary to Frankfurt and Korsgaard, we insist nonetheless that despite being powerless to convince, trusted normative criticism can still be highly effective in provoking their addressees to reconsider and subsequently replace heartfelt normative commitments. As we have briefly suggested, and shall explain in greater detail shortly, although the self's *I*-part is incapable of positively entertaining, let alone endorsing, arguments that undermine its very volitional basis, such arguments can be effective in rendering parts of that basis at least temporarily ambivalent. The option for which Frankfurt and Korsgaard fail to make room (and, as a result, are forced to detach intrapersonal normative discourse from its wider interpersonal context) is for normative criticism to be effective *despite being unpersuasive,* and in a way we would be willing to deem *rational*. But if arguments directed against heartfelt norms cannot *but* be rejected, how can they still be effective? To see how, we need to back up a little and take a closer look at the normative critical argument itself.

The Instrumental Value of Final Ends

In the usual construal of the means-ends relationship, norms and standards clearly rank among the latter. Our norms are what we live *for* and our standards, what we abide *by*. And if they are not simple derivatives of, or constraints on, higher norms and standards, then they belong not only in the category of ends, but of final ends—ends that are valued intrinsically. To criticize a person's norms or standards is to find them in some important and reasoned sense normatively problematic (as opposed to finding them merely incoherent, insufficiently explicit, or unrealistic). But if there is any truth in the characterization of problems and problemhood proposed in the previous chapter, only an arrangement of *means*—a goal-directed system—can be found problematic. To deem anything problematic, it was argued, is to deem it incapable of adequately achieving its intended ends. And if problemhood is necessarily gauged on instrumental disvalue in the usual sense of the term, an end cannot be considered problematic unless when pressed into service as a means to (or a precondition for, or a constraint on) a higher end (such as the aim of a chapter in relation to the plan of the book, the objectives of one line of products in relation to those of the firm, and, more radically, the aim of the incision—which, in all conceivable cases, clearly lacks any intrinsic value—in relation to the purpose and goals of the surgical procedure). Final ends do not bear this sort of relation to other ends. Final ends can get in each others' way, and often require careful and complex prioritizing. But postponing one final end, setting it aside, or even abandoning it altogether in favor of another is only to deem it less important, less pressing, less valuable, and so forth, not normatively wanting. Under the usual construal of the means-ends relationship, normative criticism, in the sense we seek to articulate, is inarticulable from any perspective.

But as we saw in the previous chapter, the usual construal of the means-ends relationship (late of Aristotle), misses, according to Frankfurt, the important *instrumental* value we attach to our final ends—not with respect to other final ends, but with respect to the means by which we work toward them; just as it misses the essentially *terminal* value we attach to the means we enlist in the pursuit of our final ends, by the very virtue of them being final. What a person cares about wholeheartedly, the things he cannot help but care for, form the basis for his most stable final goals,[60] those that solidify in norms, and lend his life its deepest meaning. It is in this sense that the critique of final ends, and hence of norms and standards, interestingly surpasses our goal-directed systems picture of problem-seeking and -solving, yet without undercutting the instrumental rationality on which it rests. Frankfurt makes the point nicely with respect to the problem of adopting final ends. His concise text is worth quoting in full.

> Any rational decision concerning the adoption of final ends must be
> made partly on the basis of an evaluation of the kinds of activities by

which the prospective ends would be pursued. It requires a consideration not only of the value that is inherent in these activities taken by
themselves, but also of the terminal value they possess as contributors
of meaning to life. Pursuing one final end rather than another may lead
a person to engage in activities that are in themselves more enjoyable. It
may also lead him to live a life that is more meaningful. It will do this if
it entails a richer and more fully grounded purposefulness—if, that is,
the network of activity to which it gives rise has greater complexity and
if it radiates more extensively within the person's life.

In evaluating a prospective final end, accordingly, it is essential to
consider how much terminal value that end would convey to the means
by which it had to be pursued. In this sense, *final ends must be judged
on the basis of their usefulness*. From one point of view, the activities in
which we pursue our terminally valuable final ends have only the instrumental value that is characteristic of means. From another point of view,
however, these activities are themselves terminally valuable, and they
*imbue with instrumental value the final ends for the sake of which they are
undertaken*.[61]

Frankfurt, as might be expected, limits his comments to the process of
adopting a final end, in which a person acquaints himself with the extent to which he in fact cares (and in the most interesting cases, cannot
help caring) about the end in question. And it is here, he argues, that the
usual relationship between means and end is complexified in the ways
described. These are processes of evaluation in the course of which a new
element is added to person's *I*-part, or an existing element is rendered explicit. By the same token, of course, the same could be said of processes of
devaluation, in which a person discovers that he no longer cares for a former object of care or love, and as a result abandons certain of his final
ends. Both cases boil down to the reflective reality checks typical of attempts at "getting ourselves right" in Frankfurt's sense of the term. Neither case, therefore, involves, as it stands, normative self-criticism in the
sense in which we are interested. In such processes of Frankfurtian reflective self-evaluation, a person discovers *after the event* that his *I*-part has
changed, and that he is no longer normatively committed to elements it
had formerly included. The demoted elements are not found *unworthy of
care*, but found to be, as a matter of fact, no longer *cared for*. But is it at all

possible from a Frankfurtian perspective to envisage a *prospective* process of normative demotion, one in which elements of a person's *I*-part are demoted as a result of an act of considered normative discreditation? Yes, we shall argue, but only with a little help from our (critical) friends.

Within You and Without You: The Self's Normative Dialogue

To begin with, Frankfurt's analysis of the reciprocal interchanging of instrumental and terminal value in considering final ends and the means for pursuing them is relevant to more than understanding normative self-reflection. It is equally relevant to understanding how we criticize other people's normative commitments. We regularly criticize other people's norms just as Frankfurt describes, by pointing out the normatively intolerable forms of conduct that are consequences of abiding by those norms.

There's a difference, however. From a Frankfurtian perspective, the most important difference between normative self-criticism and criticizing someone else's norms is that the latter is, in principle, unconstrained by the volitional necessities constitutive of the former. But that is to put it too mildly, for it is true of every normative judgment. People cannot be genuinely constrained by volitional necessities other than their own, even if they wanted to. They may attempt to emulate them, and even *imagine* themselves thus constrained, but the necessarily fictive, counterfactual element in so doing can never be fully eradicated (unless, of course, one's addressees' relevant volitional necessities happen to fully coincide with one's own). We can be really constrained only by the limits of our own will. The significant difference between normative criticism and normative self-criticism is that the former purports to question what the latter necessarily takes for granted. The normative critic is not merely *unfettered* by her addressee's volitional necessities, but seeks in voicing her critique to challenge, and in doing so to somehow persuade him to reconsider them. Prudent normative criticism is an attempt to subvert and destabilize by the force of reason volitional necessities constitutive of someone else's normative outlook and practical reasoning. Hence the problem to which this study boils down: how can volitional necessities be effectively reasoned against if, on a Frankfurtian showing, they are, by definition, immune to reason?

A Frankfurtian Normative Critic

As we did (following Rorty's example) with respect to Brandom's philosophy, it is useful here also to briefly imagine the thought process of a
prudent normative critic of Frankfurtian persuasion, someone who employs a thoroughly Frankfurtian picture of personal identity, reason, and
norm in dealing with both herself and others. Let us assume also that she
cares deeply for the person or people whose norms she finds normatively
questionable. Last, we shall also assume that she classifies the norms she
deems questionable as norms with which her addressees fully and wholeheartedly identify, as firm and solid components of their *I*-parts.

Care for her addressee may take one of two forms of response according to how it measures in relation to the importance she attaches
to the normative issues at hand. One, is toleration — tolerance not born
of agreement, but adopted and displayed despite substantial normative
*dis*agreement. If she resolves to put up with her addressees' conduct
and not to take action, to refrain from speaking her mind and grant her
addressees their way, she will be doing so out of respect for what she
knows they can't help caring for. Indeed, when a true Frankfurtian finds
herself in the situation described (facing someone she genuinely cares
for, whose conduct she finds problematic, but who, she believes, is acting
prudently in accord with heartfelt, wholehearted conviction, to the extent that [all things being equal] not doing so is for him unthinkable),
tolerance will be the default response. We expect tolerance to be a Frankfurtian's first option not because adherence to Frankfurt's picture of personal identity renders her more morally sensitive to a person's right to
the normative system of his choice, or, as Popperians would have it, particularly open and welcoming to the critical challenge of normative diversity.[62] The Frankfurtian incentive toward tolerance owes not to the
discourse of rights or to the idea of the open society so much as to the
way Frankfurtians ground normativity in an understanding of free will
and autonomy that, unlike more strictly Kantian depictions such as Korsgaard's, ultimately rests on the nonnegotiable volitional necessities of the
individual agent.

But even Frankfurtian tolerance has its limits. When a person's conduct is deemed to be *intolerably* wrong, even a Frankfurtian's respect
for her addressees' volitional integrity and inability to consider acting

differently is liable to give way to disapproval, dissent, and eventually explicit reproof.

In the case of ordinary criticism, a person is taken to task for not properly attending to problems within his domain of responsibility. To be effective, such criticism, we have seen, must be leveled from within that person's normative framework—either by a fellow adherent or by an outside critic doing her best to emulate her addressee's normative frame of reference. Ordinary criticism can be severe, hit deep, and have dire consequences. But, once understood, it poses no particular philosophical problem. Normative criticism is different, for it represents a reasoned challenge to the framework constitutive of its addressee's very ability to pass normative judgment. Normative criticism is a demand to reason against the very basis of one's reasoning capacity, against the necessities of one's will. From a Frankfurtian perspective more than any other, such criticism demands the impossible, and is hence, by definition, unendorsable in the usual sense of the term.

Let us stay with our imaginary Frankfurtian. Being the Frankfurtian that she is, she is aware of all this and more. She knows she cannot *convince* her addressee to adopt a different set of commitments, because she knows that wholehearted normative commitment is not something a person is at liberty to argue against. To argue against such commitment, she knows, is for her addressee's *I*-part to take a normative stand against itself, which is impossible.

And yet she continues all the same, for we are talking about a case in which for her tolerance is no longer an option—which can only mean that she considers her addressee's conduct to be not merely normatively *inappropriate* but to run up against some of *her* heartfelt commitments. Had that not been the case, she should have had no serious difficulty respecting their differences, leaving things as they are, and tolerating the deviances she detects. She opts for criticism rather than tolerance, she realizes, because what she takes her own volitional necessities to be leave her no choice.

But a prudent Frankfurtian (especially of the ideal, fully informed, imaginary variety) knows this too. She knows all too well that finding her addressee's normative conduct normatively intolerable (in conjunction with her deeming his relevant normative convictions genuinely wholehearted) bespeaks a real and unbridgeable volitional incongruity. In other words, she knows that the normative repugnance she articulates in terms of *her* normative framework cannot be translated into *his*. She knows that, as it stands, from *his* perspective the problem she detects cannot be articulated as a problem at all. Notice that the challenge of prudent normative criticism is not the general problem of the incommensurability or untranslatability of diverse frameworks as such. It is the far more specific and limited problem of the *inarticulability* from within the framework criticized of the normative *problem* its critics claim it harbors. Prudent critics (especially if Frankfurtian) do not seek to *convert* other people to their normative frameworks, but to prompt them to recognize and take action against the serious normative failings they believe plague *their* frameworks.[63]

Our Frankfurtian critic knows, in other words, that framing her critical argument from her perspective is as pointless and ineffective qua criticism, as arguing from his is impossible. She also knows that however she proceeds and whatever she does, for her criticism to somehow register and be taken rationally to heart, she must address her addressee, as far as possible, in his own terms, on the basis of premises he can recognize and deem true.

She knows all this and more. For she is also well aware of how (on a Frankfurtian showing) people identify the components of self they identify *with*, how their *I*-parts function as final normative tribunals with respect to all but themselves. She therefore concedes, at the interpersonal level, a Frankfurtian version of Comparative Irrealism that has little to do with semantics. She knows her addressee is incapable of internalizing and endorsing her criticism because the very norms she purports to prove questionable are integral components of his *I*-part, and hence of the tribunal by which he passes normative judgment. And since arguing the case from her perspective is even more futile, she reasons that her only chance of driving her point home and prompting him to reconsider is to do so from an *imaginary* point of reference, which though not completely his, and certainly not hers, poses *as if* it is his.

She will try to frame her argument from a perspective as similar as possible to his, yet sufficiently (and subtly) different from it to enable her to make her case, that is, to allow for the premises she needs for arguing that acting and living by the light of the norms she deems faulty is normatively problematic. And she will present the argument as if arguing from *his* perspective. Quentin Skinner contends that to communicate their ideas effectively, let alone win their audiences over, innovative thinkers often feel bound to conceal their radical intentions, and present their arguments by giving subtle and surreptitious new twists to a conventional vocabulary rather than presenting them by means of a new set of concepts.[64] Something similar happens in prudent and informed normative criticism. Well aware of what she is doing, our imaginary Frankfurtian critic contrives to catch her addressees off guard by quite deliberately framing her critique as if arguing from their acknowledged perspective. In more realistic scenarios (in normative criticism as in the history of new ideas) people do so unthinkingly, as a matter of course. This is because, whether we like it or not, our normative assessments of others—the expectations we frame, the disappointment and frustration we register in the light of their conduct—emphatic and open minded as they may aspire to be, are ultimately conditioned by our own normative outlooks rather than theirs. When we are disturbed by someone's conduct to the point of protesting we are measuring it by a normative yardstick *we* strongly feel *should* be his. We accuse him of betraying norms that, in the case in question, are not his own.[65] Our moral outrage owes to the fact that he fails to live up to the person we strongly believe he should be (or had believed he was). In other words, even if we are not as perceptive and calculated as our imaginary Frankfurtian, when openly and prudently criticizing elements of another person's wholeheartedly held normative scheme to his face, we will *inevitably* be arguing against him from a *picture* of his *I*-part which is importantly different from the real thing, as it were, but will do so motivated by the deep conviction that it *should* be true. And the better acquainted we are with his world of values, the truer the picture will seem to him in all other respects.

Unwittingly or not, all keen, honest, direct, and reasonably articulated normative criticism challenges its addressees with an explicit *argument* that, of itself, in principle (if the norms in question are indeed heartfelt), has no realistic hope of being convincing, but which comes accompanied by a picture implied by its premises of (the relevant part of) its addressee's *I*-part, which though true to a large extent, differs significantly from his own. Again, not every normative critic resembles our highly informed and intensely sensitive, imaginary Frankfurtian, who, fully aware of her argument's inherent ineffectiveness as a move in her addressee's space of reasons, *knowingly* crafts it with a view to conveying to him, *indirectly,* yet as effectively as possible, a largely accurate, yet not-altogether-true picture of his normative commitments. Unlike our imaginary Frankfurtian, "ordinary" normative critics almost never do so purposefully. Rather, they argue as if their arguments were capable of being endorsed directly. But this, in itself, is of little consequence. Our imaginary Frankfurtian does not enjoy any advantage as a critic by being aware of what she is doing. The result of normative criticism is always very much the same. At the receiving end—which is the end that counts, and that to which we now return—the impact of keen normative criticism (knowingly and contrived, or unaware and unintentional) consists, at best, of a meaningfully altered, yet otherwise largely true account of its receiver's *I*-part that is implicitly premised by a critical argument incapable itself of convincing. Arguing from the left, critics will surreptitiously premise certain liberal and socialist norms to make their case, while those who argue from the right will tend to smuggle in just enough conservative value to make their arguments stick.

Self-Criticism's Transformative Moment

But if normative criticism is inevitably dismissed, how can the picture conveyed by its premises still be retained? The answer is twofold. First, as noted previously, if one considers a critic trustworthy and informed, one may well deem his efforts *sincere,* even while rejecting his conclusions as unacceptable or wrong-headed. True, criticism leveled against a person's most cherished convictions is most often responded to ad hominem by defensively contesting the critics' reliability and declaring them hostile. But *trusted* criticism is different. It will also be rejected, but without undermining the critic's trustworthiness, allowing one to *dismiss* the criticism while *fully endorsing* it as conveying an honest portrayal of how one's critics see one.

Second, while the first point is true of all criticism, it is especially true of normative criticism by virtue of an important difference. When an ordinary critical argument is rationally rejected, it is argued *against*, an attempt is made to *refute* it. And, bracketing cases of alleged sloppy or invalid reasoning, to refute an argument is to refute its premises, and with them *any picture they might imply or entail.* In terms of the analogy to a playback device, the picture conveyed by a non-normative rejected critical argument resembles that of a recording device its addressees consider faulty and distortive. Such a picture will have no feedback effect, no self-critical import, even when deemed honest. If such a picture at all moves us to action, it will only be to correct the *impression* it gives of us, not to correct our ways or to admit of a mistake or an oversight. We will not be moved in any way to correct ourselves. Arguing with our critics in such cases boils down to criticizing their criticism, countering their arguments by means of counterarguments.

Normative criticism is interestingly different in this respect. Unlike ordinary criticism, normative criticism is rejected—at least in the first instance—but not by counterargument. Normative criticism is not set aside because it is deemed *refuted*, it is set aside because its conclusions are rejected—not disproved. Normative criticism is not dismissed because its *premises* are found to be unfounded but because its *conclusions* are deemed to be preposterous (or unthinkable, or repulsive)! When a stand is taken against our heartfelt normative commitments, it matters little, on a Frankfurtian showing, whether our critics' reasoning strikes us as formally valid. When prompted to think the unthinkable and act against our very will, it matters little whether or not their arguments set forth from premises that strike us as true. Although our initial response to normative criticism is, as a rule, far more resolute and unyielding than our response to ordinary criticism, it is decidedly less *reasoned* than in the ordinary case. When our norms are challenged, we normally don't argue back but rather button up and stand firm—which is both the strength and the weakness of our response. Thus, when rejected, ordinary criticism is dismantled while normative criticism remains intact. This is why the overall dismissal of normative criticism does not logically entail (for its receiver) an analogous dismissal of everything it premises, as in the ordinary case.

Cast in a more Brandomian idiom, we deal with ordinary criticism squarely within the boundaries of our space of reasons. The critical argument is either endorsed or dismissed, and in both cases, for *a reason*. When dismissed, it is because its premises are refuted along with whatever they commit or entitle us to. Normative criticism, by contrast, runs up against the normative entry points of the reasoning process itself, those that, as Frankfurt aptly puts it, *supply* us with reasons but are not entailed for us by others. The consequences of dismissing normative criticism, therefore, all lie *downstream* of our unyielding, unpremised, challenged norms. Upstream from them there is for us nothing but the rock-hard necessities of will. And thus, because they are left unrefuted, the picture of our normative identity implied by the premises of our critic's normative argument can linger on, register, and be retained uncoupled from, and without being automatically discarded along with, the argument itself.

Still, not to be formally and consciously refuted is still a far cry from being taken to heart and having an impact. To understand how the normative profile painted of us by trusted critics succeeds in moving us, involves an additional factor, one that Frankfurt, in an earlier work, notes in passing. It is an interesting passage because of the way it uncharacteristically acknowledges our normative dialogue with others. The point is raised, but to the best of our knowledge nowhere in his writing is it further developed.

> It is a salient characteristic of human beings, one which affects our lives in deep and innumerable ways, that we care about what we are. This is closely connected both as cause and effect to our enormous preoccupation with what other people think of us. We are ceaselessly alert to the danger that there may be discrepancies between what we wish to be (or what we wish to seem to be) and how we actually appear to others and to ourselves.[66]

We do not need to deem our critics' picture of us true for it to attract our attention in this way. It is enough that it is not considered *disproved*. Even though we instinctively dismiss their arguments as unfounded, their picture of us (which our Frankfurtian is aware *is* interestingly untrue!) is liable to continue to resonate, alerting us to the discrepancies between how we appear to ourselves and apparently appear to them—as Frankfurt puts it. The subtle difference that makes the difference between ordinary and normative criticism is that in the latter case, the picture they present us with, though incongruous with our own, is not one we have actively refuted and rejected. So that for the moment at least, we may find ourselves entertaining both pictures side by side. To stretch the analogy to the playback device a little further, it is as if we are struck by discrepancies between a recording and how we imagine ourselves to look and sound, but without yet being sure if the recording device is to blame (as the analogy to the ordinary case goes).

In this way, we believe, deep reaching normative criticism that is held to be prudent and honest is capable of giving rise to a sense of inner discordance and self-estrangement capable of creating the inner leeway necessary for transforming criticism by others into *self*-criticism. It is here, we believe, that the social context of heartfelt interpersonal normative discourse can be of crucial importance for creating the inner distance and perspective required for meaningful intrapersonal normative self-questioning that does not respect the Frankfurtian fault lines of our self's normal inner division.

But we have still to show how. To say that trusted normative criticism enables the mind to briefly entertain a contrasting account of its own *I*-part is not yet to explain when and how the new picture can be said to rationally dislodge the old.

The very idea of anyone being *rationally* transformed by an argument by which he is incapable of being convinced will mark for many of our readers the futile termination of this inquiry, regardless of everything we have said about the credibility we are able to grant our critics' portrayal of us from *their* perspective. Wittgenstein, who as a rule steers wide of all questions to do with the dynamics of language game *variation*, raises the question of the reasonableness and effectiveness of criticizing across language-game barriers only once, in *On Certainty* (his posthumously published response to G. E. Moore's well-known defense of commonsense realism). Wittgenstein speaks for many, in admitting only two possible outcomes when disputing across such fundamental divides. He terms such criticism "combat" *(bekämpfen)*, and sees no third option between total failure, when "each man declares the other a fool and heretic," and unreasoned "persuasion," the term he uses for "what happens when missionaries convert natives"![67] Wittgenstein's typically concise aphoristic series of rhetorical questions and brief musings neatly summarizes much of what we have been arguing—the normative grounding point of practical reason (§608); normative diversity, the principle of Comparative Irrealism, the unthinkability of denying our norms and standards (§609); the problem of normative criticism and the limits of toleration (§610–11); where reasoning gives way to "persuasion" (§612).

Wittgenstein's "persuasion" like Rorty's irony are knowing, yet reasoned forms of surrender of the rational option to which neither of them admits. For what are cherished norms, Wittgenstein's text clearly implies, if not, as Frankfurt has it, the place where reasoning ends and volitional necessity begins?

Wittgenstein and Rorty, like Frankfurt and the other thinkers whose work we have discussed, do not deny the fact that from time to time people undergo significant normative changes, but insist, some more explicitly than others, that such changes cannot, in principle, be the outcome of thoughtful consideration. They do so, however, without exception, without pausing to examine how serious, trusted, and prudent normative criticism is leveled and received. Is it still true that in the case of trusted critics who make a sincere, knowing, and considerate effort to emulate their addressee's way of thinking, and succeed in conveying to them a normative profile they are capable of recognizing as an appreciably different version *of themselves,* that the only two possible outcomes remain, as Wittgenstein would have it, a gestalt-type conversion or a futile and senseless exchange of insults?

These are certainly two possible outcomes, but are they the *only* possible outcomes? Once the scene of "combat" is internalized in the manner we have been describing, and the two irreconcilable "principles" are allowed to "meet," as described, in the mind of a single, thoughtful, and reasonably self-informed individual, rather than viewing them in dispute between differently committed individuals or communities, then, we believe, a third option does become available. For all his pragmatist openness, Rorty, like Frankfurt, describes his ironist as open to the world and to others, but not as engaged in serious, critical dialogue with others. Unlike Rorty, Wittgenstein does envisage us in conversation with others, but seems unable to imagine a conversation such as that conducted by considerate critics sensitive to the fact that they are talking across language-game barriers.[68] As we have seen, when normative criticism is leveled thus, the "irreconcilable principle" with which we are confronted is deliberately set by our critics in a tailor-made normative context that is as similar as possible to our own. What a good trusted critic allows us to experience and ponder is, as we put it before, a significantly different yet recognizable *version of ourselves,* as opposed to attempting to "combat" a full-blooded, alien "language game" in which we fail to identify anything that is us or ours. If there is any truth in the phenomenology of normative criticism outlined above, such is the nature of all serious and trusted normative criticizing. In other words, much of what Rorty and Wittgenstein all too quickly diagnose as unthinking conversion from one language game to another, and Frankfurt, as unpremeditated normative change awoken to only after the event, can in truth be a process far more thoughtful, deliberative, and considered than they envisage.

Thoughtful Ambivalence

We use the terms *thoughtful, deliberative,* and *considered,* but not *reasoned.* When a person is made aware of a normative profile he is capable of identifying as a different version of himself (in the same way we identify even a considerably distorted recording or picture as being of us), there is no *reasoned* way for him to compare the two directly and to find the new version normatively preferable to his own. That would require his still functioning *I*-part to pass negative normative judgment on itself, by itself. Internalizing the "combat" does not mitigate Comparative Irrealism. It remains impossible for a person to stand back from *both* pictures, as it were, and *compare* them normatively in a manner meaningful to both. (By means of what?) The only properly *reasoned* judgment available to him at this point is to deem the new profile his critics present him with normatively inferior to his own. If trusted normative criticism is to have *critical,* transformative impact capable of striking a middle course between all-out reasoned rejection and unreasoned conversion, it will have to be by means of a less direct route.

In Frankfurt's account, unmitigated alienation and wholehearted commitment, we have seen, are not the only options available to the self.

The self may well dither. It may dither in its self-understanding. A person may be unsure of whether he has got himself right. But selves are capable of dithering more profoundly, to be not merely uncertain of *what* they feel toward an object, but to experience definite *mixed* feelings toward it; to actually be of two minds regarding an object of love: loving and not loving it at the same time. A person, to use Frankfurt's term, may be not merely unclear or unsure, but truly *ambivalent* toward a final end or the activity required to achieve it. Here too the line between self-knowledge (epistemology) and the self itself (ontology) can prove elusive. Faced with a normative profile he recognizes as closely but not fully resembling his own, a person may well become ambivalent with respect to the points of incongruity between the two. And again, the uninteresting cases are those perceived as self-discovery, that is, cases in which a person realizes, thanks to his critics, that his commitment to the norm or standard in question was not wholehearted to start with. The cases of interest, of course, are those of the latter variety, where, as a result of his critics' efforts a person *changes his attitude* toward a well-defined final end, norm, or standard, and *renders* it ambivalent. These are the cases of normative self-transformation as opposed to normative self-interpretation.

But ambivalence is only the first step in the process. To develop ambivalence toward a norm or standard is not to *solve* the problem our critics raise. It is the self's equivalent of acknowledging and articulating it. Again, it is not a *reasoned* response to our critics' reasoned efforts—this will only come later—but it *is* a sign of critical impact. To become ambivalent toward a formerly wholeheartedly endorsed norm is a form of passing critical judgment; as if to deem it *volitionally problematic*—and we shall have more to say about this turn of phrase in a moment. But it is not a reasoned form of demotive judgment, because it does not involve the application of a standard. The norm is not demoted as a result of being measured or assessed in relation to, in comparison with, or in the light of other norms. Ambivalence, in this case, is the sheer result, one could say, of the two pictures being allowed to merge briefly in the mind; as if the profile presented by our critics is momentarily *grafted* onto our own, in a manner secured by the broad recognizable areas of identity. In the first instance the normative incongruities are not adjudicated, but sit side by side, creating ambivalence by their very juxtaposition. It is a moment in which the person's *I*-part does not sit in judgment, but merely contemplates the version it is presented with, trying it on for size, as it were, relishing the familiarity of its very strangeness, and managing to contain the incongruities as an ambivalent whole, rather than as jarring parts. This kind of ambivalence is a form of demotive verdict that is handed down not by an act of judgment but by what we might term a nonadjudicative juxtaposition of incongruous normative commitments.

The Achievement of Normative Self-Criticism

To become ambivalent toward a norm or a standard, toward the terminal value of a final end or a form of activity, is to deem them normatively undecided. This in itself does not necessarily render them problematic. Being of two minds about a goal-directed system is not to declare it flawed. What *is* rendered problematic by such a change of attitude—according to Frankfurt, severely problematic—is the self itself. Frankfurt's crisp discussion of ambivalence as a form of *self*-betrayal, brings forth the point forcefully. In "Autonomy, Necessity, and Love," Frankfurt lays down the groundwork for the intricate play between volition and necessity that serves him in later work to ground normativity in love.[69] Our passions motivate and move us, at times with overwhelming intensity and strength. However:

> The volitional attitudes that a person maintains toward his own elementary motivational tendencies are *entirely up to him.* . . . Whether a person identifies himself with these passions, or whether they occur as alien forces that remain outside the boundaries of his volitional identity, depends upon what he himself *wants his will to be.*[70]

What we love is what we want our wills to want. Hence, a person's care for his beloved

> [i]s tantamount . . . to caring about himself. In being devoted to the well-being of his beloved as an ideal goal, the lover is thereby devoted to an effort to realize a corresponding ideal in himself—namely, the ideal

of living a life that is devoted to the interests and ends of his beloved. Someone who loves justice, for instance, necessarily wants to be a person who serves the interests of justice. He necessarily regards serving its interests not only as contributing to the realization of a desirable social condition, but also as integral to the realization of his ideal for himself. His love defines for him, at least in part, the motives and preferences of his ideal self.[71]

It follows, Frankfurt goes on to argue, that a person who fails his beloved necessarily fails himself. In this context, failing is betrayal, and by the same token, betrayal of the object of love is self-betrayal, and self-betrayal entails "a rupture in his inner cohesion or unity; it means there is a division within his will."[72] For the same reason Frankfurt considers ambivalence also as a form of self-betrayal, because ambivalence too "consists in a vacillation or opposition within the self which guarantees that one volitional element will be opposed to the other, so that the person cannot avoid acting against himself."[73] A person unable to free himself of the conflict, who persists in a state of ambivalence, writes Frankfurt a decade later,

> is volitionally fragmented. His will is unstable and incoherent, moving him in contrary directions simultaneously or in a disorderly sequence.... [H]is will remains obstinately undefined and therefore lacks effective guiding authority. As long as he is unable to resolve the conflict by which he is torn, the person is at odds with himself.[74]

Ambivalence, he insists, is a grave disorder that demands urgent attention; "a disease of the mind"[75] that "tends to alarm a person and to mobilize him for an attempt at 'self-preservation.'"[76] When in a state of ambivalence a person runs up against "a quite primitive human need to establish and maintain volitional unity." Ambivalence is a threat to that unity, a "threat to the cohesion of the self."[77]

The problem with ambivalence, one might say, is that it represents a significant *weakening* of a person's capacity to conduct himself rationally. Being of two minds about a norm, a standard, or a final end renders all relevant judgment impossibly incoherent. If the necessities of wholehearted normative commitment provide the basis for a person's volitional rationality and hence the grounds for practical reasoning, then, by the same token, ambivalence generates *volitional irrationality,* which in turn obliterates his very capacity for agency in the effected areas. The deep and urgent need to free ourselves of ambivalence is no less than an insistent self-rallying to reclaim our capacity to be rational.

When trusted normative criticism succeeds in striking deep, it is capable of creating ambivalence with respect to the norms it questions. However, the problem which its addressee is consequently made to face and respond to is different from the problem his critics sought to convey. The problem *they* present him with concerns the normative failings, in their opinion, of certain of his norms, standards, or forms of conduct; the problem *he* is subsequently made to contend with concerns his inability to function rationally in those areas. In a sense, his is the more pertinent. But the solutions to the two problems add up to much the same thing, as we shall see, which renders the critical exchange more meaningful than it might now seem. But we are getting a little ahead of ourselves.

To free himself of his ambivalence, writes Frankfurt,

> it is not necessary that either of his conflicting impulses disappear. It is not even necessary that either of them increase or diminish in strength. Resolution requires only that the person become finally and unequivocally clear as to which side of the conflict he is on. The forces mobilized on the other side may then persist with the same intensity as before; but as soon as he has definitely established just where he himself stands, his will is no longer divided and his ambivalence is therefore gone. He has placed himself wholeheartedly behind one of his conflicting impulses, and not at all behind the other.[78]

For Frankfurt, normative ambivalence is deeply problematic, and exerts considerable pressure on the person to solve it by taking sides in the conflict. "If ambivalence is a disease of the mind, the health of the mind," he writes, "requires a unified will."[79] It does not matter on which side of the conflict he decides to fall, as long as his decision is firm and clear. To solve the problem is to unify the will, and to that end either side is as good as the other. But the decision on which side to fall is not, and cannot be, arbitrary. A person can no more decide what he wills by simply wanting it than he can do so by flipping a coin. To solve the problem is to become "finally and unequivocally clear as to which side of the conflict *he* is on." This is a decision rendered *by a person's I-part.* One would think, therefore, that in the case of normative criticism from without, the dice will always be loaded in favor of the prior normative commitments of which the person's *I*-part consisted from the start. But that would be to gravely underestimate the disruptive effect of normative ambivalence.

When trusted critics succeed in rendering a person truly ambivalent with respect to the points of conflict between his original *I*-part and the normative profile their arguments imply, those points of conflict cease, by definition, to function as part of his *I*-part, for they cease to be wholeheartedly identified with. Ambivalence, as we have noted, is a form of volitional demotion. When ambivalence sets in with respect to a norm or standard, our commitment to them is impaired to the point that they can no longer function in their original normatively adjudicative roles. They lose their normative authority, and are thereby denied *I*-part status. So that when a person eventually turns to address the ambivalence caused in him by his normative critics, his *I*-part will have changed and come to resemble the undisputed *intersection* between the two partly conflicting profiles. In this way his ambivalence toward the norms and standards his critics hailed questionable will be addressed by an *I*-part that, in principle, should not be biased in favor of its former configuration.

The conflict, as noted, may be resolved this way or that. When trusted normative criticism creates ambivalence in the manner described, one is liable to end up endorsing and identifying with one's critics' position and alienating oneself from one's former commitment to the norms they question, or vice versa. The important point is that there is no reason for either outcome not to be as rational and reasoned as human reflection is capable of being. Once the norms or standards that were in question no longer form a part of one's *I*-part the conflicting tendencies and motivations they now represent will be observed as it were from a distance, objectified and evaluated by one's new and leaner *I*-part, just as in any other first-order candidate. It is in this indirect way that insistent, trusted, and thoughtful normative criticism is capable of setting in motion a process by which a fully fledged, wholeheartedly endorsed component of its addressee's *I*-part can become temporarily dislodged, lose its privileged status, be stripped of normative authority, and become freely and impartially resubjected to the reflective scrutiny of his innermost volitional core.

This, however, cannot be accomplished alone. Left to our own devices, our *I*-part is incapable of splitting and subjecting a part of itself to the critical scrutiny of the other part. We are also incapable of making ourselves ambivalent toward a portion of our *I*-part at will. Ambivalence is a state we can find ourselves in, but cannot create voluntarily. As we put it above, left to our own devices, the self-critical fault lines of the reflective self are beyond control and remain rigid and unchangeable from within. But trusted criticism can change them for us. When the rich intrapersonal dialogue of the self is set in the context of an equally rich interpersonal critical dialogue with others, effective transformative normative self-criticism can become a real option.

Our imaginary Frankfurtian, who knows all this, conducts herself, therefore, not only as an effective normative critic of others, as we have described her thus far, but also, and perhaps mainly, as a knowing *consumer* of trusted criticism. For she is fully aware of how limited her ability for unassisted normative self-questioning is. She will, therefore, actively and insistently seek the critique of people whose insights and motives she trusts, because she knows that only thus is there a chance that the grip by which her norms and commitments bind her will be loosened sufficiently to allow her to subject them anew to keen normative review from within. In the first instance, the idea of actively seeking the disruptive challenge of normative criticism, *in order to* be rendered ambivalent, will undoubtedly sound very strange to Frankfurtian ears. But if there is any truth in our Frankfurtian expansion of Frankfurt's own picture, there is an important sense in which temporary ambivalence can be a valued and sought-for state—or, if you wish, set, therefore, as a desired end.[80]

As Kant has taught us, to be normatively compelled in the full sense of the term, is to comply with a norm or standard knowingly aware of the possibility of breaking it. This Kantian element of normative *self*-necessitation, enlarged upon and expanded by Frankfurt and other latter-day writers, marks the point where autonomy and necessity meet and merge. It is a semi-oxymoronic moment of *self*-compulsion, of necessity that is *willed* against a real possibility of disobedience, and awareness of getting it wrong. Though not normally a *reasoned* moment, and certainly not a critical one, it is a moment of at least fleeting reflective self-distancing, in which our freedom and responsibility are briefly glimpsed and exercised in declaring "I must." And when, confronted by knowing and trusted criticism, such moments may become permeated by a deeper sense of self-estrangement, and the mere prospect of disobedience be juxtaposed by a real alternative, then, we believe, the possibility of unquestionable commitment giving way to reflective, normative self-questioning becomes a real and a rational option.

CHAPTER NINE

Science Revisited

Taking Stock

Rationality's high point, that at which firm normative commitment is made to yield to self-critical review, is a moment of profound personal reckoning, yet one that is possible, we have argued, only within a social environment of keen, trusted normative criticism. Normative self-criticism becomes a philosophically articulable option only when a critically motivated version of Brandom's interpersonal deontic interrogation and score keeping is allowed to bear on a Frankfurtian normative dialogue of self (or some similarly hierarchical equivalent). This dependency of self-criticism on a public domain of critical exchange is in keeping with the present study's general bias toward such approaches Brandom dubs "linguistic pragmatism" that see the private realm of discursive commitment as both grounded in and explained by the public realm of discursive practice.[1] However, while it certainly preserves the linguistic pragmatist's *order of explanation*, the specific dependency of private on public argued for in the previous chapter has little to do with *grounding*. Normative self-criticism is made possible, is enabled, but is not determined by or grounded in the trusted normative criticism leveled by others. It is a dependency that sits comfortably with such collectivist approaches to the sources of norms and of meaning (interpretivist, or other), but by no means does it entail, or is it entailed by, them. (One is entitled to both, yet committed to neither, as Brandom might put it.) For ours is an account not of the sources of norms or normative commitment but of the sources of their undermining. This is why what we propose is capable of mediating between and interfacing with the pictures painted by Brandom and Frankfurt—supplementing both while jarring with neither.

The resulting amalgamation of (supplemented versions of) Brandomian discourse, Walzerian social criticism, and Frankfurtian personal identity enables us to extend the reach of critical self-reflection to our firmest normative commitments in a manner that surpasses the limitations imposed on such an extension by each of these positions when considered alone. Brandom's picture of discursive commitment, even when extended to normativity in general and interpreted as self-critically motivated, still proves incapable of extending normative self-criticism beyond deliberating the proper application of *given* norms. His attempt in later work to account for the rationality of norm determination is, we have seen, of little help in this respect, for it focuses entirely on how normative choices already made are rationalized by a retrospective appeal to history while remaining wholly unconcerned with the rationality of endorsing or dispensing with normative commitment. Rational reconstruction serves Brandom to make explicit and lend normative weight to *existing* normative dispositions and inclinations (the way common law judges justify their verdicts by selecting and reinterpreting former rulings as precedential)[2] but not to adjudicate between candidate norms, or to question given ones. Of itself, Brandom's insightful account of rational agency makes no room for and shows no interest in the very question of rationally *changing* or *modifying* normative commitment.

Walzer, by contrast, makes normative criticism central both to his interpretivist project in ethics and his account of social and political reform. But two difficulties mar his position as it stands. First, as with Brandom's expressivism,[3] Walzer's interpretivism limits normative criticism to assessments of how a given array of normative practices is understood and articulated. Its corrective scope, we have argued, is, therefore, limited, as in Brandom, to normative attitude, and remains powerless with regard to normative status—to use the latter's terminology. But Walzer's account of social criticism seems oblivious to the constraint. Unlike the ideal study partner's tame and intimate reproach described in *Avot de-Rabbi Nathan,* the fervent, Amos-like rebuke of Walzer's many examples of social criticism purports to hit far deeper than his interpretivism proves capable of supporting. Put somewhat schematically, Walzer argues that deeply transformative social criticism can be effective when leveled by *connected* critics whose efforts are understood as *interpretive*. Needless to say, we share his belief in the effectiveness of such criticism, and have argued for a related notion of connectedness (one that makes room for unconnected yet trusted critics) as well as for a similar (if more Brandomian) form of interpretivism. It is not the ingredients of his argument we find unacceptable but the argument itself. The combination of connectedness and interpretivism for which he argues lacks the critical bite required to sustain the sort of social criticism he aims at explaining.

But Walzer's account is problematic in another way, unrelated to the scope of interpretive criticism it allows. Like Brandom's, Walzer's work gives no account at all of the transformative consumption of social criticism. Even if the radical brand of social criticism of which he speaks could be accounted for in interpretivist terms, the question would still remain as to how people deeply and seriously committed to a radically different understanding of their culture can be rationally won over by such criticism. To understand the transformative effect of normative criticism is to understand how such criticism is *consumed* rather than *produced*. We know that Normative criticism can be extraordinarily effective. The question is whether its effect can be deemed *rational*. By leaving the question unattended, Walzer's account remains at best indifferent to the question that centrally exercises the present study.

In Frankfurt's rich and dynamic account of personal identity, normative commitment, and self-government, we find the natural intrapersonal counterpart to the exclusively interpersonal pictures of rational discourse and normative criticism painted by Brandom and Walzer. Yet here too, the limits of normative self-criticism follow a line worryingly similar to the Brandomian distinction between normative status and attitude. A person's *attitude* toward his wholehearted commitments may prove to have been mistaken or insufficiently informed, but on a Frankfurtian showing (alone), no amount of information and no measure of keen self-reflection are capable of rationally changing the normative *status* of such commitments. From the Frankfurtian perspective, we fully concede, the idea of a bona fide element of a person's *I*-part being self-deemed normatively wanting is a contradiction in terms. Left to their own devices, people are simply incapable of the kind of normative self-criticism we seek to articulate.

Moreover, if people are truly incapable of deeming bona fide elements of their *I*-parts normatively deficient, then, by the same token, we have argued, they are equally incapable of being convinced to do so by others. Reasoning against one's own firm normative commitments is *necessarily* impossible, not for want of a better reason, but because volitional necessity is, in principle, immune to all forms of practical reason. It matters little, it would seem, whether or not a person is exposed to the normative critique of others. If he is truly incapable of arguing against himself in this way, he will be just as incapable of endorsing such an argument when suggested by someone else. It is as simple as that.

In other words, not only do the pictures painted by Brandom, Walzer, and Frankfurt fall short of accounting for normative self-criticism when taken separately, but a simple juxtaposition of the three is to no avail either. Frankfurtian selves remain incapable of surpassing the limits of their personal normative commitments even when, as lively Brandomian participants in the game of giving and asking for reasons, they find themselves subjected to keen Walzerian critics. If there is no more to exposure to normative criticism than *reasoned* exchange, there can be no room for the kind of normative self-criticism the possibility of which this study set out to articulate.

But, as argued in the previous chapter, a closer look at the possible effects trusted critics may have on normative self-reflection reveals the interesting possibility of a truly destabilizing effect their arguments can have that has little to do with the reasoned exchange itself. For even when normative criticism is unconditionally dismissed, the normative profile implied by its premises is liable to create in its addressee sufficient self-distance (analogous, as we have argued, to the effect of a playback device) to render the norms it questions normatively ambivalent. And once rendered ambivalent, they become susceptible to the normative review of the agent's current *I*-part of which they are now no longer a part. In this way, keen external normative criticism, when trusted, can be said to facilitate normative self-criticism in the full sense of the term pursued in this study. With a little help from trusted critics we are thus able to adopt a rational stance toward the norms that govern us, not in Brandom's sense of being able and willing to *justify* them, but in the sense insisted on here, of being able and willing to hold them in critical review.

What enables going beyond Brandom (and the traditional understanding of Socratic dialogue) in this respect is the realization that reasoned discourse amounts to more than reasoned *exchange;* that rational dialogue consists in more than reasoned consideration of the soundness or fittingness of one another's reasoning; that to be rationally moved by argument is, in the first instance, not always a matter of being convinced. It is a two-stage argument, the first critical of Brandom, the second supplementary.

Against Brandom we have argued that participating and keeping deontic score in the game of giving and asking for reasons is a necessary, but not a sufficient condition for deeming the exchange rational. Taking note of people's reasons merely to acquaint oneself with, and keep track of, how they justify their actions does not count as rational discourse. When people act for a reason they act rationally, but prompting them for their reasons merely out of curiosity is not to engage them rationally. The game that counts in this respect is not that of giving and asking for reasons *simpliciter* but what Habermas calls "the language game of argumentation"[4]—that in which reasons are not merely given and noted, but *challenged*. Needless to say, engaging effectively in the former game is a prerequisite for engaging effectively in the latter. Only competent Brandomian scorekeepers can argue effectively with one another. A person's reasons cannot be competently questioned if they are not duly noted and understood.

But the game that really counts is not even the game of argumentation *simpliciter,* but the game, more specifically, of leveling and responding to criticism. Criticism is a form of argumentation, but not all argumentation is criticism. To challenge a person's reasons from one's own point of view, for example, is to engage him in argument but not to criticize. To criticize a reason, we have argued at length, is to argue against it but *from the point of view of the person whose reason it is.* To do so, a capacity for both Habermasian argument and Brandomian scorekeeping are of the essence, but in and of themselves they do not suffice.

But neither does "the language game of criticism," if we may call it so, reach all the way down. When what are called into question are a person's *norms* (i.e., his ultimate reasons), the game that counts is no longer that of leveling and responding to criticism *simpliciter*, for it is impossible to articulate a valid argument that calls the normative worth of a person's heartfelt normative commitments into question, as in ordinary criticism, strictly from his perspective. At this level, the game of leveling and responding to criticism ceases to be a strictly Habermasian matter of argument and counterargument and acquires a tacit subtext, partly articulated yet usually unacknowledged.

As the critical arguments are leveled and (because normative) inevitably dismissed, *pictures*, rather than assertions and inferences, become the currency that effectively changes hands. A normative critic reasons by portraying her addressee's normative premises subtly yet significantly differently from the way he portrays himself. People whose norms are criticized thus find themselves tacitly confronted by normative profiles they clearly recognize as theirs, despite being decidedly different from the way they portray themselves. Like the effect of a playback device, the sense of self-estrangement, the hesitance, and the eventual ambivalence to which such criticism is liable to give rise have nothing to do with the soundness of its argument or the force of its proof. One's confidence is shaken by being exposed to a picture of oneself that is too close for comfort yet at the same time sufficiently different to jar with one's own.

In the discursive games described by Brandom and Habermas, the only normative portraits produced and noted (and in Habermas's account, occasionally questioned) are *self*-portraits. One describes one's reasons on request, and does one's best to explain and justify them when challenged. If that is all there is to rational discourse, it is hard to see how Habermasian *lebenswelten* can in principle be transcended, bridged, or transformed in the ways he describes. But once it is realized how exposure to prudent normative critical discourse inherently involves exposure to the negative feedback of tacit normative counterprofiling, and the destabilizing effect it can have on normative commitment, the potential transformative influence of such discourse becomes apparent and its rationality appreciable.

In an important sense, this book thus reaches completion. It set out to articulate the possibility of rational normative change, or framework modification, and has done so, at least to the satisfaction of its authors. The site of rational normative change, we have argued, is the arena of intrapersonal deliberation; the ultimate discourse of rationality is that of the self. This in itself comes as no surprise. Insofar as 'rational' is taken, as it is taken here, as denoting a category of reasoned or considered action, it stands to reason that personal commitment can be modified or replaced *rationally* only by the person whose commitment it is. But the two further conclusions of our account are perhaps less unsurprising. The first is the absolute dependency that emerged of normative self-criticism on an interpersonal environment of trusted normative criticism. The second is the idea that the transformative high moment of rationality is not one of enlightened discovery but rather one of deeply disturbing ambivalence; a moment of inner discordance fraught with tortured dithering and painful indecision. Ambivalence, self-estrangement, and indecision are as a rule not the most inspiring and motivating states of mind, but in moments of normative crisis they become reason's defining disposition and very driving force.

The remainder of this chapter takes a closer look at both of these aspects of our account—the necessity of an environment of normative critics and the centrality of ambivalence to rational normative change—in a scientific setting, where most would claim neither of them is apparent. From the sort of Kuhnian perspective to which this study is committed, even one as advanced as Friedman's, "normal" rational scientific discourse is constituted by shared communal commitment to the science's normative framework. Who, then, are a science's trusted normative critics whose critical discourse is capable of prompting practitioners of voice and standing to reconsider normative basics? In what sense can science be at all described as operating in a critical environment capable of having the kind of transformative impact of which we have spoken? Nor does such a picture of science (or for that matter, any other major historiography of science currently employed) seem to make room or to even leave room for the type of normative ambivalence we locate at the heart of all rational normative change. The transformative moments of scientific revolution are credited, almost without exception, to the brilliant, novel, and, most of all, inspiring innovations of Copernicus, Newton, or Einstein rather than to the kind of indecision and ambivalence we locate at the heart of such transformations.[5]

Back to Science I: Meta-Frameworks, Trading Zones, and Beyond

Two of Michael Friedman's most interesting deviations from Kuhn's historiography of science will serve as our points of departure. The first, to which we first turn, has to do with the third level of discourse with which Friedman supplements Kuhn's two, namely, his notion of a meta-framework, or meta-paradigm, which serves in his account to "facilitate agreement or consensus across [a science's] different paradigms."[6] Friedman's second departure from Kuhn, with which we shall deal in the following section, is the place he assigns in the development of physics to such intermediary figures as Galileo, Helmholtz, and Poincaré.[7]

In chapter 5 we noted the inappropriateness of Friedman's employment of the terms *meta-framework* and *meta-paradigm*. Philosophy and mathematics, the two meta-frameworks on which he focuses in *Dynamics of Reason,* play no higher-order constitutive role with regard to scientific frameworks, as the term *meta-framework* would imply. In Friedman's picture, they function solely as disciplines that border on science in certain respects, to which scientists do not contribute professionally, but to which they do on occasion relate; as fields of discourse in which certain scientifically relevant ideas and possibilities are discussed that deviate sharply from those constitutive of current scientific research, that may end up being incorporated in a new scientific paradigm. They serve science as reservoirs of novel and unconventional thinking. Their great value for science, Friedman implies, lies precisely in the fact that because the work done by mathematicians and philosophers is *not* determined or constituted by the paradigms currently employed in the sciences, they are capable of thinking the scientifically unthinkable, as it were. In fields related to science such as philosophy and mathematics, ideas significantly different from those constitutive of a science are liable to be keenly discussed and pursued without the risk of running up against heartfelt commitments. Such debates— such as the discussion of non-Euclidean geometries during the nineteenth century—Friedman implies, are capable of coming to the attention of the scientific community by virtue of members who make it their business to keep informed of relevant developments outside their field.[8]

Friedman makes much of these extrascientific discourses and of the scientists whose thinking they succeed in enriching, exactly because he deems it impossible for such debates to arise and have an impact within scientific discourse proper. In this respect he is right, of course. Since no one is capable of seriously proposing and considering alternatives to the framework by which his thinking is normatively governed, framework replacement necessarily requires some sort of appeal to an external source. But we find Friedman's solution unnecessarily restrictive. First, as we have argued in some detail, if a person is seriously incapable of considering a normative alternative, having it proposed, or even argued for by others does not make it any more acceptable. Discourse conducted outside one's immediate field can become crucially important to its rational transformation only *if it poses or addresses a serious and trusted critical challenge,* not by serving merely as a source of alternative ideas. The idea that mere exposure to an alternative framework is enough to woo a person away from his own is both conceivable and common. People are regularly transformed by being thus "persuaded," as Wittgenstein uses the term. But Friedman is interested not in Wittgensteinian persuasion but in *rational* framework transition. To that end, the mere availability of alternatives will not suffice. To get beyond Rortian irony, philosophy and mathematics (to remain within the confines of Friedman's original account) must be shown to pose to science a normative critical challenge, not merely a different way of thinking. As noted in chapter 5, Friedman's account of science's engagement with philosophy and mathematics lacks any form of critical content.

In the light of our analysis, because research within a mature science is governed by a constitutive normative framework, serious engagement with disciplines and professional individuals whose work and thinking are not so determined is a necessary condition for the very possibility of normative criticism, and hence of the very possibility of rational framework replacement. But there is no reason to limit such engagement to meta-scientific disciplines such as philosophy and mathematics as much of Friedman's work does.[9] Even in the highly restricted case of theoretical physics explored by Friedman, it is wrong to assume that philosophers and mathematicians are the only professionals a working physicist is liable to engage professionally beyond the confines of his field. With respect both to the scope of relevant professional engagement outside one's field and to its critical potential, we find Peter Galison's account of scientific trading zones a more promising perspective than the meta-frameworks of *Dynamics of Reason.*

Practitioners Abroad

In *Image and Logic* (1997), Galison draws attention to the way scientists maintain professional contact with members of other disciplines relevant to their work and to the trading zones in which they conduct their "business."[10] Like Friedman, Galison's account also builds on and away from an essentially Kuhnian, "antipositivist" picture of scientific development (784), which, again like Friedman, he sees as an overreaction, and bemoans "the absence" in it, "of a continuous substratum of common practice across the break that underlies the image of 'paradigm shifts' and 'different worlds,' in which there is no overarching notion of progress" (794).[11] But unlike Friedman, Galison's account is not motivated by the problem of the *rationality* of paradigm shifts—at least not explicitly. His motives are more squarely historiographical: a desire to get the story of science right by doing justice to the sense in which physics as a whole exhibits a far greater stability and continuity across major changes in theory than Kuhn's picture allows.[12] In other words, Galison does not oppose (or at least should not oppose) the idea of a major Kuhnian paradigm shift occurring within any one of physics' subcultures—a division he minimally envisages as tripartite, comprising theory, experiment, and instrument building (799). The Kuhnian idea he does oppose is the assumption that physics instrument designers and builders or experimentalists inevitably "march in lockstep with theory" (798). "It is now commonplace that the political dislocations of the French Revolution did not alter economics, social structure, politics and cultural life in the same measure," he notes wryly, and it is, therefore, "high time that we recognize that the physics community is no less complex" (798).

In other words still, Galison remains unmoved by the problem of incommensurability *within* each of physics' subcultures, and subsequently, quite unlike Friedman's meta-paradigms, his "trading zones" appear at least not to be meant to solve it.[13] Their explanatory function, as he describes it, is to account synchronically for the "social, material, and intellectual mortar binding together the disunified traditions of experimenting, theorizing, and instrument building" (803) in physics and not, as in Friedman, to diachronically mediate "transitions between radically different [consecutive] conceptual frameworks."[14] Nonetheless, despite its apparent irrelevance to the questions that exercise both Friedman's *Dynamics of Reason* and the present study, Galison's notion of a scientific trading zone proves extremely helpful in ways he fails to anticipate.

Not unlike Friedman, Galison's "original hope" to offer a "laminated description" of physics that would "underline the heterogeneity of practice within the wider physics community while allowing continuities on one level to bridge discontinuities on another" (783) proved futile. The diversities of belief and practice between the subdisciplines of physics prove too great to reasonably claim that one community's stable paradigm could mediate the paradigm shifts of another. A discontinuity between the successive incommensurable paradigms of one community cannot be bridged by a third, incommensurable with both—even if it remains continuous across the shift. The relative unity of physics as a whole is achieved differently, argues Galison, not by "intercalating" the successive paradigms of one subculture by means of that of another, but by intercalating the subcultures themselves on the basis of their local interdependencies. Galison's key idea is to view the subcultures of physics as trading with each other in designated trading zones.

> Like two cultures distinct but living near enough to trade, they can share some activities while diverging on many others. What is crucial is that in the local context of the trading zone, *despite* the differences in classification, significance, and standards of demonstration, the two groups can collaborate. . . . Anthropologists are familiar with different cultures encountering one another through trade, even when the significance of the objects traded—and of the trade itself—may be utterly different for the two sides. And with the anthropologists, it is crucial to note that nothing in the notion of trade presupposes some universal notion of a neutral currency. Quite the opposite, much of the interest of the category of trade is things can be coordinated . . . without reference to some external gauge. (803; original emphasis)

More recently, Galison has come to acknowledge the fact (pointed out by others)[15] that scientific trading normally extends far beyond the give-and-take conducted between practitioners of the science's various "subcultures" on which he focuses in *Image and Logic*.

> We need this kind of approach not only to grasp the relation of algebraic geometers to string theorists—but also the way soil scientists speak with farmers, the way fishermen speak with fisheries regulators, the way research scientists speak with students.[16]

And the list should be extended to include all forms of professional scientific interfacing, such as "trading" for financial or public support, interacting with other scientific disciplines, offering scientific opinion in courts of law and scientific advice to all manner of public and private enterprises, and deliberating the didactics of the best way to teach one's subject,[17] as well as engaging one's students, the media, the wider public, and the historians and philosophers of one's fields.[18] Trading zones, in short, abound.

Galison's metaphor is useful, first, for the way it brings to the fore the professional, interest-driven purposefulness of such interactions, largely overlooked by Friedman. "Trading" practitioners may well become aware of and eventually endorse offerings of adjacent fields that far transcend their initial "shopping lists." But the utility and merit of these findings will always be measured against what they perceive their professional needs and interests to be. As we argued against Friedman, central as such an offering may be to its original field, its mere *availability* will not suffice to render it a scientific live option for traders on behalf of other fields. Galison's novel proposal to view engaging practitioners from different fields as *trading* rather than as mere conversation partners captures the essential self-critical element we have insisted is lacking in Sellars's and Brandom's account of the more general game of giving and asking for reasons. Professional traders frequent trading zones equipped with specific shopping lists that mark what they perceive they lack and constantly on the lookout for opportunities they failed to envisage. The trading they actually accomplish will often extend beyond their initial lists, as unanticipated offerings are brought to their attention. (Professional fairs are primarily geared to exposing potential buyers to new and unforeseen possibilities.)

But even then, the dealing will seldom be idle. Unanticipated offerings will be "purchased" only when conceived as needed, that is to say, when conceived as new solutions to existing problems or as improvements to existing solutions. The very idea of agency in trading settings usefully presupposes an inherent measure of self-critical incentive.

The second important aspect of Galison's metaphor concerns not the place but the *medium* by which such transactions are conducted. For members of different cultures and disciplines to meet and do business, more is needed than a designated "zone." In order to trade they need to be able to converse with one another. The most novel aspect of Galison's account is his analysis of how scientific trading zones, like all trading zones, operate by means of pidgins and creoles—"interlanguages" that combine simplified versions of the parties' professional "intralanguages." To coordinate their needs and expectations, they must be able to present their needs and offerings in a manner accessible to those with whom they trade.

It is at this point that Galison unwarrantedly goes on to claim that the notion of a "mediating contact language" (833) for scientific trading can serve as a philosophical corrective to more than the "block periodization" of Kuhn's account.

> Moving away from the stack periodization typical of conceptual schemes, radical translations, gestalt switches, and paradigm shifts comes at a price: we lose the vivid metaphorical imagery of totalistic transformations. In the place of such all-or-nothing mutations we need some guidance in thinking about the local configurations that are produced when two complex sociological and symbolic systems confront one another. Anthropologists are familiar with such exchanges, and one of the most interesting fields of investigation has been the anthropological linguistics of pidginization and creolization; I have used these ideas throughout the preceding chapters to characterize the border zones between different theoretical, experimental, and engineering cultures. (830–31)

Galison, we believe, is right in assuming that his notion of scientific trading zones holds an important key to overcoming the problem of rational framework replacement (i.e., that of not having to reduce all paradigm shifts to gestalt switches) but not at all in the way he implies. First, the problem of rational framework replacement is primarily not that of accounting for how "two complex sociological and symbolic systems" confront one another but that of accounting for how one is developed out of, or from within, another. (Which, as we have argued throughout this book, boils down to that of accounting for the ability of practitioners of standing to adopt a critical stance toward the norms constitutive of their speech, practice, and thinking, which in turn, we have seen, reduces to that of accounting for their exposure to trusted, potentially "ambivalating" normative criticism.)

Second, as already noted, Galison is uninterested in the diachronic problem of framework *modification*. He introduces the notion of a trading zone as a way of accounting for the synchronic coordination achieved across the boundaries between, as he puts it here, "different theoretical, experimental, and engineering cultures,"[19] which has very little to do with radical framework transitions within the confines of any one paradigm-constituted scientific subculture.

Finally, it is not at all clear what Galison means when he talks about scientific trading zones as places in which "complex sociological and symbolic systems confront one another." On the contrary, on his description, trading zones are where different practitioners come to trade, not to fight; the pidgins and creoles they develop are designed and employed to facilitate transaction, not dispute.

Still, the trading zone is a rich and fruitful metaphor that serves Galison impressively well in crafting a history of modern microphysics that endorses what he believes is right about the "antipositivist" critique of positivism while avoiding what he thinks most wrong—namely, Kuhn's theory-driven, "crazy-quilt" (51), "block-periodized . . . 'all-inclusive' breaks" (13) within physics *as a whole*. With this we have no quarrel. The problem is that the problem of the rationality of framework replacement is not confined to physics as a whole. Breaking the "lockstep" of a science's subcultures does not solve the problem of framework modification and replacement for the framework-dependency of each such subculture to itself. Galison agrees. What solves the problem, he claims (though nowhere really argues), is not breaking the lockstep, but the very ability of scientific traders to talk across their framework barriers by means of the trading zones' pidgins and creoles. Viewing a science "as a densely connected map of distinct cultures bound by interlanguages" (51), he argues in his lengthy introduction to *Image and Logic,* safeguards it from the "form of relativism" advocated late of Kuhn by Barry Barnes, David Bloor, and Harry Collins, which denies that "science [can] have any purchase on 'truth' or 'the world'" (17–18). This is a curious statement indeed coming from someone, who in the closing paragraphs of the book aligns himself philosophically with Davidson's and the later Putnam's decidedly framework-dependent accounts of truth and reality. The existence of interlanguages developed to effectively facilitate the level of communication needed for trade and transfer of know-how across disciplinary borders can have no bearing on the traditional questions of truth and realism to which Galison seems to be hinting in his opening chapter, for the simple reason that interlanguage cannot get those it serves *beyond* language. Intercalating *cultures* (by means of an interculture) and intercalating culture and reality are categorically different undertakings. Like Friedman (with respect to the diachronic axis), Galison too (across the synchronic axis) seems to think, at least in the opening chapter of *Image and Logic,* that by tuning down the radical abruptness of Kuhnian paradigm shifts, the challenge of "cultural relativism" can be somehow met.[20] As we noted in the case of Friedman, this is an illusion.

Our main problem, however, is not the traditional problem of truth and realism but that of rational framework replacement. And on this count, in view of our discussion so far, Galison's trading zones would seem to have little to offer. For the type of self-critical awareness at play here is precisely not the kind in which we are interested. The need practitioners feel to trade and exchange with neighboring disciplines pertains to the type of queries Carnap dubbed "internal," namely, questions (or as Kuhn would have it, "puzzles") that arise within a functioning field of inquiry, as opposed to "external" questions pertaining to difficulties and shortcomings perceived to plague the framework constitutive of the field. In this sense, rather than create ambivalence, trading it would seem tends to reinforce commitment to the prevailing framework.

Is there a sense in which practitioners can find themselves *challenged* in trading zone settings to the point of destabilizing their allegiance to the framework constitutive of their thinking? As it stands, Galison's analysis offers little in this respect. According to Galison, the meeting ground facilitated by the trading zone's mediating pidgins and creoles is cordoned off from the deep ontological commitments that divide the traders, creating a safe space of shared phenomenology, as he puts it. But we believe he takes his metaphor a step too far, and in doing so misses something crucial. Here is how he describes the "pidginized . . . foreigner version" of relativistic quantum field theory fashioned in 1964 by two prominent theorists, James Bjorken and Sidney Drell, as a textbook for nontheorists.

> Despite the radical difference in ontology—the set of what there is—a meeting ground exists between the experimenters and the quantum field theorists. That trading zone forms around the description of the phenomenological world of particle physics: How do photons recoil from electrons? How do electrons scatter from positrons? How do photons create pairs of electrons and positrons in the near presence of a proton? How are magnetic moments calculated for the muon? For these and similar questions, experimenters and theorists come to agreement about rules of representation, calculation, and local interpretation. Bjorken and Drell's volume 1 is an attempt to create a stable pidgin language that mediates between experimenter and theorist. Reduction of mathematical structure, suppression of exceptional cases, minimization of internal links between theoretical structures, simplified explanatory structure—*these are all ways that the theorists prepare their subjects for the exchange with their experimental colleagues.* I take these moves toward regularization to be the formal language analogues of phonetic, syntactical, and lexical reduction of natural languages. (835; emphasis added)

If Galisonian trading zones are to hold the key to normative transformation in science, we need to look less to what traders bring with them *to* the meeting ground—in terms of both their offerings and their shopping lists—and more to what they are liable to come *away* with. Galison's rendering of the made-simple, "foreigners'" edition of Bjorken and Drell concentrates exclusively on the former. It emphasizes two important aspects of the mediating work of scientific interlanguage but overlooks two others. Galison lays great stress on the "watering down" involved in making one's science simple; the way "the fullness of theoretical representation would perforce be restricted (pidginized)" (834); how major practitioners like Bjorken and Drell bring to the trading zone significantly diluted versions of their worldviews—versions that not only simplify them, but present them in a way that plays down their "radical differences" while emphasizing the phenomenology they are able to share. In this sense, foreigners' versions of a scientific language necessarily contain less than the more developed originals they purport to simplify, especially with regard to their more technical and intricate dimensions of which Galison speaks. Only those initiated into the field will possess the technical terminology, literacy, and know-how to grasp and appreciate their community's equivalent to "the fullness of theoretical representation" employed by the second quantized theorists Galison describes.

But in one important respect, consistently overlooked by Galison, foreigners' "pidgin" versions most often contain much more than their in-house, full-blooded originals. We are referring to such grounding elements of a professional community's normative framework and worldview that are so taken for granted that they are passed over in silence by practitioners among themselves: the things seasoned researchers learn *not* to justify or explain in their proofs;[21] the things that scientists learn in the course of their training go without saying in the field. These will often need to be "made explicit" when formulating a foreigners' version. (This is why textbooks are generally bad examples of full-blooded professional languages, for textbooks do not normally represent the professional language as spoken by the "natives"; they are rather texts addressed to trainees and novices that are written in the pidgins and creoles of the community's science-training trading zones.)

This is the one highly relevant aspect of talking shop to the uninitiated that Galison's interesting account of scientific trading misses completely: the way trading practitioners are often required, when abroad, to articulate in simple terms (to pidginize, if you wish) elements of their worldview that are so taken for granted back home that they remain largely unarticulated in their everyday professional discourse.[22] Not all trading zones are the same in this respect. Parties to interfaith dialogue, or peace negotiations, for instance, tend diplomatically to tread carefully so as not to offend their trading partners by unintentionally pushing too hard on matters of ideology and faith. But with regard to science, such reservations are extremely rare (such as, again, when issues of religious faith are liable to be involved, as when conducting certain curricular negotiations in certain school systems). On the contrary, when representatives of different scientific cultures trade with nonscientists or with each other, more often than not they are met with real curiosity, even fascination, and subjected to the friendly prompting and interrogation of parties who are genuinely interested in what they do and how they think, and who jump at the opportunity to receive an authoritative firsthand report.

Galison's oversight may be charged to the fact that in the "real" trading zones studied in the anthropological and sociological literature on "real" pidgins and creoles, the parties are usually far more cagey and reserved in this respect. Trading across ethnic or religious boundaries is often considered culturally threatening and potentially corrupting by at least one of the sides. But because trading is indispensable, the trading zone must be made safe by ensuring that negotiations are limited to what each side seeks to purchase from the other while cordoning off the broader cultural and other issues that sorely divide them. Trading is enabled and safeguarded by interlanguages that subtly serve the double function of both contact medium and *buffer zone*. But while scientific pidgins resemble "real" pidgins in the former sense, they hardly ever do so in the latter sense. Scientific traders engage each other with interest, fascination, and, at times, even incredulity but not with suspicion or mistrust. Unlike "real" pidgins, scientific pidgins are neither designed nor employed with a view to shielding the communicating parties from one another's worldviews. Insofar as the parties entertain "radical differences in ontology," as in Galison's example, their meeting place will be most often characterized less by a polite and considerate *bracketing* off of foundational commitment than by lively good-natured, unthreatening curiosity as to how the other side sees the world. It is hard to conceive of anything like a scientific analog to the kind of fear and suspicion typical of real trading zones.

This is not to say that making explicit one's innermost professional intuitions and commitments is always an easy or happy exercise. Many people have great difficulty articulating, let alone justifying, what they take for granted. Others find it less difficult than disconcerting. Either way, few if any in the scientific world would consider being honestly prompted by fellow academics, technicians, university management, students, grant officials, or the media to openly explain the presuppositions of their worldview as threatening or potentially corrupting as is often the case in real trading zones.

There is an important sense, then, in which scientific trading zones, and their like, offer opportunities with regard to scientific language of a nature quite different from those discussed by Galison. For it is only when "trading" with such significant others that practitioners are required to explicate, explain, discuss, and field questions and queries regarding the normative frameworks constitutive of their professional work. And it is here, when trading away from home, at the trading posts they frequent, far more than amid their professional milieus back home, that, we suggest (pace DiSalle, and going a large step beyond Galison), scientists are liable to become exposed to the kind of ambivalating normative criticism they and their peers are incapable of self-leveling. For it is here, far more than back home, that they are likely to encounter individuals who are sufficiently interested yet sufficiently impartial and, therefore, trusted whose probing, curious prompting obliges them to articulate and justify that which in the course of their scientific work requires neither.

Compensating for Galison's oversight brings to the fore a related oversight of Brandom's that can now be put right to a fuller extent than in previous chapters. It is often the case that the very act of articulation involved in making explicit a taken-for-granted norm or constitutive presupposition is enough to create the inner distance and self-estrangement required to render them ambivalent and hence subject to self-criticism.[23] In such cases, hearing oneself think aloud in response to the innocent probing of the uninitiated can suddenly and unexpectedly strike one as hollow and unconvincing. In such cases, one's own attempts at articulation seem to function as an unflattering playback. Here, explaining ourselves in the classroom or trading zone, in ways we are seldom required to do in the company of fellow researchers, we can experience how we sound and seem to others by simply listening to our own voices. But it is not as if we can become normatively self-critical merely by talking to ourselves. The kind of self-alienation we can experience in these situations is only made possible by the insistent presence, or *imagined* presence,[24] of students or trading partners.

Sellars and Brandom rightly insist on the dialogical, gamelike setting of such acts of articulation and justification. People feel obliged to explain themselves only when asked, or in anticipation of being asked.

In former chapters we have pointed out repeatedly how they both miss the central critical element that motivates most *inquiry into* other people's reasons for acting. What thinking of such exchanges in the context of the scientific trading zone reveals is a similar and even more significant potential for adopting a normatively self-critical stance in responding to such (actual or imagined) prompting; how it is possible to be rendered ambivalent and subsequently normatively self-critical without actually being normatively criticized by others, only prompted by them to explain oneself.[25]

Needless to say, not all normative self-criticism typical of scientific trading zones originates in this way. Incredulity need not be *self*-generated. More often than not practitioners prompted to explain themselves do so comfortably and confidently, making explicit their heartfelt professional norms without experiencing any initial sense of self-estrangement. In these cases it is the incredulity of their "foreign" interlocutors that may set the ambivalating process in motion. Either way, and this is the important point, it is by virtue of the special discursive conditions of the scientific trading zone, so lacking in normal in-house, professional discourse, that in being asked and willing to give their reasons, practitioners away from home are liable to become exposed to the kind of destabilizing normative critique capable of rendering them normatively ambivalent.

Thus, by joining Galison in taking a broader view of scientific discourse so as to include the diverse trading conducted by the representatives of a science with the various groups and institutions they engage professionally, it is possible, we believe, to chart a philosophically viable account of rational framework replacement in science that nonetheless remains faithful to the kind of philosophical framework exemplified in the work of the later Wittgenstein, Rorty, Sellars, Walzer, Brandom, and Friedman to which we are committed.

Back to Science II: The Force of Creative Indecision

Popper's great achievement lies in relocating rationality in troubled, destabilizing moments of earnest criticism rather than in feats of confident discovery or proof. However, he and his followers have done little to give philosophical precision, depth, or grounding to the idea of rationality as criticism, and the little they have done remains by and large almost deliberately out of touch with much of latter-day philosophy, as does Popper's own work. The attempt made here to take Popper's idea of rationality-as-criticism seriously has led us to focus attention on criticism that is both normative and self-directed—neither of which has received philosophical attention among Popperians. The previous section followed Friedman, and Galison, in exploring the possible extradisciplinary discursive contexts in which scientists are liable to be subjected to the kind of trusted normative criticism necessary for enabling them to take a normative self-critical stand.

We now turn to examine more closely the second, and more disturbing, conclusion of our analysis, certainly from a Popperian point of view: namely, that, regardless of discursive environment, in the case of normative criticism, adopting a genuinely self-critical stand is impossible from a position of firm commitment; and that normative commitment *cannot* be directly dislodged by argument. With regard to normative commitment, the truly transformative moment of rationality, we have argued, is not one of bold conjecture or keen refutation but one of disturbing, destabilizing *ambivalence;* a moment characterized by indecisive dithering—a state of mind not usually considered the most inspiring and motivating and, therefore, not usually associated with rationality. But if there is any truth in our analysis, then the creative individuals initially responsible for rationally transforming a field are to be sought among those who were lucky to be exposed to the ambivalating challenge of trusted external critics—real or imagined. But that is not enough. An individual successfully ambivalated toward what Haugeland calls his "existential commitments"[26] may end up thinking differently from his colleagues, or even considering a career change, but that in itself will not suffice to transform the field. To have an impact on the normative commitments of their home communities, it is not enough for individuals to merely *be* or *become* normatively ambivalent; their ambivalence must be capable of spreading and infecting a critical mass of their fellow researchers.

The argument in the previous section proceeded from the outside in, as it were, with the arrow of explanation pointing from the social to the personal in an attempt to characterize the kind of intersubjective discursive setting most conducive to destabilizing the intrasubjective normative commitments of *individual* practitioners. But an account of normative *communal* change, as in scientific revolutions, will not be considered complete before the direction of explanation is reversed again to account for the impact of ambivalated individuals, fresh back from the trading zones, on their home communities. Trading zones arc only visited by individuals, never by whole communities. Therefore, only individuals can be transformed outside the community; whole communities are transformed at home, from within, by members of standing and voice whose work not only reflects their own personal ambivalence, but is taken seriously enough within the community to have a corresponding ambivalating impact on a critical mass of their colleagues. (This is where we steer closest to Walzer's notion of *connected* criticism.) If there is any truth in our conclusions so far, then the role of such individuals in the history of major scientific upheavals is decisive. But their story has largely yet to be told. Current historiography of science, diverse, wide-ranging, and richly reflective as it has become in recent decades, passes such figures over in near-silence. Historians of science show little awareness of their existence, and no interest at all in the sources of their ambivalence and its effect on their peers. Telling their story raises two related questions: that of their visibility and that of the nature of their impact.

First, to visibility. Ambivalent, undecided scientists are hard to see, for both historiographical and objective reasons. Kuhn's influential historiography of paradigm shifts tends to paint vivid "before" and "after" pictures set side by side in dramatic, seemingly unbridgeable contrast, as in a weight watchers' ad. Focusing thus on steadfast adherents to the old and the new paradigm, it is easy to see how this kind of narrative structure remains virtually blind to the intermediary figures whose commitment to the old is partially waning, with no solid alternative yet in sight.[27] Those whose historiography of science leans more toward Popper than toward Kuhn are no better off. For here, again, those responsible for the intermediary moments of deliberative indecision are lost from sight in the dazzling light of the knockdown *experimentum crucis* and the novel bold conjecture. Ambiguity and indecision are simply not considered the stuff of science, or at least not the stuff capable of contributing to understanding the drama of bold scientific advancement.[28] But there are exceptions. Friedman, as we shall see immediately, is one.

But first it is important to understand that the invisibility of ambivalent, undecided scientists owes to more than historiographical blinker-
ing. It is not as if such individuals could be clearly seen had *historians* not
been looking elsewhere. For they are obscured from the sight even of their
own communities, for the simple reason that doubts and indecision are
hardly ever considered worthy of publication even by those they plague.
Modern science is a predominantly written culture whose worldview is
cultivated, enriched, expanded, modified, and proliferated primarily by
means of research papers. Scientific research papers are as a rule not
where one doubts and dithers. The vast majority of doubters and dither-
ers do not view their ambivalence and indecision worthy of scientific
publication, let alone their potential editors, referees, and readers. Indecision and doubtfulness are not regarded contributions to knowledge as
are the kind of reasoned suggestions for new developments and reasoned
challenges to old developments that are deemed publishable. It is true that
current historiography of science remains largely uninterested in the ambivalent and undecided members of the communities it studies, but it is
equally true that the ambivalent and the undecided remain hidden from
scientific view within those communities, where their work is relegated
almost entirely to the private realm of diary, journal, logbook, personal
memoir, or personal correspondence, none of which are capable of carry-
ing their master's voice effectively into the public professional domain of
scientific discourse proper.

This is not entirely true, however. Undecided, ambivalated practitioners of standing often succeed (if, as we shall see, somewhat unwittingly) in
making their indecision known to and felt by their peers in ways capable
of effectively ambivalating the field. Friedman's story of the history of
modern mathematical physics is an interesting first case in point.

In his attempt to find rationality where Kuhn (at least the Kuhn of
the "purple passages" of *Structure*)[29] finds gestalt-switch-like conversion
(of the kind Wittgenstein terms "persuasion"), Friedman, to recall, elects
to redescribe paradigm shifts as a smoother, less ruptured, "evolutionary" (to use his term) process of transition in which new frameworks are
developed naturally and gradually out of their predecessors, which they
subsequently continue to preserve as special cases. In Friedman's decidedly more leveled picture of framework replacement, figures whose work

occupies intermediate positions between the two end points of the transition become important but for reasons very different from our own. For Friedman, the importance of their work lies in furnishing the "essential intermediate stage[s]" between the old and the new framework that render the latter "actually continuous with" the former.[30] Two of his main examples are Galileo's "celebrated treatment of free fall and projectile motion," which occupied a halfway position in the transition from Aristotelian to Newtonian mechanics, and Poincaré's work on the foundations of geometry, which occupied an analogous position in the transition from classical physics to relativity theory, "without which," he submits, "it is hard to imagine how the use of non-Euclidean geometry in physics could have ever been envisioned as a real possibility."[31] Friedman rightly describes neither work as ambivalent or undecided, or as in any other way unsure or troubled. On the contrary, he presents them both as confident, well-formed, and nonproblematic positions that while retaining certain elements of the old developed certain novel departures from it that would eventually form the basis for the new. Such mediating positions, he argues, provide living disproof of the radical unbridgeability of Kuhn's depiction of the transitions they so nicely straddled.

Friedman is right not to describe the mature works of Galileo and Poincaré as anything but confident presentations of the positions to which, by the time they were published, both were fully committed. Tycho Brahe's hybrid grafting of a heliocentric planetary system on a basically geocentric cosmology would be another example of a midway position presented in genuine confidence and with full conviction—although Tycho fashioned his hybrid theory in reaction to, rather than in anticipation of, the heliocentric framework eventually adopted. But accepting this does not commit one to Friedman's account of the role of such intermediaries in the course of framework transition.

The intermediary frameworks devised by Tycho, Galileo, and Poincaré, we insist, were no more "natural developments" of those they purported to replace than were the final positions of Kepler, Newton, and Einstein natural developments of theirs. The fact that they were able to form and maintain such halfway positions only proves that even they, on whose work the old framework evidently still exerted a profound hold, had succeeded in becoming sufficiently dissatisfied with it to propose and endorse several radical departures. The relative "nearness" of the positions they formed in relation to those they abandoned as to those later adopted by their respective communities does not absolve Friedman of the need to account for their *reasons* for forming them.

Cases of such intermediary figures of standing, whose mature works attest to a strained split, or dithering between a lingering commitment to the frameworks constitutive of their earlier work, and a deeply felt need to modify those same frameworks—to which one might add such hybrids as George Peacock's strained twofold account of algebra,[32] William Rowan Hamilton's suggestion of there being two rather than one "science of dynamics,"[33] and William Whewell's equally strained two-sided "antithetical" theory of scientific truth[34]—bear vivid witness, we submit, not to how easy but to how *difficult* it must have been for them to forge and maintain such positions. Tycho's planetary theory, Galileo's analysis of projectile motion, Peacock's algebras, and Poincaré's geometrical conventionalism are indeed presented by their authors with confidence and conviction, but, we insist, there is nothing continuous or natural about their radical and painful breaking with the party-line geocentrism, Aristotelianism, algebraic realism, and Kantianism from which they were respectively distancing themselves. We prefer to see such fundamental departures as the work of deeply ambivalent practitioners, whose painful compromises mark the extent to which they were capable of going. What makes the likes of Galileo, Poincaré, and Peacock indispensable to the deeply transformative moments in which they partook is the way the highly creative yet inherently unstable hybrid systems they proposed unwittingly preserved, displayed, and, therefore, forcefully propagated the profound ambivalence that begot them, forcing other leading practitioners to take a stand.

As noted, normative doubts or ambivalence per se do not spread easily within a well-functioning scientific discipline. But confident resolutions of such doubts do. And most often the first attempts to resolve such doubts are proposed by the ambivalated individuals themselves. In Frankfurtian terms, normative ambivalence amounts to being of two minds with respect to certain elements of one's normative framework, a form of indecisive dithering regarding those elements. To the remainder of their framework (the part of their *I*-part to which they have not become ambivalent) such individuals remain wholeheartedly committed. It follows that even when their ambivalence is resolved by replacing the doubtful elements by others, the rest of their framework will remain firmly intact. Hence, the kind of hybrid, halfway solutions proposed by Tycho, Galileo, and Poincaré are exactly what one would expect in the first instance.

Modest as their suggestions might seem in retrospect, few are capable of such creative feats of rethinking and self-dividing, however deeply ambivalated they have become. It takes a Brahe to replace a fully fledged, functioning, Ptolemaic, geocentric cosmology with a heliocentric planetary system embodied within an otherwise geocentric cosmology; a Galileo to replace a two-tiered, hierarchical universe that displays for each of its two parts a different kind of natural motion, with a unitary, nonhierarchical universe that incorporates both forms of natural motion in its one part; a Peacock to propose a systematic account of modern algebra as a hybrid juxtaposition of "arithmetical algebra" viewed as a truth-governed science of number that gives rise by "suggestion" to a sufficiently general, purely formal "symbolical algebra"; and a Poincaré to replace Kant's account of the epistemic exclusivity and necessity of Euclidean geometry with an equally constitutive notion of the same "form of intuition" but adopted by convention. And, again, there was nothing "natural" or "naturally continuous" in any of these startlingly original proposals.

On the contrary, not only do such hybrids not seem natural and continuous to the fellow practitioners to whom they are addressed, but they strike them as forced and jarringly disjointed. Once the coherent unity of the old system has been broken and key elements of an alternative system have been put into play by practitioners of such standing, other members of the community are capable of becoming ambivalent with regard to larger portions of the framework, and motivated in turn to develop the transition much further, as was the case with regard to all four.

In Conclusion

From the neo-Kantian, Kuhnian perspective we share with Friedman, science, more than any other human undertaking, vividly demonstrates the thoroughly contingent, community-based framework dependency of even the best of human knowledge and practice. Yet at the same time, science is regarded as the epitome of human rationality. For a work firmly committed to both, purporting to make a case for the possibility of rational framework replacement, science poses the most serious challenge. By what scientific standards can science be said to hold its very scientific standards accountable? It was hence only natural to conclude this study by returning to science.

Friedman's *Dynamics of Reason* is an unprecedented attempt to remain maximally committed to both horns of the dilemma: not to allow science's framework dependency to impede its rationality even at moments of framework replacement and to do so without renouncing what we have here termed Comparative Irrealism. But it does so at the price of giving up on the entire project of the present study. According to Friedman, framework replacement is rational in theoretical physics only because the successive frameworks of theoretical physics bear a relationship to one another to which Comparative Irrealism does not apply. Framework replacement is rational in theoretical physics because it remains possible to reason across the divide. It follows that in cases in which Comparative Irrealism *does* apply—cases in which the new framework *cannot* be described as preserving the old as a limiting case and developing out of it "naturally"—framework transitions cannot be rational. Outside mathematical physics, Friedman more than implies, cultural relativism reigns supreme.

This study disputes both of these claims. It contests the exemption Friedman grants theoretical physics from Comparative Irrealism while making the case for the possibility of rational framework transition *in the face of* Comparative Irrealism. For us, science at-its-best is not the exception Friedman makes it out to be but a paradigmatic instance of the rule of which he elects by implication to despair. This is why for us science poses the gravest challenge.

But our main disagreement with Friedman, as with most of the thinkers whose work we have discussed, has had less to do with the extension of the rational so much as with its very nature. The central bias of this study has been to insist along with McDowell and the Popperians on locating at the heart of rationality a capacity and willingness to engage in "reflective criticism," which, to quote McDowell one last time, when fully reflective, amounts to "a standing obligation to reflect about and criticize the standards by which, at any time, [one] takes [oneself] to be gov-

erned . . . from the midst of the way of thinking one is reflecting about."[35]
It is a bias that grows from a grafting of the essentially self-critical stance
central to the reflective, free-willed self-governance on which normativity
is made to turn in the *Critique of Practical Reason* onto the neo-Kantian
realization that, despite their constitutive role, normative frameworks cannot only be *defied* but be meaningfully *changed*. And if normative frameworks can be changed or replaced, rationality must consist in an obligation not only to keeping oneself knowingly in check in the light of one's
normative commitments but also somehow to keeping knowingly in
check one's normative commitments themselves.

Hence the problem, for this is a feat no one can perform alone. If we
insist on thinking about the creative individuals responsible for changing
our way of thinking and acting as lonely "strong poets" working in isolation, then Rortian irony is indeed the only kind of self-distancing they
can hope to achieve. In terms of the Frankfurtian picture developed in
the previous chapter, most people are able to create the inner distance required for reflecting on their *I*-parts, but the measure of self-objectification
they are able to achieve will forever lack the normative bite of true reflective *criticism*. Reflective individuals are capable of standing back from
their normative commitments looking in, as it were. But from that vantage point, they can hope for no more than self-consciousness. Where we
have ventured a substantial step beyond Rorty (and Frankfurt, for that
matter) is to propose viewing such individuals as conducting their sensitive and thoughtful inner dialogues and self-monitoring in the company
of trusted normative critics, in which they find themselves prompted to
articulate their commitments, and challenged by individuals who are
committed differently. On such a construal, reflective criticism still remains an ultimately personal affair, undertaken and undergone wholly
within the confines of the intrasubjective dialogue of self. But the external, intersubjective dialogical context of trusted critics can have an ambivalating effect capable of crucially effecting its entry points, by destabilizing the I-part status of the normative commitments they criticize.
In the company of critics, we have argued at length, the playful doubtfulness of Rortian irony is liable to be replaced by the kind of anxious
normative ambivalence capable of both motivating and supporting a
truly normative self-critical stance.

And thus Normative Diversity has come interestingly of age. It started out motivating this study and then severely challenging it almost to the point of paralysis. If our norms and standards are fixed and universal, there is no sense or need to demand that reflective criticism apply to them. Conceding Normative Diversity requires it. However, conceding Normative Diversity entails Comparative Irrealism, from which it follows that sufficiently diverse normative systems are normatively unrankable. Normative Diversity, in other words, became responsible for obstructing the possibility of solving the problem to which it initially gave rise so severely that for the vast majority of relevant contributors to the discussion, it renders it insolvable.

But at the end of the day, Normative Diversity, one might say, has morphed from being the source of the problem to the key to solving it. Fully fledged normative reflective criticism can become a real possibility but only in response to the earnest and trusted normative critique of others. Only in the context of a truly normatively diverse discursive setting can a person become sufficiently ambivalated to question the norms contested by his critics. The self remains Rortian, if you wish (if much enriched by Frankfurt), but the setting, Habermasian (if much enriched by an interpretive combination of Walzer and Brandom). For although rationality ultimately resides in the intrasubjective, it becomes in an important sense intersubjectively "communicative," though not in Habermas's sense of the term. And it is a picture that fully applies to the sciences, as long as their story is narrated richly enough to include the normative diversity experienced at the science's various trading zones and the impact on the community of those who return from them sufficiently ambivalated to rethink the field.

But all this has come at a price many may not be willing to pay. Due to the logical priority of norms to logic,[36] normative criticism is powerless to convince those whose norms it challenges merely by the power of its reasoning. We have had, therefore, to find a way to account for the transformative force of a normative critical argument despite it not being endorsed. For many this would mark the end of the road. Rationality is essentially a matter of reasoning, of acting for a reason, they would argue. To dismiss, or to ignore, an argument (as opposed to attempting to *refute* it) is not an acceptable move in the space of reasons but an unreasoned, unjustifiable refusal to engage it. It is, therefore, paradigmatically a-rational if not downright irrational. Our answer has been that the rationality of normative criticism resides in a person's ability and willingness to apply *reflective* criticism to his own norms and should not be judged by his capacity and willingness to endorse someone else's argument to that effect. But that is not to argue that the arguments of his critics are, therefore, irrelevant to his capacity and willingness to engage in normative self-criticism. On the contrary, their import is crucial, we have insisted, not by virtue of the force of their logic but by virtue of the normative profiles they premise. Their logic is powerless to convince, but their implied normative profiling can have a profound ambivalating effect, capable of rendering their addressees both capable and willing to normatively reconsider the norms they question.

And thus, somewhat paradoxically, the point at which rationality asserts itself most profoundly, the point at which normative self-criticism is made possible, is precisely the point at which the rational, intersubjective game of leveling and responding to criticism exhausts itself. It is not a point of discursive continuity. Normative self-criticism is not a continuation or simple internalization of its external counterpart. It is prompted by it, caused by it, if you wish. And yet, we insist, it is rational; at least as rational as the potentially ambivalating, potentially self-correcting, indispensable effect of a playback device.

Notes

1. Polanyi 1958, especially part 2.

2. Williams 1981, 101–2. Williams's distinction between external and internal reasons is largely preserved in what follows, notwithstanding, though, his concern with the coherence of the former. If the rationality of a move is taken to turn exclusively on expert rather than on the actor's own opinion, as this view of rationality maintains it should, the reasoning involved, though external to the actor, will always, and by definition, remain internal to those who count— namely, the consulted experts. We remain unconvinced, however, with regard to Williams's main claim that the very idea of critically reviewing and justifying action one did not actually will is inherently incoherent.

3. Imre Lakatos's notion of scientific rationality is a good example of such an approach. Lakatos (1971) urges historians of science to classify as rational any scientific decision of the past that conforms with what they, the historians, believe science's true method to be, regardless of whether the scientists they are studying were, or could have been, aware of it. For criticisms of Lakatos's approach, see Curtis 1986; Garber 1986; and Fisch 1994a, 1994b. For discussion of the Hegelian aspects of Lakatos's historiography (the way rationality is conferred on one's current position by rationally reconstructing the tradition to which it belongs), see Hacking 1979/1981. For a comparison of that to Brandom 2002a and 2009, see below chapter 7, first section.

4. Brandom 2002b, 96. See also his 2009, 182 ff.

5. For a concise formulation of this position, see, e.g., Korsgaard 1997, 221.

6. Of course, "social choice"–type accounts of rationality of the first kind also foreground agency, especially those involving calculi of utility maximization. But it is not agency in acting that is required, only agency in willing or desiring the outcome of the action, which in itself could be performed unaware. See, e.g., Seligman 2000, 15 ff.

7. Unless, of course, one denies the very idea of such normative diversity. As will become apparent in the chapters that follow, we take the existence of radical normative diversity as a given.

8. Korsgaard 1996, chaps. 2 and 3. Korsgaard's concern in that work is the nature of normative obligation rather than that of rationality. She locates the source of normativity, late of Kant, in the essentially self-critical and autonomous self-governance of reason's *imprimatur* but contributes little to articulating its precise workings. One way to describe the project the present study has set itself is to turn Korsgaard's Kantian criterion of reflective endorsement on itself. For to discern the reflexive, second-order project of reason's very own normativity is to ask how it is possible for the understanding, as McDowell (1994, 81) puts it, "to reflect about and criticize the standards by which, at any time, it takes itself to be governed."

9. As Robert Audi observes, practical rationality is addressed mainly in ethical works. "Very few writers on practical reason," he observes, "have addressed the overall territory of reasons for actions, encompassing both moral and nonmoral conduct" (2001, vii). Without stating so explicitly, Audi's remark obviously limits itself to works of the second kind discussed here, as few would consider a thoughtless act moral (good, perhaps, but not *moral*). In concentrating on moral conduct these works focus more on the rational and moral selection of goals (and in doing so, often sorely conflate the two) than on the more "practical" appropriation of means to morally valued ends. As a result, value-neutral instrumental rationality is routinely frowned on for its irrelevance to ethics. In conflating the morally desirable and the rational, such accounts tend to ignore the very possibility of an amoral or even an immoral rational act. Audi himself is less concerned with separating the rational from the ethical than with globally combining theoretical and practical rationality—a commendable initiative in itself.

10. This is true whether or not the actor and approver are one and the same.

11. Galison 1997, 803–44.

12. In our discussion of scientific trading zones in chapter 9, we go a step beyond Galison in locating them as the principal sites in which scientists are liable to encounter the kind of "trusted criticism" capable of prompting normatively transformative processes of scientific rethinking within the community.

13. But even they most often exhibit interesting histories in which their rules and standards were occasionally changed with a view to improving the system. See, for example, Alan Richardson's (2002) and John Haugeland's (1998, chap. 13) insightful comparisons between the history of the rules constitutive of the game of chess (real in Richardson's case, imaginary in Haugeland's) and those of science.

14. This is true even in the case of final ends, as we shall see, following the work of Harry Frankfurt, in chapter 7, third section, and especially chapter 8, third section below. For Frankfurt's insightful problematization of the means-ends relation, see Frankfurt 1992.

15. "The notion of and arrangement of ends and means," writes Frankfurt, "comprehends both the purposefulness and the rationality that are essential features of our active nature; and it also facilitates considering the relationship by which they are connected" (1992, 82).

16. E.g., Rorty 1989, 44; 1996.

17. On Rorty's explicit rejection of cultural relativism, see Rorty 1999, 15. Elsewhere in his work, however, he appears to come uncomfortably close to endorsing it—at least by implication. See, e.g., Rorty 1990.

18. Cf. Korsgaard 1996, 96–100; and the discussion of her position in Moran 2001, 138–51.

19. The formulation is Rorty's, describing the extent of his agreement with Hilary Putnam. See Rorty 1993, quote at p. 45. The framework dependency of all normative evaluation and reasoning, as well as the multiplicity of such frameworks, is also an idea central to Charles Taylor's *Sources of the Self* and the work leading up to it. See especially Taylor 1977, sec. 2; and 1989, part 1.

20. Rorty 2000a, 23–24. The point, of course, is, for Rorty (as it was for Dewey), a quite general one concerning all manner of normative obligation and judgment. Rorty's slide in the passage, from talk of "unconditional obligation" in general to that of "context-independent *validity*" is due the specific debate with Habermas, Davidson, and Putnam of which it is part.

21. For an interesting and equally forceful formulation of the same idea, see Wittgenstein 1974, §608–12—at least as we read him (see chapter 8, sixth section; and see also Dilman 1971). Unlike Rorty, Wittgenstein reserves the term *persuasion* to the unreasoned variety. "At the end of reasons," he writes, "comes *persuasion*" (§612).

22. Rorty 1989, 47, 48. The point is a delicate and complex one, however, that Rorty himself saw fit to subtly reformulate in later work. Here is how he puts it in discussing the views of Apel, Habermas, Putnam, and especially Albrecht Wellmer several years later. On the one hand, he declares, "I whole-heartedly

accept" the claim "that the very idea of incompatible, and perhaps reciprocally unintelligible, language-games is a pointless fiction, and that in real cases representatives of different traditions and cultures can always find a way to talk over their differences." ("This is the point," he adds in an accompanying footnote, "made in Davidson's 'The Very Idea of a Conceptual Scheme.'") "I entirely agree with Wellmer," he continues, citing Wellmer (1998, 150), "that 'rationality—in any relevant sense of the word cannot end at the borderline of closed language-games (since there is no such thing)'" (2000a, 12). However, what (Wellmer and) Rorty could mean by "rationality" in this context is quite unclear, for Rorty immediately goes on to argue, as shall we in detail later, that, on the other hand, bilateral intelligibility is, of itself, no guarantee for the possibility of reasoned agreement:

> The fact that there are no mutually unintelligible language games does not, in itself, do much to show that disputes between racists and anti-racists, democrats and fascists, can be decided without resort to force. Both sides may agree that, although they understand what each other says perfectly well, and share common views on most topics . . . there seems no prospect of reaching agreement on the particular case in hand. (2000a, 13)

In *this* sense, that of reasoned second-order, normative *debate*, rationality, it appears, cannot *but* end at the borderline of normatively closed language games.

23. Putnam 1990, 28. Putnam's immediate concern in this passage is realism rather than relativism. What is fatally compromised, he argues there, is "the very project of representing ourselves as being 'mappers' of something language-independent."

24. As Brandom (2000b, xv) aptly observes, despite the seeming all-out rejection of Kantian representationalism by Rorty (1979), Rorty "follows Kant in sharply distinguishing issues of *causation* from issues of *justification*. Enforcing this distinction between the natural and the normative (according to the lessons he learned from Sellars's 'Empiricism and the Philosophy of Mind') is what leads Rorty to insist that our environment can at most *cause* us to form beliefs, not *justify* them. In his reliance on this fundamental distinction Rorty is a Kantian, even as he deploys this tool to criticize the epistemological tradition Kant represents" (original emphasis).

25. Rorty 1989, 73.

26. On Davidson's alignment with Rorty, see text to note 40 below.

27. Friedman 2001 and Brandom, first in his *Articulating Reasons* (2002a, 12 ff.) and more fully in the third of his 2007 Woodbridge lectures, now published

as chapter 3 of *Reason in Philosophy* (2009), respectively. The interesting affinity between the two is explored in chapter 5 below.

28. Sliding effortlessly between reference to "the ironist" and "we ironists." See, e.g., pp. 79–81.

29. Rorty insists that as in the arts, the "anxiety of influence"—as Harold Bloom famously dubbed the fear of unoriginality—be considered the major incentive for all manner of creative reform. See Rorty 1989, 24–25, for his reference to Bloom (1973).

30. On this point Rorty's rhetoric can be misleading, as, for example, when speaking of "the gradual trial-and-error creation of . . . the sort of vocabulary developed by people like Galileo, Hegel, or the later Yeats" (Rorty 1989, 12). However, it is clear from his description of the three men's work in the very next passage that he uses the term "trial-and-error" very differently from the Popperian notion of a problem-driven process of conjecture and refutation. For Rorty, as we shall see shortly, a final vocabulary can only be deemed problematic from without, never from within. Errors may come to light but only retrospectively from the new perspective of an aimlessly hit on solution. For another similarly misleading utterance, see his attribution to Kuhn of the idea "that science, like politics, is problem-solving" (Rorty 1999, xxi).

31. Rorty 1997, 175, 188–89. See also Rorty 1999, 35–36.

32. Kuhn 1993, 330, cited approvingly by Rorty (1990, 67).

33. Rorty 1998, 68. See especially Rorty 1979, 322–42; see also 1989, 28; 1999, xvi, 35–36; 1997.

34. The same conflation between inquiry and acceptance, we shall argue in chapter 5, plagues the account of scientific rationality proposed by Kuhn's most important philosophical successor, Michael Friedman.

35. Rorty 1989, 6; emphasis added.

36. This is not to say that the first question is purely sociological. For an early and lively discussion of the philosophical significance and ramifications of what he dubs "the sociological problem of induction," see Harry Collins's now-classic *Changing Order* (1985). We discuss Michael Friedman's equally "collectivist" reading of Kuhn in some detail in chapter 5 below.

37. Elsewhere, though, he is clearer. See, e.g., Rorty 1989, 20; 1998, 339 n.14.

38. Rorty 1989, 6; original emphasis.

39. Rorty 1989, 12–13; emphasis added. In some of his later work, especially when writing in favor of Habermas's distinction between "subject-centered" and "communicative" accounts of rationality and preference for the latter (cf. Habermas 1987, Lecture 11), Rorty might seem to be less decisive on this point than he was in 1989. In his 2007 work, *Philosophy as Cultural Politics,* for instance, he

characterizes his position thus: "On the view of culture I am suggesting, intellectual and moral progress is achieved by making claims that seem absurd to one generation into the common sense of the later generations. The role of the intellectuals is to effect this change by explaining how the new ideas might, if tried out, solve, or dissolve, problems created by the old ones[,] . . . by explaining how the new institution or the new theory might solve problems that the old institutions or theories could not handle" (85–86). But the change of heart is but apparent. There is nothing to indicate that his position had changed in this respect between the publication of *Contingency, Irony, and Solidarity* and that of his most recent collection of essays. The giveaway phrase in the passage quoted is of course "if tried out." Only from the vantage point of the new can the problems created by the old be appreciated and the new not "seem absurd."

40. Davidson 1982.

41. Rorty 1989, 49.

42. Ibid., 48–49; emphasis added. Charles Taylor's notion of personal normative advancement (limited in his case to the intrasubjective level of what he terms "strong evaluation") is more carefully analyzed than Rorty's but is also made to turn exclusively on self-(re)interpretation and, therefore, just like Rorty's, lacks critical bite. The constant attempt to make explicit one's inchoate desires and motivations inevitably lends them new form, meaning and direction, and is constitutive of what will by hindsight be deemed progressive. See especially Taylor 1971; 1977; 1985a, chap. 2. We chose to focus on Rorty at this point for two reasons. First, because of how, unlike Taylor (but squarely in line with the concerns of the present study), he explicitly raises the question of the *rationality* of normative change while unequivocally identifying rationality with self-criticism. And second, for the full generality of his account, which, unlike Taylor's, by no means excludes the natural sciences. For a pointed critique of Taylor along these lines, see Geertz 1995.

43. Which we locate in chapter 5 as the major drawback of Friedman's account of the rationality of scientific framework replacement.

44. In an essay published shortly after *Contingency, Irony, and Solidarity*, Rorty 1992 (later retitled "Rationality and Cultural Difference" and republished as chap. 10 of his 1998), he defines rationality anew rather than merely drop the term. He distinguishes three senses of the term, none of which remotely relates to the notion of critical appraisal discussed here. What he terms "rationality$_1$," is "an ability that squids have more than amoebas," namely, "the ability to cope with the environment by adjusting one's reactions to environmental stimuli in complex and delicate ways." Rationality$_2$ is "the name of an extra added ingredient that human beings have and brutes do not," an ingredient that "sets goals

other than mere survival." Rationality$_3$, according to Rorty, is "roughly synonymous with tolerance" and the ability "not to be overly disconcerted by differences from oneself, not to respond aggressively to such differences" (Rorty 1992, 186–87). All three of Rorty's senses of rationality have little to do with the self-conscious, self-doubting, reflective use of one's reasoning ability.

45. Our use of "external" in this context requires some qualification. We use the term here to describe positions similar to Korsgaard's for whom, following Kant, certain foundational values, whose source remains wholly *internal* to individual normative reflection, are nonetheless viewed as *transcending* individual reflection or communal commitment. They are thus normative absolutists in the manner described, while wholly rejecting the idea (often dubbed "moral realism") that normative commitment be attributed to an independent normative reality. For further discussion of moral realism within a Kantian framework, see Korsgaard 1997, 240–43. However, there is a fundamental difference between attributing transcendental, and hence transcultural, value to certain norms and merely acknowledging the existence of a "minimal code" of values contingently shared by all communities by virtue of their members' shared human nature. There is nothing *transcultural* and hence no reason to bestow normatively *supracultural* status to a value merely because it happens to be shared. The difference between acknowledging a minimal code and resisting all forms of normative absolutism (from an interpretivist perspective) is explored in greater detail in chapter 4 below.

46. Cf. Walzer 1987; 1996: chap. 1; Dworkin 1983. See also Dworkin 1986, 424–25; 1996.

47. That is not to say, however, that while engaging a form of life radically different from her own, a person cannot become attracted and eventually commit herself to new and formerly unanticipated normative possibilities that she comes to realize her own vocabulary lacks (e.g., the value of hospitality in Muslim societies, forms of equality found in some single-sex marriages, or some of the so-called knightly virtues). This is certainly a commonplace, unproblematic, and undeniably rational form of normative enrichment. But, as we argue below, such cases of framework *supplementation* are not in violation of Comparative Irrealism because they do not require normatively *faulting* any part of one's functioning framework and therefore are irrelevant to cases of norm *replacement*. We thank Lorraine Daston for forcefully raising this point in private communication but beg to disagree with her suggestion that all forms of framework transition are explicable along such lines.

48. In talking of action we include all manner of endeavor, including such voluntary mental acts as endorsing a belief or committing oneself.

49. Hence the immediate relevance to this study of the sharp distinction (late of Kant and central to the work of Sellars, Brandom, McDowell, and many others) between exercising one's agency in the "space of reasons" and being merely subject to the "space of law."

50. Here, of course, we show our colors as firm supporters of the second approach to rationality. However, as we argued at the outset, although the two approaches sorely differ with regard to first-order rational endeavor, they converge (on the second approach) with respect to second-order acts of rational *norm revision*, on which this study primarily focuses.

51. Korsgaard clearly formulates what she calls "the problem of the normative" in terms of this sense of the priority of reason to action. However, Sellars, Brandom, and McDowell locate rationality in the essentially timeless inferential relations that obtain at any one moment within a person's set of commitments (or as Brandom [2009: 44 ff.] now calls it late of Kant, her "synthetic unity of apperception").

52. Or as Taylor would have it: ordinary goods in the light of "hypergoods." See below note 54.

53. See note 47 above.

54. We prefer Walzer's interpretivism to Taylor's because of Walzer's explicit focus on the transformative effect of normative *criticism* and the nature of its communal disputative context. Taylor's interpretivism is primarily intrasubjective, and, as previously mentioned, his early work locates its normative transformative force, not unlike Rorty, in essentially noncritical acts of self-redescription and rearticulation. In *Sources of the Self* a decidedly self-critical form of normative self-adjustment is added to his earlier account of strong evaluation in the form of what he terms "hypergoods"—goods that "are not only incomparably more important than others but provide the standpoint from which these must be weighed, judged, decided about" (1989, 63). Taylor admits, however, that such normative criticism can only convince those whose hypergoods they are. Their normative force is hence inevitably internal, and, therefore, begs the question of the rationality of their own endorsement and modification. "A hypergood," he maintains (not unlike Brandom's Hegelian Wiggism), "can only be defended" genealogically "through a certain reading of its genesis" (73), namely, from the necessarily circular perspective of those who are "morally moved" by it.

55. Robert DiSalle, who otherwise fully concedes Friedman's account, calls him to task for overlooking how practitioners keenly engage in "dialectical confrontation with prevailing conceptions" (2002, 204) with a view explicitly to "revealing the hidden presuppositions of the old conception, and exhibiting the internal difficulties that must be resolved by the new" (2010, 528). DiSalle,

however, shows no awareness of the difficulties involved in adopting such a self-critical stance, especially from the neo-Kantian perspective he supposedly shares with Friedman.

56. Following Sellars, Brandom, as is well known, centrally identifies rationality, or sapience, with the capacity and willingness to engage in the game of giving and asking for reasons, which, taking his cue from Lewis (1979), he further identifies in *Making It Explicit* (chap. 3 §IV) with the ability to keep score of the deontic, inferential structure of one's fellow players' commitments and entitlements. "Being rational," he writes there, that is, "understanding, knowing how in the sense of being able to play the game of giving and asking for reasons—is mastering in practice the evolution of the score. Talking and thinking is keeping score in this kind of game" (1994, 183). Here, we argue, the self-critical motivation for doing so remains wholly implicit. But in later work, most notably in his Woodbridge Lectures, the emphasis is shifted away from an ability to keep score of other players' reasoning (which is dropped altogether) to the *responsibility for* articulating and integrating one's own commitments into an inferentially structured "synthetic unity of apperception" (e.g., 2009, 37) in dialogue with others. Here, we argue, the critical and self-critical aspects of rational engagement become far more apparent in Brandom's exposition but in a manner that wholly sidesteps the problem of normative self-criticism, because the critical dimension of normative change and development is reduced to troubleshooting for coherence.

57. This, we argue, remains true of Brandom's later work in which a supposedly intrasubjective Kantian account of apperception is placed in an intersubjective Hegelian context of communal appraisal.

58. McDowell 1994, 81.

59. With regard to science, Popper and his school arguably fall in the first group—denying Normative Diversity in science and treating all elements of scientific knowledge as unproblematically criticizable. Lakatos, whose philosophy of science retains much of Popper's, departs from him sharply on this point by at least acknowledging the existence of a potentially different "hardcore" of empirically irrefutable beliefs at the heart of every "scientific research programme." Lakatos, however, (not unlike Quine) overlooks the *constitutive* role of the hard core with regard to the program's succession of theories, concentrating exclusively on its immunity to empirical test. In his view, therefore, an entire research program can be rationally faulted—hardcore included—by force of instrumental considerations of fruitfulness operating between programs.

Interestingly, in the *Open Society* Normative Diversity is not only acknowledged by Popper with regard to ethical and political ways of life, but is prized for its critical, rationally, self-correcting potential. But because his philosophy of science motivates his political theory, rather than the other way around, the problem of normative self-criticism remains unacknowledged.

Part I. Introduction

1. Or as Sellars and his followers would have it, the motivating force of desire belongs in the space of law or causes, not in the space of reasons.

2. For Harman's defense of moral relativism, see part 1 of Harman 2000. For a weaker version of antirealism with regard to value, see Lewis 1989.

3. We here follow Harman 1978.

4. Harman 1978, 34.

5. Though different from Harman's, David Wong's defense of moral relativism, for instance, similarly combines both noncognitivism and antirealism. See Wong 1984.

Chapter 2. Comparative Irrealism and Community-Based Semantics

1. In order to avoid attempts to dismiss the possibility of conversion between the two communities as a "dead option," we imagine them sharing the same territory and in constant contact. Under such conditions some will surely rate such conversions a dead option, but others may well not. Compare Bernard Williams's "The Truth in Relativism," reprinted in his *Moral Luck* (1981, 140–43).

2. Wallace 2002, 434. For the full discussion, see Scanlon 1998, chap. 1; we cite Wallace since the examples and arguments advanced by Scanlon suggest that what is really at issue is the relation between general and specific normative and evaluative concepts. Scanlon presents the issue slightly differently. For one thing, Scanlon's commitment to the primacy of the thick is doubtful. See also Dworkin's (2002) discussion of Scanlon's position.

3. We here ignore views that insist on not treating morality as an inherently normative domain. For such views, see Brink 1988, chap. 3; Railton 1986b.

4. Wallace 2002, 463.

5. Ibid., 455. For a similar position, see Hurley 1992, chap. 1.

6. Although we generally follow Williams's lead in defending the thick/ thin distinction, we find a major aspect of his discussion unconvincing. Williams characterizes thick normative thought as nonreflective; we think that adherence to a network of thick concepts might be thoroughly reflective. See, for instance, Williams 1986, 147–48, where he claims that reflection (utilizing thin concepts) destroys ethical knowledge (formulated in terms of thick predicates). Our account, as will become apparent in chapters to come, bears more resemblance

to Walzer's. See Walzer 1996, chap. 1. For an interesting criticism of the distinction, see Scheffler 1987.

7. We have no intention of pursuing a full-blown, general semantic account of thin predicates but only to list certain of their features that any such theory would be required to explain.

8. Compare the account of ethical outlooks proposed by Sreenivasan (1998, sec. 1). Sreenivasan's interpretivism will be taken up in some detail in chapter 4 below.

9. We define incompatible forms of life in this way in order to silence attempts to view *b* as prima facie desirable due to being creative and prima facie undesirable due to being immodest. For an analysis of prima facie judgments and their role in practical reasoning, see Donald Davidson, "How Is Weakness of the Will Possible?" in Davidson 1980, chap. 2.

10. Williams 1986, 141.

11. We do think that they are wrong, though. They deny the normative reality of the thick, since their criterion for reality seems to us to be biased toward scientific realism. See Blackburn 1990, 1992; Gibbard 1992.

12. The more common version of the Wilde story describes him as having been accused of blasphemy rather than obscenity. See Robert Brandom citing Jonathan Bennett in Brandom 2000a, 70. In the case of blasphemy, however, one can certainly imagine someone thus accused who claims not to have use for the concept yet uses it positively.

13. For a technical elucidation of the practice of using other people's words and applying other people's concepts, see Benbaji 2004a, 2004b.

14. For a similar analysis, see Brandom 2000a, 69–71. Cast in a more Kantian idiom, it is the difference between understanding a concept, including its normative import, and it playing a constitutive role in one's form of life. See the distinction made by Tsou (2003) between incommensurability of meaning and of value discussed in chapter 5, n. 32, below.

15. Scheffler (1987) claims that Williams himself is not fully committed to this view.

16. Williams 1995b, 237.

17. See Wiggins's reply in Lovibond and Williams 1996.

18. Wiggins's monism is formulated exclusively with reference to ethics. Even if he remains unconvinced with regard to ethics, it is still an open question whether he would extend it to all forms of normative diversity. We seriously doubt that anyone would be willing to do so.

19. Kripke 1982.

20. Here is a very partial list: McGinn 1984; Goldfarb 1985; Baker and Hacker 1984; Wright 1984; Zalabardo 1997; Soames 1998; Wilson 1998.

21. Kripke's challenge as we construe it cannot be met by McDowell's "platonic naturalism." According to McDowell (1984), our concepts are observable to those who are absorbed in "our" form of life. Yet this does not answer the question posed by the '+' case, which is deliberately constructed to involve differences of meaning that fall outside the normal boundaries of perceivable conduct. If the two functions differ with respect only to huge numbers, chances are that we will never know whether our colleagues add or quad. See in this respect Crispin Wright's (1992, 92) response to McDowell's argument. For another attempt to block Kripke's argument with primitivism, see Goldfarb 1985, 548–49.

22. Kripke 1982, 96–97; original emphasis.

23. Ibid., 97; original emphasis.

24. For different readings of the community view and of the arguments against the solitary conception of meaning, see Boghossian 1989, 519–22.

25. Kripke 1982, 96.

26. These very sketchy remarks do not constitute a theory of meaning—and as many have noted, it is far from clear that any coherent sketch for an account of meaning has been really laid down. See especially Goldfarb 1985.

27. Kripke 1982, 69–70. As noted above, much of the discussion of Kripke's book focuses on the viability of his interpretation of Wittgenstein. Such, for its most part, is the nature of McGinn's response. However, McGinn makes it clear at points that one of his reasons for doubting the ascription of the "skeptical solution" to Wittgenstein is that the very idea of the impossibility of a private rule makes no sense. For a recent restatement of this argument, see McGinn 2002, chap. 5, esp. 146–55.

28. This aspect is justly emphasized by McDowell (1984, 334–36).

29. Cf. Canfield 1996. Brandom, whose inferential semantics is thoroughly practice based in the manner described, disagrees that the notion of communal mistake is meaningless. We discuss his distinction between normative status and attitude, as well as his disagreement with Wright (1980), in chapter 6, second section, below.

30. Kripke 1982, 77–78.

31. Ibid., 91.

32. As will become apparent in upcoming chapters, from a community-based perspective, moving from semantics (i.e., accounts of conceptual propriety or conceptual norms, to use Brandom's terms) to talk of normativity in general requires further discussion (e.g., as to whether conceptual normativity is paradigmatic of all normative commitment [as implied by Stout 2004, chap. 12], in which case the move is justified without further ado, or is merely a necessary condition for normative commitment, in which case it is not). Here, however, the argument goes from conceptual propriety in general to that of a particular type

of *concept* (rather than norm), namely, that of the thin, normatively compara-tive variety.

33. Note that our argument is not based on the science/ethics dichotomy, and, therefore, much of the criticism that Williams's form of "cultural" relativism has attracted is irrelevant. See Williams 1986, 135 ff.; and the critical comments in McDowell 1986 and especially Hilary Putnam's "Objectivity and the Science/ Ethics Dichotomy" (1990, 163–78), his "Bernard Williams and the Absolute Con-ception of the World" (1992, 80–107), and most recently Putnam 2002.

34. This line of thought is implicit in Putnam's pragmatism: "truth is to be identified with ... idealized justification, as opposed to justification on the pres-ent evidence" (1990, xvii). It is more than implicit (if put somewhat differently) in Friedman's claim (late of Cassirer) that the framework transitions in physics from Aristotle's to Einstein's and beyond represent a regulative, "convergent se-quence" of constitutive principles in which the consensus reached by each "pre-sent scientific community" must view itself "as an approximation to a final, ideal community of inquiry ... that has achieved ... the ideal limit of scientific prog-ress" (Friedman 2001, 64).

35. Williams, "What Does Intuitionism Imply?" in Williams 1995a, 186.

36. For a defense of this line of thought, see also Wright 1992, chap. 4. For an attack on it, see Dworkin 1996. We find Dworkin's defense of absolutism uncon-vincing. According to Dworkin, it is not the case that all mistakes have cognitive explanations. In many philosophical debates, he argues, we do not tend to pre-sume cognitive shortcuts, despite being convinced that our opponent is mistaken. Yet the dis-analogy between the cases is straightforward: conservatives take im-modest behavior to be paradigmatically bad. If liberals are mistaken with respect to such an obvious truth, there must be a cognitive explanation for their mistake.

37. Kripke 1982, 98.

38. See note 6 above.

39. Williams 2000, 490–41.

40. Putnam 2001, 46.

41. Rorty 1989, 48.

Chapter 3. **Factuality without Realism**

1. Hurley 1992, 53, quoted in Sreenivasan 2001, 7. According to Sreeni-vasan, Hurley's argument is based on what he terms the "crucial assumption," which sets forth from Davidson's claim that "we cannot take even a first step to-wards interpretation without knowing or assuming a great deal about the speaker's

belief" (1984a, 196). The crucial assumption is that the set of beliefs required in order to make the first step toward interpretation is so large as to render radical Normative Diversity impossible. One aim of the present chapter is to show that one can reject the crucial assumption while fully maintaining a Davidsonian framework.

2. Our sketch here is a short summary of the basic idea underlying Bernard Williams's "external and internal reasons" (Williams 1981, 101–13) and Darwall et al. (1996, 363–71), which he restated later as follows: a claim of the form "x has reason to A" is true, if and only if x "could reach the conclusion that he should A . . . by a sound deliberative route from his actual motivational set" ("Internal Reasons and Obscurity of Blame," Williams 1995a). Williams's argument is clearly circular, as argued by Hooker (1987), Cohon (1986), Millgram (1996), and others. Following McDowell, we present the internalism/externalism debate by asking whether a conversion—a radical change in the agent's "basic" preferences—can be explained by appealing to reasons. Cf. McDowell 1995a.

3. Davidson 1982, 305; emphasis added. Cf. Rorty 1989, 49.

4. Cf. Davidson 1985.

5. This short statement is very controversial, and we will not even try to enumerate the issues that it raises, let alone discuss them. The idea to analyze meaning by appealing to the theory of translation is Quine's. See Quine 1960, especially chaps. 1 and 2. For a short defense of this idea, see Quine 1970a. A modified version of this move is impressively elaborated in Davidson 1984a. Some philosophers, most notably Dummett, do not find radical interpretation a useful imaginative device in the philosophy of language. See, "Dummett's Replies" in McGuinness and Oliveri 1994. We are also aware that our formulation of the "meaning theorems" ("*Q* in *L* means that *p*") is only one of several possible formulations.

6. Not to be confused with Walzer's essentially community-based interpretivist approach to normativity dealt with in detail in the following chapter.

7. This is, of course, a simplification. In practice, collecting this kind of "data" is inherently part of the process of interpretation.

8. Davidson 1990a, 320.

9. Cf. Michael Williams 1988–89, 185.

10. Davidson himself would make more explicit use of systematicity and holism at this point, to explain why *Q1* means that it is raining and not, for example, that a certain prayer has been answered, or that it is wet, or that it is good weather for gardening, and so on. We, however, are not sure that this is the case. The causal relations the interpreter is after are based on lawlike generalizations. Such generalizations support counterfactuals: "had it not been raining, he would

not hold true *Q1*." And in verifying such counterfactuals, interpreters would use systematicity and holism.

11. For the original version of the argument, see Davidson 1974. The argument is often misread. See, e.g., Hacker 1996. According to Hacker (pp. 303–6), Davidson denies that there might be concepts that can be expressed in one language but be inexpressible in another. On our reading, the argument secures only a *partial* overlap of *observational* concepts. Cf. Davidson's replies to Stroud and Genova in Hahn 1999, 163–64, 193–94.

12. For a defense of the claim that justification is a logical relation among beliefs, see Davidson 1986a. Cf. Michael Williams 1988–89, 186.

13. Davidson 1990a, 332.

14. In the polemical context of trying to distinguish his own "distal" theory of meaning from Quine's "proximal" theory, Davidson says, "A distal theory connects meaning directly to the conditions that make sentences intersubjectively true or false. . . . [T]he causal relations between the world and our beliefs are crucial to meaning . . . because they are often apparent to others and so form the basis for communication" (1990b, 75–76). For a defense of Davidson's externalism, see Bilgrami 1992, 201 ff.

15. Davidson, "Knowing One's Own Mind," in Davidson 2001, 15–38, at 16.

16. The distinction is Harry Frankfurt's. See Frankfurt 1971.

17. This is an assumption, which Davidson accepts. See the three principles he enumerates in his "How Is Weakness of the Will Possible?" in Davidson 1980, 21–42.

18. There are, of course, thoroughly perverted and bizarrely irrational individuals whose outlandish preferences we do not share, yet we believe we can interpret, at least to some degree. This is as much a problem for a Davidsonian theory of meaning as accounting, in the descriptive part of language, for a blind person's use of color words. It is a matter of degree, of course. Can the blind be said, in principle, to possess color concepts similar to those who can see? Can a person who seems to enjoy pain and vile food be said to at all understand what painful or tasty mean? Masochists, for instance, seem to feel pain, and wince and cry, but also to seek out such pain and give other tokens of enjoying it. To be sure, most facts about meaning and belief are soft, but that in itself will not suffice to topple the Davidsonian conceptualization of the interpretive process.

19. Behaviorists do not think that pain is observable any more than color sensations are. In their view, what is observable are the circumstances that cause pain and the typical behavior of one who is in pain. We, like many, disagree, yet nothing of substance depends on this.

20. Davidson's work on the structure of practical reasoning grew out of an inquiry into how weakness of the will is possible. See Davidson 1980, 21–42.

However, compare Davidson 1982 and 1986b, in which he seems to give up the idea defended in the earlier article.

21. Generally, the interpretation of Q5-like sentences does not have to be based on *more basic* beliefs and desires; it could proceed from (or as part of) the interpretation of other beliefs and desires of the same level as Q5. Yet, in any actual process of interpretation, there is a point in which the interpreter is required to go beyond the basic level. At this point she will be making use of knowledge she had gained in the earlier stages of interpretation in order to interpret this Q5-like sentence.

22. See Frankfurt 1971.

23. With the exception, of course, as we shall argue immediately, of cases of scientific framework revision, such as those studied by Kuhn and Friedman, in which concept employment is discontinued, similarly to the case of the reformed biker. In other words, the distinction made here between radical theoretical and normative shifts should not be taken to imply that science is somehow immune to radical shifts in its *normative* vocabulary. We discuss such transitions in science in some detail below, first in chapter 5 and again in chapter 9.

24. Here, as in the previous chapter, the "view of normativity" presented is limited to the purely descriptive task of analytically characterizing the relations obtaining between the old and the new normative vocabularies employed at either side of a radical divide of change of heart. Questions concerning the nature of normative commitment, and change of commitment, and especially those concerning the possibility of rationally bridging such divides and facilitating such changes of heart, are dealt with in upcoming chapters.

25. For a very different view, see Friedman 2001, 83–84, endorsed and discussed below in chapter 5, third section.

26. Note that in other contexts a subject might maintain his prejudgmentt even after realizing that the less probable eventuality had happened. Many failed analysts rightly continue to justify their predictions and recommendations after they have been proven false. But the case under discussion is importantly different. The best interpretation of the senior staff's phrase "probable" is such that, had they known the future, they would have hailed their original all-things-considered judgment a grave mistake, which they now explain as having been caused by an unwarranted bias. They would have awakened to the misconception that was leading them astray.

27. Davidson 2001, 16.

28. From an interview with Davidson, *Inquiry* 37 (1994): 216.

29. Davidson develops this idiolect-based conception of meaning in his "First Person Authority" (1986c). Dummett seems to believe that, due to being truth-oriented, the Davidsonian theories are bound to be idiolect-based. The

idiolect-based conception of meaning, he claims, was first advocated by Frege: "there is, in Frege's theory, no room for explaining the sense which an expression has in some language otherwise than as the sense all, or most, individual speakers . . . attach to it. Thus, . . . the basic notion really is that of an idiolect" (Dummett 1978, 424). The claim that theories that identify truth and meaning deny the social character of language is the main thesis of Strawson (1970). The history of the debate starts with Davidson's (1979, 1984b) response to the convention-based conception of meaning and ends (at least for Davidson) in Davidson 1994. See Dummett's reply there.

30. Davidson 1992, 111.

31. For an amusing example, see Sellars's parable of John the necktie salesman (1956, §14–20).

32. We thank Bill Child for bringing this important point to our attention in private correspondence.

33. McDowell's criticism of Davidson in *Mind and World* turns on an accusation that the "coherentist" inferential element in the latter's account of conceptual content is so dominant as to render it spinning frictionlessly in a void. On such a reading, the only "truth by correspondence" to which a Davidsonian approach ultimately admits is that between the inferential schemes of interpreter and interpretee. Davidsonian "triangulation" is conducted not with reality *simpliciter* occupying the third corner but with reality *as perceived by the interpreter.* According to McDowell, Davidson's account of meaning is coherentist all the way down, as it were.

34. See, e.g., Burge 1989; Dummett 1989.

35. Davidson 1991, 199.

36. Davidson 1984c, 12.

37. This is, of course, not the only way to incorporate a notion of a shared language into a conception of meaning. See, e.g., McDowell 1984, 1987. A related move is developed by Charles Taylor in various places; see, e.g., Taylor 1993.

38. See Davidson's replies in Stoecker 1993, 118.

39. Goldfarb 1985, 484.

Part II. **Introduction**

1. Most accounts of rationality written by philosophers of mind, language, action, science, and ethics lack a critical dimension altogether. Thus, to take four very different examples, criticism makes no appearance at all in the "three senses of rationality" delineated in Rorty 1992, in the "five conceptions of rationality"

discussed in the introduction to Brandom 2002a, in John Searle's book-length study of "rationality" in action (2000), or in Michael Friedman's account of the rationality of framework transitions in science (2001). And when criticism does make an appearance in such accounts, it is most often confined to troubleshooting for incoherence or inconsistency as in McDowell 1994 and Brandom 2009—both of which will be studied a little closer in upcoming chapters.

2. McDowell 1994, 124–26.

3. McDowell's response to Robert B. Pippin in Smith 2002, 276. See also McDowell 1994, 81; and our discussion of that pertinent passage in chapter 6, first section, below.

4. The affinity between an interpretive account of normativity (including Taylor's) and Brandom's expressivist account of the embeddedness of inferential semantics in a normative pragmatics, though striking, has yet to be appreciated. (The "interpretivist" elements of Brandom's thought that are discussed in the literature refer to Davidson's interpretive semantics, which is a different matter entirely, of course. See, e.g., Ramberg 2004.)

5. Which is ultimately what enables Friedman to adopt Habermas's well-known notion of communicative rationality as the basis for his account. Communicative rationality is about rationally reaching a consensus between adherents to different *lebenswelten*. It has little to offer in situations in which alternatives are sought for but are not yet in sight.

6. As noted above (chap. 1, note 54), Robert DiSalle criticizes Friedman on this point, yet despite Friedman's seeming endorsement of his criticism shows no awareness of the philosophical difficulties involved in adopting such a stance. See Fisch 2010 n. 7.

7. Equipped with an account of rational, normative self-criticism developed in chapter 8, we return in chapter 9 to consider scientific framework transitions anew in a manner that builds on and away from Friedman.

8. As perceptively pointed out by one of the anonymous readers of this work.

9. See Stout 2002; 2004, chap. 12; and especially Brandom 2009, chaps. 1–3.

10. Brandom 2009, 39.

11. Ibid., 2–3; original emphasis.

Chapter 4. The Limits of Connectiveness

1. From the start, we refrain from restricting the intrepretive approach to ethics, and apply it, as far as possible, to normativity in general.

2. These two elements of the interpretive account on which we focus are elaborated separately in Walzer's work. The first in Walzer 1987, the second in Walzer 1996, chap. 1. Our deep debt to these works will become apparent in what follows.

3. Walzer 1987, 30.

4. See especially Williams 1979, 1986.

5. By "context," we mean here the "Kaplanian" context: a set that includes the speaker of the utterance, the time, the place, and the world in which the utterance occurred.

6. This exposition relies heavily on Sreenivasan 1998.

7. Sreenivasan 1998, 145–46. It is noteworthy that schemes of values are attributed first and foremost to communities, and only derivatively to their individual members. Apart from *sittlichkeit,* the community as a whole is conceived as having a *weltanshauung.* The scheme of values is, in a clear sense, institutionalized: its presence is a social fact, an element of the furniture of the community's moral world. The community has an accepted standard of interpretation of its practice. This is the sense in which disagreement presumes a shared "text." In this sense, the communal brand of interpretivism brought here to the fore late of Walzer differs from more intrasubjective accounts of normative *self-interpretation,* such as Taylor's interpretive elaboration of Harry Frankfurt's account of agency. See especially Taylor 1977, 1985a, chap. 2. See below notes 8 and 10.

8. As noted, the interpretive account of ethics late of Walzer discussed and substantiated in the present chapter adopts a wholly community-based approach to normativity, as does the intricate philosophical elaboration it receives in Brandom's "expressivist," practice-based semantics, as we shall argue in chapter 6. But not all interpretive accounts of normativity adopt a communal approach. Taylor's widely discussed interpretive account of agency and personal identity is a case in point. Although Taylor pictures the individual "strong self-evaluator" as self-constituted interpretively against the backdrop of a shared, "objective" communal scheme of values, his account shows little interest in the role of interpretation in forming and maintaining the latter or in the nature of its social grounding. Anderson (1996) offers an insightful analysis of the difficulties involved in bridging within a Taylorian framework Taylor's tripartite "stated commitment to the individuating role of personal commitment, to the need for some appeal to nonsubjective standards of evaluative reasons, and to the endlessly transformative character of self-interpretation" (34). For Taylor's interpretivism, see especially Taylor 1971; 1977; 1985a, chap. 2; 1985a, part 1. For reasons that will become apparent in the upcoming chapters (among them our general bias toward what Brandom dubs "linguistic pragmatism," the view that sees the private realm of

discursive commitment as both grounded in and explained by the public realm of normative discursive practice), our commitment to the interpretive approach (as well as our criticism of it) will be extended from the communal to the personal only in chapter 8, where we shall return to Taylor's account of personal identity and human agency in the course of discussing the later work of Harry Frankfurt (an interpretivist of sorts himself, as we shall argue, but whose interpretivism remains largely implicit). For an interesting, if overly systematic attempt, late of Walzer and Taylor, to outline a comprehensive interpretive account of the social, institutional, personal, and bodily "bearers of norms, values and meanings," see Rosa 1996 and especially 2004.

9. Walzer 1987, 12–14. For Rawls's explicit reliance on Kantian morality, see Rawls 1975, 1980.

10. Taylor's far more linguistically motivated interpretivism is presented, by contrast, in similarly explicit opposition, not to universalist accounts of value late of Kant, but to what McDowell (1994, e.g., 67) dubs the "bald naturalism" that typifies "the ambition to model the study of man on the natural sciences" (Taylor 1985a, 1). He characterizes such approaches (as in the case of "the contemporary fashion of computer-modelled explanations" of human agency) as "so flagrant and so bizarre, that only very strong preconceptions could mask" (1985a, 5). Cast in Sellars's terminology, we might say that while Walzer's community-based interpretivism reacts against absolutist depictions of "the space of (ethical) reasons," Taylor's subjectivist approach reacts against attempts to reduce it to the "realm of law." For one of several clear statements of Taylor's dismissive impatience with "the strange continuing obsession with this wildly implausible approach to the science of man," see his "Self Interpreting Animals" (1985a, chap. 2)—citing p. 51.

11. As Rawls (1971, 18) puts it, we "should not be misled . . . by the somewhat unusual conditions which characterize the original position. The idea here is simply to make vivid to ourselves the restrictions that it seems reasonable to impose on arguments and principles of justice" in order to "incorporate [our] commonly shared presumptions." See Kymlicka 1989, 65–66.

12. For the epistemological analogy between justice and grammar, see Rawls 1971, 47, 50. The analogy between our sense of justice and our sense of grammaticality was developed in detail by Gilbert Harman (1999). Rawls believes that having a sense of justice is what distinguishes humans from animals, who do not take part in the hypothetical contract that yields the just principles. Those who can give justice are owed justice. See Rawls 1971, 504–12.

13. Sreenivasan 1998, 145.

14. Cohen 1986, 467.

15. Needless to say, assessing and evaluating practices reliably from a perspective different from one's own, especially when critical, requires a good insider's grasp of, and acqaintance with, the form of life in question. This is more than a merely epistemological observation. Walzer, as we shall see, makes much of the difference between the trust and potential effectiveness of the insider's "connected" normative criticism, as opposed to that of any outsider. Normative criticism, we shall argue in chapters to come, must be *trusted* in order to be effective, but we shall contest Walzer's identification of trusted and connected criticism as overly rigid.

16. Sreenivasan 1998, 149. Sreenivasan employs Dworkin's notion of interpretation of social practice, which Dworkin considers to be irrelevant to ethical reasoning. On the essential mutual underdetermination of "the self-interpretations of the explicit realm of ideas and those implicit or 'hidden' in our institutions," see Rosa 2004, 695.

17. The idea that an interpretation does not determine simpliciter but purports to articulate the true meaning of its interpretandum, thus leaving the viability and truth of an interpretation forever an open question, is nicely captured, as we shall see, in Brandom's distinction between normative statuses and normative attitudes. Taylor, who stresses the normatively *constitutive* (as opposed to explicatory) function of self-interpretation (e.g., Taylor 1985a, 68–76) leaves little room for meaningful normative deliberation and disagreement. (Or, in other words, runs up against the problem of normative self-criticism from the very start!)

18. See Geertz 1973, chap. 1. Thick description in Geertz's sense is what anthropologists, as opposed to "natives," must do in order to satisfy the requirement for cultural involvement. So one cannot get the criterion of interpretive adequacy from Geertz's notion as it stands. And see Williams 1986, 140–43.

19. In such a case, the belief that x is immodest should be abandoned. This is *not* to say that S should believe that x is *not* immodest. (After all, if x is paradigmatically immodest, doing so might be rationally impossible for a person who understands what modesty is.) Rather, if the *value* of modesty is not part of the community's ideally interpreted ethical outlook, its members should refuse to use the concept of modesty as if it was their own. They should claim that this is not "one of their words," as Oscar Wilde is reputed to have claimed with respect to obscenity—see above chap. 2, note 12.

20. The literature is vast. For one pertinent discussion, see the special issue of *Mind and Language* devoted to Stanley and Szabó (2000a, 2000b) and discussion there by Bach (2000) and Neale (2000).

21. Thus, if you say, "He had a rotten life," what you are really saying is that it was sorrowful, or boring, or plagued by illness; when you say "God's creation

is good" you mean that it is complex, beautiful, fascinating, and so forth. Note that the thesis is very close to the widely discussed "buck-passing" account of goodness that originated in Scanlon (1998, chap. 1, §9). For a similar statement, see Hurley 1992, chap. 1.

22. Another question that lies beyond the scope of this project is that of interpretive underdetermination: might there not be incompatible but equally good ways of interpreting or understanding a practice? A positive answer seems very plausible. But if so, how can the (bivalent) truth of normative statements be made dependent on the idea of interpretation?

23. See Sreenivasan 1998, 147–50; Locke [1689] 2006; Walzer 1987, 53.

24. Sreenivasan 1998, 167–69.

25. On this point Walzer and Taylor again steer unacknowledgedly close to each other. Cf. Taylor 1991b, 17–18.

26. Walzer takes the point to the limit: "Morality provides those basic prohibitions—of murder, deception, betrayal, gross cruelty. . . . [W]e can . . . study the actual historical processes by which they came to be recognized and accepted, for they have been accepted in virtually every human society" (1987, 24). As we shall argue shortly, this seems to us an overstatement of the interpretive position.

27. Here the interpretive approach late of Walzer and Taylor converges interestingly with Davidson's brand of interpretivism, where the ascription of meaning and values to others derives from a *self*-understanding of what we inevitably share.

28. See Nagel 1970; Parfit 1995; Korsgaard 1996, 142–45; Rachels 2002, sec. 4).

29. The term is Walzer's. See Walzer 1987, 24.

30. Regan 2003, 661 n. 24.

31. To be considered agents (as opposed to mere "mechanisms generating behavior" [653]), argues Regan on Moore's behalf, we must be able to ask "the desire transcending question" (653), namely, whether our highest-level desires are worth pursuing. It is a question, he believes, that can only be answered by a transcendental argument (655), namely, with reference to "some Archimedean standpoint outside all of our brute desires (of whatever order) if we are to choose our actions. . . . [I]f we are to regard ourselves as agents . . .we need some concept that . . . must constitute a standard for our will which is grounded independently of our desires" (654). Regan's Moorean position thus far transcends the "Weak Absolutism" of the "Kantian Liberals."

32. Regan 2000, 652.

33. The terminology is ours, but Regan says so all but explicitly in claiming (contra Korsgaard's [1996, 44] classing of Moore as a "substantial realist"

according to whom we have normative concepts because we are able to spot normative entities, as if they "were wafting by") that "good," for Moore, "is more like 'true' than like 'yellow,' and the concept of 'truth' is not something wafting in the air" (656).

34. Regan 2000, 658 ff.

35. Ibid.

36. Ibid., 677.

37. Wallace 2002, 463.

38. Regan 2003, 660–61; emphasis added.

39. Ibid.; Jackson 1998, 41. Jackson himself seeks to prove much more than we do: we try to show that facts about goodness are reducible to thick normative facts, while he believes that they can be fully expressed with the help of purely descriptive predicates.

40. We knowingly use the term *idiosyncratically*. I. C. Jarvie (1986, 50 ff.), for example, uses it in contradistinction to relativism to denote a position not dissimilar from our own (though argued for from a Popperian perspective).

41. Scanlon 1982, 118.

42. Walzer 1987, 22–23.

43. Ibid., 30.

44. For our argument in the following section we are indebted to Rosati 2003, especially pp. 491–500, and to the more developed arguments against the informed-desires satisfaction theory of individual goodness found in Rosati 1995a, 1995b.

45. Griffin 1986, chap. 2.

46. Frankfurt 1982, 93–94.

47. See Frankfurt 1982, 93–94. Rosati (1995a, 511) claims that "autonomous agents have the capacity to reflect on . . . the sort of persons they are, they may come to want to be different." This picture of agency was initially portrayed in Frankfurt 1971, 1987. For similar accounts of agency, see Dworkin 1970; Taylor 1976; Korsgaard 2009. For a detailed discussion of the bearings of Frankfurt's later work on the concerns of the present study, see below chapter 8.

48. The austere and artificial setting of deliberating what a person cares for or should do "under conditions of full information" tends to obscure a point Taylor makes insistently in his early work on human identity and agency, concerning "the constitutive relation" between "our descriptions of our motivations and our attempts to formulate what we hold important." It is that our "very attempts to formulate what we hold important must, like descriptions, strive to be faithful to something. But what we strive to be faithful to is not an independent object with a fixed degree and manner of evidence but rather a largely inarticulate sense of what is of decisive importance. According to Taylor, the very act of

articulation inherently involved in deliberating the Socratic question "shapes our sense of what we desire or what we hold important" in ways formerly unavailable to us (1977, 35–36).

49. Though it will be considered in our discussion of his work in chapter 8 below.

50. It might be objected that our consistency claim is false, that had the agent known all the relevant facts about himself at time *t*, he would have known what he cares about at any later time. Thus, if we identify a person's individual goodness with the satisfaction of his informed desires (and insist that caring is a mode of desired desiring), the person who knows all the relevant facts about himself at a certain time would know what is good for him, at *any* time. Following Broadie and Rosati, we reply that this might be so, especially if the world is deterministic. Yet, when a person knows at *t* the facts that determine what he will care about later, he can no longer deliberate, since he will experience his future as closed. So our very capacity to deliberate is such that as agents we must assume that it is not the case that at any time everything about our future desires is settled. Hence, only if our basic belief as deliberative agents is true can the question whether satisfying the current set of informed desires is good for us be reopened. See Broadie 2002. On the essential difference in this respect between first- and third-person perspectives on normativity, freedom, and deliberation, see Korsgaard 1996, 96–100; and the discussion of her position by Moran (2001, 138–51).

51. Moreover, unlike the obsessive pursuit for its own sake of valueless projects (like avoiding stepping on the cracks on the sidewalk) the former social climber's newly found social unpretentiousness is valuable. This goes against Frankfurt's own position in his early work, according to which the things we care about are necessarily important to us. For there are things that we care about but that are not made important by our caring about them. Valueless projects are one example. A better way of putting Frankfurt's point would be that a person will be said to rationally care about a thing only if he believes that by caring about it he will make it important to himself. In the final sections of Frankfurt 2006, the possible discrepancies between what we care about and make important are acknowledged as ways in which a person is liable to get himself wrong. This, as we shall argue in chapter 8, is the only form of normative self-criticism for which Frankfurt makes room.

52. The real/notional distinction is Williams's. See Williams 1975; 1986, chap. 8. We give a slightly different content to this notion.

53. We shall have much more to say in chapter 8 both about the need for "Socializing Harry," as Dan-Cohen (2006) nicely puts it, and about the role of normative criticism in bringing about such volitional changes, but only after a

richer and better-grounded picture of the function and explication of communal normative frameworks late of Friedman and Brandom is in place.

54. Or, as Taylor would have it, *articulating* the desire.

55. It turns out that, in the interpretive view, the context-dependency of thin normative judgments is subtler than was suggested above. The semantic account of purely normative sentences presented there was, "*x* is good" is true if there is a specific value (in *S*'s ideally interpreted ethical outlook) instantiated by *x*. The bracketed addendum—the contribution of the extralinguistic context—should now be amended thus: "expressed in the speaker's ideally interpreted *current* ethical outlook."

Chapter 5. Rationality as Agreement

1. As Brandom (2000a, 4) aptly puts it, pragmatists aspire to "to explain ... the content by the act, rather than the other way round."

2. First presented in Friedman 2001, chap. 1, and most recently in Friedman 2010a and 2010b. In what follows, page references in the text are to Friedman 2001.

3. See especially Friedman 1996 and 1998 and his reference to the work of Sellars and McDowell in *Dynamics of Reason* (2001), 55, 85.

4. On Friedman's (1999) "revisionist" reading of Reichenbach, Schlick, and Carnap as offering "not a radical form of empiricism (the 'received view'), but a relativized conception of the a priori," see Tsou 2003, 592 n. 1.

5. Friedman 2001, 30–31. For an insightful comparison of Putnam's notion of a priori "framework principles" developed during the 1960s and 1970s in response to Quine's two dogmas argument and Friedman's latter-day appropriation of Reichenbach's notion of relativized a priori principles in science, see Tsou 2010. For Putnam's position, see Putnam 1962, 1976.

6. Friedman 2001, 31–32; Carnap 1950.

7. Quine 1951.

8. For an explicit statement to this effect, see Friedman 2002, 182. Don Howard makes the interesting suggestion that the reason for the exclusively historical nature of Friedman's argument may well run deeper. In making the case for the contingent a priori, Howard points out, Friedman relies on historical evidence rather than on the kind of transcendental arguments one would have expected from an avowed neo-Kantian. The reason, he suggests, is that since the conclusion of a transcendental argument is invariably "universal and eternal, . . . transcendental arguments do not yield contingent conclusions."

Therefore, "historical evidence could well be the only possible evidence for the contingent a priori" (Howard 2010 351 n. 1). Howard's comment, of course, far transcends the nature of Friedman's response to Quine to the inclusion of his entire project.

9. Quine 1970b, 7. More interestingly, as Tsou (2010) points out, this also marks the main difference between Friedman's relativized a priori and Putnam's "framework principles" (see note 5 above). Putnam (1976), following Quine, stresses their necessity—that is, their immunity to empirical refutation relative to the framework. The defining feature of such statements, he writes several years later, is that they "cannot be overthrown merely by observations, but can only be overthrown by thinking of a whole body of alternative theory as well" (Putnam 1994, 251). For Friedman, by contrast, their defining feature is not their immunity per se to empirical findings but their being *constitutive* of such findings. Friedman's relativized a priori principles do not merely stand aloof from and untouched by the facts, it is by them that the facts' very facticity is normatively established! Therefore, transitions from one scientific framework to another represent for Friedman, far more than for Putnam, a replacement of scientific *standards* that appears so profound as to defy reason. For a detailed account of the stable and the changing elements in Putnam's work on these topics, see Mueller and Fine 2005, esp. §III.

10. The close affinity between central aspects of the work of Carnap and Kuhn as well their acknowledgment of each other's work have been brought to light in recent years by a number of historians of philosophy of science. See especially Reisch 1991; Earman 1993; Galison 1995. See also Friedman 1993; 2001, 18–19, 42–43, and additional references therein.

11. Carnap 1952, 219, cited by Galison 1995, 30. (See also the quote in Earman 1993, 11, from Carnap's notes to a letter he wrote to Kuhn in April 1962, as associate editor of the *International Encyclopedia of Unified Science*, after reading the completed manuscript of *Structure*.) Galison takes this to mean that for Carnap such external questions simply "have no cognitive content" (1995, 30–31). Friedman's paraphrase seems closer to the mark: for Carnap, he asserts, external questions "can only be decided conventionally on the basis of broadly pragmatic considerations of convenience or suitability for one or another given purpose" (32). For an insightful latter-day conventionalist grounding of the a priori, see Stump 2003.

12. Earman 1993, 19, with reference to, e.g., Kuhn 1970, 94, 150, 151.

13. Friedman 2001, 42, referring, among others, to Kuhn's assertion, "The transfer of allegiance from paradigm to paradigm is a conversion experience that cannot be forced" (1970, 150).

14. Kuhn 1993, 314, in which, as Conant and Haugeland note, one finds "some of the central ideas of [his] long promised but never finished new book— on which he continued to work until he no longer could" (Conant and Haugeland's "Editor's Introduction" to Kuhn's posthumous 2000, 9).

15. Kuhn 1993, 338–39.

16. Friedman 2001, 49–50 (emphasis added), quoting Barnes 1982 and Barnes and Bloor 1982.

17. A similar ambiguity in Friedman's presentation occurs in the clear (if no less perplexing—see following note) change of heart that is evident in the way his argument is presented two years later in Friedman 2002 in which Kuhn's instrumentalist universalism is openly and explicitly accepted.

18. Curiously, in Friedman 2002 both of these points are taken back and wholly reversed. Only the third is retained. "For it is surely uncontroversial," he writes there, "that the scientific enterprise as a whole has in fact become an ever more efficient instrument for puzzle-solving in Kuhn's sense—for maximizing quantitative accuracy, precision, simplicity, and so on in adjusting theoretical predictions to phenomenological results of measurement" (184). It remains quite unclear how Friedman, who there seems wholly to accept Kuhn's instrumentalist universalism, does so in the face of his arguments here to the effect that the diversity of human ends renders impossible the very existence of such trans-paradigmatic criteria of scientific success or the means rationally to apply them. As far as we know, Friedman (2002) postdates both parts of *Dynamics of Reason*—originating in the Ernan McMullin Perspectives Lecture he delivered at the University of Notre Dame in April 2001 (see Richardson 2002, 253). *Dynamics of Reason*, on the other hand, originated two years earlier—part 1 in the Kant Lectures Friedman delivered at Stanford in 1999 and part 2 in discussions of those lectures and other of Friedman's writings at Göttingen later that year. It is possible, however, that the change of heart evident in Friedman (2002) occurred already between the two parts of *Dynamics of Reason*. Commenting on Kuhn's talk of "the unproblematic increase of 'puzzle-solving' success across scientific . . . paradigm shifts," in chapter 3 of part 2, Friedman notes that "it is entirely uncontroversial . . . that this kind of purely instrumental success does indeed accrue to the later paradigm" (95). Be this as it may, nowhere is the sharp discrepancy between these texts explained or even noted by Friedman.

19. Friedman 2001, 83. Indeed, Kuhn (1993, 330–31) says so explicitly in response to McMullin (1993). See also Rorty 1988, in which he disputes Bernard Williams's (1986, 136) claim that contrary to ethics, the success of science prompts us to conclude that "in scientific inquiry, there should ideally be convergence on an answer, where the best explanation of the convergence involves the idea that the answer represents how things are."

20. The idea that empirical truth can be warranted relative to a framework, though not attested by science's impressive instrumental success, adds an ironic twist to the debate on instrumentalism between Rorty and Williams referred to in note 19 above.

21. Kuhn 1993, 330–31.

22. Friedman's approach would be in violation of Comparative Irrealism, of course, had he insisted that the criterion for choosing between rival frameworks be *comparative*. But he is careful not to do so, arguing insistently that the problem of rational framework choice is that of justifying moving to the new from *within the old*. In framing the question the way he does, Friedman could well be read as motivated by awareness of the pitfalls of Comparative Irrealism.

23. Rorty 1989, 55.

24. Ibid., 12–13.

25. Richardson 2002, 263.

26. Galison 1997, 14.

27. McMullin 1993, 75–76.

28. Kuhn 1993, 330.

29. Ibid., 319.

30. Ibid., 331, quoting Friedman 1993, 50.

31. Ibid., 319.

32. Ibid., 324–25. Sankey (1998) dubs the semantic version of the incommensurability thesis developed in Kuhn's later works "taxonomic incommensurability." In his extensive work on Kuhn—especially Sankey 1993 and 1998—he criticizes Kuhn's contention that taxonomic incommensurability "entails the falsity of the realist idea of progress as increase of truth about a fixed set of entities" (Sankey 1998, 8). For a similar position even more strongly put, see Devitt 2001. For criticism of Sankey's reading leveled from a neo-Kantian interpretation of Kuhn, see Hoyningen-Huene 1993 and especially Hoyningen-Huene, Oberheim, and Andersen 1996. Tsou (2003) also distinguishes between the two Kuhnian "theses": that of "the incommensurability of values" as opposed to that of "the incommensurability of meaning." Tsou's main criticism of Friedman's theory of the communicative rationality of science is that "it only has persuasive force" against the latter, thus leaving unattended the problem of rationality with regard to the former (Tsou 2003, 590).

33. Kuhn 1993, 330; original emphasis.

34. Ibid., 331, noted above in text to note 21.

35. See above notes 18, 19, and 20.

36. Kuhn 1993, 324.

37. Ibid., 314; original emphasis.

38. Ibid., 336.

39. Ibid., 338.

40. In *Dynamics of Reason* but not in Friedman 2002.

41. For a single exception, see p. 45, where he notes that during "deep conceptual revolutions," the constitutively a priori principles come "under intense pressure . . . from new empirical findings and especially anomalies." But even here, it is not the pressure from such findings that is said to prompt or to motivate the conceptual revolution. The reverse direction of explanation is implied: in periods of revolution, the constitutive framework is said to come under pressure.

42. See above note 32.

43. Friedman 2001, 85 n. 18.

44. Citing Kant's *Critique of Pure Reason* Bxxvi n.

45. The distinction between logical and real possibility and the twofold space of reasons they generate is worked out in considerable detail in the later pages of section 2 of part 1 of Friedman 2001, with special reference to general relativity.

46. As noted, the theory of lexicons and lexical change outlined in "Afterwords" is described by Kuhn as a sketch "both dogmatic and incomplete" of the "rapid series of significant breakthroughs" he reports on having made since giving the Shearman Lectures at University College London in 1987; breakthroughs, he went on to say, that form the basis for the book he was working on. As we have learned from James Conant, coeditor of Kuhn 2000, in private correspondence, that manuscript is unfortunately not yet accessible.

47. Friedman 2001, 45.

48. Habermas 1984, 13.

49. Ibid., citing Pollner 1974, 47.

50. Habermas 1984, 15.

51. Ibid., 15–23.

52. Ibid., 22. Schnädelbach (1991, 12–13) argues forcefully that the cognitivist qualification in the latter part of Habermas's remark can, from a Habermasian perspective, be given up in the theory of rationality. After all, argues Schnädelbach, "we can . . . also classify utterances and actions as rational if the estimations on which they are based prove to be erroneous." The full quote from Habermas reads worryingly thus: "[R]ationality is understood to be a disposition of speaking and acting subjects that is expressed in modes of behavior for which there are good reasons or grounds. This means that rational expressions admit of objective evaluation."

53. Taylor 1991a, 23. See also Thomas McCarthy's assessment of Habermas's project as representing "an explicit shift to the paradigm of language—not to language as a syntactic or semantic system, but to language-in-use or speech" (translator's introduction to Habermas 1984, ix).

54. Habermas 1984, 277.

55. Or, for that matter, that of Brandom, who unlike all other speech-act theorists reverses the direction of explanation, premising, late of Sellars, the pragmatics of asserting and inferring to the semantics of assertion and inference.

56. Habermas 1984, 278; original emphasis.

57. E.g., Habermas 1984, 96, 336–37.

58. Habermas 1984, 101. Writing fourteen years later, Habermas remains firm and clear on this point. Communicative rationality, he writes,

> is a peculiar rationality, inherent not in language as such but in the communicative use of linguistic expressions, that can be reduced neither to the epistemic rationality of knowledge (as classical truth-conditional semantics supposes) nor to the purposive rationality of action (as intentionalist semantics assumes). This *communicative rationality* is expressed in the unifying force of speech oriented toward reaching understanding, which secures for the participating speakers an intersubjectively shared lifeworld, thereby securing at the same time the horizon within which everyone can refer to one and the same objective world. (Habermas 1998, 315; original emphasis)

See below note 60.

59. Habermas 1998, 320–26.

60. Maeve Cooke's introduction to Habermas 1998 usefully charts the sense in which Habermas's "universal pragmatics" aspires to be at once universal and yet inherently pragmatic; how the validity claims—descriptive, normative, expressive—of communicating subjects can be "context-transcendent" and at the same time "circumscribed contextually." How, in other words, not to lose "sight of the potential power of validity claims to explode actual contexts of justification . . . while retaining an internal relation between truth and [context-dependent] justifiability" (8, 10–13). McCarthy rightly stresses its essential universalist core, and in doing so puts significant distance between Habermas's approach and the kind of comparative normative irrealism with which the present study deals. Although "the turn to the sociological matrix of individual action orientations brings Habermas face to face with the cultural and historical variability of lifeworld structure," McCarthy insists that "Habermas argues that our ability to communicate has a universal core—basic structures and fundamental rules that all subjects master in learning to speak a language" (Translator's introduction to Habermas 1984, x–xi).

61. Rorty 2000a, 7, 18.

62. Habermas 2000, 47–48.

63. Ibid., 48; emphasis added.

64. Ibid.; emphasis added.

65. Ibid., 46.

66. Ibid.; emphasis added.

67. For a detailed and nuanced discussion of Habermas's theory of rationality with special emphasis on its universalist elements, see the exchange on justification and truth between Habermas (2000) and Rorty (2000a, 2000b).

68. Friedman 2001, 54, citing Habermas 1984, 10. Friedman's English rendition of the passage contains several departures from McCarthy's original translation.

69. More precisely, for such transitions to be considered communicatively rational, it must be shown (a) that practitioners of the new can formulate and argue for their position in an idiom *understandable* to those of the old and (b) that the latter, in turn, be able eventually to *justify* a transition to the new from their own perspective. Friedman, we shall argue, succeeds in making a case for (a) but ultimately fails with respect to (b).

70. Nonetheless, at one point, in his eagerness to prove just how much more (communicatively) rational science is from other enterprises, Friedman's rhetoric takes a rather amusing and wholly uncalled-for universalist turn. In a footnote to the paragraph cited above, in which periods of normal science are praised for achieving "a situation of communicative rationality far exceeding that possible in other areas of intellectual and cultural life" (57–58), Friedman recalls Rorty asking him at Stanford, "whether other cultural enterprises, such as jurisprudence, for example, might not have achieved an equal situation of communicative rationality?" Friedman answers: "[T]his may be true within particular national traditions during particular historical periods, [but] I do not see how anything approaching the trans-national and trans-historical communicative rationality characteristic of the mathematical exact sciences has been attained anywhere else" (58 n. 70). This is a curious statement indeed coming from a professed neo-Kantian. First, the size of a community of discourse is irrelevant to the degree of communicative rationality its inner dialogue achieves, or is capable of achieving. If size is indicative of anything, it is of the vocational appeal of science rather than of its greater *rationality*. If one is at all to talk about degrees of communicative rationality, the initial diversity of opinion within the community would seem a better measure than the sheer number of its members.

By the same token, neither should the level of communicative rationality achieved or achievable by science be made a function of how *prolonged* its periods of uncritical adherence are to a particular linguistic framework. From Friedman's perspective, one would think that if anything the kind of distinction he aspires to make between the rationality of science and that of other enterprises would have less to do with the way functioning scientific frameworks function than in the rational manner they are *replaced* from time to time—which, of course is what the project of *Dynamics of Reason* is all about. Many intellectual, cultural, and especially religious enterprises display admirable levels of the sort of intraframework rationality Friedman finds in normal science, namely, protracted, widespread, and unquestioned conformity to well-formed frameworks constitutive of their discourses. Legal and ritual deliberation in conservative, traditionalist religious communities is a good example.

71. Of course, on a Habermasian showing, such disputes could go either way. Habermas's model is wholly symmetrical across the inter-*lebenswelt* divide. There is nothing to ensure in advance that the revolutionaries will carry the day and, just because they are out to revolt, will not eventually be reeled back in by the force of the old guard's arguments. The history of *failed* scientific revolutions, though far less studied for lack of "whiggish" appeal, is just as interesting a topic for exploring the rationality of science. From a Kuhnian or Carnapian perspective, decisions to stick with a functioning framework are no more rationally explicable than decisions to replace it, while from Friedman's point of view, both are just as easily dealt with. Friedman, however, gives no sign of being aware of this particular historiographic possibility.

72. By which we mean members of standing and voice, whose arguments in favor of the transition are capable of at least commanding the attention of the opposition.

73. See section 5 of the postscript to the second edition of *Structure* (Kuhn 1970, 202) and his description of paradigm shifts as shifts between different lexicons of kind-terms in Kuhn 1993. For Friedman's reference to Kuhn's comparison, see Friedman 2001, 95.

74. In *Dynamics of Reason,* Friedman does not present his argument as clearly as we reconstruct it. At crucial junctures he seems to lose sight of its main objective, namely, to make a case for the type of dialogical reasoning that constitutes communicative rationality. To argue for their *communicative* rationality is to argue, at the very least, that such transitions are, in principle, debatable and decidable by both parties involved. Hence, to argue, as Friedman does, that adherents of the new framework "are always in a position to understand and rationally justify—at least in their own terms—all the results of earlier stages" (96) is largely beside the point. For the transition from old to new to be considered communicatively rational, practitioners of the latter must certainly be capable of understanding the results of the former, but not to "rationally *justify* them." On the contrary, they should be doing their utmost to justify their *abandonment* of the former perspective in ways convincing to their adversaries.

75. The timebound terminology is misleading, of course. At the point at which the possible transition between a functioning and a newly proposed framework is being negotiated, the two perspectives cannot, and should not, be described as forward or backward looking. Communicative rationality is not about the community's ability retrospectively to rationalize its choices after the event but about the reasoned manner in which its choices can be said to have been debated and *made*. Throughout his book Friedman wisely allows the history and historiography of science to act as a corrective to philosophy. Here, however, the timebound language of historical sequence serves to obscure rather than correct the vital timelessness of the philosophical analysis of rationality.

76. This is a requirement very different from, say, Popper's demand that the predictive and explanatory powers of a candidate theory be at least as great as the theory it aspires to replace (e.g., Popper 1994, 12). Friedman's demand that the old be preserved as an approximation of the new is designed as a first small step toward somehow bridging the gap between the alien concepts of reality (scientific "lifeworlds"?) constituted by the two frameworks—a problem Popper and his followers generally do not even acknowledge. Popper's unwillingness to seriously engage, or properly acknowledge, the philosophical challenges of the linguistic turn dealt with in the present study and by Friedman is most evident in his "The Myth of the Framework" (1994, chap. 2). See also Fisch 2008.

77. As indicated in note 76 above, Popper's views to the contrary are irrelevant to the present study, because he denies the neo-Kantian presuppositions of the picture of science subscribed to by Carnap, Kuhn, Friedman, and ourselves.

78. Declaring in summary that "despite the important kernel of truth in Kuhn's doctrine of incommensurability or non-intertranslatability, there is still considerably more rational continuity in the revolutionary transitions in question than either Kuhn or the post-Kuhn conceptual relativists allow" (117).

79. In later work, especially Friedman 2010b, the list of external fields relevant to scientific rethinking is extended from mathematics and philosophy to other fields, including religion.

80. Indeed, in later works the terms *meta-framework* and *meta-paradigm* are dropped in favor of the less misleading *meta-scientific level*—e.g., Friedman 2010a, 718.

81. Similarly dissatisfied with the "block-periodized accounts" of "all-inclusive breaks," late of Carnap and Kuhn, that depict science as "a collection of island empires each under the rule of its own system of validation" (1997, 12–13), Galison, not unlike Friedman, stresses the interdependence of and collaboration between scientific subcultures and their neighboring disciplines. He suggestively portrays them (in metaphorical rather than full-fledged philosophical response

to the implied relativism of Kuhn's "meaning incommensurability") as exchanging knowledge in "trading zones" by means of pidgin and creole versions of their professional vocabularies. Galison's metaphor has the advantage of bringing to the fore the professional, interest-driven purposefulness of such interactions that is largely overlooked by Friedman. Viewing the interface between a science and its relevant neighboring cultures in Galison's commercial idiom further emphasizes the point we have made that central as it may be to its original field, the mere availability of an offering outside science will not suffice to render it a scientific "live option" except in the most rudimentary and unhelpful sense of the term.

We return in the final chapter of this book to the insight shared by Friedman's meta-paradigms and Galison's trading zones regarding the importance of a science's professional engagements with other fields and professions to its development and prospects of rational renewal. Needless to say, unlike Friedman or Galison, our concern will be with the role such discourses can play in motivating normative self-criticism among practitioners, a topic neither of them addresses. For an initial outline of the argument see Fisch 2008, esp. §9–10, which is further developed in Fisch 2010.

82. A story traced by Friedman in detail (e.g., 107–15).

83. As noted in chapter 1 (n. 54) as well as in the introduction to Part II, DiSalle, who otherwise fully concedes Friedman's position, stands alone in criticizing him on precisely this point, urging him to "reconsider the role of philosophy in the evolution of science—not merely as an external source of general heuristic principles and new conceptual possibilities, but, at least in the most important revolutionary developments, as an objective tool of scientific inquiry" (2002, 192). In a series of publications—notably, DiSalle 2002, 2006, 2010—DiSalle argues that, in addition to the role attributed to philosophy by Friedman as a source of new conceptual possibilities, the history of the transition from Aristotle to Einstein exhibits significant moments of keen "dialectical confrontation with prevailing conceptions" (2002, 204) performed by major practitioners with a view explicitly to "revealing the hidden presuppositions of the old conception, and exhibiting the internal difficulties that must be resolved by the new" (2010, 528). He portrays physicists as being, not merely alert and open to "the rational discussion of theoretical alternatives" (527) by others, but as actively partaking in that discussion as part of their work as physicists. DiSalle shows in considerable detail how Galileo, Newton, and Einstein all fashioned their conceptual innovations in response to shortcomings they perceived in the prevailing framework. And in doing so, he clearly implies that with regard to framework replacement in science, *two* questions of rationality need to be addressed: that alongside

the question addressed by Friedman, of practioners of the old opting rationally for the new, that of the creative individuals initially responsible for fashioning the new in place of old, clearly implying that this form of rationality, wholly lacking from Friedman's account, must turn *prospectively* on an agent's ability to (noncomparatively) fault elements of her own constitutive framework.

DiSalle, however, shows no awareness of the thorny difficulties involved in the very possibility of adopting such a critical stance, especially from the neo-Kantian perspective he supposedly shares with Friedman. DiSalle's suggestions are an important complement to Friedman's picture, which the latter justly if not wholeheartedly welcomes (see Friedman 2010a, 718–29). Perhaps Friedman's hesitance indicates an uneasiness on his part with the total nonchalance with which DiSalle introduces his protagonists' ability to criticize the frameworks constitutive of their thinking.

84. Brandom 1994, 231.

Chapter 6. **Toward a Critical Pragmatism**

1. Two additional points raised by Friedman that will prove pertinent to what follows will be built on in the final chapter of the book, in which we return to the problem of the rationality of scientific framework replacement: (a) the place he assigns to intermediary figures such as Galileo and Poincaré and (b) that assigned to science's professional engagements with other disciplines. Both factors, we shall argue there (differently from Friedman), are centrally relevant to the possibility and possible outcome of normative self-criticism.

2. E.g., Friedman 2001, 54.

3. See Friedman 2001, 106–7, for a comparison of science and philosophy in this respect.

4. Rational action and successful action, we argue in what follows, are not synonymous. Reasoned action is rational, but reasoning per se, even at its very best, cannot warrant success. Serious, thoughtful, yet ultimately unsuccessful attempts to solve a thorny mathematical problem, for example, could well be a model of rational endeavor, despite failing painfully.

5. Michele Dillon (1999), who emphasizes the centrality of reflective self-criticism in Habermas's communicative rationality, sharply criticizes Habermas for excluding religion "as anathema to rational critical discourse." Her references to Fisch (1997) in this respect render her work relevant to the present study, despite the Habermasian emphasis she lays on social consensus as the rational goal of communicative action rather than on legal or theological improvement, as does Fisch.

6. Friedman 2001, 98.

7. Ibid., 64–65.

8. Following Ross's (1954) English rendition of Aristotle's *'phronēsis'.*

9. McDowell 1994, 79.

10. Ibid., 81. Haugeland (1998, 360 n. 26) also rightly draws attention to McDowell (and wrongly to Kuhn) in this respect but does so disappointingly to make an unjustified special case for empirical science. Notice how, in Haugeland's text, the contrast shifts dramatically from games such as chess and baseball, which are his prime examples, to all human endeavor other than science:

[W]hat is most important, the *essential* difference between science and games, is that the enterprise itself is always in question. In science, unlike in any game, the repair and improvement not only of mundane but also of constitutive skills is always potentially (and often in fact) an issue. The responsibilities entailed by an empirical constitutive commitment thus necessarily extend to the very skills and concepts that are the form and substance of the domain itself. It is this empirical responsibility for the terms in which the enterprise can so much as be conducted, grounded in an existential constitutive commitment, that most deeply distinguishes genuine empirical research from all other human endeavors. (1998, 343; original emphasis)

In a footnote he describes this paragraph as "elaborating on a theme sounded (but not elaborated) in both Kuhn and McDowell." Interestingly, the passage he quotes from the latter differs from the passage quoted here (which is mentioned but not cited), in referring not to thinking in general but to the process of squaring one's worldview with experience.

11. McDowell 1994, 81–82.

12. Davidson 1982; Rorty 1989, 48–50.

13. See in particular McDowell 2009a, chaps. 14–16, 18, and 19; and 2009b, chap. 6.

14. Which he takes to be a (transcendental) question about the possibility of empirical *content* rather than a(n epistemological) concern about empirical *warrant,* and hence crucial to the self-critical nature of empirical accountability rather than the self-assuring nature of empirical attestation. See most recently McDowell 2009a, 243–44.

15. McDowell 2009a, 244–45.

16. McDowell 1994, 77.

17. E.g., McDowell 1994, 66.

18. McDowell 2009a, 249.

19. McDowell 2009b, 6.

20. E.g., McDowell 1994, 94–95, 178.

21. Toward the end of his Woodbridge Lectures (now published as part 1 of Brandom 2009), Brandom makes the same point about perceptual judgments being constrained and "their evolution . . . subject to friction" by the "normative attitudes" that "practitioners are trained to acquire . . . non-inferentially." "Under the right circumstances," he explains, "properly trained observers are reliably disposed to respond to perceptible states of affairs by acknowledging commitments to corresponding perceptual judgments." But he steps more cautiously than McDowell in adding immediately that they are not granted special ontological status by being immediate: "Like any other judgments, immediate perceptual judgments amount to petitions for recognition. The authority they claim may or may not be recognized by being incorporated in later rational integrations. But they exert constraint or friction just by making that petition for recognition" (Brandom 2009, 96).

22. Thus construed, Robert Brandom's "social practice theory of discursive commitments" (1994, 54), to which we turn immediately, clearly falls under the interpretive rubric. A person forms "normative attitudes" by articulating, or "making explicit," the relevant social practice. However, although constitutive of his thought and speech, normative attitudes, according to Brandom, may be found incorrect in comparison to the "normative statuses" they purport to denote.

23. E.g., Walzer 1987, 22. In a telling passage further down he explains why:

What makes [social] criticism a permanent possibility, according to this account, is the fact that every ruling class is compelled to present itself as a universal class. . . . This self presentation of the rulers is elaborated by the intellectuals. Their work is apologetic, but the apology is of a sort that gives hostages to future social critics. It sets standards the rulers will not live up to, cannot live up to, given their political ambitions. . . . Ideology strains toward universality as a condition of its success. (40–41)

24. Brandom 1994, 55.

25. Ibid., xi.

26. Nonetheless, we shall argue that his inattendence to the questions and challenges of Normative Diversity lends his theory an unfortunate "Habermasian" semblance, as if there is no stopping point between the ability to *understand* the commitments and entitlements of others and that of finding them relevant to one's own. We shall also argue that inattendence to the question of normative self-criticism deprives the important communal aspect of his account, late of Hegel, of its vital critical bite.

27. We thank a perceptive anonymous reader for the Press for prompting us to acknowledge how Brandomian our reading of Brandom is, as well as for the suggestive phrase.

28. Jeffrey Stout (2002, 2004) anticipates our reading of Brandom in extending his account of conceptual norms to normativity in general. However, in his most recent work—especially his Woodbridge Lectures—Brandom himself makes the point far more explicitly than in the past.

29. Brandom 2009, 39.

30. Brandom 1994, 30; original emphasis. Or as Kant puts it: "Everything in nature works according to laws. Only a rational being has the power to act according to his conception of laws, i.e. according to principles, and thereby has he a will" ([1785] 1981, 412). This is not a distinction between norm and fact, however—neither in Kant nor in Brandom—but one "between the realm of regularity and the realm of responsibility"; between "that which can acknowledge rules only implicitly by obedience . . . and those that can acknowledge them explicitly by the use of concepts" (624).

31. Brandom 1994, 31.

32. Ibid., 19–20 (original emphasis)—a view he also attributes to Frege (11–13).

33. Ibid., 52.

34. Ibid., 52–53 (original emphasis), referring to the culmination point of the normative element in Wittgenstein's well-known private language argument. I could be right or wrong to describe a certain painful sensation of mine as rheumatic, for example. (And the assessment of the rightness of my description could also be deemed right or wrong.) But, argues Wittgenstein, when, in order to keep track of the occurrence of a certain sensation, I record it in my diary as S, "I have no criterion of correctness. One would like to say: whatever is going to seem right to me is right. And all that means is that here we can't talk about 'right'" (Wittgenstein 1958, §258). The point is further developed in the second chapter of Brandom 2009.

35. Wright 1980, 220, cited by Brandom 1994, 53 .

36. Ibid.

37. Brandom 1994, 54.

38. Ibid. For a similar position, see Haugeland 1998, esp. chap. 13.

39. Brandom 1994, 54.

40. Stout 2004, chap. 12.

41. Ibid., 274. See also the illuminating comparison of chess to science in Richardson 2002, and especially Haugeland's (1998, chap. 13) analysis of the various forms of normativity involved in games (primarily baseball and various modifications of chess).

42. Haugeland (1998) criticizes Brandom's "ingenious version of social pragmatism" (357) for not distinguishing sufficiently between what he terms "instituted" and "constituted" norms—namely, between norms that govern, for example, the appropriate maneuver called for in a certain circumstance in a free-form folk dance and those that, for example, govern a color-identifying response (315–16). As a result, argues Haugeland, despite claims to the contrary (e.g., Brandom 1994, 606–7), Brandom proves incapable of distinguishing between the "two fundamentally distinct sorts of normative constraint: social propriety and objective correctness (truth)" (317). In his more recent work, Brandom attempts to better address this point by showing "of-intentionality"—namely, the *representational* dimension concerning what one is thinking or talking *about*—to be "a necessary sub-structure of inferential that-intentionality," that is, the *expressive* dimension concerning the *content* one attributes to what one is thinking or talking about. By taking responsibility *for* a judgment, one makes oneself responsible, or answerable, to the objects implied by it—which he considers "the punchline" of the first of his Woodbridge Lectures (2009, 42–45). What Brandom's dispute with Wright brings to the fore, and receives further emphasis from Stout's extension of his thesis, is that the fundamental notion of objectivity for Brandom is that of an objective *norm* rather than an object or a state of affairs. The problem we find with his position, as opposed to Haugeland, is in the way he reduces normative objectivity to the objectivity of normative *application*. Like Brandom, Haugeland also presents the distinction he makes between social propriety and objective correctness as a corrective to the "fatal flaw" he finds in Wright's (reading of Wittgenstein's) inability to "give sense to the possibility of everyone being consistently wrong about something" (315). Interestingly, in doing so he cites McDowell's (1984) criticism of Wright rather than Brandom's. See Brandom (2009, 63–64) for forcefully distinguishing between the attitude-dependency of a norm's *force* from the attitude independency of its *content*.

43. Brandom 2009, 33; original emphasis on "contents" and "is."

44. Ibid., 35–36; original emphasis.

45. Ibid., 35.

46. The subtitle of the Woodbridge Lectures and of part 1 of Brandom 2009.

47. Brandom 2009, 53; "concepts" and "conceptual" emphasized in the original.

48. See especially Brandom 2000a, 7–12; 2009, 27–32.

49. Brandom 2002a, 7.

50. See especially his elaborate Sellarsian inferentialist account of perception, representation, and the noninferential application of concepts in observational reports in Brandom 1994, chaps. 4 and 8, I; 2000a, 165–83; and in the closing paragraphs of his study guide to Sellars (1956).

51. Responding to McDowell, Brandom (2005) refers explicitly to the question of the place of conceptual norms in normative practices. He answers with an unqualified "yes" the question (not to be confused with Stout's point) of whether there can "be implicitly normative practices of attributing and undertaking commitment without there being specifically *conceptual* norms in play[.]" This, of course, marks his parting of ways late of the later Wittgenstein with Kantian regulism. The point we attribute to Stout is different and concerns the question of whether there can be normative practices of *assessing* the application of attributing and undertaking commitment without there being specifically *conceptual* norms in play?—to which we join Stout in answering with an unqualified "no."

52. To use the phrase he himself employs to describe the "common thought" he sees in Brandom (2002a, 348–49) as underlying the most important arguments deployed in Sellars (1956), referred to in note 50 above.

53. McDowell (2005, 122–23) strongly objects to Brandom's attribution of this reductive element of his theory to Wittgenstein.

54. Brandom 1994, 199–200; original emphasis.

55. Ibid., 624.

56. Ibid., chap. 2, vi,1.

57. Chapter 1, "Toward a Normative Pragmatics," precedes chapter 2, "Toward an inferential Semantics." However, the argument *up* from Kantian normativity *toward* "a normative pragmatics" to which chapter 1 is devoted stops short of concluding that "the practices in which [conceptual norms] are implicit . . . depend on the social articulation of the inferential practice of giving and asking for reasons." This, writes Brandom in chapter 1, turns out to be the case "according to the answer elaborated in Chapter 8" (54).

58. Brandom 1994, 230–31.

59. Brandom 2002a, 350–51; original emphasis.

60. "Right" or "correctly" are used in this context as context-dependent, thin normative terms, which do not necessarily connote perfect, excellent, or maximal performance. Often the order of the day will be minimal or partial compliance due to special circumstances or other duties.

61. Brandom 1994, 5. See also Brandom 2009, 55–60.

62. Brandom 2000a, 81; emphasis added.

63. Brandom 2002a, 6.

64. Ibid., 12.

65. Korsgaard 1996, 68.

66. Walzer (1987, chap. 1) famously compares three "paths" in moral philosophy: those of discovery, invention, and interpretation, arguing that most often the first two are "disguised" versions of the third. "The moralities we discover and invent," he submits,

always turn out to be, and always will turn out, remarkably similar to the morality we already have. Philosophical discovery and invention (leaving aside divine revelation) are disguised interpretations; there is really one path in moral philosophy. . . . Our categories, relationships, commitments, and aspirations are all shaped by, expressed in terms of, the existing morality. (20–21)

And it is in relation to the existing morality, to "the shared understanding of a people expressed . . . in its historical ideals, its public rhetoric, its foundational texts, its ceremonies and rituals" (29), that the fruits of invention and discovery are ultimately judged.

 67.　Walzer 1987, 77–78.
 68.　Ibid., 89–90.
 69.　Brandom 1994, 4–5.
 70.　Ibid., 644–45.
 71.　Ibid., 645.
 72.　Ibid., 645–49; 2002a, 6–8.
 73.　Brandom 1994, 242.
 74.　E.g., Brandom 1994, 142.

Chapter 7.　**The Critical Stance**

 1.　Brandom 2002a, 12. Brandom (2009, 65 ff.) attributes to Kant "adopting a characteristic rationalist order of explanation" the idea that in order to judge or to act, the "empirical consciousness always already has available a stable of completely determinate concepts" (65)—a point Hegel, he argues, centrally criticizes. In what follows page references in the text are to Brandom 2002a.

 2.　The common law judge analogy is further developed in Brandom 2009, 84–90. It is also mentioned briefly in Brandom 1994, 130, but to a different end.

 3.　Lakatos 1971. For a detailed assessment of Lakatos's philosophy and historiography of science, see Hacking 1979. For the Hegelian aspects of Lakatos's approach to the history of science and philosophy, see pp. 383 ff.

 4.　Despite "the absolutely pivotal role" Kant plays for Brandom "in the larger narrative" to which he sees the essays comprising *Tales of the Mighty Dead* "as contributing," the book surprisingly lacks a chapter on Kant, whose "watershed innovations" it "skips over . . . between the Leibniz work and the Hegel work" (45–46). The lacuna has since been partly filled by Brandom 2006 and more so by the first chapter of Brandom 2009.

5. On Brandom's (and Heidegger's) "tendency to treat their predecessors as partial and sometimes confused versions of themselves," see Haugeland 2005, quote at 421.

6. Brandom (2009, 7) presents the project of his Woodbridge Lectures as an attempt to "reanimate" some of the ideas that animated the tradition "anchored and epitomized by Kant and Hegel" "by retrospectively, rationally reconstructing a coherent, cumulative trajectory of thought, carving it out of the context in which it is embedded, ruthlessly ignoring elements near and dear to Kant and Hegel that are not essential to the line of thought on which I am focusing."

7. Brandom 2009, 105–7.

8. Ibid., 60.

9. Ibid., 52.

10. Ibid., 71.

11. Ibid., 70; original emphasis.

12. Ibid., 71.

13. Ibid., 84.

14. Brandom (2009, 82–84) adopts a firm Hegelian, anti-Carnapian line, in rejecting all out the "two-phase story about meaning and belief, language and theory" advocated by Carnap (and endorsed by Friedman), in favor of a Quinean approach late of Hegel, according to which the process of applying concepts is also the process by which the concepts applied are determined. Seen from the perspective of the actor, we argue immediately, we seriously doubt his account can sustain such a radical taking of sides.

15. See Fisch 1994a and 1997, chap. 1, which contain rough and preliminary sketches of parts of what follows, written, though, from an unhelpful Popperian perspective.

16. Briskman 1977 is one of the very few works on rationality that forcefully distinguishes between doubt and "concrete criticism" as the basis for combating the problem of the rational critique of standards in explicit acknowledgment of Normative Diversity (see esp. §5). It is also one of the very few works that aspires to do so, as proposed here, by treating rational endeavor as "a goal-directed and aim-oriented activity" (§4). However, he attempts to do so with a view to overcoming rather than succumbing to Comparative Irrealism. As a result he unhelpfully understands criticism as the problem of choice between incompatible alternatives rather than as an argument aimed to demonstrate the existence of a failing.

17. Hattiangadi 1978–79 remains the most substantial theory of problems and problem-solving published to date. But by formally reducing problems to logical contradictions, his account is rendered incapable in principle of

distinguishing between problems large and small, pressing and nonpressing, and solutions full or partial. More promising, yet far less developed, is the account of problem-solving as "crossing a logical gap" suggested by Polanyi (1957) whose general approach to defining problems partly anticipates the approach presupposed in what follows.

18. We disagree, therefore, with Agassi's contention (1987, 250) that "it seems obvious that no teaching is rational, that rationally we may exchange opinions, offer intellectual excitement, and so on, but never teach, *never try to convince*" (emphasis added). The question of the rationality of instruction may be an open one for critical rationalism, but we fail to see how it is possible to "view rationality as criticism" as Agassi does (Agassi and Jarvie 1987, 247), yet view attempts to convince as nonrational. For what is criticism, if not an attempt to convince one's addressee that something is amiss?

19. For a similar point, see Moran 2002, 200–202.

20. An ability to understand and argue knowingly from another person's perspective does not require full "connectedness" in Walzer's sense of the term. As we have seen in the preceding chapter, Comparative Irrealism does not prohibit mutual *understanding*. In what follows we shall be arguing for a more lenient account of knowing, trusted, and, therefore, effective normative criticism than that of Walzer's member-critic.

21. Brandom 2009, 36.

22. Ibid., 40.

23. See above note 17.

24. Within the premises of this study, their factuality remains framework dependent, of course.

25. This crucial point is systematically ignored by what usually goes under the name of "instrumental" conceptions of rationality. As Nozick (1993) puts it, quoting Russell (1954, viii: "Reason . . . has nothing to do with the choice of ends") and Simon (1983, 7–8: "Reason is wholly instrumental. It cannot tell us where to go; at best it can tell us how to get there"), "about the goals themselves, an instrumental conception has little to say" (64). Instrumental rationality "gives us no way to evaluate the rationality of . . . goals, ends, and desires themselves, except as instrumentally effective in achieving further goals taken as given" (139). His attempt toward the end the book to "take a few tentative steps toward a theory of substantive rationality of desires and goals" (139–51) accomplishes little due to his failure (typical of the standard instrumental approach) to distinguish between the rationality of action and that of its fruits. In this case he fails to distinguish between setting a rational goal and setting a goal rationally.

26. Frankfurt 1992, 82–83.

27. Ibid., 83; original emphasis.

28. Ibid., 85.

29. Ibid., 86.

30. Interestingly, Martha Nussbaum (2006, 73) makes a similar point arguing for her "capabilities approach" against "the economic-Utilitarian approaches." By focusing on the state of satisfaction, she argues, "[u]tilitarianism shows a deficient regard for agency. Contentment is not the only thing that matters in a human life; active striving matters, too." Nussbaum goes on to cite Nozick's reductio ad absurdum "pleasure-machine" thought experiment (Nozick 1974, 42 ff.) in which by hooking up to the machine people experience contentment without doing anything. This reversal of the means-end relationship goes unnoticed in Christine Korsgaard's otherwise excellent "The Normativity of Instrumental Reasoning" (1997).

31. See Frankfurt 1994; and esp. 1999, chap. 14.

32. "The significance to us of *caring* is . . . more basic than the importance to us of *what* we care about. Needless to say, it is better for us to care about what is truly worth caring about than it is to care about things that are inconsequential or otherwise unworthy or that will bring us harm. However, the value to us of the fact that we care about various things does not derive simply from the value or the suitability of the objects about which we care. Caring is important to us for its own sake, insofar as it is the indispensably foundational activity through which we provide continuity and coherence to our volitional lives . . . [and] its essential role in making us the distinctive kind of creatures that we are" (Frankfurt 1999, 162–63).

33. Frankfurt 2006, 3. For his summary statements to this effect with respect to morality, see pp. 45–48.

34. For an illuminating account of the historiographical implications of the dynamics of concept change and redeployment, see Skinner 1969 and 1980 and the discussion of his views in Tully 1988. See also Buzaglo 2002.

35. He termed this sort of explanatory surprise a "consilience of inductions" (Whewell 1847, II, 65). For differing latter-day assessments of Whewell's claim, see Hesse 1971; Butts 1977; Fisch 1985a, 1985b; and more recently Snyder 2006, 173–202.

36. Whewell 1847, II, 65.

37. For an articulation of the possible support enjoyed by hypotheses by virtue of explanatory surprise (as opposed to novel prediction), see Fisch 1985b.

38. Restricting its domain of application, on the other hand, *is* often a corrective measure taken with a view to reducing some of the system's undesired consequences.

39. Except when done as a decoy, for instance, to draw attention away from the system's prime application.

40. For an insightful analysis of how such moves are negotiated across the scientific disciplinary and subdisciplinary boundaries, see Galison 1997, esp. chap. 9. For a first assessment of the relevance and bearing of this aspect of Galison's work on normative self-criticism, see Fisch 2008; for a more substantial discussion, see Fisch 2010 and chap. 9 below.

41. Their neutrality with respect to Normative Diversity does not in any way diminish that diversity. There being a common language by which to accommodate and analyze processes of all manner of problem-seeking and problem-solving is irrelevant to arguments for Comparative Irrealism.

42. This is true even in the case of coerced action.

43. Polanyi 1958, 56.

44. In the case of normative criticism, Comparative Irrealism bars this option for sufficiently diverse alternatives.

45. We hence agree, in principle, with Kekes's (1977, 268) proposal to regard problem-seeking and problem-solving as the external standard of rationality.

46. Collingwood 1939, chap. 5.

47. Walzer 1987, 57.

48. Ibid., 59.

Chapter 8. **The Achievement of Self-Criticism**

1. Taylor's notion of personal "strong evaluation" (see esp. Taylor 1977) is both thoroughly normative and explicitly self-critical in ways that Brandom's system is not. However, not unlike Brandom, in building on and away from Frankfurt (15–16) Taylor's notion of personal normative self-criticism is made to rest solidly on a stratified "onology" of a realm of given communal norms, for which, like Brandom, he offers no account of their critical review and modification. On this weakness of Taylor's interpretivism, see Anderson 1996.

2. Carol Rovane (2006) is a case in point. The "one overarching normative requirement of rationality on persons," she argues in almost Brandomian idiom, is "the normative requirement to achieve overall rational unity" by "resolving contradictions among one's beliefs; working out the implications of one's beliefs and other attitudes; and ranking one's preferences in a transitive ordering" (101).

3. For two relatively recent sets of important engagements with Frankfurt's thinking see Buss and Everton 2002 and the "comments" of Christine Korsgaard, Michael Bratman, and Meir Dan-Cohen appended to Frankfurt 2006.

4. For a useful summary of his position on human self-reflection and the way it generates the two main foci of his work see the introduction to Buss and

Everton 2002, esp. xi–xiii. For one of several earlier formulations, see Frankfurt 1999, 99–100. Korsgaard's account of normativity also sets forth from a close study of "the authority of reflection" (to quote the title of the last of the three lectures comprising her *The Sources of Normativity*). Hers, however, is a picture directed primarily not to the forging of personal identity, as is Frankfurt's, but to accounting in Kantian fashion for the grounding of ethics in free will. More on the agreements and disagreements between Korsgaard and Frankfurt below.

5. Frankfurt 2006, 3–4.

6. Ibid., 4.

7. Ibid., 5.

8. Ibid., 4–5.

9. Buss and Overton 2002, xi–xii; original emphasis.

10. Commenting on Frankfurt's notion of self-identification, Moran (2002, 201–2) compares the activity and "specifically first-person responsibility" a person relies on in making his own desires "answerable to and adjustable in the light of some sense of good to pursue" to those relied on in "ordinary reasoning" with others. Here, as in his influential 2001 work, Moran concentrates on comparing and contrasting first- and third-person knowledge but does not raise the question of the possible *bearing* of the latter on the former.

More helpfully, Dan-Cohen (2006) writes of the need to expand "Frankfurt's focus on individual psychology" so as "to take account of the intersubjective or the social" (91). The need arises, according to Dan-Cohen, because "[t]he shape of the self is at least in part the product of what we may call *constitutive* practices, including those of law and morality" (96; original emphasis), which may well be in conflict with a person's own account.

11. This particular formulation of Frankfurt's two-tier delineation of the self derives from Dan-Cohen 2006, 91–92.

12. Ibid., 6.

13. Ibid., 10.

14. Frankfurt, "Reply to Richard Moran" (Buss and Overton 2002, 219). The idea of identification as constitutive of agency is expressed most vividly in Frankfurt (1987, 170): "in making a decision by which he identifies with a desire [the person] *constitutes himself*" (emphasis Frankfurt's).

15. Except to distinguish interestingly between what in his later work he calls volitional rationality and the strictures of pure reason. See Frankfurt 1988, chap. 13; 2006, 29 ff.

16. We are referring to the four brief paragraphs he devotes to normative self-correction toward the end of his second Tanner Lecture (Frankfurt 2006, 48–50), which we discuss in some detail below.

17. See, for instance, the analogy he draws between "a person who is uncertain whether to identify himself with one or with another of his desires" and a person uncertain about the outcome of a problem in arithmetic (Frankfurt 1987, 167–69).

18. Frankfurt 1987, 164.

19. Ibid., 165.

20. See, for example, his reply to Moran in Buss and Overton (2002, 219): "[I]t is true that identification and reasons are essentially related," but it is not "because the former depend essentially on the latter as their indispensable ground. The relationship of dependency goes the other way around."

21. Frankfurt 1987, 165; original emphasis.

22. Frankfurt 1994, 139.

23. A point overlooked, or at least underestimated, we believe, by G. A. Cohen (1996, 187–88).

24. Frankfurt 2004, 46.

25. Frankfurt 1982, 182.

26. Frankfurt 2004, 48; emphasis added. For a detailed analysis and constructive critique of Frankfurt's grounding of normativity in love, see Korsgaard 2006.

27. Bratman 2006, 78.

28. For "the reflective endorsement method" in Hume, Bernard Williams, and John Stuart Mill, see Lecture 2 in Korsgaard 1996; for it being, for Kant, "not merely a way of justifying morality [but] *morality itself*," see Lecture 3 (original emphasis). In that book (99 n. 8) Korsgaard notes in passing, citing Frankfurt (1971), that "the affinity of my account with Frankfurt's should be obvious." Ten years later, in her comments on Frankfurt's Tanner Lectures, Korsgaard spells out the extent of the affinity in some detail. The points of agreement are listed as follows: (i) "that the distinguishing feature of human life is . . . our capacity to take our own mental states and activities as the objects of our attention"; (ii) "that this form of self-consciousness is the source of the distinctively human tendency to self-assessment and the resulting capacity for normative self-government"; (iii) "that this kind of self-consciousness is the source of normativity, or anyway makes normativity possible; (iv) "is the source of the freedom of the will"; (v) the rejection of "the kind of normative realism which holds that (to use Frankfurt's own phrase) 'volitional necessities are a response to an independent normative reality'"; and (vi) "that all normativity springs from the will" (Korsgaard 2006, 55). However, she disagrees with Frankfurt that "the normativity of morality for any given agent is contingent on whether that agent cares about morality," arguing, by contrast, "that the logic of caring commits us to universal

shared values, and so to morality (76), thus purporting to argue for the Kantian thesis of *Sources of Normativity* from within Frankfurt's framework.

29. Brandom 1994, 19–20.

30. As summarized nicely by Geuss (Korsgaard 1996, 189–90), that we must go a step beyond Kant by driving a wedge between the categorical imperative— namely, that "a free will must choose a maxim that it can regard as the law"— and the moral law—namely, a commitment to "the kind of thing all rational beings could agree to act on together in a working cooperative system" (189, citing Korsgaard 1996, 99–100).

31. See Frankfurt 2006, 46.

32. Ibid., 11.

33. Ibid., 28–29; emphasis added.

34. Herman 2002.

35. Buss and Overton 2002, 276–78. Herman (2002, 258–59) suggestively points out that the authority of Frankfurtian volitional necessities is "the practical analogue of the Cartesian norm of clear and distinct ideas"—an idea Frankfurt warmly embraces in his response (278 n. 1), and reiterates in the concluding remarks of Frankfurt 2006, 51–52.

36. Frankfurt 2006, 33.

37. Ibid., 42; emphasis added.

38. Ibid., 51–52.

39. Ibid., 48.

40. Ibid., 34–37.

41. Ibid., 38–39.

42. Ibid., 49.

43. Ibid.

44. Ibid. See also Frankfurt 1999, 158–59.

45. Frankfurt 2006, 49.

46. In Brandom's later work, as we have seen at the outset of the previous chapter, due to the Hegelian twist he gives his position in Brandom 2002 and especially 2009, personal normative attitude is seen to contribute prospectively to social normative status by virtue of the reciprocal-recognition model of the latter. But even there, it is always, for Brandom, a matter of differently explicating a *given* practice, and in a manner wholly devoid of normative criticism *of* that practice.

47. See, e.g., Frankfurt 2006, 48.

48. Frankfurt 2006, 20. Benbaji (2001) challenges this claim of Frankfurt's, which Frankfurt purports to meet in notes 1 and 3 on p. 105 of that work.

49. Frankfurt 2006, 23.

50. The importance of vitamins to people who lived before they were discovered is Frankfurt's example of how something can be important to a person who does not, and even cannot, care about it directly. However, had they not cared about their health, for example, it would no longer be true that vitamins were important to them. Cf. Frankfurt 2006, 20.

51. See especially Wolf 2002; Dan-Cohen 2006.

52. Korsgaard 2006, 56, quoting Frankfurt 2006, 32. For a more detailed discussion of moral realism, see Korsgaard 1997, 240–43.

53. To borrow Moran's terminology, for Frankfurt "getting the proper alignment of the self as agent to the self as spectator" presupposes seeing the self exclusively as spectator with regard to the volitions and necessities that ground its norms. See Moran 2001, esp. chap. 2. Quotation at p. xxxiii.

54. Korsgaard 1996, 93; original emphasis.

55. Frankfurt 1987, 175.

56. Frankfurt himself sometimes calls this a person's "essential nature" or "essential identity." See Frankfurt 1994, 138.

57. This subsection knowingly borrows its title from that of Dan-Cohen 2006.

58. Frankfurt 2006, 51.

59. Cf. Korsgaard 2006, 55; Frankfurt 2006, 32. See also the latter's (explicitly neo-Kantian) distinction between heteronomy and autonomy (Frankfurt 1994, 132–33). "Someone is heteronymous," he writes, "when what he wills is not determined exclusively by the inherent nature of his will but at least partly by considerations that are . . . logically external to it. . . . To that extent, he is passive. The person is active, on the other hand, insofar as his will determines itself."

60. On the connection between caring and the continuity and stability of self, see, e.g., Frankfurt 2004, 16.

61. Frankfurt 1992, 91; emphasis added. See also Frankfurt 2004, 55–59. Frankfurt's analysis of final ends bears an interesting affinity to John Haugeland's discussion of what he terms existential, or constitutive commitment. Haugeland (1998, chap. 13, §16) distinguishes between a "deontic" commitment to play by the rules of a game, and a "constitutive commitment" to the game that "is not an agreement to play by the rules, on pain of being rejected, but rather an involved insistent way of responding and playing . . . on pain of 'giving up on the game'" (342).

62. For a discussion and comparison of the two positions in the political realm, see Fisch 2003.

63. On a Frankfurtian showing, the problems brought to the fore in prudent normative criticism do not at all resemble the sort of anomalies, of which Kuhn speaks, that are recognizable as such and set aside by members of the

community. Once deemed worthy and adopted, a wholeheartedly applied norm or standard cannot give rise to conduct that could be considered anomalous from *that* perspective.

64. See, e.g., Skinner 1976, 77–78.

65. Again, the acute problem of normative self-criticism is to explain our ability to *normatively* question norms by which we in fact wholeheartedly abide, as opposed to reconsidering them in the light of new *information* about ourselves or the things we care about, or questioning their priority in relation to other of our norms and standards.

66. Frankfurt 1987, 163.

67. Wittgenstein 1974, 80e–81e. We thank Nehama Verbin for drawing our attention to this passage. The entire text reads as follows:

608. Is it wrong for me to be guided in my actions by the propositions of physics? Am I to say I have no good ground for doing so? Isn't this precisely what we call a 'good ground'?

609. Supposing we met people who didn't regard that as a telling reason. Now, how do we imagine this? Instead of the physicist, they consult an oracle. (And for that we consider them primitive.) Is it wrong for them to consult an oracle and be guided by it?—If we call this "wrong" aren't we using our language-game as a base from which to *combat* theirs?

610. Are we right or wrong to combat it? Of course, there are all sorts of slogans which will be used to support our proceedings.

611. Where two principles really do meet which cannot be reconciled with one another, then each man declares the other a fool and heretic.

612. I said I would 'combat' the other man,—but wouldn't I give him *reasons*? Certainly; but how far do they go? At the end of reasons comes *persuasion*. (Think what happens when missionaries convert natives.) (Original emphasis.)

68. This is perhaps not an entirely fair assessment of Wittgenstein's position. Close to the outset of *On Certainty,* Wittgenstein (in response to Moore 1925 and 1939), begins his discussion of the framework dependence of the meaning of "I know," by noting that:

"I know" often means: I have the proper grounds for my statement. So if the other person is acquainted with the language-game, he would admit that I know. The other, if he is acquainted with the language-game, *must be able to imagine how one may know something of this kind.* (Wittgenstein 1974, 4e; original emphasis on "how")

Wittgenstein here imagines the necessary conditions of acquaintance for *understanding* someone playing a different language game. What he fails to do, here and elsewhere, is to consider how such understanding may facilitate effective normative criticism across the barrier—unless, of course, we have misinterpreted his notion of persuasion.

69. In the closing paragraphs of Frankfurt 1994 the necessities of love and those of the moral law are viewed on a par as compelling us analogously, through the mediation of respect. "With regard to love, the situation is quite similar" to the moral law, he writes,

> The necessities of love are not rational, of course, but volitional; love constrains the will rather than the understanding. But just as the moral law cannot be other than it is, so we cannot help loving what we love. Moreover, the dictates of love, like the requirements of the moral law, enjoy an unconditional authority. In radically distinct but nonetheless closely parallel ways, each tells us what we must do. (141)

In Frankfurt 2006 (esp. 46–48), however, the two are no longer presented as distinct yet parallel. Here "the truths of morality" are presented as derivative, owing their entire authority to the necessities of will.

70. Frankfurt 1994, 137; emphasis added.

71. Ibid., 139.

72. Ibid.

73. Ibid., 139 n. 9.

74. Frankfurt 2004, 92.

75. Frankfurt 2006, 95.

76. Frankfurt 1994, 139.

77. Ibid.

78. Frankfurt 2004, 91.

79. Ibid., 95.

80. In his otherwise laudatory review of Frankfurt (2004), Quinn (2004) remarks that Frankfurt's preoccupation with "restlessness, uncertainty, indecisiveness, irresolution, ambivalence, fragmentation, instability, disorder, and similar psychic conditions" and cherishing of "such things [as] harmony, unity, clarity, stability, and repose" are perhaps exaggerated. "Our lives would be impoverished," counters Quinn, "if we did not allow room in them for a measure of restless striving toward a kind of self-transcendence that is bound to put the unity of the self at risk . . . maybe our aim should be successful management of internal volitional conflict, not elimination of such conflict for the sake of having a

unified and harmonious volitional character. Considerations such as these lead me to suspect that Frankfurt's picture of how human lives can be rendered meaningful is too simple and one-sided." When, as proposed here, Frankfurt's picture is enriched in the direction indicated by Quinn, our lives are not merely rendered more meaningful, but more *rational*.

Chapter 9. Science Revisited

1. See, e.g., Brandom 2000a, 5–7.

2. Brandom 2002a, 13–15; 2009, 84 ff.

3. Expressivism in Brandom's sense of the term. See Brandom 2000a, 7–34.

4. Habermas 2000, 43. In that paper the language game of argumentation is alluded to not in connection with rationality but (in disputing Rorty) with regard to truth.

5. Whewell's 1837 *History of the Inductive Science from the Earliest to the Present Time*, the first ever comprehensive history of science, set the tone by viewing the history of every science as punctuated by a series of "inductive epochs," in which a novel idea was discovered successfully to "colligate" a body of formerly unconnected fact. Whewell's epochs are flanked on either side by "preludes" of work preparatory to the discovery and "sequels" in which its consequences were worked out in detail. In Whewell, as in virtually all history of science written to date, scientific development is conceived solely in terms of scientific *achievement*. Moments of indecisive dithering have no place at all in Whewell's narrative schema (and, consequently, find no place in the semi-Kantian philosophy of science he later articulated "founded on their history"). One self-conscious exception to the rule is the role assigned to intermediary figures in Damerow et al. 2004.

6. Friedman 2001, 58.

7. Which, as we shall see, is far more a departure from the Kuhn of *Structure* than from the Kuhn of the study of Plank (1987).

8. Friedman (2010b) extends the list beyond philosophy and mathematics to show "how some of the developments in modern science and philosophy . . . were inextricably entangled with technological, institutional, and political developments" outside science (503–4). The case study he explores builds on Heilbron (1999) and focuses on "how the Gregorian reform was . . . inextricably entangled with the new mathematical astronomy" (505).

9. On the role of "'transcendental' meta-disciplines" in Friedman's account, see Van Dyck 2009.

10. Galison 1997, esp. chap. 9. Page numbers in the text that follows refer to this work.

11. Or as he puts a few pages earlier: the idea "that theoretical and linguistic changes of science shifted with the abruptness of a gestalt switch. Just as the duck became a rabbit, experiments showing the absence of Phlogiston now became experiments displaying the presence of oxygen" (790).

12. "Thus, *for historical reasons,* instead of searching for a positivist central metaphor grounded in observation, or an antipositivist central metaphor grounded in theory, I suggest that we admit a wider class of periodization schemes, in which three (or more) levels are intercalated" (799; emphasis added). Indeed, Galison's arguments against the two "central metaphors" as well as those he mounts in favor of his own are predominantly historical rather than philosophical.

13. However, at critical moments, Galison's presentation takes a far more radical philosophical stand against Kuhnian antipositivism, such as his brief attack on incommensurability between theoreticians in Harman and Galison 2008, discussed briefly in note 19 below, and his more sustained philosophical self-alignment, in the last section of Galison 1997 with "a historicized neo-Kantianism" (described in terms similar to Friedman's notion, late of Reichenbach, of a relativized a priori [842]) and "the justly influential work of Donald Davidson and Hilary Putnam." However, even there, he describes his project as "manifestly more historical" (840) than philosophical. We discuss below a third, even more radical such moment located in the introductory chapter to Galison 1997.

14. Friedman 2001, 105.

15. Notably Gorman 2002; Collins, Evans, and Gorman 2007.

16. Harman and Galison 2008, 568–69.

17. For a detailed account of the transformative role such didactic deliberations played in the formation of William Whewell's understanding of mathematical physics, see Fisch 1991, chap. 2; and below note 25.

18. For a usefully nuanced typology of all such interactions, see Collins, Evans, and Gorman 2007.

19. In Harman and Galison 2008, 568, Galison very briefly applies the trading zone metaphor within a single subculture of physics rather than between two subcultures. His example is the way Poincaré and Lorentz engaged each other's work. But his comments are far too brief to be instructive. He does not clarify what actual trading they conducted, the nature of the pidgin or creole they employed, or how their views were transformed by the exchange if at all. If all he purports to claim is that despite their differences (that remained in place throughout), they simply "did not, in fact, meet each others' work with gaping-mouth incomprehension," he is not claiming much. As Friedman argues con-

vincingly, the problem of interframework discourse is not that of understanding but that of convincing and transforming.

20. Friedman in a sense succeeds in doing so but only at the price of following Cassirer in returning to a more orthodox Kantian position, according to which science is such that, when properly conducted, its successive paradigms will display such "inter-paradigm convergence" (66) as to render "our present scientific community . . . an approximation to an ideal limiting community of inquiry acknowledging similarly ideals standards of *universal, trans-historical* communicative rationality" (68; emphasis added). This is evidently not an option for Galison, who dissociates himself explicitly from the sense in which "Kant's 'transcendental' suggests conditions that are beyond history." "The entirety of the last eight chapters," he writes of *Image and Logic,* "speaks against such an assumption" (842).

21. A point made nicely in Andrew Warwick's (2003) insightful study of the training of mathematical physicists in nineteenth-century Cambridge. See esp. chaps. 2–5.

22. For an insightful account of the taken-for-grantedness of a scientific community's basics, see the section "Wittgenstein and Rules" in Collins 1985, 12–16.

23. Taylor, as we have noted, lays great stress on the role of self-interpretation in normative change and realization. His account remains thoroughly interpretive, however, and makes no reference to normative ambivalence or normative criticism. See, e.g., Taylor 1971; 1985a, chap. 2.

24. As when preparing a lecture or writing a textbook.

25. The account of Whewell's early mechanics textbook writing, and the crucial role it played in the formation of his historiography and philosophy of science proposed by Fisch (1991, chap. 2), provides a striking example of the normative transformative power of such attempts at self-articulation in a pedagogical and didactic context.

26. Haugeland 1998, 340 ff.

27. Lakatos's historiography of scientific research programs resembles the later Kuhn in subjecting transitions from one research program to another to purely instrumental considerations of predictive fruitfulness. Commitment within a program to the program's "hardcore" is normative in the sense that it is rendered immune to empirical refutation by the ad hoc construction of "auxiliary hypotheses." Commitment to the program itself, however, is, for Lakatos, not a matter of empirical testing but of empirical *fertility.* For his methodology and historiography of scientific research programs, see Lakatos 1971, 1978. For a recent exposition of Lakatos's position in comparison to Kuhn's, see Gattei 2008, 56 ff. For reference to criticisms of Lakatos, see above chap. 1, note 3.

28. See note 5 above.

29. Earman 1993, 19, with reference to, e.g., Kuhn 1970, 94, 150, 151—noted above, chap. 5, note 12.

30. Friedman 2001, 61.

31. Cf. Friedman 2001, 60–63. Galileo's intermediary role lies in preserving the two basic Aristotelian forms of natural motion—naturally accelerated motion toward the center of the earth and naturally uniform circular motion directed at right angles to it—while discarding "the hierarchically and teleologically organized Aristotelian universe" (61). According to Friedman, Galileo's notion of circular inertial motion rendered "the modern conception of rectilinear natural inertial motion . . . actually continuous with the preceding Aristotelian conception of natural motion" (61). On Galileo as an intermediary figure, see also Damerow et al. 2004, chap. 3, esp. §3.7.

To Poincaré's *Science and Hypothesis* (a book he maintains Einstein was "intensively reading . . . immediately before his revolutionary breakthroughs in 1905") Friedman attributes the neo-Kantian idea that although geometry functions as "a constitutive framework making properly empirical discoveries first possible," the fact that "there is more than one such constitutive framework" can only mean that the choice between them is "based on a convention" (simplicity) and not on "some innate necessity of the human mind" (62). In this way, "Einstein's introduction of a radically new constitutive framework for space, time, and motion again grew naturally out of, and is thus quite continuous with, the preceding framework it replaced" (63).

32. On the formation of George Peacock's *Treatise on Algebra* during the 1810s and 1820s presented as "a case of creative indecision," see Fisch 1999.

33. See Fisch 1991, 63–67, and references there.

34. See Fisch 1985a; 1987; 1991, 93–98.

35. McDowell 1994, 81.

36. In Brandom's system, logic is grounded in and abstracted from the *material* inferences implicit in the norms implicit in community practice (see, e.g., Brandom 1994, chap. 6, §I). In Frankfurt's account, volitional necessity grounds practical reasoning (see, e.g., Frankfurt 2004, chap. 2). In both accounts, normative commitment cannot be normatively argued against from within. For criticism of Brandom's position, see Carus 2003.

Bibliography

Agassi, Joseph. 1987. "Theories of Rationality." In Agassi and Jarvie 1987, 249–63.

Agassi, Joseph, and Ian C. Jarvie, eds. 1987. *Rationality: The Critical View*. Nijhoff International Philosophy Series, vol. 23. Dordecht: Martinus Nijhoff.

Altham, J. E. J., and Ross Harrison, eds. 1995. *World, Mind and Ethics: Essays on the Ethical Philosophy of Bernard Williams*. Cambridge: Cambridge University Press.

Anderson, Joel. 1996. "The Personal Lives of Strong Evaluators: Identity, Pluralism, and Ontology in Charles Taylor's Value Theory." *Constellations: An International Journal of Critical and Democratic Theory* 3 (1): 17–38.

Audi, Robert. 2001. *The Architecture of Reason: The Structure and Substance of Rationality*. Oxford: Oxford University Press.

Awodey, Steve, and Carsten Klein. 2003. *Carnap Brought Home: The View from Jena*. Chicago: Open Court.

Bach, Kent. 2000. "Quantification, Qualification and Context—A Reply to Stanley and Szabó." *Mind and Language* 15 (2–3): 262–83.

Baker, Gordon P., and Peter M. S. Hacker. 1984. "On Misunderstanding Wittgenstein: Kripke's Private Language Argument." *Synthese* 58: 407–50.

Barnes, Barry. 1982. *T. S. Kuhn and Social Science*. New York: Columbia University Press.

Barnes, Barry, and David Bloor. 1982. "Relativism, Rationalism and the Sociology of Knowledge." In Hollis and Lukes 1982, 21–47.

Barret, Robert B., and Roger Gibson, eds. 1990. *Perspectives on Quine*. Oxford: Blackwell.

Benbaji, Yitzhak. 2001. "The Moral, the Personal and the Importance of What We Care About." *Philosophy* 76: 415–33.

———. 2004a. "Using Others' Words and Drawing the Limits of the Thinkable." *Dialogue* 43: 125–45.

———. 2004b. "Using Others' Words." *Journal of Philosophical Research* 29: 93–112.

Benbaji, Yitzhak, and Menachem Fisch. 2004. "Through Thick and Thin: A New Defense of Cultural Relativism." *Southern Journal of Philosophy* 62: 1–24.

———. 2005. "Factuality without Realism: Normativity and the Davidsonian Approach to Meaning." *Southern Journal of Philosophy* 43: 505–30.

Ben Menahem, Yemima, ed. 2005. *Hilary Putnam.* Cambridge: Cambridge University Press.

Bilgrami, Akeel. 1992. *Belief and Meaning.* Oxford: Blackwell.

Bjorken, James, and Sidney Drell. 1964. *Relativistic Quantum Mechanics.* New York: McGraw-Hill.

Blackburn, Simon. 1990. "Hume and Thick Connexions." *Philosophy and Phenomenological Research* 31: 237–50.

———. 1992. "Through Thick and Thin." *Proceedings of the Aristotelian Society* 66 (Suppl.): 285–99.

Bloom, Harold. 1973. *The Anxiety of Influence: A Theory of Poetry.* Oxford: Oxford University Press.

Boghossian, Paul A. 1989. "The Rule-Following Considerations." *Mind* 98: 507–49.

Brandom, Robert B. 1994. *Making It Explicit: Reasoning, Representing, and Discursive Commitment.* Cambridge, MA: Harvard University Press.

———. 2000a. *Articulating Reasons: An Introduction to Inferentialism.* Cambridge, MA: Harvard University Press.

———, ed. 2000b. *Rorty and His Critics.* Malden, MA: Blackwell.

———. 2002a. *Tales of the Mighty Dead: Historical Essays in the Metaphysics of Intentionality.* Cambridge, MA: Harvard University Press.

———. 2002b. "Non-Inferential Knowledge, Perceptual Experience, and Secondary Qualities: Placing McDowell's Empiricism." In Smith 2002, 92–105.

———. 2005. "Responses." *Pragmatics and Cognition* 13 (1): 227–49. Special Issue, "The Pragmatics of *Making It Explicit.*"

———. 2006. "Kantian Lessons on Mind Meaning and Rationality." *Southern Journal of Philosophy* 44 (Suppl.): 49–71.

———. 2009. *Reason in Philosophy: Animating Ideas.* Cambridge, MA: Harvard University Press.

Bratman, Michael E. 2006. "A Thoughtful and Reasonable Stability—A Comment on Harry Frankfurt's 2004 Tanner Lectures." In Frankfurt 2006, 77–90.

Brink, David O. 1988. *Moral Realism and the Foundation of Ethics.* Cambridge: Cambridge University Press.

Briskman, Larry. 1977. "Historicist Relativism and Bootstrap Rationality." *Monist* 60: 509–39.

Broadie, Sarah. 2002. "Alternative World-Histories." *Philosophical Papers* 31: 117–44.

Buchwald, Jed Z., ed. 1995. *Scientific Practice, Theories, and Stories of Doing Physics.* Chicago: University of Chicago Press.

Burge, Tyler. 1989. "Wherein Is Language Social." In George 1989, 175–91.

Buss, Sarah, and Lee Overton, eds. 2002. *Contours of Agency: Essays on Themes from Harry Frankfurt.* Cambridge, MA: MIT Press.

Butts, Robert E. 1977. "Consilience of Inductions and the Problem of Conceptual Change in Science." In Colodny 1977, 71–88.

Buzaglo, Meir. 2002. *The Logic of Concept Expansion.* Cambridge: Cambridge University Press.

Calhoun, Craig J., Edward LiPuma, and Moishe Postone, eds. 1993. *Bourdieu: Critical Perspectives.* Chicago: University of Chicago Press.

Canfield, John V. 1996. "The Community View." *Philosophical Review* 105: 469–88.

Carnap, Rudolph. 1934. *Logische Syntax der Sprache.* Vienna: Verlag Springer. (English trans. *The Logical Syntax of Language.* London: Routledge & Kegan Paul, 1937.)

———. 1950. "Empiricism, Semantics, and Ontology." *Revue Internationale de Philosophie* 11: 20–40.

———. 1952. "Empiricism, Semantics, and Ontology." In Linsky 1952, 208–28.

Carus, André W. 2003. "Sellars, Carnap, and the Logical Space of Reasons." In Awodey and Klein, eds., 2003, 317–56.

Cohen, George A. 1996. "Reason, Humanity, and the Common Law." In Korsgaard 1996, 167–88.

Cohen, Joshua. 1986. Review of *Spheres of Justice,* by Michael Walzer. *Journal of Philosophy* 83: 457–68.

Cohen, Robert S., Paul K. Feyerabend, and Marx W. Wartofsky, eds. 1976. *Essays in Memory of Imre Lakatos.* Boston Studies in the Philosophy of Science, vol. 39. Dordrecht: Kluwer Academic.

Cohon, Rachel. 1986. "Are External Reasons Impossible?" *Ethics* 96: 545–56.

Collingwood, Robin George. 1939. *An Autobiography.* Oxford: Oxford University Press.

Collins, Harry M. 1985. *Changing Order: Replication and Induction in Scientific Practice.* London: Sage.

Collins, Harry M., Robert Evans, and Michael Gorman. 2007. "Trading Zones and Interactional Expertise." *Studies in History and Philosophy of Science* 38 (4): 657–66.

Colodny, Robert G., ed. 1977. *Logic, Laws, and Life: Some Philosophical Complications.* Pittsburgh: University of Pittsburgh Press.

Cullity, Garret, and Berys Gaut, eds. 1997. *Ethics and Practical Reason.* Oxford: Clarendon Press.

Curtis, Ronald C. 1986. "Are Methodologies Theories of Scientific Rationality?" *British Journal for the Philosophy of Science* 35: 135–61.

Damerow, Peter, Gideon Freudenthal, Peter McLaughlin, and Jürgen Renn, eds. 2004. *Exploring the Limits of Preclassical Mechanics. A Study of Conceptual Development in Early Modern Science: Free Fall and Compounded Motion in the Work of Descartes, Galileo, and Beeckman.* 2nd enl. and rev. ed. Heidelberg: Springer.

Dan-Cohen, Meir. 2006. "Socializing Harry." In Frankfurt 2006, 91–103.

Darwall, Stephen, Allan Gibbard, and Peter Railton, eds. 1996. *Moral Discourse and Practice: Some Philosophical Approaches.* Oxford: Oxford University Press.

Davidson, Donald. 1974. "On the Very Idea of a Conceptual Scheme." *Proceedings and Addresses of the American Philosophical Association* 47: 5–20. Reprinted in Davidson 1984a, 183–98; pagination according to reprint.

———. 1979. "Moods and Performances." In Margalit 1979, 9–20. Reprinted in Davidson 1984a, 109–21.

———. 1980. *Essays on Actions and Events.* Oxford: Oxford University Press.

———. 1982. "Paradoxes of Irrationality." In Wolheim and Hopkins 1982, 289–305.

———. 1984a. *Inquiries into Truth and Interpretation.* Oxford: Oxford University Press. (2nd ed. 2001.)

———. 1984b. "Communication and Convention." *Synthese* 59: 3–17.

———. 1984c. "First Person Authority." *Dialectica* 38: 101–11. Reprinted in Davidson 2001, 3–14.

———. 1985. "Incoherence and Irrationality." *Dialectica* 39, 345–54.

———. 1986a. "A Coherence Theory of Truth and Knowledge." In LePore 1986, 307–19.

———. 1986b. "Deception and Division." In LePore 1986, 138–48.

———. 1986c. "A Nice Derangement of Epitaphs." In LePore 1986, 459–76.

———. 1990a. "The Structure and Content of Truth." *Journal of Philosophy* 87: 281–328.

———. 1990b. "Meaning Truth and Evidence." In Barret and Gibson 1990, 68–79.

———. 1991. "Epistemology Externalized." *Dialectica* 45: 191–202. Reprinted in Davidson 2001, 193–204.

————. 1992. "The Second Person." *Midwest Studies in Philosophy* 17, 255–67. Reprinted in Davidson 2001, 107–122, pagination according to reprint.

————. 1994. "The Social Aspect of Language." In McGuinness and Oliveri 1994, 1–16.

————. 2001. *Subjective, Intersubjective, Objective.* Oxford: Oxford University Press.

Devitt, Michael. 2001. "Incommensurability and the Priority of Metaphysics." In Hoyningen-Huene and Sankey 2001, 143–57.

Dillon, Michele. 1999. "The Authority of the Holy Revisited: Habermas, Religion, and Emancipatory Possibilities." *Sociological Theory* 17: 290–306.

Dilman, Ilham 1971. "On Wittgenstein's Last Notes (1950–51): *On Certainty.*" *Philosophy* 46 (176): 162–68.

DiSalle, Robert. 2002. "Reconsidering Kant, Friedman, Logical Positivism, and the Exact Science." *Philosophy of Science* 69 (2): 191–211.

————. 2006. *Understanding Space-Time: The Philosophical Development of Physics from Newton to Einstein.* Cambridge: Cambridge University Press.

————. 2010. "Synthesis, the Synthetic A Priori, and the Origins of Modern Space-Time Theory." In Domski and Dickson 2010, 523–51.

Domski, Mary, and Michael Dickson, eds. 2010. *Discourse on a New Method: Reinvigorating the Marriage of History and Philosophy of Science.* Chicago: Open Court.

Dummett, Michael. 1975. "What Is a Theory of Meaning." In Guttenplan 1975, 97–138.

————. 1978. *Truth and Other Enigmas.* Cambridge, MA: Harvard University Press.

————. 1989. "Language and Communication." In George 1989, 192–212.

Dworkin, Ronald. 1970. "Acting Freely." *Nous* 4: 367–83.

————. 1983. "To Each his Own" (Review of Walzer 1983). *New York Review of Books,* 14 April. Reprinted as "What Justice Isn't," in Dworkin 1985, 214–20.

————. 1986. *Law's Empire.* Cambridge, MA: Harvard University Press.

————. 1996. "Objectivity and Truth: You'd Better Believe It." *Philosophy and Public Affairs* 25 (2): 105–8.

————. 2002. "Contractualism and the Normativity Principles." *Ethics* 112: 471–82.

Earman John. 1993. "Carnap, Kuhn, and the Philosophy of Scientific Methodology." In Horwich 1993, 9–36.

Feigl, Herbert, and Michael Scriven, eds. 1956. *The Foundations of Science and the Concepts of Psychology and Psychoanalysis.* Minnesota Studies in the Philosophy of Science, vol. 1. Minneapolis: University of Minnesota Press.

Fisch, Menachem. 1985a. "Necessary and Contingent Truth in William Whewell's Antithetical Theory of Knowledge." *Studies in History and Philosophy of Science* 16: 275–314.

———. 1985b. "Whewell's Consilience of Inductions: An Evaluation." *Philosophy of Science* 52: 239–55.

———. 1987. "Il collegamento dei fatti: La nozione non necessaria di verità empirica di William Whewell." In Simili 1987, 39–63.

———. 1991. *William Whewell, Philosopher of Science.* Oxford: Clarendon Press.

———. 1994a. "Towards a Rational Theory of Progress." *Synthese* 99: 277–304.

———. 1994b. "Trouble-Shooting Creativity." *History and Philosophy of the Life Sciences* 16: 141–53.

———. 1994c. "The Emergency Which Has Arrived: The Problematic History of 19th-Century British Algebra—A Programmatic Outline." *British Journal for the History of Science* 27: 247–76.

———. 1997. *Rational Rabbis: Science and Talmudic Culture.* Bloomington: Indiana University Press.

———. 1999. "The Making of Peacock's *Treatise on Algebra:* A Case of Creative Indecision." *Archive for History of Exact Science* 54: 137–79.

———. 2003. "A Modest Proposal: Toward a Religious Politics of Epistemic Humility." *Journal of Human Rights* 2 (1): 49–64.

———. 2008. "Taking the Linguistic Turn Seriously." *European Legacy* 13 (5): 605–22. Special Issue, "The Languages of Science and the Humanities," edited by Oren Harman.

———. 2010. "Toward a History and Philosophy of Scientific Agency." *Monist* 93 (4): 518–44. Special Issue, "Philosophical History of Science."

Frankenberry, Nancy K., ed. 2002. *Radical Interpretation in Religion.* Cambridge: Cambridge University Press.

Frankfurt, Harry G. 1971. "Freedom of the Will and the Concept of a Person." *Journal of Philosophy* 68: 5–20. Reprinted in Frankfurt 1988, 1–25.

———. 1982. "The Importance of What We Care About." *Synthese* 53: 257–90. Reprinted in Frankfurt 1988, 80–94.

———. 1987. "Identification and Wholeheartedness." In Schoeman 1987, 27–45. Reprinted in Frankfurt 1988, 159–76; pagination according to reprint.

———. 1988. *The Importance of What We Care About.* Cambridge: Cambridge University Press.

———. 1992. "On the Usefulness of Final Ends." *Iyyun: The Jerusalem Philosophical Quarterly* 41: 3–19. Reprinted in Frankfurt 1999, 82–94; pagination according to reprint.

———. 1994. "Autonomy, Necessity, and Love." In Fulda and Horstmann 1994, 433–47. Reprinted in Frankfurt 1999, 129–41; pagination according to reprint.

———. 1999. *Necessity, Volition, and Love.* Cambridge: Cambridge University Press.

———. 2004. *The Reasons of Love.* Princeton: Princeton University Press.

———. 2006. *Taking Ourselves Seriously and Getting it Right.* Edited by Debra Satz, with comments by Christine M. Korsgaard, Michael E. Bratman, and Meir Dan-Cohen. Stanford: Stanford University Press.

Friedman, Michael. 1993. "Remarks on the History of Science and the History of Philosophy." In Horwich 1993, 37–54.

———. 1996. "Exorcising the Philosophical Tradition: Comments on John McDowell's *Mind and World.*" *Philosophical Review* 105 (4): 427–67. Reprinted in Smith 2002, 25–57.

———. 1998. "Kantian Themes in Contemporary Philosophy." *Supplement to the Proceedings of the Aristotelian Society* 72 (1): 111–30.

———. 1999. *Reconsidering Logical Positivism.* Cambridge: Cambridge University Press.

———. 2001. *Dynamics of Reason: The 1999 Kant Lectures at Stanford University.* Stanford: CSLI Publications.

———. 2002. "Kant, Kuhn, and the Rationality of Science." *Philosophy of Science* 69 (2): 171–90.

———. 2010a. "Concluding Essay." In Domski and Dickson 2010, 571–813.

———. 2010b. "A Post-Kuhnian Approach to the History and Philosophy of Science." *Monist* 93 (4): 497–517.

Fulda, Hans Friedrich, and Rolf-Peter Horstmann, eds. 1994. *Vernunftbegriffe in der Moderne—Stuttgarter Hegel-Kongress 1993.* Stuttgart: Klett-Cotta.

Galison, Peter L. 1995. "Contexts and Constraints." In Buchwald 1995, 13–41.

———. 1997. *Image and Logic: A Material Culture of Microphysics.* Chicago: University of Chicago Press.

Garber, Daniel. 1986. "Learning from the Past: Reflections on the Role of History in the Philosophy of Science." *Synthese* 67: 91–114.

Gattei, Stephano. 2008. *Thomas Kuhn's "Linguistic Turn" and the Legacy of Logical Empiricism: Incommensurability, Rationality, and the Search for Truth.* Hampshire, UK: Ashgate.

Geertz, Clifford J. 1973. *The Interpretation of Cultures: Selected Essays.* New York: Basic Books.

———. 1995. "The Strange Estrangement: Taylor and the Natural Sciences." In Tully 1995, 83–95.

George, Alexander, ed. 1989. *Reflections on Chomsky.* Oxford: Blackwell.

Gibbard, Allan F. 1992. "Morality and Thick Concepts." *Proceedings of the Aristotelian Society* 66 (Suppl.): 267–83.

Goldfarb, Warren D. 1985. "Kripke on Wittgenstein and Rules." *Journal of Philosophy* 82: 471–88.

Goldman, Alvin, and Jaegwon Kim, eds. 1978. *Values and Morals.* Dordrecht: D. Reidel.

Gorman, Michael. 2002. "Levels of Expertise and Trading Zones." *Social Studies of Science* 32 (6): 933–38.

Griffin, James. 1986. *Well-Being: Its Meaning, Measurement, and Moral Importance.* Oxford: Oxford University Press.

Guttenplan, Samuel, ed. 1975. *Mind and Language.* Wolfson College Lectures 1974. Oxford: Clarendon Press.

Habermas, Jürgen. 1984. *The Theory of Communicative Action,* vol. 1: *Reason and the Rationalization of Society.* Translated by Thomas McCarthy. Boston: Beacon Press.

———. 1987. *The Philosophical Discourse of Modernity: Twelve Lectures.* Translated by Frederick Lawrence. Cambridge, MA: MIT Press.

———. 1998. *On the Pragmatics of Communication.* Edited by Maeve Cooke. Cambridge, MA: MIT Press.

———. 2000. "Richard Rorty's Pragmatic Turn." In Brandom 2000b, 31–55.

Hacker, Peter M. S. 1996. "On Davidson's Idea of a Conceptual Scheme." *Philosophical Quarterly* 46: 289–307.

Hacking, Ian. 1979. "Imre Lakatos's Philosophy of Science." *British Journal for the Philosophy of Science* 30 (4): 381–402. Extracts republished, with revisions, as "Lakatos's Philosophy of Science," in Hacking 1981, 128–43.

———, ed. 1981. *Scientific Revolutions.* Oxford Readings in Philosophy. Oxford: Oxford University Press.

Hahn, Lewis E. 1999. *The Philosophy of Donald Davidson.* Library of Living Philosophers, vol. 27. Chicago: Open Court.

Harman, Gilbert. 1978. "What Is Moral Relativism?" In Goldman and Kim 1978, 143–61. Reprinted in Harman 2000, 20–38.

———. 1999. "Moral Philosophy and Linguistics." *Proceedings of the 20th World Congress of Philosophy,* vol. 1: *Ethics,* edited by Klaus Brinkmann, 107–15. Reprinted in Harman 2000, chap. 13.

———. 2000. *Explaining Value and Other Essays in Moral Philosophy.* Oxford: Oxford University Press.

Harman, Oren, and Peter L. Galison. 2008. "Epistemic Virtues and Leibnitzian Dreams: On Science, Faith, and the Humanities." *European Legacy* 13 (5):

551–75. Special Issue, "The Languages of Science and the Humanities," edited by Oren Harman.

Harris, Henry, ed. 1995. *Identity: Essays Based on Herbert Spencer Lectures Given in the University of Oxford.* Oxford: Clarendon Press.

Harrison, T. Ross, ed. 1979. *Rational Action: Studies in Philosophy and Social Science.* Cambridge: Cambridge University Press.

Hattiangadi, Jagdish N. 1978–79. "The Structure of Problems." *Philosophy of the Social Sciences* 8: 345–65 (pt. 1); 9: 49–76 (pt. 2).

Haugeland, John. 1998. *Having Thought: Essays in the Metaphysics of Mind.* Cambridge, MA: Harvard University Press.

———. 2005. "Reading Brandom Reading Heidegger." *European Journal of Philosophy* 13 (3): 421–28.

Heilbron, John L. 1999. *The Sun in the Church: Cathedrals as Solar Observatories.* Cambridge, MA: Harvard University Press.

Herman, Barbara. 2002. "Bootstrapping." In Buss and Overton 2002, 253–74.

Hollis, Martin, and Steven Lukes, eds. 1982. *Rationality and Relativism.* Oxford: Blackwell.

Honneth, Axel, and Hans Joas, eds. 1991. *Communicative Action: Essays on Jürgen Habermas's "The Theory of Communicative Action."* Cornwall: Polity Press.

Hooker, Brad. 1987. "Williams' Argument against External Reasons." *Analysis* 47: 42–44.

Horwich, Paul, ed. 1993. *World Changes: Thomas Kuhn and the Nature of Science.* Cambridge, MA: MIT Press.

Howard, Don A. 2010. "'Let me briefly indicate why I do not find this standpoint natural': Einstein, General Relativity, and the Contingent A Priori." In Dickson and Domski 2010, 333–55.

Hoyningen-Heune, Paul. 1993. *Reconstructing Scientific Revolutions: Thomas S. Kuhn's Philosophy of Science.* Chicago: University of Chicago Press.

Hoyningen-Heune, Paul, Eric Oberheim, and Hanne Andersen. 1996. "On Incommensurability." *Studies in History and Philosophy of Science* 27: 131–41.

Hoyningen-Heune, Paul, and Howard Sankey. 2001. *Incommensurability and Related Matters.* Dordrecht: Kluwer Academic.

Hurley, Susan L. 1992. *Natural Reasons: Personality and Polity.* Oxford: Oxford University Press.

Jackson, Frank. 1998. *From Metaphysics to Ethics: A Defense of Conceptual Analysis.* Oxford: Oxford University Press.

Jarvie, Ian C. 1986. *Thinking about Society: Theory and Practice.* Boston Studies in the Philosophy of Science, vol. 93. Dordecht: D. Reidel.

Kant, Immanuel. [1781] 2003. *Critique of Pure Reason.* Translated by Norman Kemp Smith, with introduction by Howard Gaygill. New York: Palgrave Macmillan.

———. [1785] 1981. *Grounding of the Metaphysics of Morals.* Translated by L. Ellington. Indianapolis: Hackett. Pagination according to the Prussian Academy numbering.

———. [1788] 2003. *Critique of Practical Reason.* Translated and edited by Mary Gregor, with introduction by Andrews Reath. Cambridge: Cambridge University Press.

Kekes, John. 1977. "Rationality and Problem-Solving." *Philosophy of the Social Sciences* 7 (4): 351–66. Reprinted in Agassi and Jarvie 1987, 265–79; pagination according to reprint.

Koertge, Noretta. 2009. "How Should We Describe Scientific Change? Or: A Neo-Popperian Reads Friedman." In Dickson and Domski 2009, 511–22.

Korsgaard, Christine M., with G. A. Cohen, R. Guess, Thomas Nagel, and Brian Williams. 1996. *The Sources of Normativity.* Edited by O. O'Neill. Cambridge: Cambridge University Press.

———. 1997. "The Normativity of Instrumental Reasoning." In Cullity and Gaut 1997, 215–54.

———. 2006. "Morality and the Logic of Caring: A Comment on Harry Frankfurt." In Frankfurt 2006, 55–76.

———. 2009. *Self-Constitution: Agency, Identity, and Integrity.* Oxford: Oxford University Press.

Kripke, Saul. 1982. *Wittgenstein on Rules and Private Language.* Cambridge, MA: Harvard University Press.

Kuhn, Thomas S. 1970. *The Structure of Scientific Revolutions.* International Encyclopedia of Unified Science, vol. 2, no. 2. 2nd enl. ed. Chicago: University of Chicago Press.

———. [1978] 1987. *Black-Body Theory and the Quantum Discontinuity, 1894–1912.* Chicago: University of Chicago Press.

———. 1993. "Afterword." In Horwich 1993, 311–41.

———. 2000. *The Road since Structure: Philosophical Essays, 1970–1993, with an Autobiographical Interview.* Edited by James Conant and John Haugeland. Chicago: University of Chicago Press.

Kymlicka, Will. 1989. *Liberalism, Community, and Culture.* Oxford: Oxford University Press.

Lakatos, Imre. 1971. "History of Science and Its Rational Reconstructions." In *Proceedings of the 1970 Biennial Meeting of the Philosophy of Science Association,* vol. 1970, 91–136. Boston Studies in the Philosophy of Science, vol. 8. Dordecht: D. Reidel. Reprinted in Lakatos 1978, 102–38.

———. 1978. *The Methodology of Scientific Research Programmes: Philosophical Papers,* vol. 1. Cambridge: Cambridge University Press.

LePore, Ernest, ed. 1986. *Truth and Interpretation: Perspectives on the Philosophy of Donald Davidson.* Oxford: Blackwell.

Lewis, David. 1979. "Scorekeeping in a Language Game." *Journal of Philosophical Logic* 8 (1): 339–59.

———. 1989. "Dispositional Theories of Value." *Proceedings of the Aristotelian Society* 63 (Suppl.): 113–37.

Linsky, Leonard, ed. 1952. *Semantics and the Philosophy of Language.* Urbana: University of Illinois Press.

Lipton, Peter. 2001. "Kant on Wheels." *London Review of Books,* 19 July, 30–31.

Locke, John. [1689] 2006. "A Letter Concerning Toleration." In *John Locke: An Essay concerning Toleration: And Other Writings on Law and Politics, 1667–1683,* edited by John R. Milton and Philip Milton, 11–52. Oxford: Clarendon Press.

Lovibond, Sabina, and Stephen G. Williams, eds. 1996. *Essays for David Wiggins: Identity, Truth, and Value.* Oxford: Blackwell.

Lynch, Michael. 1998. *Truth in Context: An Essay on Pluralism and Objectivity.* Cambridge, MA: MIT Press.

Macdonald, Cynthia, and Graham Macdonald, eds. 2006. *McDowell and His Critics.* Oxford: Blackwell.

Margalit, Avishai, ed. 1979. *Meaning and Use.* Dordrecht: D. Reidel.

McDowell, John. 1984. "Wittgenstein on Following a Rule." *Synthese* 58: 325–63. Reprinted in McDowell 1998, 221–62.

———. 1987. "In Defense of Modesty." In Taylor 1987, 59–80. Reprinted in McDowell 1998b, 87–107.

———. 1994. *Mind and World.* Cambridge, MA: Harvard University Press.

———. 1995a. "Might There Be External Reasons?" In Altham and Harrison 1995, 387–98. Reprinted in McDowell 1998a, 95–111.

———. 1998a. *Mind, Value, and Reality.* Cambridge, MA: Harvard University Press.

———. 1998b. *Meaning, Knowledge, and Reality.* Cambridge, MA: Harvard University Press.

———. 2005. "Motivating Inferentialism: Comments on *Making It Explicit* (Ch. 2)." *Pragmatics and Cognition* 13 (1): 121–40. Special Issue, "The Pragmatics of *Making It Explicit.*"

———. 2009a. *The Engaged Intellect: Philosophical Essays.* Cambridge, MA: Harvard University Press.

———. 2009b. *Having the World in View: Essays on Kant, Hegel, and Sellars.* Cambridge, MA: Harvard University Press.

McGinn, Colin. 1984. *Wittgenstein on Meaning: An Interpretation and Evaluation.* Oxford: Blackwell.

———. 2002. *The Making of a Philosopher: My Journey through Twentieth-Century Philosophy.* New York: HarperCollins.

McGuinness, Brian, and Gianluigi Oliveri, eds. 1994. *The Philosophy of Michael Dummett.* Dordrecht: Kluwer.

McMullin, Ernan, ed. 1988. *Construction and Constraint: The Shaping of Scientific Rationality.* Notre Dame: University of Notre Dame Press.

———. 1993. "Rationality and Paradigm Change in Science." In Horwich 1993, 55–76.

Millgram, Elijah. 1996. "Williams' Argument against External Reasons." *Nous* 30: 197–200.

Mischel, Theodore, ed. 1977. *The Self: Psychological and Philosophical Issues.* Oxford: Blackwell.

Moore, George E. 1925. "A Defence of Common Sense." In Muirhead 1925, 193–22.

———. 1939. "Proof of an External World." *Proceedings of the British Academy* 25: 273–300.

———. [1903] 1993. *Principia Ethica.* Rev. ed. Edited by Thomas Baldwin. Cambridge: Cambridge University Press.

Moran, Richard. 2001. *Authority and Estrangement: An Essay on Self-Knowledge.* Princeton: Princeton University Press.

———. 2002. "Frankfurt on Identification: Ambiguities of Activity in Mental Life." In Buss and Overton 2002, 189–217.

Mueller, Axel, and Arthur Fine. 2005. "Realism, beyond Miracles." In Ben Menahem 2005, 83–124.

Muirhead, J. H. 1925. *Contemporary British Philosophy: Personal Statements (Second Series).* London: Allen and Unwin.

Nagel, Thomas. 1970. *The Possibility of Altruism.* Oxford: Clarendon Press.

———. 1984. *The View from Nowhere.* Oxford: Oxford University Press.

Neale, Stephen. 2000. "On Being Explicit: Comments on Stanley and Szabó, and on Bach." *Mind and Language* 15 (2–3): 284–94.

Niznik, Jozef, and John T. Sanders, eds. 1996. *Debating the State of Philosophy: Habermas, Rorty, and Kolakowski.* Westport, CT: Praeger.

Nozick, Robert. 1974. *Anarchy, State, and Utopia.* New York: Basic Books.

———. 1993. *The Nature of Rationality.* Princeton: Princeton University Press.

Nussbaum, Martha C. 2006. *Frontiers of Justice: Disability, Nationality, Species Membership.* Cambridge, MA: Harvard University Press.

Parfit, Derek. 1995. "The Unimportance of Identity." In Harris 1995, 13–45.

Polanyi, Michael. 1957. "Problem Solving." *British Journal for the Philosophy of Science* 8 (30): 89–103.

———. 1958. *Personal Knowledge: Towards a Post-Critical Philosophy.* London: Routledge & Kegan Paul.

Pollner, Melvin. 1974. "Mundane Reasoning." *Philosophy of the Social Sciences* 4: 35–54.

Popper, Karl Raimund. 1994. *The Myth of the Framework: In Defence of Science and Rationality.* London: Routledge.

Putnam, Hilary. 1962. "The Analytic and the Synthetic." In *Minnesota Studies in the Philosophy of Science,* edited by H. Feigl and G. Maxwell, 358–97. Minneapolis: University of Minnesota Press. Reprinted in Putnam 1975, 33–69.

———. 1975. *Mind, Language, and Reality: Philosophical Papers.* Vol. 2. Cambridge: Cambridge University Press.

———. 1976. "'Two Dogmas' Revisited." In Ryle 1976, 202–13. Reprinted in Putnam 1983, 87–97.

———. 1983. *Realism and Reason: Philosophical Papers.* Vol. 3. Cambridge: Cambridge University Press.

———. 1990. *Realism with a Human Face.* Edited and introduction by James Conant. Cambridge, MA: Harvard University Press.

———. 1992. *Renewing Philosophy.* Cambridge, MA: Harvard University Press.

———. 1994. *Words and Life.* Edited and introduction by James Conant. Cambridge, MA: Harvard University Press.

———. 2001. *Enlightenment and Pragmatism.* Assen: Koninklijke Van Gorcum. Reprinted as part 2 of Putnam 2004.

———. 2002. *The Collapse of the Fact/Value Dichotomy and Other Essays.* Cambridge, MA: Harvard University Press.

———. 2004. *Ethics without Ontology.* Cambridge, MA: Harvard University Press.

Quine, Willard V. O. 1951. "Two Dogmas of Empiricism." *Philosophical Review* 60: 20–43. Reprinted in Quine 1953, chap. 2.

———. 1953. *From a Logical Point of View: Nine Logico-Philosophical Essays.* New York: Harper & Row.

———. 1960. *Word and Object.* Cambridge, MA: MIT Press.

———. 1970a. "On the Reasons for Indeterminacy of Translation." *Journal of Philosophy* 67: 178–83.

Quinn, Philip L. 2004. "The Reasons of Love [Review of Frankfurt 2004]." *Notre Dame Philosophical Reviews,* March 12. http://ndpr.nd.edu/review.cfm?id=1400.

Rachels, Stuart. 2002. "Nagelian Arguments against Egoism." *Australasian Journal of Philosophy* 80: 191–208.

Railton, Peter. 1986a. "Facts and Values." *Philosophical Topics* 14: 5–31.
———. 1986b. "Moral Realism." *Philosophical Review* 95: 163–207. Reprinted in Darwall et al. 1996, 137–64.
Ramberg, Bjørn. 2004. "Naturalizing Idealizations: Pragmatism and the Interpretivist Strategy." *Contemporary Pragmatism* 2: 1–63.
Rawls, John. 1971. *A Theory of Justice*. Cambridge, MA: Harvard University Press.
———. 1975. "A Kantian Conception of Equality." *Cambridge Review* 96: 94–99. Reprinted, with an addition by the author, in Held 1980, 198–208; and in Rawls 2001, chap. 13.
———. 1980. "Kantian Constructivism in Moral Theory." *Journal of Philosophy* 77: 515–72. Reprinted in Rawls 2001, chap. 16.
———. 2001. *Collected Papers*. Edited by Samuel Freeman. Cambridge, MA: Harvard University Press.
Regan, Donald H. 2003. "How to Be a Moorean." *Ethics* 113: 651–77.
Reichenbach, Hans. 1920. *Relativitätstheorie und Erkenntnis apriori*. English translation: *The Theory of Relativity and Apriori Knowledge*. Berkeley: University of California Press, 1965.
Reisch, George. 1991. "Did Kuhn Kill Logical Empiricism?" *Philosophy of Science* 58 (2): 264–77.
Richardson, Alan. 2002. "Narrating the History of Reason Itself: Friedman, Kuhn, and a Constitutive A Priori for the Twenty-First Century." *Perspectives on Science* 10 (3): 253–74.
Ricks, Christopher, and Leonard Michaels, eds. 1980. *The State of Language*. Berkeley: University of California Press.
Rorty, Amélie O., ed. 1976. *The Identity of Persons*. Berkeley: University of California Press.
Rorty, Richard. 1979. *Philosophy and the Mirror of Nature*. Princeton: Princeton University Press.
———. 1988. "Is Natural Science a Natural Kind?" In McMullin 1988, 49–74. Reprinted in Rorty 1991, 46–62, pagination according to reprint.
———. 1989. *Contingency, Irony, and Solidarity*. Cambridge: Cambridge University Press.
———. 1990. "Another Possible World." *London Review of Books*, 8 February, 21. Reprinted as "On Heidegger's Nazism," in Rorty 1999, 190–97.
———. 1991. *Objectivity, Relativism, and Truth: Philosophical Papers*. Vol. 1. Cambridge: Cambridge University Press.
———. 1992. "A Pragmatist View of Rationality and Cultural Difference." *Philosophy East and West* 42: 581–96. Reprinted as "Rationality and Cultural Difference," in Rorty 1998, 186–201; pagination according to reprint.

————. 1993. "Putnam and the Relativist Menace." *Journal of Philosophy* 90: 443–61. Reprinted as "Hilary Putnam and the Relativist Menace," in Rorty 1998, 43–62; pagination according to reprint.

————. 1996. "Relativism: Finding and Making." In Niznik and Sanders 1996, 31–47. Reprinted in Rorty 1999, xvi–xxxii.

————. 1997. "Thomas Kuhn, Rocks, and the Laws of Physics." *Common Knowledge* 6: 6–16. Reprinted in Rorty 1999, 175–89; pagination according to reprint.

————. 1998. *Truth and Progress: Philosophical Papers.* Vol. 3. Cambridge: Cambridge University Press.

————. 1999. *Philosophy and Social Hope.* London: Penguin Books.

————. 2000a. "Universality and Truth." In Brandom 2000b, 1–30.

————. 2000b. "Response to Jürgen Habermas." In Brandom 2000a, 56–64.

————. 2007. *Philosophy as Cultural Politics: Philosophical Papers.* Vol. 4. Cambridge: Cambridge University Press.

Rosa, Hartmut. 1996. "Cultural Relativism and Social Criticism from a Taylorian Perspective." *Constellations* 3: 39–60.

————. 2004. "Four Levels of Self-Interpretation: A Paradigm for Interpretive Social Philosophy and Political Criticism." *Philosophy and Social Criticism* 30 (5–6): 691–720.

Rosati, Connie S. 1995a. "Naturalism, Normativity, and the Open Question Argument." *Nous* 29: 46–70.

————. 1995b. "Persons, Perspectives, and Full Information Accounts of the Good." *Ethics* 105: 296–325.

————. 1996. "Internalism and the Good for a Person." *Ethics* 106: 297–326.

————. 2003. "Agency and the Open Question Argument." *Ethics* 113: 490–527.

Ross, David. 1954. *The Nicomachean Ethics of Aristotle.* Oxford: Oxford University Press.

Rovane, Carol. 2006. "Personal Identity, Ethical, not Metaphysical." In Macdonald and Macdonald 2006, 95–114.

Russell, Bertrand. 1954. *Human Society in Ethics and Politics.* London: Allen and Unwin.

Ryle, Gilbert, ed. 1976. *Contemporary Aspects of Philosophy.* Stocksfield, UK: Orion Press.

Sankey, Howard. 1993. "Kuhn's Changing Concept of Incommensurability." *British Journal for the Philosophy of Science* 44 (4): 775–91.

————. 1998. "Taxonomic Incommensurability." *International Studies in the Philosophy of Science* 12 (1): 7–16.

Scanlon, Thomas M. 1982. "Contractualism and Utilitarianism." In Sen and Williams 1982, 103–28.

————. 1998. *What We Owe to Each Other.* Cambridge, MA: Harvard University Press.

Scheffler, Samuel. 1987. "Morality through Thick and Thin." *Philosophical Review* 96: 411–34.

Schnädelbach, Herbert. 1991. "The Transformation of Critical Theory." In Honneth and Joas 1991, 7–22.

Schoeman, Ferdinand, ed. 1987. *Responsibility, Character, and Emotions: New Essays in Moral Psychology.* Cambridge: Cambridge University Press.

Searle, John R. 2000. *Rationality in Action.* Cambridge, MA: MIT Press.

Seligman, Adam B. 2000. *Modernity's Wager: Authority, the Self, and Transcendence.* Princeton: Princeton University Press.

Sellars, Wilfrid. 1956. "Empiricism and the Philosophy of Mind." In Feigl and Scriven 1956, 253–329. Reprinted, with introduction by Richard Rorty and study guide by Robert Brandom. Cambridge, MA: Harvard University Press, 1997. Pagination according to reprint.

Sen, Amartya, and Bernard Williams, eds. 1982. *Utilitarianism and Beyond.* Cambridge: Cambridge University Press.

Simili, Raffaella, ed. 1987. *L'epistemologia di Cambridge (1850–1950).* Bologna: Societa Editrice il Mulino.

Simon, Herbert. 1983. *Reason in Human Affairs.* Stanford: Stanford University Press.

Skinner, Quentin. 1969. "Meaning and Understanding in the History of Ideas." *History and Theory* 8: 3–53.

————. 1980. "Language and Social Change." In Ricks and Michaels 1980, 562–78.

————. 1988. "A Reply to My Critics." In Tully 1988, 231–88.

Smith, Nicholas H., ed. 2002. *Reading McDowell on "Mind and World."* London: Routledge.

Snyder, Laura J. 2006. *Reforming Philosophy: A Victorian Debate on Science and Society.* Chicago: University of Chicago Press.

Soames, Scott. 1998. "Facts, Truth Conditions, and the Skeptical Solution to the Rule-Following Paradox." *Philosophical Perspectives* 12: 313–48.

Sreenivasan, Gopal. 1998. "Interpretation and Reason." *Philosophy and Public Affairs* 27: 143–71.

Stanley, Jason, and Zoltán Gendler Szabó. 2000a. "On Quantifier Domain Restriction." *Mind and Language* 15 (2–3): 219–61.

————. 2000b. "Reply to Bach and Neale." *Mind and Language* 15 (2–3): 295–98.

Stoecker, Ralf. 1993. *Reflecting Davidson: Donald Davidson Responding to an International Forum of Philosophers.* Berlin: W. de Gruyter.

Stout, Jeffrey. 2002. "Radical Interpretation and Pragmatism: Davidson, Rorty, and Brandom on Truth." In Frankenberry 2002, 25–52.

———. 2004. *Democracy and Tradition.* Princeton: Princeton University Press.

Strawson, P. F. 1970. *Meaning and Truth.* Oxford: Clarendon Press.

Stump, David. 2003. "Defending Conventions as Functionally A Priori Knowledge." *Philosophy of Science* 70: 1149–60.

Taylor, Charles. 1971. "Interpretation and the Sciences of Man." *Review of Metaphysics* 25 (1): 3–51. Reprinted in Taylor 1985b, 15–57; pagination according to reprint.

———. 1976. "Responsibility for Self." In Rorty 1976, 81–99.

———. 1977. "What Is Human Agency." In Mischel 1977, 103–35. Reprinted in Taylor 1985a, 15–44; pagination according to reprint.

———. 1985a. *Human Agency and Language: Philosophical Papers 1.* Cambridge: Cambridge University Press.

———. 1985b. *Philosophy and the Human Sciences: Philosophical Papers 2.* Cambridge: Cambridge University Press.

———. 1989. *Sources of the Self: The Making of Modern Identity.* Cambridge, MA: Harvard University Press.

———. 1991a. "Language and Society." In Honneth and Joas 1991, 23–35.

———. 1991b. *The Ethics of Authenticity.* Cambridge, MA: Harvard University Press.

———. 1993. "To Follow a Rule." In Calhoun, LiPuma, and Postone 1993, 45–60. Reprinted in Taylor 1995, 165–80.

Tsou, Jonathan Y. 2003. "A Role for Reason in Science." *Dialogue* 42: 573–98.

———. 2010. "Putnam's Account of Apriority and Scientific Change: Its Historical and Contemporary Interest." *Synthese* 176 (3): 429–45.

Tully, James, ed. 1988. *Meaning and Context: Quentin Skinner and His Critics.* Cambridge: Polity Press.

———, ed. 1995. *Philosophy in an Age of Pluralism: The Philosophy of Charles Taylor in Question.* Cambridge: Cambridge University Press.

Van Dyck, Maarten. 2009. "Dynamics of Reason and the Kantian Project." *Philosophy of Science* 76 (5): 689–700.

Wallace, R. Jay. 2002. "Scanlon's Contractualism." *Ethics* 112: 429–70.

Walzer, Michael. 1987. *Interpretation and Social Criticism.* Cambridge, MA: Harvard University Press.

———. 1988. *The Company of Critics: Social Criticism and Political Commitment in the Twentieth Century.* New York: Basic Books.

———. 1996. *Thick and Thin: Moral Argument at Home and Abroad.* Notre Dame: University of Notre Dame Press.

Warwick, Andrew. 2003. *Masters of Theory: Cambridge and the Rise of Mathematical Physics.* Chicago: University of Chicago Press.

Wellmer, Albrecht. 1998. *Endgames: The Irreconcilable Nature of Modernity. Essays and Lectures.* Cambridge, MA: MIT Press.

Whewell, William. 1847. *The Philosophy of the Inductive Sciences Founded on Their History.* 2 vols. 2nd ed. London: John W. Parker.

Williams, Bernard A. O. 1975. "The Truth in Relativism." *Proceedings of the Aristotelian Society* 75 (Suppl.): 215–28. Reprinted in Williams 1981, 132–43; pagination according to reprint.

———. 1979. "Internal and External Reasons." In Harrison 1979, 17–28; Williams 1981, 101–13; and Moser 1990, 387–97.

———. 1981. *Moral Luck: Philosophical Papers, 1973–1980.* Cambridge: Cambridge University Press.

———. 1986. *Ethics and the Limits of Philosophy.* Cambridge, MA: Harvard University Press.

———. 1995a. *Making Sense of Humanity and Other Philosophical Papers, 1982–1993.* Cambridge: Cambridge University Press.

———. 1995b. "Truth in Ethics." *Ratio* 8 (3): 227–42.

———. 2000. "Philosophy as a Humanistic Discipline." *Philosophy* 75: 477–96.

Wilson, George M. 1998. "Semantic Realism and Kripke's Wittgenstein." *Philosophy and Phenomenological Research* 58: 99–122.

Williams, Michael. 1988–89. "Scepticism and Charity." *Ratio,* n.s., 1–2: 176–94.

Wittgenstein, Ludwig. 1958. *Philosophical Investigations.* 3rd ed. Translated by G. E. M. Anscombe. Oxford: Blackwell.

———. [1969] 1974. *On Certainty.* Edited by G. E. M. Anscombe and G. H. von Wright, translated by Denis Paul and G. E. M. Anscombe. Reprinted with corrections and indices. Oxford: Blackwell.

Wolf, Susan. 2002. "The True, the Good, and the Lovable: Frankfurt's Avoidance of Objectivity." In Buss and Overton 2002, 227–44.

Wolheim, Richard, and James Hopkins, eds. 1982. *Philosophical Essays on Freud.* Cambridge: Cambridge University Press.

Wong, David B. 1984. *Moral Relativity.* Berkeley: University of California Press.

Wright, Crispin. 1980. *Wittgenstein on the Foundations of Mathematics.* Cambridge, MA: Harvard University Press.

———. 1984. "Kripke's Account of the Argument against Private Language." *Journal of Philosophy* 81: 759–78.

———. 1992. *Truth and Objectivity.* Cambridge, MA: Harvard University Press.

———. 1993. *Realism, Meaning, and Truth.* 2nd ed. Oxford: Blackwell.

Zalabardo, Jose L. 1997. "Kripke's Normativity Argument." *Canadian Journal of Philosophy* 27: 467–88.

Index

normativity
and causation vs. justification,
305n.24
conceptual norms, 170–75, 178,
181, 339n.34, 341n.51
of considered reasoning, 8
Davidson on (*see* Davidsonian
approach to meaning)
free will as ground of, 230, 237,
255, 299, 346n.4
as a human universal, 21, 95
Kantian, linked with giving and
asking for reasons, 175–81, 187,
341n.57
logic's priority, 300, 356n.36
normative mistakes, 171–73, 242
via reciprocal group recognition,
192, 199–200, 349n.46
regress-of-rules argument, 169–70
regulism about norms, 169–70, 237
statuses vs. attitudes, 170–71, 179,
199, 241, 246, 322n.17, 339n.34,
349n.46
volitional necessity as ground of,
238–39, 244, 350n.53, 356n.36
Nozick, Robert, 344n.25, 345n.30
Nussbaum, Martha, 345n.30

open question argument, 108,
109–17, 324nn.47–48,
325nn.50–51, 326nn.54–55
Overton, Lee, 232, 349n.35

pain
and interpretivism, 103–6,
323n.26
and pleasure, 69, 316n.19
as prima facie bad, 98, 103–6
paradigm cases, 37–38, 40, 43, 160

paradigm shifts
vs. evolutionary framework
transitions, 132, 135–36,
154–55, 158, 294–95, 335n.83,
356n.31
Kuhn on, 13–14, 89, 124–25, 281,
293, 327n.13
See also scientific framework
transitions
Parfit, Derek, 104
Peacock, George, 296–97
performative utterances, 205
Pirkei Avot (Mishna's Book of
Principles), 223–24
Plato, 248
platonic naturalism, 165, 313n.21
Poincaré, Jules Henri, 279, 295–97,
336n.1, 354n.19, 356n.31
Polanyi, Michael, 2, 219, 344n.17
Pollner, Melvin, 138
Popper, Karl Raimund
on criticism as exposing problems,
202–3
normative diversity denied by, 30,
310n.59
on piecemeal social engineering,
205
on problems as facts, 203
on rationality as criticism, 291–92
on scientific transitions,
334nn.76–77
on trial and error, 306n.30
positivism, 281, 285, 354nn.12–13
practical rationality, 303n.9
practical wisdom, 162–63
pragmatism
of Brandom, 25–26, 320n.8,
331n.55 (*see also* expressivist
pragmatism)

MENACHEM FISCH

is Joseph and Ceil Mazer Professor of History and Philosophy
of Science at Tel Aviv University in Israel.

YITZHAK BENBAJI

is associate professor on the law faculty and in the philosophy
department at Bar-Ilan University in Israel.